Little VISITS

VOLUME ONE

365 FAMILY DEVOTIONS

CONCORDIA PUBLISHING HOUSE · SAINT LOUIS

Copyright © 2002 Concordia Publishing House
3558 S. Jefferson Avenue, St. Louis, MO 63118-3968

Manufactured in the United States of America

Library of Congress Cataloging-in-Publication Data

365 family devotions.
    p. cm. -- (Little visits ; v. 1)
    ISBN 0-7586-0291-X
    1. Family--Prayer-books and devotions--English. 2. Devotional
calendars. I. Series.
    BV255 .A14 2002
    249--dc21   2002006608

3 4 5 6 7 8 9 10   11 10 09 08 07 06 05 04

Versions of these devotions originally appeared in various volumes of the magazine, *My Devotions.* This book is dedicated to the authors of these devotions, who have contributed their God-given time and talents to nurturing the faith of God's children. ⸙

Preface

For a number of years, the title *Little Visits* has been associated with devotions that share the saving Gospel of Jesus Christ with children. From the very first edition of *Little Visits with God* to this current volume, these devotions reinforce scriptural truths and faith concepts centered on God's love for us through Christ.

Setting aside time for devotions is an excellent way to lead children to the Savior and to bring them face-to-face with God's Word. In Romans 10:7, we read that "faith comes from hearing the message, and the message is heard through the word of Christ."

Find a time that best suits your family and be consistent. Set a format that is most harmonious with the ages and stages of your children. Using the order of worship provided on the facing page will build a sense of tradition and ritual into your family devotions. Developing such rituals or traditions helps to lay important building blocks for faith formation and creates a link between worship in the family of faith and worship within your own family.

These devotions have been written by pastors and educators who have drawn upon their experiences to provide illustrations from daily life and link them to God's Word. May you and your children be blessed as the Holy Spirit works through these words to teach your minds and to touch your hearts.

The Editors

Daily Devotion for Family Use

Parents may feel free to adapt according to the children's ages and ability to participate.

_____ The Invocation

The parent may open the devotion with a call to worship.
Leader: In the name of the Father and of the Son and of the Holy Spirit.
Family: Amen.

_____ The Hymn

The family may sing together a related hymn or song of praise.

_____ The Scripture Reading

The designated Scripture may be read by parent or child.

_____ The Devotional Reading

The designated devotion may be read by parent or child.
The parent may lead the family in discussion using the questions provided.

_____ The Closing Prayer

The parent may lead the family in the closing prayer.

january

Contributors for this month:

Kenneth Braun

Julie Dietrich

Suzanne Falk

Carla Fast

Jim Hahn

Gail Marsh

Cindy Wheeler

Judy Williams

Off to a Great Start

Have you ever seen a starfish? Most of them have five arms, but some have as many as 12. The starfish's arms can easily snap off, but losing an arm isn't a problem for the starfish. God created it with the ability to grow a new arm when necessary.

God gives us something new today—the first day of a brand new year. Each day God gives is a gift, but sometimes we forget to remember this. We may get out of bed without even thinking about God's blessings. We get very busy just going through the motions. Just like a starfish that loses an arm, we can give up a whole day without thinking about God.

God doesn't forget the starfish. And He won't forget us. He remembered us by sending His Son, Jesus, to die on the cross for our sins. He gives us new days to remember Him. In fact, today He is giving us the start of a whole new year filled with many days.

Let's start each day of this year right. Before getting out of bed each morning, thank God for the new day. Ask Him to lead you on the right path. God will hear your prayer and He will be your guide every day. You'll be off to a great start!

_____Let's do: Write Psalm 118:24 on an index card. Place the card by your bed. Start each day by saying this verse.

_____Let's pray: Dear God, thank You for Your gift of a new year. Help us begin each day with You. In the name of Jesus, our Lord and Savior. Amen

J. D.

Read from God's Word

This is the day the LORD has made; let us rejoice and be glad in it. ... You are my God, and I will give You thanks; You are my God, and I will exalt You. Psalm 118:24, 28–29

Words, Words, Words

Read from God's Word

Likewise the tongue is a small part of the body, but it makes great boasts. Consider what a great forest is set on fire by a small spark. The tongue also is a fire, a world of evil among the parts of the body. It corrupts the whole person, sets the whole course of his life on fire. ... It is a restless evil, full of deadly poison. With the tongue we praise our Lord and Father, and with it we curse men, who have been made in God's likeness. Out of the same mouth come praise and cursing. My brothers, this should not be. James 3:5–10

An old saying goes: "Sticks and stones may break my bones, but words can never hurt me." *Wrong!* Words can and do hurt. Lies can ruin a reputation. Talking behind someone's back can make you lose a friend. Teasing can make others angry. Words that complain or brag tire us out.

If words are so dangerous, maybe we should try another famous saying: "Hold your tongue." Go ahead. Try it. Try saying your name while holding onto your tongue. That's hard to do. The saying "Hold your tongue" really means that we should not hurt others with our words. But controlling our words can seem as impossible as actually holding onto our slippery tongue.

Only God the Holy Spirit can help us hold our tongues—that is, stop sinning with our words. He helps us stop bragging and teasing. The Spirit helps us tell the truth and not lie. God alone gives us the power to defend a friend rather than join the gossip. The power of God changes our tongues into messengers of good.

When Jesus was accused by others, He didn't talk back to them. His silence showed that He was willing to become guilty of all our sins. Because Jesus took the punishment for our sins, we are free to speak to others in kind and loving ways.

_____Let's talk: Have your words hurt someone lately? What words can Jesus help you say to heal that hurt? What specific words could you say to bring peace and joy to others today?

_____Let's pray: Lord Jesus, sometimes we say things that hurt others. Please forgive us, and help us use our words in ways that please You. Amen.

G. M.

Yes, You Can!

I t's impossible!" complained Juanita as she hung up the phone. "I can't be friends with Cassie. She makes me so mad. I just can't be her friend."

"I can't ride this bike," grumbled Juanita's little brother, Carlos. Carlos pushed his new Christmas bicycle and it landed on its side in the corner of the garage. He stomped into the kitchen wearing a big frown.

"My checkbook isn't balancing," Dad announced. "I've checked and rechecked the figures all evening, but I just can't get it to come out right."

The words "I can't" do not appear in today's Bible reading although everything seems to be going wrong! Instead of complaining, the writer is able to rejoice. That's because He believes that "the Sovereign LORD is my strength."

Jesus wants us to know that He is able and willing to help us with every problem or situation. To remember this important truth, try this: Print the words "I can't" on a slip of paper. Then carefully tear off the letter *t*. Tape it above the words, "I can." See how the letter *t* looks like a cross? The next time you feel like saying "I can't," remember that with Jesus' help you *can!* He hung on a cross for you, and He is your strength.

Read from God's Word

Though the fig tree does not bud and there are no grapes on the vines, though the olive crop fails and the fields produce no food, though there are no sheep in the pen and no cattle in the stalls, Yet I will rejoice in the LORD. I will be joyful in God my Savior. The Sovereign LORD is my strength; He makes my feet like the feet of a deer. He enables me to go on the heights. Habakkuk 3:17–19

_____Let's talk: Have you or your family members ever felt like Juanita and her family? What happened?

_____Let's pray: We know You can help us, Jesus. Please change our *can'ts* into *cans*, with Your help. Thank You. Amen.

G. M.

Read from God's Word

Love is patient, love is kind. It does not envy, it does not boast, it is not proud. It is not rude, it is not self-seeking, it is not easily angered, it keeps no record of wrongs. Love does not delight in evil but rejoices with the truth. It always protects, always trusts, always hopes, always perseveres.
1 Corinthians 13:4–7

Record Keeping

From the day we were born until the day we die, people keep records about us. Parents write information in our baby books: first tooth, first word, first steps. Doctors keep records about us too: height and weight, diseases, vaccinations. Some of us even keep our own records in diaries and journals.

Think about all the numbers used to keep things straight. Moms and dads have Social Security numbers from the government. The numbers on a credit card record what we buy so we know how much to pay. There are numbers on every car's license plate and every driver's license. Our homes have numbers. Our communities are assigned zip codes with one-of-a-kind numbers. No one else has a telephone number like ours so if a record needs to be updated, people can notify us.

It seems that everyone is keeping track of everything. All except for God. That's right—God does not keep track. He doesn't record our sins. If you don't believe it, check out what He tells us in His Word for today. Or read Psalm 130:3–4 and Isaiah 43:25.

God, in Jesus, forgives and forgets every one of our sins. No records are kept. Our page in God's *Sin Record Book* will always be blank because Jesus died on the cross for us. Praise God for His love, forgiveness, and grace!

_____Let's talk: Sometimes we keep track of all the times others hurt us. We remember what someone has done and we refuse to forgive and forget. But remember what God has done for us. Is there someone you need to forgive? Ask God to help you do it.

_____Let's pray: Dear God, thanks for not keeping track of our sins. Help us forgive when others sin against us. In Jesus' name. Amen.

G. M.

It's No Joke

Read from God's Word

When you were slaves to sin, you were free from the control of righteousness. What benefit did you reap at that time from the things you are now ashamed of? Those things result in death! But now that you have been set free from sin and have become slaves to God, the benefit you reap leads to holiness, and the result is eternal life. For the wages of sin is death, but the gift of God is eternal life in Christ Jesus our Lord. Romans 6:20–23 ↩

A while back some jokes got started that were called good news/bad news jokes. Here's a sample: *Good news:* You've been chosen to be on the football team. *Bad news:* Your job is to be the football.

Or how about this one: *Bad news:* The food we planted did not grow, and there is nothing to eat except worms. *Good news:* There aren't enough to go around.

When you stop to think about it, we could talk about our own lives using a good news/bad news statement:

Bad news: We sin and deserve God's anger and punishment. *Good news:* Jesus took the punishment for our sins when He suffered and died on the cross. Now we have forgiveness and eternal life.

The Good News, or Gospel message, certainly is no joke! Our very lives here on earth depend on Jesus. He forgives, helps, and comforts us every day. Our eternal life also depends on Jesus—the Savior who will one day take us to live forever with Him in heaven.

———Let's talk: Do you know someone who needs to hear God's message of salvation? How might Jesus help you share the Good News with this person?

———Let's pray: Thank You, Jesus, for taking away the bad news of sin and giving us Your Good News of forgiveness, power, and eternal life—all good gifts from You. Help us share this news with others. It's the best news ever! Amen.

G. M.

Read from God's Word

You are all sons of God through faith in Christ Jesus, for all of you who were baptized into Christ have clothed yourselves with Christ. There is neither Jew nor Greek, slave nor free, male nor female, for you are all one in Christ Jesus. If you belong to Christ, then you are Abraham's seed, and heirs according to the promise. Galatians 3:26–29

The Perfect Gift

Look what came in the mail," Mom announced as she held up a neatly wrapped box. "Aunt Jessica may be a little late, but her Christmas gifts are always a nice surprise."

The family huddled close as Mom removed the brown wrapping paper. "Look," Steve said, "there's a note inside."

"'One gift fits all,'" Mom read aloud. "Hmm. Strange. Isn't it supposed to say, 'One size fits all'?"

"Aunt Jessie is sometimes hard to figure out, Mom. Let's open the package." Steve was eager to see what was inside the box.

Mom removed the last of the wrapping paper while Steve and Kate watched with anticipation. "A puzzle?" asked Kate as she looked at the hundreds of jumbled puzzle pieces inside the plain red box. "But how will we put it together without a picture to look at?"

Aunt Jessica's gift turned out to be a perfect "fit" for the family. Although it took several days to put the puzzle together, everyone enjoyed working on the project. Steve and Kate did their homework quickly each night so they could work on the puzzle. Fitting the pieces together helped Mom relax after a hard day at work. When the 500 pieces were finally joined together, the family could see a beautiful picture of Jesus and the Wise Men. It reminded them that God's best gift of all was sending Jesus to be their Savior.

_____Let's talk: Today is Epiphany, the day we celebrate the Wise Men's visit to the Christ Child. Epiphany reminds us that the Savior is God's gift to all people. Why is Jesus the perfect gift for all? (See Romans 3:23–24.)

_____Let's pray: Father in heaven, thank You so much for sending us the perfect gift—Jesus. Amen.

G. M.

Really Listening

Supper was ready, but no one was coming to the table. "Sarah! Come for supper!" Mom called for the third time. "Joey! Chad! Supper is ready!"

Mom went to find the three children. Sarah was in her beanbag chair, listening to music. "Sarah!" Mom called loudly.

"Oh, sorry, Mom." Sarah sat up quickly. "Is supper ready?" She followed Mom to the family room.

Joey and Chad were watching television. "Boys!" Mom chided. "Supper is getting cold. Didn't you hear me calling you?" Joey and Chad had heard Mom call but didn't answer.

Did the children really hear Mom's voice? To really hear means more than just receiving the noise that enters our ears. To really hear means that our hearts make us want to listen.

Sometimes we get so used to hearing God's Word that we no longer take it to heart. We hear God speak to us when we read the Bible, listen to a sermon, or attend Sunday school. The words go in our ears, but we don't really listen. Then, one day, we realize what God is saying to us.

Our loving God has so many things to tell us. He tells us that He is with us and for us. He tells us that Jesus has rescued us from the worst things that could happen to us. Let's really listen with our hearts!

Read from God's Word

[Jesus said] "This is why I speak to them in parables: Though seeing, they do not see; though hearing, they do not hear or understand.' In them is fulfilled the prophecy of Isaiah: "'You will be ever hearing but never understanding; you will be ever seeing but never perceiving. For this people's heart has become calloused; they hardly hear with their ears, and they have closed their eyes. ...'" But blessed are your eyes because they see, and your ears because they hear." Matthew 13:13–16 ✐

———Let's talk: Why is it sometimes hard to truly listen to God? Is God trying to tell you something right now? How can you respond?

———Let's pray: Jesus, sometimes we hear only with our ears, not our hearts. Help us listen—really listen—to what You say. Amen.

G. M.

The Frozen Chosen

After a three-inch snowfall one night, my children woke the next morning to a white playground outside. Quickly, they bundled up in their snow gear. They rushed out the door, looking forward to the thrill of the new snow.

A few minutes later the doorbell rang. It was my four-year-old daughter. "Mommy, I'm cold," she complained. "Why can't the snow be hot? Then I could play in it all day."

We are God's chosen people, but we sometimes grow cold toward Him. The Lord warms us with His love and gives us the fire of faith. But sometimes we do wrong things and the coldness of sin makes us freeze God out.

God chose us to be His children. He makes us His very own through the water of Holy Baptism. But we are not perfect—we are sinners. The Lord knows His chosen can become frozen in their faith, but God forgives us when our faith gets cold. He sent His only Son to suffer on the cross to forgive our sins.

Even more, God gives us the Holy Spirit to light a faith fire in us that stays hot. As we hear God's Word, the Holy Spirit acts as antifreeze to keep our faith from becoming frozen. In God's warm love and mercy, the "frozen chosen" can feel a "burning yearning" for the Lord.

_____Let's talk: How does God keep our faith active and growing? What can we do when we feel cold toward Him?

_____Let's pray: Dear Lord, thank You for choosing us as Your children. Help us grow in our faith in You. For Jesus' sake. Amen.

J. D.

Different, Yet the Same

Read from God's Word

May the God who gives endurance and encouragement give you a spirit of unity among yourselves as you follow Christ Jesus, so that with one heart and mouth you may glorify the God and Father of our Lord Jesus Christ. Accept one another, then, just as Christ accepted you, in order to bring praise to God. Romans 15:5–7 ✍

Firecrackers! It sounded like exploding firecrackers! And the popping sound was coming straight from Tad's bedroom. Pop—pop—pop—pop—pop! Cindy went to investigate.

"Tad, what's that noi ..." Cindy's words stopped as she saw what caused the popping sound.

Tad stopped, grinned, and breathlessly sputtered, "Packing bubbles. I'm stomping on packing bubbles. Come on! Help me make noise!"

Although Cindy was usually the quiet one in the family, she was soon stomping and laughing aloud.

Many families are like Cindy's. Some members are quiet and others are not so quiet. Sometimes the differences in our personalities cause problems. Cindy could have complained that Tad was making too much noise. Instead, God helped her make a better choice.

God creates many kinds of people: quiet, loud, bold, shy, silly, serious, and more. God also helps us get along with family members and friends who are different from us. It would be a pretty boring world if all people were exactly the same.

Although we are all different, there is one thing that is the same for all Christians. We are all God's children through faith in Jesus. St. Paul urges us: "As dearly loved children ... live a life of love, just as Christ loved us and gave Himself up for us" (Ephesians 5:1–2). Praise God for this kind of sameness!

———Let's talk: Can you identify different personalities in your family? When do these differences cause problems? How might God help you respond in love?

———Let's pray: Lord, help us rejoice in the differences You've created in people. Amen.

G. M.

Keep Going!

Read from God's Word

I can do everything through Him who gives me strength. ... And my God will meet all your needs according to His glorious riches in Christ Jesus. To our God and Father be glory for ever and ever. Amen. Philippians 4:13, 19–20 ✐

Tiffany shook some snow out of her mittens. Then she dropped her ice skates to the floor. "How'd it go?" Mom wanted to know. It was Tiffany's first try at ice-skating.

"Actually, falling down wasn't too hard," Tiffany replied. "But getting up sure was!"

Getting up and sticking with something is often hard. It's easier to just give up, stop, or quit. Think about it. It's easy to close the math book; it's hard to stick with it and figure out a complicated problem. It's easy to end a friendship; it's hard to work out your differences. It's easy to quit the team; it's hard to practice and become as good as you can be. It's easy to over-look someone who needs help; it's hard to take time to lend a hand.

Paul says in today's Bible reading, "I can do everything through Him who gives me strength." The secret is trusting in Jesus. *Through Him* we find strength to go on. Did Jesus give up when He faced great pain and a scary, cruel death? No, He kept going to win the victory for us.

Our Savior wants us to seek His help in everything we do. He'll lead us to make God-pleasing decisions and help us succeed. Then our actions will give Him glory.

———Let's talk: What hard things face you right now? Pray for help. Ask God to help you glorify Him in all you do.

———Let's pray: Dear Lord, we don't always want to do the right thing. Sometimes the right thing seems too hard. Help us, Father. Give us Your power to succeed. Amen.

G. M.

Rescued from the Market

I t happened rather suddenly. After school had been dismissed for the day, Jim went to deliver a message to the teacher. There in the hallway sat a huge pink stuffed pig that had been part of Farm Day.

The school teacher sadly informed him that the pig was on its way to the "market," the local Goodwill store. When he asked why, the teacher shared that the pig was taking too much space and needed to go.

Jim was more than happy to provide a new home for the huge pig. It now sits in a corner of his office. It has caused many people to stop and ask about the pig.

Because of our sin, we were just like that pig—unwanted, on the way out. We were being sent away to live a life apart from God.

But God still loved us and wanted us. He rescued us by sending His own Son, Jesus, to die for us and rise again.

Read from God's Word

But God demonstrates His own love for us in this: While we were still sinners, Christ died for us. Since we have now been justified, by His blood, how much more shall we be saved from God's wrath through Him! For if, when we were God's enemies we were reconciled to Him through the death of His Son, how much more, having been reconciled, shall we be saved through His life! Not only is this so, but we also rejoice in God through our Lord Jesus Christ, through whom we have now received reconciliation. Romans 5:8–11 ✍

We can thank God every day that our sins have been forgiven by His grace and mercy. Now there is a place all ready for us in His big home. In fact, because of Jesus, God has a place for us to sit with Him in His heavenly kingdom (see Ephesians 2:6).

———Let's talk: Have you ever rescued or saved something? What was it? Why was it important to you? What did it cost for us to be rescued from sin and death?

———Let's pray: Dear God, thank You for rescuing us by sending Jesus to die on the cross for our sins. Help us live according to Your will and depend on Your grace. In Jesus' name. Amen.

J. H.

Read from God's Word

This is what the LORD says—your Redeemer, the Holy One of Israel: "I am the LORD your God, who teaches you what is best for you, who directs you in the way you should go." Isaiah 48:17 ↩

A Gentle Leader

Not long ago a family received a new puppy. His name was Rootbeer. As a puppy he was soft and cuddly, but over time Rootbeer changed. Each time he went to the veterinarian for some shots, he had gained 10 pounds.

Rootbeer quickly became a large, strong dog. He pulled people along whenever they walked. They needed to do something soon if they were going to control Rootbeer rather than letting Rootbeer control them.

The problem was solved by buying a special collar for leading him. Rootbeer resisted the new collar, but his behavior soon started to change. There was no more pulling, lunging, or tugging. Rootbeer followed their gentle leading.

In many ways we resist God and try to go our own way. We think we know what is best. We don't like being told in the commandments what we should or should not do. But God knows best and cares for us. He gently leads us in the way we should go. He sent Jesus to be our Savior. Because of Jesus, our sins are forgiven when we try to go our own way. Every day we can thank God for His gifts of love and forgiveness.

_____Let's talk: When have you resisted God and gone your own way? Did you later feel sorry and want to follow God's will?

_____Let's pray: Heavenly Father, forgive us for those times when we try to leave You. Thank You for Your love and for gently leading us back to You. Help us accept Your will for our lives. Amen.

J. H.

One of a Kind

Read from God's Word

For You created my inmost being: You knit me together in my mother's womb. I praise You because I am fearfully and wonderfully made; Your works are wonderful, I know that full well. My frame was not hidden from You when I was made in the secret place. When I was woven together in the depths of the earth, Your eyes saw my unformed body. All the days ordained for me were written in Your book before one of them came to be. Psalm 139:13–16

Anyone who lives in a place like Minnesota during winter can be sure of two things—cold temperatures and lots of snow. Each snowflake is special, one of a kind, as it falls from the sky.

Most people in Minnesota look forward to the first snowfall. There are contests to guess which will be the first day of enough snow to measure. They can't wait to go outside and enjoy the fresh snow.

But as winter gets longer and the snow gets deeper, the people start to change. Instead of getting excited each time it snows, they groan and complain, "Not again!" The snow stops being special.

In today's Bible reading, David described how special we are in God's eyes. God created each of us as one of a kind. We are fearfully and wonderfully made. Even more amazing, God knows everything about us; He knew us even before we were born.

Although people might get tired of seeing snowflakes, God never gets tired of seeing us. He loves to see us reading His Word, praying, singing songs of praise, worshiping, and serving others. How special we are that God made us and takes care of us! Because Jesus took our place and suffered on the cross for us, we will someday join Him in the place He has already prepared for us—His heavenly home.

_____Let's do: Sit in a circle with your family. Give each person a clear glass, and let him or her grasp it. Carefully hold the glass up to a light and look for the lines that form "one of a kind" fingerprints.

_____Let's pray: Creator God, we praise You for having wonderfully made us to be so special. We thank You for Your continuing care of us. Help us appreciate the uniqueness of each person as a member of Your family. In Jesus' name. Amen.

J. H.

Read from God's Word

Jesus said, "Have the people sit down." There was plenty of grass in that place, and the men sat down, about five thousand of them. Jesus then took the loaves, gave thanks, and distributed to those who were seated as much as they wanted. He did the same with the fish. When they had all had enough to eat, He said to His disciples, "Gather the pieces that are left over. Let nothing be wasted." So they gathered them and filled twelve baskets with the pieces of the five barley loaves left over by those who had eaten. John 6:10–13

Lots from Little

Imagine Andrew's surprise when Jesus said the people should sit for a meal. All together there were 5,000 men, plus women and children! Philip pointed out that it would cost eight months of wages to feed the crowd! The only food available was a young boy's lunch, and that was barely enough for him.

Yet from this little lunch, Jesus created a lot. He gave thanks to His heavenly Father, who blessed the bread and fish. The Bible tells us everyone received more than just a little lunch. They all ate as much as they wanted—maybe even second and third helpings!

Impossible? Yes, for us, but not for God. He can use even small things for His purposes. God used a small boy and his lunch to miraculously feed the people, and there was even food left over.

Young or old, God can use us as He used the boy in the Bible story. God works through us to help others in need, to offer words of encouragement, to pray for the sick, to bring cheer to someone who may be sad.

God will bless the little things we do in response to His love and mercy to us. He helps us be a blessing to many. We are servants of our Lord Jesus, who served us by giving His life for us.

_____Let's talk: What are some things your family might do for one another today? What are some little things your family might do to help others?

_____Let's pray: Dear God, thank You for letting us serve as Your helpers on earth. May what we do bring glory to You, and may Your love reach others through us. For Jesus' sake we ask this. Amen.

J. H.

Learning from Clowns

A number of years ago Jim led a small group of young people who became interested in clowning. They spent lots of time learning about the history of clowns and the types of clowns. They also went to watch some clowns in action.

One of the most interesting things they learned was how to apply make-up to create a clown face. The base makeup that a clown puts on is a white paint that covers the face. On top of the white paint, the clown adds many colors to create the look of the clown face. The faces were transformed, or made to look different than before.

When the young people were made up in their clown faces, they became different people. It wasn't just their faces that were different. They acted in new and different ways. They became like clowns. In today's Bible reading, Paul writes about a change in people who have received faith in Jesus by the work of the Holy Spirit. They are new; they are different.

Read from God's Word

Those who live according to the sinful nature have their minds set on what that nature desires; but those who live in accordance with the Spirit have their minds set on what the Spirit desires. ... You, however, are controlled not by the sinful nature but by the Spirit, if the Spirit of God lives in you. ... And if the Spirit of Him who raised Jesus from the dead is living in you, He who raised Christ from the dead will also give life to your mortal bodies through His Spirit, who lives in you. Romans 8:5–11 ✍

When we have faith, Christ lives in us and our "old self" dies. We no longer want to live for ourselves, instead we want to live for Jesus and others. We become changed people. Jesus' love and goodness cover our sinful selves and a "new self" is created.

_____Let's talk: What makes new things special to you? How are you different because Christ lives in you? What kinds of things have you done that show others you are God's new creation?

_____Let's pray: Dear Father in heaven, how happy we are that You have made us new creations in Your Son, Jesus! May our lives truly reflect His living in us. Amen.

J. H.

Part of the Team

The last day of tryouts was over! Scott waited for the coach to announce the players who had made the team. "Scott, left field."

Suddenly Scott realized that he made the team. But he wasn't as happy as he thought he'd be. "I can't play left field," he muttered to himself. "I'm a pitcher. Besides, left fielders aren't as important as pitchers."

Scott walked toward the exit. The coach caught up with him and explained, "Scott, you're very important to the team. You were chosen to play left field because you can throw the ball long distances. You're needed a lot."

We are all needed on God's team. God has chosen each of us to be part of His family. We never have to try out or wait to see if we've made it onto God's team. Jesus took care of everything when He died on the cross for us. Our sins are forgiven. We belong to God forever.

As part of God's team, each of us is important. We can all work together to tell others about Jesus, our Savior. As our Bible reading says, each of us is part of the body of Christ. Many parts form one body, just as many players form one team. Ask God to help you play your best every day. Be proud to be on God's team!

_____Let's talk: What are some ways you can serve the Lord? Think of activities you like to do. How could you use those to tell others about Jesus?

_____Let's pray: Dear God, thank You for making each one of us part of Your team through Your Son, Jesus. Help us always do our best to share Your love and tell others about You. Amen.

S. F.

The Greatest Party

Read from God's Word

"Then I saw a new heaven and a new earth, for the first heaven and the first earth had passed away, and there was no longer any sea. I saw the Holy City, the new Jerusalem, coming down out of heaven from God, prepared as a bride beautifully dressed for her husband. And I heard a loud voice from the throne saying, 'Now the dwelling of God is with men, and He will live with them. They will be His people, and God Himself will be with them and be their God. He will wipe every tear from their eyes. There will be no more death or mourning or crying or pain, for the old order of things has passed away.'" Revelation 21:1–4

Close your eyes. Think about the best party you've attended. Who was there? What did you do? What made it the best party ever?

Was it a party with your family or friends? Were there bright, colorful decorations? Did you eat lots of yummy food? Did you laugh a lot?

The party you remembered was probably great, but there is something that's even better! Imagine a place where no one gets hurt, no one dies, and no one cries. In this place, everyone is always happy. No one is sad or lonely. Everyone is part of a gigantic family and has millions of friends.

Does a place like that sound unbelievable? Would you like to live there? This place is called heaven. And everyone who believes that Jesus is his or her Savior will someday live in heaven.

While we wait to enter heaven, we love and serve Jesus here on earth. But not everything is perfect. We are sinners. We hurt others by what we say, think, and do. However, Jesus died on the cross and rose again for the forgiveness of our sins.

Get ready for the party. Live life praising and serving God. Pray for the Holy Spirit so you can share the Good News of Jesus with others. Then even more people will be able to enjoy the greatest party of all!

_____ Let's talk: What question would you like to ask God when you get to heaven? Tell someone about heaven and how to get there.

_____ Let's pray: Dear Jesus, we're sorry for our sinful acts, words, and thoughts. Forgive us. Fill our hearts with Your Spirit as we excitedly wait to live with You in heaven. Amen.

S. F.

God's Path Is Best

Read from God's Word

Show me Your ways, O LORD, teach me Your paths; guide me in Your truth and teach me, for You are God my Savior, and my hope is in You all day long. Remember, O LORD, Your great mercy and love, for they are from of old. Remember not the sins of my youth and my rebellious ways; according to Your love remember me, for You are good, O LORD. Psalm 25:4–7 ✐

Squish. Splash. Crunch. Tires rolled slowly through the snow and ice. The cold wind whistled outside. Snowflakes fell. Seven plow trucks battled the snowstorm, plowing the snow off the road. Some cars moved patiently behind the trucks. These plow trucks guided and directed the cars along the right path.

However, other cars chose not to follow. They swerved in and out. Although it was dangerous, the drivers wanted to go their own way.

We are like the cars and God is like the plow trucks. God the Father sent Jesus to go before us and to battle something much more powerful than a snowstorm. He battled Satan and won when He died and rose again. Now through the Holy Spirit, God guides and directs us on life's path.

But sometimes we choose not to follow where God leads us. Maybe we're in too much of a hurry or we think that going our own way is better than following God's direction. This can be very dangerous.

When this happens, we need to ask God for forgiveness and direction in our lives. He knows what's best for us and He promises to be with us always. As we read and study God's Word, God prepares us for the situations we face every day. He safely leads us through any and every storm.

_____Let's talk: What are some times when you have not followed the way God wants you to live? Give examples of how you can show your trust in God.

_____Let's pray: Heavenly Father, help us trust in You. Forgive us when we don't stay on the path You want us to follow. You know what's best for us. Amen.

S. F.

Someone Special

As Sarah flipped through her magazine, she stared at the beautiful models. She dreamed about being like them. She got up to look in the mirror. She wondered. "Why can't I look like those models?"

Zachary watched the other boys on the playground. He was so short next to them. He knew he would never be a basketball star. He watched TV shows and movies and wished he could be fast and strong.

Have you ever felt like Sarah or Zachary? Do you sometimes wish you were like somebody else?

The Bible tells us that when God created people, He made them in His image (Genesis 1:26). How special we must be if God made us like Him! In today's Bible reading Jesus says, "even the very hairs of your head are all numbered." *Wow!* That's pretty amazing! Could you begin to count all the tiny hairs on your head? God can. God does!

Read from God's Word

[Jesus said] "Are not two sparrows sold for a penny? Yet not one of them will fall to the ground apart from the will of your Father. And even the very hairs of your head are all numbered. So don't be afraid; you are worth more than many sparrows." Matthew 10:29–31 ✍

Every day we can remember that we belong to God and that He made us. He loves us just as we are. He knows what we are thinking and how we feel. And no matter what we look like or what we can or cannot do, we are precious in God's eyes because of Jesus. He died to take away our sins. We are forgiven. Special and precious? Indeed we are!

———Let's talk: Look at each other's thumbprints. Now look at your own. Is it exactly like anyone else's? Name some other things that make each of you unique.

———Let's pray: Creator God, You made us in Your image and gave Your Son for us. You have made each one of us special. Help us to be more like Jesus in everything we say and do. In His name. Amen.

S. F.

Copycat

One day Thomas and his sister, Dawn, went on a hike with Dad. They came close to a pond and something huge caught Thomas's eye.

"Look at that bird!" Thomas shouted.

"Look at that bird!" Dawn repeated.

"Don't copy me," Thomas yelled with an angry look on his face.

"Don't copy me," said Dawn, imitating the look on Thomas's face.

"Dad, Dawn's copying me!" whined Thomas.

"Dad, Dawn's copying me!" laughed Dawn.

Just then seven ducklings waddled by, carefully following their mama. Thomas and Dawn watched closely. The ducklings did everything like their mother. If she turned, they turned. If she stopped, they stopped. When she showed them how to float in the water, one by one the ducklings followed.

"Have you learned anything, kids?" Dad asked. "Each duckling copied everything their mother did. But their copying was pleasing to their mother. Dawn, the way you copied your brother was not appropriate." Dad continued, "It makes me think of the Bible verse that says 'Be imitators of God ... as dearly loved children and live a life of love, just as Christ loved us.'"

"I get it!" Thomas exclaimed. "We're like the ducklings, except that we're God's children. He wants us to imitate Him."

"Remember," Dad said, "if you want to copy someone, copy Jesus. His is the best example of love!"

_____Let's talk: What are some things your family can do to show Jesus' love to others? Choose one of those ideas and carry it out.

_____Let's pray: Lord Jesus, thank You for loving us so much that You died for us. Make us more like You so others will see Your love through us. Amen.

S. F.

God Feeds Pelicans–and Us

Grandpa spent a whole day showing Jose where he lived in Florida. One of the places Grandpa showed him was a long pier stretching out into the Gulf of Mexico. Jose could see people fishing from the end of the pier.

As they walked closer, Jose noticed some gray birds with long, bulging bills. "What are those, Grandpa?"

"Those are pelicans," Grandpa answered.

"Why are so many of them swimming under the pier?"

Grandpa smiled. "They're waiting for God to feed them."

Jose looked up to see God drop food down to the funny-looking birds.

"No, no!" said Grandpa. "Not like that. After folks catch fish, they clean them. They throw the small fish and the parts they don't want into the water. God uses people who fish to feed the pelicans."

Lots of times we forget that every good thing we receive comes from God. Food, new jeans, a bike, a new pencil for school—God gives it all.

And what a loving God He is! He keeps it coming even when we don't pray for it. Jesus, our merciful and forgiving Savior, taught us the Lord's Prayer. In one part we pray, "Give us this day our daily bread." Even when forget to pray the prayer, the bread still comes. Every day God gives us everything we need!

Read from God's Word

How many are Your works, O LORD! In wisdom You made them all; the earth is full of Your creatures. There is the sea, vast and spacious, teeming with creatures beyond number—living things both large and small. There the ships go to and fro, and the leviathan, which You formed to frolic there. These all look to You to give them their food at the proper time. When You give it to them, they gather it up; when You open Your hand, they are satisfied with good things. Psalm 104:24–28

_____Let's talk: Every good thing is a gift from God. What are some of the good things God has given your family? Why are you happy that God sent His Son as His best gift?

_____Let's pray: Father, for everything You have given us, we thank You. Forgive us for not seeing everything we have as a gift from You. Help us use all You give to strengthen us to serve You. In Jesus' name. Amen.

K. B.

Look! No Mess!

Rachel tucked Peter and Ozzie, the two boys she was baby-sitting, into bed for the night. As she sat down to munch some goodies, she looked at the book about Goof-off Goose she had just read to the boys.

In the story, Goose's yard was a mess. Her neighbors were very upset and wanted her to clean it. Finally, Goose promised she would do it "tomorrow." But when tomorrow came, Goose looked out the window and saw the mess covered with newly fallen snow. She said, "You can't see the mess in my yard. The snow has kept my promise!"

The story reminded Rachel of a promise about snow that her Sunday school teacher had read. It's the Bible reading for today. God promised He would cover all the wrong things we do, sort of like snow covers things.

God sent His Son, Jesus, who lived His whole life without doing anything wrong. His perfect life made up for all the times we have messed up. Now when God looks at us, He sees what His Son did for us. In the story, Goose's mess was still under the snow. But when God covers our sins, He gets rid of them completely.

When the snow melts, Goose will still have the mess to clean up. But Jesus has forever wiped our sins away. What is more, He is with us each day, helping us live in ways that are pleasing to Him. What a wonderful God and Savior we have!

_____Let's talk: Talk about some things you did today that were wrong. Now remind one another that God loves you and forgives you. After someone confesses a sin, recite today's Bible verse.

_____Let's pray: Jesus, Savior, wash away,
All that has been wrong today;
Make me more like You each day
In all the things I do and say.

J. W.

Perdiddle

Pretend you are riding in a car at night, looking for any cars, vans, and trucks with just one working headlight. The first one to spot three vehicles with only one headlight shining can shout, "Perdiddle!"

One mile down the road you see the first dark headlight. Shh! Don't let on that you've seen it. Look! The very next truck is missing a headlight too. More than five miles go by. You start to think there will never be another one. You know it's just a matter of time, but it's hard to be patient for that third dark headlight.

Waiting for something can be hard. Maybe you prayed for someone to get better. Maybe you prayed for Dad to get a new job. Jesus knows we will sometimes get impatient. But because He died for us on the cross, all of our sins—even our impatience—are forgiven.

In today's Bible reading, St. Paul tells how patient Jesus is with sinners. He came into the world to save even the worst of sinners. Even when we get impatient, Jesus shows mercy and love to us. He helps us get through the struggle and gets us ready to practice patience.

There may not always be a winner in the game of Perdiddle. But we pray that Christ's strong light will always shine brightly in us and through us.

Read from God's Word

Here is a trustworthy saying that deserves full acceptance: Christ Jesus came into the world to save sinners—of whom I am the worst. But for that very reason I was shown mercy so that in me, the worst of sinners, Christ Jesus might display His unlimited patience as an example for those who would believe on Him and receive eternal life. Now to the King eternal, immortal, invisible, the only God, be honor and glory for ever and ever. Amen. 1 Timothy 1:15–17 ✍

———Let's do: Play a game of Perdiddle with your family or friends. While waiting for vehicles to pass, think of ways to show patience.

———Let's pray: Dear Jesus, be with us every day. Give us patience as we serve You and others around us. Amen.

J. D.

God's Wonderful Creation

Jacob could hardly believe his eyes when he looked out the window. He saw snow, but it never snows in Alabama—well, hardly ever. Jacob quickly called Alex and Aaron. All three of them decided to meet at the park and have fun in the snow before it melted.

The three boys made a snowman, built a fort, and had a snowball fight. They laid in the snow and made snow angels. What a wonderful time!

By the time they finished, the boys' clothes were soaked. But they didn't mind. It had been a perfect day already—and when they walked in the house, Jacob's mom announced she had made snow milkshakes.

"Mm-m-m good!" they shouted as they each grabbed a glass. But before the boys started sipping, they gave praise and thanks to God for a wonderful, snowy day in Alabama.

No matter where we live, we can see signs of God's wonderful creation. Our Bible reading is a psalm of praise, telling about the great wonders of God's creation, such as mountains, seas, meadows, and grain-covered fields.

But the psalm writer praises God for something else too. Read verse 3: "When we were overwhelmed by sins, You forgave our transgressions." God is also the one who brings salvation from sin through His Son, Jesus. The blessings of God are never-ending. He has loved us from before He made the world and He will love us through eternity.

_____Let's talk: Does it snow where you live? If so, what do you like to do in the snow? If it doesn't, what *would* you like to do in the snow?

_____Let's pray: Lord, we praise You for Your loving care. You are our God forever! Amen.

J. W.

My Dad's in Prison

Read from God's Word

Jesus said to him, "Today salvation has come to this house, because this man, too, is a son of Abraham. For the Son of Man came to seek and to save what was lost." Luke 19:9–10 ✍

Well, Mark's dad wasn't in prison yet, but the jury had reached a verdict yesterday. They found his dad guilty of robbery. It was all over the front page of the paper. Mark wondered how he could face all the kids at school.

Sometimes Mark got so mad at his dad. He wondered how his dad could have let his friend talk him into doing it. Mark thought about what how hurt he and his mom felt. He didn't want to go today, but Mom said he had to.

It didn't take long to walk to school. He just kept walking and looking at the ground. He decided to go right into school and see if he could help Mrs. Jackson hand out papers or something.

"Hi, Mark!" said Mrs. Jackson. "How about helping me get a couple of things ready for class?"

"Sure," he answered. But before Mark could do anything, Mrs. Jackson gave him a hug. She said she wanted Mark to know she loved him, and if he wanted someone to talk to, she would be glad to listen.

A friend! Mark had really needed a friend. Maybe today wouldn't be as bad as he thought. Isn't it great that God knew just what Mark needed?

———Let's talk: Do you know someone like Mark who really needs a friend? What would Jesus want you to do? What will Jesus help you do? What example did Jesus give in today's Bible reading about how to treat others who feel alone because of sin. Read about it in Luke 19:1–10.

———Let's pray: Dear Jesus, You know that sin brings so much sadness into the world. That's the whole reason You came—to live a life without sin and to suffer and die for all sins. Thank You for being our friend. Help us follow Your example and reach out to others who are hurting because of sin. In Your name we pray. Amen.

J. W.

Teaching That Saves Lives

Read from God's Word

Therefore, since we are surrounded by such a great cloud of witnesses, let us throw off everything that hinders and the sin that so easily entangles, and let us run with perseverance the race marked out for us. Let us fix our eyes on Jesus, the author and perfecter of our faith, who for the joy set before Him endured the cross, scorning its shame, and sat down at the right hand of the throne of God. Consider Him who endured such opposition from sinful men, so that you will not grow weary and lose heart. Hebrews 12:1–3

Every fall and spring, Mr. Moss teaches a Montana Hunters Safety class to 12-year-olds. He teaches how to survive in the mountains, just in case a young hunter becomes separated from other hunters.

This actually happened to one of the students. His name was Scott. He was hunting with his dad, but they got separated. When his dad couldn't find Scott, he went for help. Search teams looked for three days in below-freezing weather. Family and friends joined in prayer, asking God to keep Scott safe.

On the third day, a helicopter spotted Scott. He was in great shape, except for frostbite on his toes. When asked how he survived, Scott said, "I just did what Mr. Moss told us to do."

The lessons Mr. Moss taught probably saved Scott's physical life. But there are other lessons that are more important—the lessons that teach us about eternal life with Jesus, our Savior. For example, the Bible tells us that when sin clings to us like a heavy weight, we need to look to Jesus. Why? Because He is "the author and perfecter of our faith, who for the joy set before Him endured the cross, scorning its shame" (Hebrews 12:2).

When we remember how much Jesus suffered in our place, we won't feel like giving up. With His help we'll be strengthened so we can survive.

_____Let's talk: Who's the best teacher you ever had? Why did you choose that person? Who's the best spiritual helper you ever had? Why did you choose that person?

_____Let's pray: Thank You, dear God, for the many teachers You have given us. Help us listen so we may learn lessons we need to know for our physical life and especially for eternal life with You and Your Son. In His name we pray. Amen.

J. W.

A Hug for You

Tim crawled into bed. Then he waited. After Tim was ready for bed, his dad always came by for a bedtime talk, a prayer, and a hug.

Tim heard Dad coming down the hall. He came into Tim's room with the usual "Are you ready for bed, son?"

Tim enjoyed this time when he could tell Dad what had happened that day. Then Tim and Dad would pray together, thanking God for the good things that had happened, telling God about the sad and bad things, and asking God for forgiveness. After that Dad would give Tim a big hug and say, "I love you, Tim."

Tim always replied, "I love you too, Dad." Now Tim was ready for a good night's sleep.

In today's Bible reading, a group of children experienced a big hug from Jesus. Just like Tim's dad, Jesus took time to talk with the children. Then He picked them up in His arms and blessed them. In other words, He gave them a loving hug.

Read from God's Word

People were bringing little children to Jesus to have Him touch them, but the disciples rebuked them. When Jesus saw this, He was indignant. He said to them, "Let the little children come to Me, and do not hinder them, for the kingdom of God belongs to such as these. I tell you the truth, anyone who will not receive the kingdom of God like a little child will never enter it." And He took the children in His arms, put His hands on them and blessed them. Mark 10:13–16

These same arms that gently hugged the children were later stretched out on a cross, where Jesus died for the sins of all people. What a loving, caring, hugging God we have! Now we can be ready for anything!

_____Let's talk: Why did Jesus hug the children? Why do people today give one another hugs? Plan to give someone you love a hug to show how much you care for them and how much God loves and cares for them too.

_____Let's pray: Lord Jesus, since You love me, Now spread Your wings above me And shield me from alarm.
Though Satan would devour me, Let angel guards sing o'er me: This child of God shall meet no harm.

J. W.

Do You Understand?

Now an angel of the Lord said to Philip, "Go south to the road ... that goes down from Jerusalem to Gaza." So he started out, and on his way he met an Ethiopian eunuch, an important official ... sitting in his chariot reading the book of Isaiah the prophet. The Spirit told Philip, "Go to that chariot and stay near it." Then Philip ran up to the chariot and heard the man reading Isaiah. ... "Do you understand what you are reading?" Philip asked. "How can I," he said, "unless someone explains it to me?" So he invited Philip to come up and sit with him. Acts 8:26–31 ✑

Draw a capital *O* on top of the curve of a lower case *h*. Then place a *small* capital *M* on top of the capital *O*. Finish with a small sideways *s* in the center of the capital *O*. What do you have?

"*A big mess!*" Shelley crumpled the paper and tossed it into the trash can.

"What's wrong, dear?" her mother asked.

"Oh, it's this puzzle. I just can't do it. I need someone to explain it to me."

Her mother walked over to Shelley's desk, picked up the wad of paper, and smoothed it out. "Let's see what we have here. Hmmm ... Look, Shelley, here's how it works..."

Do you sometimes read something but have no idea what it means? You're not the only one. Today's Scripture reading tells about an Ethiopian man who couldn't understand what he was reading from the Bible. What did God do? He sent Philip to help him. Philip sat with the man and explained the Scriptures. He told him how Jesus was sent to suffer, die, and live again for all people. That includes each of us.

Does God help *us* when we have trouble understanding Scripture? Yes, all the time. He gives us parents, pastors, and teachers to share the Gospel with us and lead us to a better understanding of His Word. God blesses us through them in the same way that He blessed the Ethiopian through Philip.

_____Let's do: The next time you have a question about something in the Bible, study it as a family. It's fun digging into Scripture together!

_____Let's pray: Heavenly Father, thank You for sending Your Son to be our Savior. Thank You also for the gift of parents, pastors, and teachers who nurture us in the Christian faith. In Jesus' name. Amen.

(Try Shelley's puzzle. Did you get a picture of a cat sitting on a chair?) C. F.

Build on the Rock

The headlines in the morning paper read "House and Street Slide into Gully!" It was hard to believe. Cars had driven on the street just the day before. Now no one could drive on the street.

The house had been built on a type of soil called *loess*, which is very sandy. After days of rain, the ground gave way. The building and half the street slid down into a gully, where they broke into pieces.

Loess soil is not a good foundation. A foundation needs to be firm and secure so it can stand strong against any kind of problem. If the foundation is weak, anything built on top of it will fall.

Jesus told about a wise man who built on a foundation of rock. A rock is firm and strong. It will not give way in any kind of weather. But Jesus wasn't just talking about things like houses. He was talking about life. Many people trust in other things besides Jesus to save them. But these things do not last. They give way just like the loess soil.

There is only one foundation that is solid—Jesus, *the* rock. Jesus is our foundation. He is firm and strong and sure. When our lives are built on Jesus, nothing can harm us. Not even sin, death, or the devil can make us slip or slide away. Jesus is our rock. We can depend on Him.

_____ Let's talk: What are some things people build their lives on, other than Jesus? Why did Jesus warn people not to do this?

_____ Let's pray: Dear God, we are weak, but You are strong. Thank You for being our rock, our solid foundation. In Jesus' name we pray. Amen.

C. F.

Read from God's Word

[Jesus said] "Therefore everyone who hears these words of Mine and puts them into practice is like a wise man who built his house on the rock. The rain came down, the streams rose, and the winds blew and beat against that house; yet it did not fall, because it had its foundation on the rock. But everyone who hears these words of Mine and does not put them into practice is like a foolish man who built his house on sand. The rain came down, the streams rose, and the winds blew and beat against that house, and it fell with a great crash." Matthew 7:24–27 ✑

New Snow

New snow! Joey was excited as he peeked out his window. He ran to the kitchen. "Dad," Joey begged, "help me get my snow stuff on! I want to go outside right now!"

Dad helped Joey into his clothes. First came thermal underwear, then jeans and two shirts. On top went the snow pants, parka, boots, and mittens. Finally, Dad tied Joey's hood strings and wrapped a warm scarf around his head.

Joey stepped onto the front porch. How beautiful everything was! Snow clung to the electric wires, frosted the tree branches, and piled along the house and tool shed.

Suddenly, kersplat! Joey saw blue sky. A big clump of snow had fallen on Joey. He was lying flat on his back!

"Are you okay, Joey?" Dad called from the door.

"Yeah, Dad, all the piles of clothes protected me from getting hurt. Besides, I kinda like the view from here!"

Sometimes we are surprised when things happen. God's love for us is full of surprises, giving more than we expect. Because of our sins we deserve God's punishment. But, through Jesus' death and resurrection, God in love erased our sins. Instead we receive forgiveness and the promise to live with God forever in heaven.

God always provides us with more than we expect or deserve. How can we help but praise Him for His wonderful love?

_____Let's talk: Share about a time when you were surprised. How has God surprised you? When have you been aware of God's protection?

_____Let's pray: (Complete the sentence stems with your own words.) Loving God, thank You for … Please protect us from … In Jesus' name we pray. Amen.

C. W.

Read 'Em and Weep

Read 'em and weep!" Often these words are said by the tough, card-playing cowboy in the old Western movies. Sometimes these words led to fist fights or a gunfight at sundown. In the movies the cowboys never backed down from a fight. Money, power, pride, and even a cowboy's horse were worth protecting with a fight to death.

"Read 'em and weep" are also the words of Jesus in today's Scripture lesson, but they mean something entirely different. Jesus had purposely waited until it was too late to come and help His friend Lazarus. Lazarus died and had already been buried by the time Jesus arrived. His sisters, Mary and Martha, were very sad. Jesus *reads* their sadness and responds with His own *weeping*.

But Jesus didn't stop there. He went with Mary and Martha to the tomb of Lazarus. There He confidently prayed to God the Father and called Lazarus to walk out of the tomb. He called Lazarus from death to life.

Read from God's Word

"Lord," Martha said to Jesus, "if You had been here, my brother would not have died. But I know that even now God will give You whatever You ask." Jesus said to her, "Your brother will rise again. Martha answered, "I know he will rise again in the resurrection at the last day." Jesus said to her, "I am the resurrection and the life. He who believes in Me will live, even though he dies; and whoever lives and believes in Me will never die. Do you believe this?" "Yes, Lord," she told Him, "I believe that You are the Christ, the Son of God, who was to come into the world." John 11:21–27 ✍

Only a short time later Jesus hung on the cross for us. He didn't come to the cross because of silver or gold, power or pride. Jesus faced this punishment because of us, His lost and sinful children. He took our place in the fight against sin because He knew we could not win the fight on our own. He won the victory for us. Read 'em and rejoice!

———Let's talk: How did Jesus show He is truly the Son of God? How did Jesus also show that He is true Man? (You can read the complete Bible story in John 11:1–44.)

———Let's pray: Thank You, Jesus, for defeating sin, death, and the devil for our sake. Work within each of us the faith to believe in You and to trust You for all things. Amen.

C. W.

february

You Mean the World to Him

For God so loved the world ..." You know that verse, don't you? You probably memorized it a long time ago. It's an important verse. To know and believe this verse is a matter of life and death—eternal life and eternal death. Have you ever stopped to think about what the word *world* means?

A few years ago a teacher asked a class of sixth graders in a Christian school what they thought the word *world* in this Bible verse meant. In other words, whom does God love so much that He sent His Son to die for them so they could live in heaven forever with Him? Some of the students said *world* means *everything*; others answered *everybody*; some didn't know.

"What about you?" the teacher asked. "Does *world* include *you*? Could you place your names in that verse in place of *the world*?"

One student named Susan said, "Oh, no. I wish I could do that, but I don't think it means me." The teacher had Good News for Susan that day.

What about *you*? Could *you* put your name in that verse, replacing *the world*? Try it. Say, "God so loved *(your name)* that He gave His one and only Son, that whoever believes in Him shall not perish but have eternal life."

It's true. Believe it. It's God's Good News for you today and every day. You mean the world to Him!

Read from God's Word

[Jesus said] "For God so loved the world that He gave His one and only Son, that whoever believes in Him shall not perish but have eternal life. For God did not send His Son into the world to condemn the world, but to save the world through Him. ... Everyone who does evil hates the light, and will not come into the light for fear that his deeds will be exposed. But whoever lives by the truth comes into the light, so that it may be seen plainly that what he has done has been done through God." John 3:16–21 ☙

_____Let's do: Use a bright piece of construction paper and a black marker to write out John 3:16, replacing the words *the world* with your name. Place the verse where your family will be sure to see it every day. Read the verse aloud at least once a day.

_____Let's pray: God of love, sometimes it's hard to believe You love us so much that You gave Your Son to die for our sins. Help us believe this and live every day in the joy of knowing we belong to You. In Jesus' name. Amen.

K. B. M.

Read from God's Word

Simeon took Him in his arms and praised God, saying: "Sovereign Lord, as You have promised, You now dismiss Your servant in peace. For my eyes have seen Your salvation, which You have prepared in the sight of all people, a light for revelation to the Gentiles and for glory to Your people Israel." Luke 2:28–32 ✍

A Holiday and a Holy Day

Today is a holiday, but it is not about groundhogs, the end of winter, or anything like that. The word *holiday* comes from *holy day*, and *holy* means "set apart for God's use." That means a *holy day* is a day set apart for us to think about what God has done for us.

Today marks the Presentation of Our Lord, the day when Mary and Joseph brought baby Jesus to the temple to be presented, or devoted, to God. They were following God's command to bring the firstborn son to the temple. But this was no ordinary firstborn son. This was God's Son, born to do the most important work of all.

Simeon and Anna were in the temple that day. Anna was an elderly woman who lived there, worshiping God night and day. After seeing Jesus, Anna spoke to many people about God's plan for Him to be the Savior of all people. God had promised Simeon that he wouldn't die until he had seen the Savior. The Bible reading tells us that Simeon knew He had seen the Savior and was assured of God's salvation. Now he was ready to die in peace.

This is a holy day for us too. It's a day to recall that because Jesus gave His life for our sins, we are holy to God. We are special, set apart for God's use. We belong to Him!

_____Let's do: Pray Simeon's words in Luke 2:29–32 as your family prayer. Then ask God to help you live as the holy people He made you through Christ.

_____Let's pray: Blessed Savior, thank You that because You are holy and gave Your life for us, we are holy to God. Help us live as Your children, holy and precious to You. Amen.

K. B. M.

Good Food

Once there was a woman who went to the pet store to buy a talking bird. The owner showed her a beautiful bird. "But will it talk?" she asked.

"Of course," said the owner. "Just talk to it a lot and soon it will be talking."

The woman took her bird home. After a week she went back to the pet store. "The bird won't talk even after I talked to it all week," she told the shop owner.

"Try this mirror," he said. "When the bird sees itself in the mirror, it will start talking."

Another week passed, and the bird still didn't talk. The woman got angry. "I thought you told me this bird would talk!" she shouted at the pet-store owner.

"I have one more thing for you to try," he told her. "Put this ladder in your bird's cage. After it gets some exercise, it will start talking. If not, bring it back, and I'll give you a new bird." The next week the woman came in to the pet store. "The bird died," she told the owner.

"I'm very sorry," he said. "Did it say anything before it died?"

"Well, yes," she told him. "It said, 'Don't they have any food at that pet store?'"

We can have many things like money, food, friends, good grades, and a happy family. But if we are missing God, nothing else matters. Jesus said, "I am the bread of life. He who comes to Me will never go hungry" (John 6:35).

Read from God's Word

Jesus said to them, "I tell you the truth, ... it is my Father who gives you the true bread from heaven. For the bread of God is He who comes down from heaven and gives life to the world." "Sir," they said, "from now on give us this bread." Then Jesus declared, "I am the bread of life. He who comes to Me will never go hungry, and he who believes in Me will never be thirsty. But as I told you, you have seen Me and still you do not believe. All that the Father gives Me will come to Me, and whoever comes to Me I will never drive away." John 6:32–37

_____Let's talk: What things get in the way of our family feeding on God's Word? What can we do to get those things out of the way?

_____Let's pray: Dear Jesus, thank You for loving us and giving Your life to save us. Help us treasure Your Word and feast on it often. In Your name we pray. Amen.

K. B. M.

For the word of God is living and active. Sharper than any double-edged sword, it penetrates even to dividing soul and spirit, joints and marrow; it judges the thoughts and attitudes of the heart. Nothing in all creation is hidden from God's sight. Everything is uncovered and laid bare before the eyes of Him to whom we must give account. Hebrews 4:12–13 ✐

Naked but Not Ashamed

One winter day a college student got up early to go to class. She didn't want to wake her roommate, so she got dressed without turning on any lights. She put on her coat and went.

When she got to class, she started to take off her coat. Suddenly she stopped. She had forgotten to put on her skirt! Needless to say, she didn't hang up her coat. She wrapped it snugly around her until class was over.

We cover ourselves to keep from being embarrassed in front of others. The Bible reading talks about another way people cover themselves. Some people think they can hide from God by pretending they do nothing wrong or by making excuses for the wrong things they do.

Here are some excuses people use to cover their sins: "I didn't mean it"; "Everyone else does it"; "I couldn't help it"; "I didn't know it was wrong." Maybe you've used some of these excuses yourself.

But we can't hide from God. He looks right through our excuses and sees our sins—every wrong act and every wrong thought. We are totally naked before God, and that's a good thing. God sent His Son, Jesus, to die for all our wrongs and all our excuses. He loves us and forgives us. Jesus is all the covering we need to stand before God and not be ashamed.

_____Let's do: Take some time to talk about how to confess to God the wrongs you did today. Then read 1 John 1:8–9 and trust that God loves each of you and forgives you.

_____Let's pray: Loving Father, thank You for loving us and forgiving us for Jesus' sake. Amen.

K. B. M.

How Does Your Garden Grow?

Read from God's Word

[Jesus said] "The seed is the word of God. Those along the path are the ones who hear, and then the devil comes and takes away the word from their hearts, so that they may not believe and be saved. Those on the rock are the ones who receive the word with joy when they hear it, but they have no root. They believe for a while, but in the time of testing they fall away. The seed that fell among thorns stands for those who hear, but as they go on their way they are choked by life's worries, riches and pleasures, and they do not mature. But the seed on good soil stands for those with a noble and good heart, who hear the word, retain it, and by persevering produce a crop." Luke 8:11–15 ✐

Rosa was miserable. She was always arguing with her mother. She was tired of being told what to do and wanted to be left alone. She didn't even care about school anymore, just about hanging out with her friends or watching TV.

Rosa used to like going to church, but she didn't like it anymore. After all, none of her friends went to church. Rosa had also stopped reading the Bible. She wanted more fun things to read.

Do you know why Rosa was miserable? Her faith couldn't grow without God's Word. The longer she was away from it, the worse she felt.

Here's an experiment to try: Plant some seeds in four different pots. Do not water the first pot. Flood the second pot with water, keeping the soil super-wet. Pour milk on the third pot. And put just the right amount of water on the fourth pot. Watch the pots for one month. The seeds in the fourth pot will grow, but watch to see what happens to the others.

God's Word is the food you need to grow in Christ. Without it, your faith will dry up. With it, your faith will grow until you're bearing fruit for God.

Jesus is the vine; we are His branches. He tells us: "Remain in Me, and I will remain in you" (John 15:4). When we stay connected to our Savior, we have a life that continues forever.

_____ Let's talk: What does it mean to be connected to Christ? Can we do this on our own? How does it happen?

_____ Let's pray: Lord Jesus, thank You for planting Your Word in our hearts. Give us Your Holy Spirit so we can grow strong in You and bear the fruit of good works. In Your name we pray. Amen.

K. B. M.

A Friend Who Never Leaves

"That's the worst possible day to move!" Gabe shouted, exploding into tears. Gabe's parents told him they would be moving to another state September first. "School starts September second. I won't even be able to say good-bye to my friends," Gabe sobbed, heartbroken at the thought of leaving the friends he had been in school with since kindergarten.

Gabe's mom felt sad too. "I wish we could wait, but we have to move then so Dad can start his new job. We will invite some of your friends over before we move. I know it will be hard to leave them, but at least you can say good-bye."

Gabe's family moved, and for a while Gabe felt lonely. But soon he started making new friends, and it seemed he'd forgotten all about the friends he'd left. Then one day Gabe said to his mom, "I wish some of my friends from back home could come to visit."

Gabe's mom understood. "Moving away from good friends is hard, isn't it?" she said. "Things will never be just like they were. But some things are the same and will never change. Dad and I love you, your brothers love you, and best of all, Jesus loves you. Jesus is the Friend who never leaves. He has promised to be with you always, even if we move 100 times."

Gabe smiled. "That's a good thing to remember," he said.

_____Let's talk: Whom have you had to say good-bye to in the last year? Do you know someone who may be having a hard time leaving someone else? If so, pray for that person.

_____Let's pray: Dear Jesus, You are our forever Friend. You even laid down Your life for us. Thank You for Your promise to be with us always. Help each one of us be a friend to others, especially those who are lonely. In Your name we pray. Amen.

K. B. M.

The Tempting Cupcake

Peter's mom bought four chocolate cupcakes for the family's supper. Two-year-old William wanted one as soon as he spotted them. "No," Mom told him, "those are for dessert."

Mom, Dad, and William all had a cupcake after supper. Peter said he wanted to save his for later. So Mom put Peter's cupcake on the counter, out of William's reach.

Not long after supper was over, William began begging for the remaining cupcake. "No, William, that's Peter's cupcake," Mom reminded him. "You may have a cookie if you like."

But William didn't give up on getting that last cupcake. As soon as everyone else was out of the kitchen, he pushed a chair to the counter, climbed up, and ate Peter's cupcake.

Temptations to do wrong come to us all. Perhaps you have been tempted to cheat in school when you had not studied well. Or maybe you have been tempted to lie to your parents to keep them from finding out about something you did wrong.

The Good News for today is that Jesus was tempted too. He understands the temptations each one of us meets and is with us to help us face them. Jesus never gave in to temptations to sin. When we do give in to sin, we can know He forgives us and will help us face the next temptation that comes along.

_____Let's do: Make a list of the most difficult temptations some of you face. Take them to God in prayer, and ask Him to give each one of you power to say "No!" to them.

_____Let's pray: Dear Jesus, we thank You that You never gave in to temptation. You earned forgiveness for our sins through Your dying on the cross. Be with us today in all that we do, especially as we meet temptation. In Your strong name we pray. Amen.

K. B. M.

Read from God's Word

Therefore, since we have a great High Priest who has gone through the heavens, Jesus the Son of God, let us hold firmly to the faith we profess. For we do not have a high priest who is unable to sympathize with our weaknesses, but we have one who has been tempted in every way, just as we are—yet was without sin. Let us then approach the throne of grace with confidence, so that we may receive mercy and find grace to help us in our time of need. Hebrews 4:14–16 ༒

Read from God's Word

... *A centurion came to [Jesus], asking for help. "Lord," he said, "my servant lies at home paralyzed and in terrible suffering." Jesus said to him, "I will go and heal him." The centurion replied, "Lord, I do not deserve to have You come under my roof. But just say the word, and my servant will be healed. ..." Then Jesus said to the centurion, "Go! It will be done just as you believed it would." And his servant was healed at that very hour. Matthew 8:5–9, 13* ✍

Undeserved Blessings

Sam worked hard to earn enough money to buy a new bike. He mowed lawns in the summer, raked leaves in the fall, and shoveled snow in the winter. By spring, he had only half the money he needed. "I'll never have enough money for that bike," Sam fretted.

One day Sam came home and saw the bike he was saving for in the garage. Sam couldn't believe his eyes! Was it for him? He hadn't earned enough money to buy it. It wasn't even his birthday.

When Sam's mom came home from work, he raced out to meet her. "Yes, it's for you," she told him.

"But I didn't earn it. And it's not my birthday," Sam said. "Why did you get this for me, Mom?"

"Because you're my son, and I love you. Is that a good enough reason?" Mom replied. "Now go and enjoy your bike."

Why does God give us good things? Because we're cute or smart? Because we try hard to obey and do the right things? Because we go to church on Sundays and have devotions during the week? Nope—none of these is reason.

The answer to the question is simple. God loves us. He made each one of us and we belong to Him. He wants us to enjoy life that will never end because of what Jesus did for us on the cross at Calvary.

_____Let's talk: What are some things God has given you that you don't deserve? How can you show your thanks for these blessings?

_____Let's pray: Loving Father, You are so good to us. Thanks for all the good things we enjoy in life. Thank You especially for the gifts of forgiveness and life with You. Help us live as Your children who belong to You. In Jesus' name we pray. Amen.

K. B. M.

Time-Out

Ⓐ young girl was very excited about moving to a new house. She jumped up and down and said, "A new house—with a bedroom of my own and a place for all my toys!" Suddenly she stopped jumping. "Dad," she asked quietly, "does our new house have corners?"

She was thinking about the times she had messed up and had to have a time-out in the corner. Our parents and teachers show us love by setting limits and disciplining us when we mess up. When this happens, we may not feel like they love us, but they discipline, or teach, in order for us to learn from our mistakes.

Do you think our heavenly Father ever makes us do "time-out?" In chapter 12 of Hebrews, we read: "The Lord disciplines those He loves."

Some days we show hatred instead of love; we push and shove instead of giving hugs. The wrong things we do make us feel alone, separated from God. But our heavenly Father doesn't leave us alone in the corner. He sent His Son, Jesus, to suffer the punishment for our sins on the cross. Jesus lovingly waits with us in the corner, helping us to see what was wrong and to teach us with His lessons of love.

Taking our hand, Jesus helps us up. He hugs us ever so dearly. His Holy Spirit helps us give hugs of love to others.

Read from God's Word

And you have forgotten that word of encouragement that addresses you as sons: "My son, do not make light of the Lord's discipline, and do not lose heart when He rebukes you, because the Lord disciplines those He loves, and He punishes everyone He accepts as a son." Endure hardship as discipline; God is treating you as sons. ... God disciplines us for our good, that we may share in His holiness. No discipline seems pleasant at the time, but painful. Later on, however, it produces a harvest of righteousness and peace. ... Hebrews 12:5–11 ᕤ

_____Let's do: Take a "time-out" every day to be with God. Thank Him for His love. Remember the grace of your Baptism when He adopted you as His very own.

_____Let's pray: Thank You, heavenly Father, for being with us always. We are glad that You discipline us in love. Amen.

C. D.

In God's Workplace

Read from God's Word

But because of His great love for us, God, who is rich in mercy, made us alive with Christ even when we were dead in transgressions—it is by grace you have been saved. And God raised us up with Christ and seated us with Him in the heavenly realms in Christ Jesus, in order that in the coming ages He might show the incomparable riches of His grace, expressed in His kindness to us in Christ Jesus. Ephesians 2:4–7 ✍

One day Brianna went with her mom to work. It was "Take Your Daughter to Work" day. She sat swiveling in her mom's chair and helped her work on the computer.

Brianna enjoyed the pizza, the make-your-own ice cream sundaes, and the half-day off from school. Her mom enjoyed laughing and talking with Brianna. It was a good day.

We have a heavenly Father who invites us each day to watch Him at work. Every morning He paints a beautiful sunrise for us to enjoy. He shapes snow sculptures and ice designs for our delight. God creates things in our lives.

Some days, though, we can't see God at work. Our sin keeps us from seeing God. We feel all alone, hopeless, and afraid.

But our Father forgives our sins and helps us to see Him at work once again. He does this because His Son, Christ Jesus, died and rose again for our sins.

Where is Christ now? He ascended into heaven. He sits today at His Father's right hand. Where are we, God's children? According to our Bible verse, we are sitting with Christ.

What a grand seat Christ has ready for us! From by His side we can see our Father at work. The Holy Spirit shares with us the riches of God's wisdom and teaches us His work of love.

What a good day! What a grand day, each day we spend with our Father.

_____Let's talk: With whom can you share the news about the best seat in the universe?

_____Let's pray: Thank You, loving Father, for inviting us into Your workplace, Your kingdom. We love being with You. Amen.

C. D.

Knit Together in Love

Today was Friday, and Suzanne loved Fridays. This afternoon she would visit Mrs. Gordon, her mother's friend from church.

Everyone in the church knew Mrs. Gordon as the Knitting Lady. Whenever a baby was born, the Knitting Lady gave a blanket to the parents. She made scarves and mittens for the fall clothing drive. All the Sunday school students had knitted bookmarks for their Bibles. And this winter, on Friday afternoons, Mrs. Gordon was giving Suzanne "how to knit" lessons.

At first, handling the long needles didn't feel right. But before long, Suzanne got used to them. She learned to cast on stitches, the difference between "knit" and "purl," and how to change yarn colors. It was fun to see her knitting grow with every row of stitches.

"Knitting is like making a long chain, Suzanne," said Mrs. Gordon. "The first stitch is the anchor. Even if the other stitches unravel, the anchor holds tight so you can make the chain again."

St. Paul wrote that Christians are to be united, or knit together, in love. Christ is the anchor. As we live in Him, we grow in faith with others who also believe. Like a knitted blanket or sweater, God's people grow together as they love one another. The Bible says that we love because Jesus first loved us and gave Himself to save us.

Read from God's Word

I want you to know how much I am struggling for you and for...all who have not met me personally. My purpose is that they may be encouraged in heart and united in love, so that they may have the full riches of complete understanding, in order that they may know the mystery of God, namely, Christ, in whom are hidden all the treasures of wisdom and knowledge...so then, just as you received Christ Jesus as Lord, continue to live in Him, rooted and built up in Him, strengthened in the faith as you were taught, and overflowing with thankfulness. Colossians 2:1–3, 6–7 ✍

_____Let's do: Look closely at a sweater or other knitted piece. No matter how hard you look, the anchor stitch usually can't be found when the project is finished. But maybe you can see how the stitches are joined together like a chain.

_____Let's pray: Thank You, Jesus, for being the anchor stitch that holds all believers together. And thank You for loving us first so we can love one another. Amen.

D. N.

Silence and Speaking

Read from God's Word

"Be still, and know that I am God; I will be exalted among the nations, I will be exalted in the earth." Psalm 46:10

There is a time for everything, and a season for every activity under heaven ... a time to be silent and a time to speak. Ecclesiastes 3:1, 7 ◌

Nearly everyone likes to visit the zoo. Seeing wild animals, and sometimes even getting close to them, can be fun. Some animals even look quite strange.

One favorite zoo animal is the giraffe. That tiny head on top of that v-e-r-y long neck and those thin, wobbly legs—way cool! Giraffes are huge and powerful, and at 18 or 20 feet tall, they are taller than any other living being. What's best is that they do not attack or hurt other animals just because they are so big. In fact, they are mostly plant-eaters.

Another amazing thing about giraffes is that they are mostly silent. They make tiny noises to communicate with one another but no roars or screeches to scare other creatures.

Our everyday world is pretty noisy. There is so much going on around us that sometimes we can hardly hear our own thoughts. The psalm writer says we should sometimes be still. Being quiet lets us think about God and meditate on the gift of His Son, Jesus.

Ecclesiastes 3:7 reminds us that although it's good to be quiet at times, sometimes we should speak. First we need to learn all we can about how God loved us so much He sent the Savior. Then, like giraffes, we can use our voices—not to scream and shout, but to tell others the wonderful Good News of Jesus, who came to seek and rescue lost sinners.

_____Let's talk: Have each person name his or her favorite animal. Talk about ways each creature reminds you of the way we live as Christians.

_____Let's pray: Thanks, dear Lord, for the beauty of this world and the variety of creatures You have made. Help us know when to be silent and when to speak. Through Jesus we ask this. Amen.

D. N.

How Snoopy Is Like Us

Read from God's Word

When you were slaves to sin, you were free from the control of righteousness. What benefit did you reap at that time from the things you are now ashamed of? Those things result in death! But now that you have been set free from sin and have become slaves to God, the benefit you reap leads to holiness, and the result is eternal life. For the wages of sin is death, but the gift of God is eternal life in Christ Jesus our Lord. Romans 6:20–23 ✑

Do you like to read comic strips? A favorite cartoon character for many people is Snoopy, the floppy-eared beagle in *Peanuts*. But most people don't know that the artist who created Snoopy wanted to have readers see some things in Snoopy that were like being a Christian.

Snoopy is not perfect. Sometimes he steals the blanket Linus clutches. He makes fun of Charlie Brown and kisses Lucy when she doesn't want him to. He also teases his little bird friend, Woodstock. And he brags about the furniture and paintings in his doghouse.

But at the same time Snoopy is a loyal friend to Charlie Brown. He sticks by him when things go wrong. He forgives everyone who hurts him. And he "dances for joy" to show his happiness and to thank God for blessing him.

Is Snoopy like a real Christian? He's only make-believe, of course. But his cartoon character is similar to how we can be good and bad at the same time. By ourselves we are self-centered and can't help being sinful. But God made us His children in our Baptism. The Holy Spirit now works in us to help us live as "little Christs," sharing God's love with others. We are sinners and saints at the same time because Jesus Christ died and rose again.

What if we called each other saints? Maybe it would help us remember to dance for joy in thanksgiving to God. Think it over.

_____Let's do: Look in the newspaper or in a library book for *Peanuts*. See if you can find examples of a character acting like a little Christ.

_____Let's pray: Thank You, God, for washing us clean in Baptism. Help us live to be more like Your saints, for Jesus' sake. Amen.

D. N.

Read from God's Word

Dear friends, let us love one another, for love comes from God. ... Whoever does not love does not know God, because God is love. This is how God showed His love among us: He sent His one and only Son into the world that we might live through Him. This is love: not that we loved God, but that He loved us and sent His Son as an atoning sacrifice for our sins. Dear friends, since God so loved us, we also ought to love one another. No one has ever seen God; but if we love one another, God lives in us and His love is made complete in us. 1 John 4:7–12 ✐

Happy Valentine's Day

Did you know that Valentine was a real person? He was a priest who lived in Rome about 250 years after Jesus was born. There are many stories about St. Valentine, and after so many years we can't be sure exactly which ones are true. But we do know that he was a martyr who refused to give up his Christian faith. He died on February 14, the day that has been called St. Valentine's Day for the last 1,500 years.

Over the years, Valentine's Day has helped many people celebrate love and friendship. Some think it's because Valentine helped young people get married. Whatever the reason, today we use cards, candy, and flowers to say "Be my valentine." Red hearts have become the symbol of love.

St. John tells us that love comes from God Himself. We would not be able to love others if God had not loved us first. And the way God chose to show His love was by sending His one and only Son into the world. What a valentine gift from God! Because Jesus was the sacrifice for us, we can now love one another. And when we love each other, God lives in us.

Trading valentines is fun. Some of the ones for sale are silly, and a few might even be mean. But mostly they help us show our friendship and love for one another. Maybe we should pretend it's Valentine's Day every day!

_____Let's talk: Write a valentine letter or poem that explains how God's love helps your family to love one another.

_____Let's pray: God of love, help us love others as You have loved us. In Jesus' name. Amen.

D. N.

Hooray for Hoops

K now what I like best about February?" Bryant asked his dad. "There are so many basketball games to play and watch."

"I agree," said Dad.

"Me too!" chimed in twins Betsy and Billie.

"Let's make that unanimous," said Mom. "Besides Bryant's games at school and you girls in the Y-league, we watch cousin Jared's college team. This family sees so much basketball, we must love it!"

What's so special about "hoops?" Although individual players some-times make spectacular plays, it's a game that depends on teamwork. Each person has a special role to play. Some players may not score many points. They help the team as they dribble or pass the ball, guard the opponents, or cheer from the bench. One player may be the star who gets the most atten-tion. But that person cannot play the game alone—everyone is needed.

Read from God's Word

Just as each of us has one body with many members, and these members do not all have the same function, so in Christ we who are many form one body, and each member belongs to all the others. We have different gifts, according to the grace given us. If a man's gift is prophesying, let him use it in proportion to his faith. If it is serving, let him serve; if it is teaching, let him teach; if it is encouraging, let him encourage; if it is contributing to the needs of others, let him give generously; if it is leadership, let him govern diligently; if it is showing mercy, let him do it cheerfully. Romans 12:4–8

In a way, believers in Jesus are like a huge team. As the Bible says, we are members of the body of Christ, but we don't have the same roles. You may be a leader or a supporter. Or maybe you encourage and help others.

We have different gifts. And no one is more valuable or more impor-tant than another. The only "star" in the body of believers is its head, Jesus Christ. He once offered Himself on the cross to pay for all our sins. And that offering makes the entire body whole.

_____Let's talk: Do you enjoy playing or watching team sports? How is your fam-ily like a team? What does the picture of Christians as a team help you understand about your family? About the church?

_____Let's pray: Holy Spirit, be with us as we serve together in the body of Christ. Help us appreciate others who have different gifts and roles than we do. In Jesus' name. Amen.

D. N.

Long-Distance Sisters

Read from God's Word

For this reason, ever since I heard about your faith in the Lord Jesus and your love for all the saints, I have not stopped giving thanks for you, remembering you in my prayers. I keep asking that the God of our Lord Jesus Christ, the glorious Father, may give you the Spirit of wisdom and revelation, so that you may know Him better. I pray also that the eyes of your heart may be enlightened in order that you may know the hope to which He has called you, the riches of His glorious inheritance in the saints, and His incomparably great power for us who believe.
Ephesians 1:15–19 ✎

Ginger couldn't wait to check the mail every day. Her class had written to an organization that matched pen pals all over the world. Finally, one day there was an envelope from Australia.

The letter came from a girl named Bronwyn. She was the same age as Ginger. "Wow, Mom," said Ginger, "this is amazing! Did you know that February is in the middle of summer in Australia?"

The girls wrote lots of letters telling each other about their two countries. They described their families and friends. They wrote about school, hobbies, and special experiences. It was like having a long-distance sister to share things with.

One day Ginger wrote about how exciting it was to play the part of Mary in last year's Christmas pageant. Ginger also wrote about how she believed in Jesus as her Savior. It was the first time she had written about her faith.

How wonderful it was when Bronwyn wrote back, "I am so glad to know that you're a Christian too!" After that, the girls also shared prayers and songs, and told about Sunday school lessons. They discovered that despite many things that were different between them, they were united by the love of God.

They agreed that some day they would meet in person and greet each other as sisters in Christ. Because Jesus died for the sins of the whole world, He is the strongest link. He holds believers together.

_____Let's talk: Talk about some of the different people and friends with whom you can talk about Jesus. When are some good times to talk about Jesus with others in your family? Read more of Paul's encouragement in his letter to the early Christians in Ephesians 1:19–23.

_____Let's pray: Thank You, God, for making us sisters and brothers in Christ. Help us tell others about our Savior. Amen.

D. N.

Just Laugh!

B ecky's family had always lived in the South. Now they had moved to a northern town. It was exciting to see the first heavy snowfall.

Making snowballs and playing in all that white stuff was fun. But walking on icy sidewalks was not. Becky fell down lots of times before learning how to bend her knees and take tiny, careful steps. Her teacher said, "When you start to fall, Becky, just laugh! It will make you feel better."

Laughter is good for us. It helps us stop worrying, relaxes our bodies, and makes us feel good.

Did you know that children laugh more than adults do? When boys and girls hear and see things that seem funny, they just start to laugh. But when people get older, they think they should be more serious. Sometimes they even keep themselves from laughing out loud.

Maybe grown ups worry more than children do. Maybe they forget that God is in charge of our lives. Psalm 121 teaches that He cares for us and always watches over us. It's true that we all have troubles, but Jesus is the proof that God loves us. He came to save us from sin and any harm that could ever threaten us. Even death will not separate us from God's love.

Worry and happiness usually don't go together. So if you fall on the ice or some other trouble comes along, put your trust in God. And just laugh!

_____Let's talk: What keeps you from feeling happy? How does reading Psalm 121 help your family remember God's care for you?

_____Let's pray: Heavenly Father, we know You love us. Thank You for Your Son, Jesus, who makes us sure of Your love and care. Help us be good examples of showing happiness for others. Amen.

D. N.

Read from God's Word

I lift up my eyes to the hills— where does my help come from? My help comes from the LORD, the Maker of heaven and earth. He will not let your foot slip—He who watches over you will not slumber; indeed, He who watches over Israel will neither slumber nor sleep. The LORD watches over you—the LORD is your shade at your right hand; the sun will not harm you by day, nor the moon by night. The LORD will keep you from all harm—He will watch over your life; the LORD will watch over your coming and going both now and forevermore. Psalm 121

Predicting the Future

Read from God's Word

... A slave girl ... had a spirit by which she predicted the future. She earned a great deal of money for her owners by fortunetelling. This girl followed Paul and the rest of us, shouting, "These men are servants of the Most High God, who are telling you the way to be saved." She kept this up for many days. Finally Paul became so troubled that he ... said to the spirit, "In the name of Jesus Christ I command you to come out of her!" At that moment the spirit left her. When the owners of the slave girl realized that their hope of making money was gone, they seized Paul and Silas and ... brought them before the magistrates... ."
Acts 16:16–20 〰

Fifty years ago, the first computers filled a whole room. The engineers who worked with one of the world's first computers made a prediction. They said that by the year 2000, computers would weigh only 3,000 pounds. Wouldn't they be surprised to see the computers we have today! Some fit on a desk. Others are easily carried from one place to another.

People have always wanted to predict the future, but it's seldom possible. Lots of people try to make good guesses. Some people even pay others to tell them what will happen in the future. But no one can count on what they say. If they knew what would happen, they could be almost like God.

King Nebuchadnezzar once asked the prophet Daniel to explain a dream and reveal the future. But Daniel told him, "No wise man, enchanter, magician or diviner can explain to the king the mystery he has asked about, but there is a God in heaven who reveals mysteries" (Daniel 2:27–28).

Our lives are full of mysteries, with both troubles and wonderful surprises ahead of us. But Christians don't have to worry about the future. We *know* God cares for us and wants us to be with Him forever. Although we are sinners, we *know* that Jesus died on the cross for our sins. So, we *know* we *will* live with God. That's a future we *can* predict.

———Let's talk: What are some wonderful surprises your family has experienced? Are there any troubles you predicted that never happened?

———Let's pray: Thank You, dear God, for caring for us. Please stay with us during all the unknowns of the future. Through Jesus we pray this. Amen.

D. N.

No Need to Fear

Mrs. Waters began to pass out a thick stack of papers. As she approached, Carol wanted to jump up and run away. When the teacher put the paper on her desk, Carol's worst expectations came true. She had tried hard on this paper. And yet here she was, looking at a glaring bad grade.

Carol knew she was disappointed, and she knew her mom would be disappointed too. What would she say? Would she be ashamed? Would she be angry? She didn't want to find out.

On the short walk home she thought and thought, planning what she would say to Mom. As she passed her church, she noticed a new sign. It said, "God says, 'Do not fear; I will help you.'"

What? She thought. *Is that really true? God, I know You help when terrible things happen, but how about now? A poor grade is not exactly a world crisis, but I'm really worried about telling Mom. Jesus, even though this isn't a big problem, could You help me right now?*

Read from God's Word

"For I am the LORD, your God, who takes hold of your right hand and says to you, Do not fear; I will help you. Do not be afraid, O worm Jacob, O little Israel, for I Myself will help you," declares the LORD, your Redeemer, the Holy One of Israel. Isaiah 41:13–14 ✍

Looking up from her thoughts and prayer, she realized she was home. Carol started to feel afraid once again. But then she remembered God's promise on the sign, "Do not fear; I will help you." She took a deep breath, stood up tall, and asked God to help. She slowly went through the doorway and called, "Mom ..."

_____ Let's talk: Think about a time when you were afraid of something. What did you do about it, or whom did you ask for help? What ways does God use to remind us that He is always with us?

_____ Let's pray: Dear Father, often we're afraid when bad things happen. Because You gave Your only Son for us, You will freely give us everything else we need. Help us remember that You are always with us, always helping us. In Jesus' name. Amen.

C. H.

Cloudy Skies

Read from God's Word

"Whoever would love life and see good days must keep his tongue from evil and his lips from deceitful speech. He must turn from evil and do good; he must seek peace and pursue it. For the eyes of the Lord are on the righteous and His ears are attentive to their prayer, but the face of the Lord is against those who do evil." 1 Peter 3:10–12

One day Cheryl took a plane trip to visit her parents. She relaxed and watched the scenery go by. But after awhile, things on the ground began to get blurry and unclear. Clouds were moving in to block her view.

Cheryl tried to keep looking to see the ground, but as they traveled she could see less and less. Finally, she couldn't see anything on the ground. Then she started to notice the clouds. They were beautiful! They were light and fluffy and very bright from the sun. Cheryl began to enjoy her new view. Soon she forgot all about the earth-view for which she had been striving.

Sometimes our relationship with God is like that. We keep ourselves focused on Jesus until something moves in to block our vision. Usually that thing is so wonderful that it's easy to take our eyes off our Lord. It happens gradually, not all at once. We forget about wanting to be closer to God. These things that distract us are like clouds that are waiting to storm into our lives.

But the Good News is that although these stormy distractions sometimes keep us from seeing God, He never stops seeing us. His vision is never blocked. Jesus suffered and died on the cross and then rose again. Now and forever, God will look at us through the "clear skies" of Jesus and His love for us.

_____Let's talk: What are some distractions that keep you from seeing God? What can you do when these distractions begin to blur your vision?

_____Let's pray: Dear Father, we are sometimes distracted by the things of this world. Thank You that although we sometimes lose sight of You, You always keep us clearly in Your sight. In Jesus' name. Amen.

C. H.

No Puzzle at All

Tim was sitting at the kitchen table when in walked his mother. "What are you doing, Tim? I didn't think you had any homework today."

"Oh, I'm not doing homework, Mom. I'm doing something fun."

Tim's mom took a look at his paper. She saw a jumble of letters in rows and columns. "Oh, a word-find puzzle!" she exclaimed. "I love word-find puzzles."

"I do too," said Tim, "but sometimes I get mad when I can't find the words. Sometimes I want to give up and throw the puzzle away."

Have you ever been frustrated like Tim? You look and look for something and just can't find it. You struggle so hard that you get frazzled. Then you're tempted to give up.

God never wants us to have to hunt for Him. He showed His Son, Jesus Christ, to the whole world. For three years Jesus met and helped many people. At the end of those three years He died on the cross for all of our ugly sins.

God's love for us has never been a secret. He gave us 66 books in the Bible to show His heart of mercy toward us. He doesn't want us to become frustrated looking for Him, so He comes to us.

Many things in the world are puzzling and difficult to understand. But God makes no puzzle of His love for us. His grace and love are offered to us freely and openly through Jesus, our Savior.

Read from God's Word

In the beginning was the Word, and the Word was with God, and the Word was God. ... The Word became flesh and made His dwelling among us. We have seen His glory, the glory of the One and Only, who came from the Father, full of grace and truth. ... From the fullness of His grace we have all received one blessing after another. For the law was given through Moses; grace and truth came through Jesus Christ. No one has ever seen God, but God the One and Only, who is at the Father's side, has made Him known. John 1:1, 14–18

_____Let's talk: Think about a time when you felt frustrated. How did God help you through that time? How does it help us to know that God loves us so much?

_____Let's pray: Dear Father, we are thankful that You have revealed Your love for us so openly, through Your Son, Jesus Christ. Help us be truly content in Him. Amen.

C. H.

Jomo's Secret

Jomo knew he was risking his life every night when he went to Peter Young's hut. Gamal, the witch doctor, had threatened to kill anyone who went near the missionary.

"Peter," asked Jomo, "if Paul changed from someone who persecut-ed Jesus to someone who loved Jesus, can Gamal be changed too?"

"Yes," answered Peter, "but some-one has to tell him. He is afraid that if the people know that Jesus loves them and died for them, he will lose his power. Are you brave enough to tell him that he is wrong?"

About a month later, everyone in the village was excited. The mayflies were back. People happily headed toward the river. They grabbed the mayflies and put them in their mouths. Mayflies were a delicacy among the tribal people.

Peter and his family stood by the river too. Gamal held a mayfly in his hand and offered it to Peter. Peter put the bug in his mouth and took a big gulp. Down it went. The people let out a loud cheer!

The next morning Jomo burst through the door. "Peter, Gamal said we will not die if we talk to you! I don't have to be afraid anymore. Let's get to work."

Many years later, Peter came to thank a grown-up Jomo for helping to translate the Bible into the tribe's language. And guess what? Gamal was now the pastor of the village church.

_____Let's talk: Why was Jomo afraid? Some people today are risking their lives to spread God's Word. How can your family help them?

_____Let's pray: Lord, be with everyone who translates the Bible into other languages. Give them success in sharing Your message of love through Jesus, in whose name we pray. Amen.

E. S.

Mom's Wisdom

Read from God's Word

Therefore, if anyone is in Christ, he is a new creation; the old has gone, the new has come! All this is from God, who reconciled us to Himself through Christ and gave us the ministry of reconciliation: that God was reconciling the world to Himself in Christ, not counting men's sins against them. And He has committed to us the message of reconciliation. We are therefore Christ's ambassadors, as though God were making His appeal through us. We implore you on Christ's behalf: Be reconciled to God. God made Him who had no sin to be sin for us, so that in Him we might become the righteousness of God. 2 Corinthians 5:17–21*

Mom, Shelly won't share her candy bar with me," whined Karen.

"Share with your sister now," prompted Mom.

"Mom! Shelly gave me the small piece," yelled Karen.

"Okay, girls, from now on one of you can split the candy bar in half and the other one can choose which half she wants."

"Cool, Mom. That sounds fair," said Shelly.

"Yeah, if I get to pick, I know Shelly will divide it evenly," said Karen.

Once again Mom had come to the girls' rescue. In a much greater way, God comes to our rescue. God created people to be perfect. We were made to love, care, and share. But the first people fell into sin. We are sinners too. Sometimes we hate, hurt one another, and cheat. If things don't go our way, we grumble. There is nothing we can do to take away our sins.

In His wisdom God takes our sins and faults and trades them for the riches of His love and forgiveness through Jesus Christ. He placed our sins on Jesus who died on the cross. In exchange God gives us eternal life! All who believe in Jesus as their Savior have the forgiveness of sins here on earth and will live eternally in heaven.

Filled with His love for us, God helps us use His love and wisdom to serve others, care for their needs, and joyfully share our blessings with them.

———Let's talk: Think of a time when you didn't feel like sharing. Now, can you think of a time when God helped you want to share? What's the best reason for giving of our possessions to help others?

———Let's pray: Dear Jesus, help us share Your love and our possessions with others. Give each of us a generous heart because of Your generous blessings to us every day. Amen.

P. L.

Splinters and Specks

Read from God's Word

[Jesus said] "Why do you look at the speck of sawdust in your brother's eye and pay no attention to the plank in your own eye? How can you say to your brother, 'Brother, let me take the speck out of your eye,' when you yourself fail to see the plank in your own eye? You hypocrite, first take the plank out of your eye, and then you will see clearly to remove the speck from your brother's eye." Luke 6:41–42 ✍

One day Katelyn rushed into the house. "My thumb! The tree house! It hurts bad!" she cried.

After the tears stopped, Katelyn's aunt looked at her thumb. "I don't see anything," she said. "Let's try soaking your hand."

Katelyn's hand soaked until it was shriveled. They looked again and saw nothing. "It's there, Aunt Carol," Katelyn sobbed. "It hurts a lot."

Her aunt squeezed her finger a bit and saw a tiny speck of a splinter. Bravely, they headed to the medicine cabinet. They gathered supplies for an operation: alcohol, tweezers, and a needle. After five minutes of agony, the splinter was out.

Today's Bible reading tells us to take the big planks out of our own eyes. How do we do that? By searching for our own faults and confessing them to God. He forgives us for the sake of His Son, Jesus, who died on the planks of a cross for all our sins.

The Holy Spirit give us "speck-tackles" to see other people's hurts. He helps us share God's Word with others. His love and forgiveness provide healing—great medicine from our Great Physician.

_____Let's talk: Can you think of some encouraging actions or words to help others? Write them down and ask God to help you put them to use.

_____Let's pray: Lord, forgive us for criticizing and hurting others. Help us see those around us through Your eyes. In Jesus' name we pray. Amen.

C. D.

Smiling Faces

Kelley sat staring at her bedroom walls. Her mom had given her permission to decorate the room as she pleased. She decided to paint the walls white and add great big yellow faces. She wanted a room full of happy faces.

Kelley asked all her friends and family members to draw their faces on the yellow circles and sign their names. Her friend Keri drew a big mouth on her face. But cousin Betsy sketched hers with the tongue sticking out. Katie drew eyes with tears falling from them. And her brother's face was hairy and grim.

"I wanted a happy room," Kelley groaned, her own face unhappy.

Like Kelley's room, the world has people with all kinds of faces. Smiles turn into frowns when we see evil. Evil has an ugly face—proud eyes, a lying tongue, and ears that refuse to listen. Everyone adds to the frowns of life. We all sin.

But our heavenly Father looks on us with love. He sent His Son to die for us. Jesus won forgiveness for us on the cross. His sacrifice washes away the guilt of our sins. His Spirit replaces our gloom with joy. God promises us a heavenly home, where He will wipe every tear from our eyes.

God is with us through good times and bad times. He will never let us down. Seeing God's smile puts a smile on our face. Strengthened by the Holy Spirit, we face life with hope.

Read from God's Word

Therefore, since we have been justified through faith, we have peace with God through our Lord Jesus Christ. ... And we rejoice in the hope of the glory of God. Not only so, but we also rejoice in our sufferings, because we know that suffering produces perseverance; perseverance, character; and character, hope. And hope does not disappoint us, because God has poured out His love into our hearts by the Holy Spirit, whom He has given us. You see at just the right time, when we were still powerless, Christ died for the ungodly. ... But God demonstrates His own love for us in this: While we were still sinners, Christ died for us. Romans 5:1–8 ✐

———Let's talk: Do you know someone who needs a smile? Are smiles contagious? Try giving some.

———Let's pray: Dear Father, thank You for loving us. Pour Your love into our hearts so we can share it with a smile. Amen.

P. L.

Read from God's Word

"Be perfect, therefore, as your heavenly Father is perfect." Matthew 5:48

Jesus answered, "I am the Way and the Truth and the Life. No one comes to the Father except through Me. John 14:6

Spelling Bee

"Christine, it's your turn to spell. Your word is *excellent*," announced the teacher.

Christine stood up and pronounced, "Excellent, e-x-c-e-l-e-n-t, *excellent.*"

"I'm sorry; you are incorrect," said her teacher. "*Excellent* has two *l*s."

It was clear from her tears that Christine was upset about misspelling the word. She had hoped to be the champion. She really wanted to spell all the words perfectly.

Sometimes we feel just like Christine. No matter how hard we try to be perfect, we fail. Matthew 5:48 tells us: "Be perfect ... as your heavenly Father is perfect." But how can we be perfect? We fail God's commands. So often we think of ourselves first and forget about God and others.

That's when we can remember the spelling word a Sunday school teacher once gave to a class. "How do you spell *salvation?*" the teacher asked. But before anyone could answer, he said, "The only way to spell salvation is J-e-s-u-s C-h-r-i-s-t."

Then the teacher asked the class to look up John 14:6. There Jesus says, "I am the Way and the Truth and the Life. No one comes to the Father except through Me."

It's true—the only way to spell *salvation* is J-e-s-u-s C-h-r-i-s-t. Because He took away our imperfections (our sins) by His suffering and death, God says we are now holy and righteous (forgiven). Through faith in Jesus we're safe with God eternally.

_____Let's talk: Have you ever been in a spelling bee? How did you feel when you missed a word? How do *you* spell *salvation?*

_____Let's pray: Dear Jesus, thank You for giving us Your perfection so we can be saved from our sins and mistakes. Help us trust only in You as the way to heaven. Amen.

P. L.

All Will Be Different!

Michael's team had just finished their warm-ups and the big basketball game was about to start. Michael took off his glasses and laid them on the bench while he wiped the sweat off his forehead.

Whomp! Someone threw a heavy bag of balls on the bench, smashing his glasses into little pieces. "No!" Michael yelled as he rescued the pieces of glass from under the bag. Tears ran down his face as he realized he couldn't even *see* the ball without his glasses, much less shoot it.

Everyone has sad times like this—and even worse ones. Grandparents die, parents divorce, bikes are stolen, or people get hurt. But life will not always be this way. When Jesus Christ comes the second time, He will change everything. There will be no more crying or pain. All these "old" things will be gone forever.

In heaven there won't be glasses because Jesus will give us perfect bodies. There won't be fights or divorces because we will all know how to love one another. There will be no funerals because no one will ever die.

Everything will be different because Jesus died on the cross to take away sin and give us eternal life. He rose from the dead to proclaim victory over sin, death, and the power of the devil. We can feel God's comfort even when sad things happen, knowing that Christ helps us and will soon end all pain and problems.

> **Read from God's Word**
>
> *Then I saw a new heaven and a new earth. ... I saw the Holy City, the new Jerusalem, coming down out of heaven from God. ... And I heard a loud voice from the throne saying, "Now the dwelling of God is with men, and He will live with them. They will be His people, and God Himself will be with them and be their God. He will wipe every tear from their eyes. There will be no more death or mourning or crying or pain, for the old order of things has passed away." He who was seated on the throne said, "I am making everything new!" Revelation 21:1–5*

——Let's talk: What troubles, pains, and problems do you have now? What does Jesus promise to do for you *now?* How will things be different when Jesus returns?

——Let's pray: Heavenly Father, thank You for sending Jesus, who gives us hope in the middle of problems and who promises to come again to take away all pain and problems. In His name. Amen.

J. J.

Do You Make Excuses?

"Who will do the dishes today?" asked Dad.

"Not me," said Joy. "I did them yesterday."

"What about you, Melissa?"

"I can't do them now, Dad," she answered. "My favorite show is on TV. Tell James to do them."

"Not me, Dad," James whispered. "I'm too tired."

Most of us do not like to do household chores, so we make excuses. But what would happen if someone didn't wash the dishes, cut the grass, or take out the trash? We would have to eat off dirty dishes, and we couldn't find our beds under all the trash! That would not be good at all!

When Jesus calls people to follow and obey Him, some people make excuses: "I don't know if my family would like it if I spent more time at church"; "I don't want to give offerings for God's work—I'd rather keep the money." Lots of times our excuses keep us from following Jesus.

But Jesus didn't make excuses, even when the Father asked Him to do hard things like suffer and die on the cross for our sins. The Savior loved us so much that He helped us even when it hurt Him. Now He sends us His Spirit to help us do the hard things too.

As surely as God has forgiven us, He will also help us avoid making excuses and willingly follow Him.

_____Let's talk: What excuses have kept you from following Jesus? How do you know that God has forgiven you?

_____Let's pray: Almighty God, we thank You that Jesus Christ gave up His life and everything He had for us. Help us to trust and serve You with our whole heart. We pray in Jesus' name. Amen.

J. J.

Do You Like to Wait?

A re we there yet?"
"When is my birthday?"
"How many days until spring?"
"The bus is late again!"

Every day we have to wait for something. Sometimes it seems to take so long. We get frustrated, or we feel like quitting. When we wait for a happy event like a birthday or Christmas, the closer we get to the time, the longer it seems to take.

We even wait for God to do things He has promised to do. We wait for Jesus Christ to come and take us to heaven, and we wait for answers to our prayers. Sometimes we wonder why it seems to take so long.

But God isn't slow or forgetful. Instead, He is patient and wise. He is waiting for just the right time to make His move. Before He answers a prayer, He makes sure that everything is ready. Before Christ comes back to take us to heaven, He waits patiently for nonbelievers to become Christians so they won't be condemned.

Read from God's Word

In the last days scoffers will come. ... They will say, "Where is this 'coming' He promised? ... Everything goes on as it has since the beginning of creation." ... But do not forget this one thing, dear friends: With the Lord a day is like a thousand years, and a thousand years are like a day. The Lord is not slow in keeping His promise, as some understand slowness. He is patient with you, not wanting anyone to perish, but everyone to come to repentance. 2 Peter 3:3–9 ✎

People in Old Testament days waited a long time for the Savior to be born at Bethlehem. Finally, Jesus came to take away the sins of the world. The people were happy they had trusted God and had waited patiently. Waiting may be hard for us, but it's good for us. It means that God loves us enough to wait for just the right time to help us.

_____Let's talk: Have you ever prayed for something then waited a long time for it to happen? Why does God sometimes take a long time to do what He has promised? Why is it better for us to wait patiently than to complain?

_____Let's pray: Lord God, thank You that You do what You have promised at just the right time. Help us trust You and wait patiently for You to act. Amen.

J. J.

march

Contributors for this month:

Gene Friedrich

Pat List

Phillip T. Miksad

Carolyn Sims

Gregory R. Williamson

The Lord of Victory

Read from God's Word

For none of us lives to himself alone and none of us dies to himself alone. If we live, we live to the Lord; and if we die, we die to the Lord. So, whether we live or die, we belong to the Lord. For this very reason, Christ died and returned to life so that He might be the Lord of both the dead and the living. Romans 14:7–9 ༄

One day there was a funeral. It wasn't a funeral for an elderly person or someone who had been sick for a long time. It was for a high school student named Laura.

Several hundred young people from Laura's school came to the funeral. Many cried when the pastor gave the message. But people often cry at funerals. What was unusual was that although Laura was in high school, she was a "baby" Christian. If she had died a few years ago, she wouldn't be in heaven with Jesus. That's because a few years ago Laura didn't know Jesus as her Savior.

Laura's friends had come to church regularly and attended many of the youth group activities. Over and over again they invited Laura to join them, and finally she agreed. Laura started coming to church, Bible class, and other activities with her friends. Then she went to the pastor's information class and was confirmed.

Laura's friends will miss her, but they are happy she is now in heaven with Jesus. He is the Lord of victory, who defeated death and the grave so we can live forever.

Do you know someone who needs to hear of God's love and forgiveness? Maybe you are the person the Holy Spirit will use to share the Gospel with him or her. Young Christians, as well as adults, can tell their friends and relatives about God's love.

_____Let's talk: Did you know God can work through you to reach someone else? Name one way you can be God's helper.

_____Let's pray: Dear Jesus, thank You for sharing Your victory with us. Make us willing to pass on this great gift. Help us show our excitement about You and the promise of eternal life. Be with us and help us use the right words. In Your name we pray. Amen.

P. L.

Read from God's Word

This is good, and pleases God our Savior, who wants all men to be saved and to come to a knowledge of the truth. For there is one God and one Mediator between God and men, the man Christ Jesus, who gave Himself as a ransom for all men—the testimony given in its proper time. 1 Timothy 2:3–6

Out with the Old, In with the New

Mom and the children had a great time at the mall. It was fun buying new spring clothes. It was even more fun to model them for Dad.

"Where are you going to put all these new things?" he joked. "We'll have to get rid of some old clothes just to make room for these new ones. After all, our closets have only so much room!"

"You're right," Mom laughed. "It's out with the old and in with the new."

Sara had a puzzled look on her face. "Is that the way it works with everything, Mom?" she asked. "I sure hope not."

"Well," Mom said, "most houses don't have enough space to continue adding new things without getting rid of some of the old stuff. Why do you ask?"

"Remember last week when the Millers' new baby was baptized?" Sara asked. "Does God need to get rid of some of the old Christians to make room for the new ones? If so, how does God decide whom to get rid of?"

"Oh, Sara. It doesn't work that way at all. God has plenty of room in His family. He wants everyone to be in His family. That's why He sent His Son, Jesus, to die for everyone in the world. There will never be a time when there are too many Christians."

"I'm glad it works that way, Mom," Sara replied. "Now, let's see which clothes we can take to the clothes bank."

_____Let's talk: Why does God want everyone in heaven? Will heaven ever get filled up?

_____Let's pray: Dear Lord, we are glad You always have room for more Christians in heaven. Help us lead the kind of life that shows others what being a Christian is all about. As we grow in size and knowledge, help us also grow stronger in our love for You. In Jesus' name we pray. Amen.

P. L.

Different Points of View

Read from God's Word

Consequently, just as the result of one trespass was condemnation for all men, so also the result of one act of righteousness was justification that brings life for all men. For just as through the disobedience of the one man the many were made sinners, so also through the obedience of the one Man the many will be made righteous. Romans 5:18–19 ✍

I s rain good or bad?" asked Frank. "It depends on your point of view," Mrs. Harris said. "If you want plants to grow, rain is good. But if you are planning a picnic, then it's bad."

"What about sunshine?" Frank continued.

"I guess it's the same thing," Mrs. Harris said. "If you want the puddles dried up, sunshine is good. But if you don't have any shade, it might be bad."

"It sounds like there could be two ways of looking at everything, doesn't it?" Frank thought out loud.

Many things in life can be good in some circumstances and bad in others. But some things will always stay the same. One example of something that stays the same is sin. Sin is always wrong. It doesn't matter if it's a little sin or a big sin. In God's eyes, a sin is a sin, and it's always wrong. Sin gets in the way and separates us from God.

That's why God sent Jesus to die on the cross for us. He took the punishment for our sin. When we go to God and ask His forgiveness, He remembers that Jesus paid the price for that sin, and He forgives us. Forgiveness and God's love are two very important things that will always stay the same.

_____Let's talk: Make a list of things that could have a good side and a bad side. Then make a list of things that are always right or always wrong. How can you tell the difference?

_____Let's pray: We thank You, heavenly Father, that Your love for us is always the same. You never grow tired of loving us, helping us, and forgiving us. We sin every day, and we need Your forgiveness daily. We are thankful that You are always willing to listen to our prayers. Make us truly sorry for all our sins. In Jesus' name we pray. Amen.

P. L.

Read from God's Word

For the grace of God that brings salvation has appeared to all men. It teaches us to say "No" to ungodliness and worldly passions, and to live self-controlled, upright and godly lives in this present age, while we wait for the blessed hope—the glorious appearing of our great God and Savior, Jesus Christ, who gave Himself for us to redeem us from all wickedness and to purify for Himself a people that are His very own, eager to do what is good. Titus 2:11–14 ✍

Garbage In, Garbage Out

One day in Sunday school Mrs. Stouffer said, "Today we are going to make milkshakes. How many of you would like one?" Almost every hand went up.

But the hands went down when they saw what Mrs. Stouffer was putting into the blender. There were moldy banana pieces, milk that smelled terrible, and vinegar. Then she added lumpy gravy. "Who's ready?" Mrs. Stouffer asked. The class groaned.

Then Mrs. Stouffer started over. She measured ice cream, flavoring, and fresh fruit. Soon everyone was enjoying the wonderful treat.

Mrs. Stouffer used the milkshakes to explain the idea of "garbage in, garbage out." When she used bad ingredients, the result was awful. When she used good ingredients, the result was great.

In a way, it's like that with our minds. If we watch TV shows with bad words and actions, we may be tempted to do or say bad things. If we watch TV shows or read books with a Christian message, that is the message that will come out of us.

If you're not sure what's right, ask yourself, "Would I want Jesus to watch or read this with me?" If the answer is yes, go ahead and do it. The Bible says, "Jesus Christ ... gave Himself for us to redeem us from all wickedness and to purify for Himself a people that are His very own, eager to do what is good" (Titus 2:13–14).

_____Let's talk: Every time you are trying to decide whether to do something, think "garbage in, garbage out."

_____Let's pray: Dear Jesus, help us keep garbage out of our lives. Make every thought, word, and deed be ones we would proudly share with You. Remind us that You are always there beside us, helping us make the right decisions. In Your name we pray. Amen.

P. L.

A Little Goes a Long Way

Mary Anna didn't like green peppers. Her mom knew that and understood. Whenever she made something for dinner with green peppers in it, she set aside part of it for Mary Anna and then added peppers to the rest.

One day a girl named Sandy moved next door. She and Mary Anna became friends and played together often. "Would you like to stay for dinner tonight?" Sandy's mom asked Mary Anna one afternoon. After a quick phone call to Mary Anna's mom, the plans were made. What fun the girls had that afternoon as they set the table and helped with the salad!

But Mary Anna's joy turned to embarrassment when she took the first bite of her dinner. Although she couldn't see the pieces of green peppers, Mary Anna knew they were there. Even a tiny bit of the peppers made the whole dinner seem awful to her.

In our lives a little bit of bad can go a long way. Just like the peppers, even a little bad in us can cause us to sin again and again and make our lives awful. Can we always be successful in keeping bad things out of our lives? The answer is no. That's why Jesus came to earth to suffer and die in our place. As we ask God's forgiveness for our sins, He remembers Jesus' suffering, and all the sin is removed from us in His name.

Read from God's Word

But even if you should suffer for what is right, you are blessed. "Do not fear what they fear; do not be frightened." But in your hearts set apart Christ as Lord. Always be prepared to give an answer to everyone who asks you to give the reason for the hope that you have. But do this with gentleness and respect ... For Christ died for sins once for all, the righteous for the unrighteous, to bring you to God. He was put to death in the body but made alive by the Spirit. 1 Peter 3:14–15, 18 ✍

____Let's talk: Although Mary Anna couldn't see the green peppers, how did she know they were there? Our sins may be very little, does that make them all right?

____Let's pray: Heavenly Father, forgive our sins for Jesus' sake. Help us stay away from those things that are not pleasing to You. Amen.

P. L.

Scrubbing Out the Dirt

Read from God's Word

If You, O LORD, kept a record of sins, O LORD, who could stand? But with You there is forgiveness; therefore You are feared. Psalm 130:3–4 ✎

When Sean's family bought their new house, it was a mess. The people who lived there before them didn't keep things very clean, so Sean and his family had a lot of work to do.

"We're going to scrub and clean everything," Mrs. Lindsay said. "There won't be any dirt left at all."

Every evening Sean and his family worked on the house. Bucket after bucket of soapy water became dark from the dirty floors. Soon the hard work made a big difference. When the house was clean, Sean's family moved in. What a hard job it had been, but it was worth it.

When we were born, there was dirt in our hearts, called sin. There was no way we could scrub ourselves clean of this sin. That's why we needed Baptism. Through Baptism, God washes us clean. He did the work we couldn't do. Now when He looks at us, He sees His children cleansed from sin through Jesus' blood.

Did Sean's house always stay clean? No, of course not. Every day it needs to be cleaned a little. Sometimes the floors need vacuuming or the furniture needs dusting.

Do our lives stay free from sin because we were baptized? No, of course not. Every day we sin. When we ask God to forgive our sins, He always says yes. He knows that Jesus suffered and died for those sins, and He always forgives them. Then we are clean again.

_____Let's talk: Why doesn't Sean's house stay clean all the time?
Why can't we stay clean from sin?

_____Let's pray: We don't want to have sin in us, dear Lord. We want to be clean. But, Lord, we were born sinners, and we sin daily. Remind us of our Baptism and how You scrubbed us clean. Then give us peace in knowing we are forgiven. Amen.

P. L.

Witness Wear Days

Read from God's Word

Then the eleven disciples went to Galilee, to the mountain where Jesus had told them to go. When they saw Him, they worshiped Him; but some doubted. Then Jesus came to them and said, "All authority in heaven and on earth has been given to Me. Therefore go and make disciples of all nations, baptizing them in the name of the Father and of the Son and of the Holy Spirit, and teaching them to obey everything I have commanded you. And surely I am with you always, to the very end of the age." Matthew 28:16–20 ∽

All week the students at St. John's School were talking about what they would wear on Friday. The student council had planned a "Witness Wear Day," and students were encouraged to wear something that showed they were Christians.

When Friday came, it was fun to see what everyone was wearing. David wore a shirt with a big frog on it. Under the frog was the question "Where are you going when you croak?" Benjie wore his "Jesus loves you" shirt. Instead of the word *loves*, there was a big heart. Some students wore jewelry with Christian symbols. Many wore cross necklaces.

Janine wore a WWJD bracelet. She eagerly shared its message with others: "This stands for 'What Would Jesus Do?' When I have to make a decision, I ask Jesus to help me think about what He would do if He were in the same situation."

Our whole lives are a witness. When people see us doing something wrong, it's like we are saying that God really isn't that important in our lives. When we help someone or say something kind about others, we are showing how God's love shines through us. That's the kind of witness God wants His children to be.

But no matter how hard we try, we can't do the right thing by ourselves. But Jesus loves us and forgives us. On the cross He paid for all our misdeeds. Ask Him to help you be a witness to His love today.

_____ Let's talk: Are there times when you wouldn't want someone to see or hear what you're doing? How can you be a Christian witness no matter where you are?

_____ Let's pray: Dear Father, help us remember that no matter where we are, people see us. Inspire us to do and say things that will give You glory. For Jesus' sake, forgive us when we do wrong. In His name we pray. Amen.

P. L.

Who's in Control?

Read from God's Word

The fool says in his heart, "There is no God." They are corrupt, and their ways are vile; there is no one who does good. God looks down from heaven on the sons of men to see if there are any who understand, any who seek God. Everyone has turned away, they have together become corrupt; there is no one who does good, not even one. ... Oh, that salvation for Israel would come out of Zion! When God restores the fortunes of His people, let Jacob rejoice and Israel be glad!
Psalm 53

One day on the way to school, Kali was riding with her mom behind a large pickup truck. The driver of the truck had hung his jacket on a small hook behind him. Kali watched the truck for a long time and then started to laugh. "Look at the way that man's jacket is hanging," she said. "It hides the driver so it looks like the truck is driving itself."

Some people say there is no God. They think the world just made itself and keeps itself going. That doesn't make any more sense than thinking a truck could drive itself. The Bible tells us that God created everything and keeps the world going. He decides when it should rain and when the sun should shine. He brings children into the world and welcomes people to Himself when they die.

God also knew that the first people He made would sin. He planned to send His Son, Jesus, to die for them. He knew this was the only way for all of us to be saved.

The season of Lent is a time during the church year when we think of how hard it was for Jesus to suffer and die for us. We look forward to the joyful celebration of Easter, when we praise Jesus for rising from the dead for us. We can thank God for being in control of everything, especially our salvation.

_____Let's talk: Sometimes people give up something for Lent, perhaps a favorite food or pastime. This reminds them that Jesus gave up His life for them. Is this something you could do?

_____Let's pray: Help us remember, Jesus, that You gave up Your life for us. You loved us enough to save us. Thank You! Amen.

P. L.

A Lesson from Grapefruit

O n Saturdays Mrs. King and her children usually went grocery shopping. The children helped choose which fruits and vegetables to buy. Sometimes they chose golden bananas or bunches of big green grapes.

One day a salesperson was cutting up fresh grapefruit samples for shoppers. The samples were delicious, and the children knew right away which fruit to buy.

At first the grapefruit was stored in the front of the refrigerator, and everyone remembered to eat them. But as the days went by, the rest of the grapefruit got pushed farther and farther back. Pretty soon no one remembered they were there.

One day Mrs. King discovered one last grapefruit, way in the back. One side looked good, but the other had a big patch of mold on it. Into the trash it went. Although the grapefruit had been good, it had not lasted forever.

Read from God's Word

[Jesus said] "For God so loved the world that He gave His one and only Son, that whoever believes in Him shall not perish but have eternal life. For God did not send His Son into the world to condemn the world, but to save the world through Him."
John 3:16–17

Most things in the world are like that grapefruit. They look good at first, but things go wrong. They may even have to be thrown away. Food gets moldy; metal gets rusty; clothes get torn and dirty. Even favorite toys break.

There's one thing that does last forever. That's God's love for us. He loved us before we were born, He loves us right this minute, and He will love us forever. God loved us so much He sent His Son, Jesus, to die for our sins and rise again. That's the kind of love that will take us to heaven.

_____Let's talk: God's promises last forever. What are some of them?

_____Let's pray: You loved us even before we were born, dear Lord, and You will love us forever. You prepared a place in heaven for us, and You even planned a way for us to get there. Thank You, Lord, for sending Jesus. You surely have a lot of love. In Jesus' name we pray. Amen.

P. L.

Read from God's Word

Peter replied, "Repent and be baptized, every one of you, in the name of Jesus Christ for the forgiveness of your sins. And you will receive the gift of the Holy Spirit. The promise is for you and your children and for all who are far off—for all whom the Lord our God will call." With many other words he warned them; and he pleaded with them, "Save yourselves from this corrupt generation." Those who accepted his message were baptized, and about three thousand were added to their number that day. Acts 2:38–41 ⸙

Time to Rejoice

Sasha's school was raising money for new equipment for the computer lab. A poster hung on the wall to help students see how the project was coming. The poster looked like a giant thermometer. Along the side were numbers showing how much money was needed. Each day, as money was raised, the thermometer was colored in.

Every morning students hurried in to look at the poster. Cheers went up each time the color in the thermometer grew closer to the goal. At last the color reached the top and the computer equipment was ordered. Joyful students could hardly wait for the boxes to arrive. At last they would be able to use their new computers.

The Bible tells us about another kind of celebration. It says that the angels rejoice over one sinner who repents. Acts 2 reports a time when 3,000 people were baptized. Just imagine the celebration in heaven that day!

Think of the excitement we experience when something wonderful happens. Yet nothing can match the joy of knowing that one more person is on his or her way to heaven. We can have that joy as we share how Jesus saved the whole world by offering up His own life. We can rejoice with the angels when another person comes to faith in Christ as their Savior and Lord.

_____Let's talk: Do you know someone who may not know that Jesus is the only way to heaven? What can you say or do to tell this person about the salvation won by Jesus?

_____Let's pray: Heavenly Father, help us know what to say or do so Your message of love and forgiveness can make a difference in someone's life. Make us strong when we're afraid to speak to someone about You. In Jesus' name we pray. Amen.

P. L.

Get the Message?

E ight-year-old Tommy raced out the front door to see where the loud noise was coming from. He looked up to see flashing lights. They were very close, and they didn't seem to move.

What could it be? Tommy wondered. *Is it a flying saucer? Are aliens coming? Wait! The lights are moving away. They seem to be spelling out a message! They say . . . "Buy Goodyear tires."*

Tommy's mysterious lights spelled out a message on the Goodyear Blimp. When the blimp was directly overhead, the words were impossible to read. It was sending Tommy a message, but he couldn't figure out what it was.

Jesus brought a message to God's people. He told them He was the Savior, the promised Messiah. He turned water into wine; He healed the sick; He even raised people from the dead. But many people still did not understand.

Read from God's Word

For we know in part and we prophesy in part, but when perfection comes, the imperfect disappears. When I was a child, I talked like a child, I thought like a child, I reasoned like a child. When I became a man, I put childish ways behind me. Now we see but a poor reflection as in a mirror; then we shall see face to face. Now I know in part; then I shall know fully, even as I am fully known. 1 Corinthians 13:9–12 ✍

God sends us messages too. On our own, we can't figure out what they are. But God sends His Spirit into our hearts. He washes away our sins through the waters of Baptism. He opens our hearts to receive the Gospel message that Jesus has overcome sin and death for us.

There are many things about God we can't understand. But one day, when we get to heaven, we will understand. "Now we see but a poor reflection as in a mirror; then we shall see face to face" (1 Corinthians 13:12). That's an event we do not want to miss!

———Let's do: Make a list of things you don't understand about God. Ask someone for help in understanding them.

———Let's pray: Thank You, Lord, for giving us the message of Jesus. Help us spread the Good News to others. Amen.

G. F.

Read from God's Word

Therefore God again set a certain day, calling it Today, when a long time later He spoke through David, as was said before: "Today, if you hear His voice, do not harden your hearts." For if Joshua had given them rest, God would not have spoken later about another day. There remains, then, a Sabbath-rest for the people of God; for anyone who enters God's rest also rests from his own work, just as God did from His. Let us, therefore, make every effort to enter that rest, so that no one will fall by following their example of disobedience. Hebrews 4:7–11 ✎

A Promised Rest

Nigel felt achy all over. He wasn't sick enough to miss school, but he was having a tough time getting through the day. He managed to survive gym class, language arts, and Mr. Fairweather's math class.

What kept Nigel going? His mother had made him a promise that morning. She had encouraged him with the guarantee of after-school warmth and comfort. "Nigel," she had said, "when you get home from school, you can sit in the window seat under the warm, blue and white comforter. There will be some hot chocolate for you too."

God has given each of us a promise of rest. It keeps us going when we struggle to get through the bitter times in our lives.

Some kids have to live with other families because of unstable conditions in their home. Some children and teens suffer physical or mental challenges and need counseling. All of us have disappointments and setbacks at times.

We will enjoy God's rest completely when we're home in heaven. But each day we have the assurance that Jesus loves us and stands with us. Through Baptism we are united with our Savior. He gives us His Spirit, the heavenly Comforter, to see us through times when we think there's no way out. When we rest in the Lord, we can be full of hope and joy.

_____Let's talk: How will God's promise of rest help you manage today? What aren't you going to worry about? What will see you through hard times?

_____Let's pray: Dear Jesus, heaven is our home because of Your gift of faith. Help us get through difficult days because of Your promise of rest. Wrap us in the comfort of Your eternal love. Amen.

G. R. W.

Computer Breakdown

Computers are good only when they work. When they break down, they aren't much help. We can't do our homework; we can't send e-mail; we can't surf the 'net. Sometimes when we try to fix the problem, we only make it worse. So we have to call in an expert, a computer technician.

God's marvelous creation broke down as well. Adam and Eve sinned, and God's perfect world no longer worked perfectly. Our connection with God was lost.

But because God loves us, He sent the Master Technician to restore our connection with Him. God had a plan for Adam and Eve and for everyone who came after them. From Noah to Abraham to Isaac to Jacob to Joseph, God carried forth His plan for our salvation. Jesus fulfilled that plan. He came to earth and was born in a cattle stall. He was whipped and beaten. He was nailed to a cross.

Read from God's Word

But the gift is not like the trespass. For if the many died by the trespass of the one man, how much more did God's grace and the gift that came by the grace of the one man, Jesus Christ, overflow to the many! Again, the gift of God is not like the result of the one man's sin: The judgment followed one sin and brought condemnation, but the gift followed many trespasses and brought justification. For if, by the trespass of the one man, death reigned through that one man, how much more will those who receive God's abundant provision of grace and of the gift of righteousness reign in life through the one man, Jesus Christ. Romans 5:15–17

Soon we will celebrate Easter—the completion of God's plan, Jesus' victory over the devil. Yes, Jesus died. But He also rose from the dead. He showed He was more powerful than the devil. Jesus, the Master Technician, fixed what we could not fix. He restored our connection with the Father.

When a technician fixes our computer, we're glad to have it back. We hope it won't break again. When Jesus fixes something, it stays fixed. It will never break again. God's promise is sure. Praise the Lord for our Master Technician, Jesus!

_____Let's do: Use your computer to tell someone how Jesus has restored your connection with the Father.

_____Let's pray: We deserve eternal punishment for our sins, Lord. Thank You for sending Jesus to take our place. Amen.

G. F.

Touched by Jesus

John was playing "Hide and Seek" on his uncle's farm. He started to crawl along the top of the wooden fence between the barn and the pigpen. But he lost his grip and fell into the slippery, smelly, messy muck. He was covered with filth from head to toe.

"Yuck! What happened to you?" cried Carol as she came around the corner.

"I had an accident," John replied miserably.

"Well, look on the bright side," Carol said. "You don't have to worry about getting caught. Nobody will want to tag you!"

In Jesus' time there were people who were considered unclean. They had a disease called "leprosy." People believed leprosy was spread by touching someone who had it. People with leprosy were usually sent away to live.

Listen to what Jesus did one time. "A man with leprosy came and knelt before Him and said, 'Lord, if You are willing, You can make me clean.' Jesus reached out His hand and touched the man. 'I am willing,' He said. 'Be clean!' Immediately he was cured of his leprosy" (Matthew 8:2–3).

Isn't that amazing? Jesus could simply have said, "Be healed." Yet He chose to reach out and touch the man.

Jesus touches us too. Sin makes our souls filthy. Even when we try to do something right, we mess up. Who would want to touch us? Jesus. He makes us clean and heals us by His power. What love we have received!

_____Let's talk: How can you help someone around you who needs your touch?

_____Let's pray: Thank You, Jesus, for touching us with Your love. Help us touch others by sharing Your love with them. Amen.

G. F.

Where's the Fire?

D ad! Dad! There's a fire down the street!" Jenny cried. They heard the siren as they ran down the street. A cement truck working at a new house had caught fire.

A minute later the fire truck raced past them. The firefighters dashed to extinguish the blaze. In a few minutes their work was done.

"Well, the action is over. Let's go home, Jenny," her dad said. As they turned to leave, Jenny couldn't believe her eyes! More than a hundred people were watching the fire.

"Wow, Dad!" Jenny exclaimed. "Where did all these people come from? How did they know there was a fire?"

"The siren told them," Dad explained. "They followed the smoke and the fire truck. This reminds me of another fire a long time ago. Jesus had ascended into heaven. His disciples were gathered together in a room when suddenly there was a loud sound like a rushing wind. Tongues of fire appeared on the disciples' heads. Many people came to find out what the excitement was, just like people came to watch the fire today.

"The disciples began to tell people from many nations how they had sinned and how Jesus came to save them. Peter told them to repent and be baptized. The Holy Spirit worked in the hearts of many people that day, just like He works in our hearts today. Aren't you glad the Holy Spirit has made His home in you and me?"

Read from God's Word

When the day of Pentecost came, they were all together in one place. Suddenly a sound like the blowing of a violent wind came from heaven and filled the whole house where they were sitting. They saw what seemed to be tongues of fire that separated and came to rest on each of them. All of them were filled with the Holy Spirit and began to speak in other tongues as the Spirit enabled them. Acts 2:1–4 ✍

_____Let's talk: Do you know of any other times God used fire to spread the Word? How can we be "on fire" for God?

_____Let's pray: Thank You, Lord, for living in us. Keep us on fire with Your Gospel message. Amen.

G. F.

Be Glad, Not Mad

Read from God's Word

Therefore each of you must put off falsehood and speak truthfully to his neighbor, for we are all members of one body. "In your anger do not sin": Do not let the sun go down while you are still angry, and do not give the devil a foothold. Ephesians 4:25–27

Zing! Crash! The checkers bounced off the walls and clattered to the floor. Tyler and Austin must have played a hundred games, and Tyler had lost every single one of them. He stormed into his house and plopped into a chair.

"Austin beat me at checkers again," he told his mom. "He acts so big. I think he cheated. I never want to see him again!"

"Do you really mean that? Austin is your best friend. Besides, God tells us we shouldn't let the sun go down on our anger."

"I don't want to be angry," Tyler said, "but I don't know how to make the anger go away."

His mom answered, "My dad always told me that when I was angry with someone, I should pray for him. It's hard to stay angry with someone when you pray for him."

Later, in his room, Tyler prayed, "Dear Lord, please make Austin lose every game of checkers for the rest of his life!"

No, no, no, he thought; *that's not right. Let me try again.* "Dear Lord, please let Austin win at checkers except when he plays me."

No, no, no, he thought again; *that's not right either.* He realized that he was wrong for being angry and needed God's forgiveness. "Dear Lord," he prayed. "I'm sorry I got angry at Austin. Thank You for forgiving me because Jesus died for me. Help me remember that Austin is my best friend no matter who wins at checkers."

_____Let's do: Ask Jesus to forgive you when you're angry with a family member or a friend. Pray for that person and ask God to make things better.

_____Let's pray: Thank You, Lord, for forgiveness when we're angry. Give us Your love to replace our anger. In Jesus' name. Amen.

G. F.

God's E-Mail

Read from God's Word

By faith Noah, when warned about things not yet seen, in holy fear built an ark to save his family. By his faith he condemned the world and became heir of the righteousness that comes by faith. By faith Abraham, when called to go to a place he would later receive as his inheritance, obeyed and went, even though he did not know where he was going. By faith he made his home in the Promised Land like a stranger in a foreign country; he lived in tents, as did Isaac and Jacob, who were heirs with him of the same promise. For he was looking forward to the city with foundations, whose architect and builder is God. Hebrews 11:7–10 ✍

Isn't e-mail a wonderful thing? All you have to do is type your letter on your computer, make sure to add the correct e-mail address, and hit the "send" button. The next thing you know, your friend has your letter, whether he or she lives next door or around the world.

Did you ever wonder how e-mail works? Hitting the "send" button sends an electric signal out of your computer and into the telephone lines. But where does it go from there? And how does it get to the right address? When you send an e-mail message, you just have to have faith it will get to the right place.

Our faith in God is like that. We can't prove God is real. We can't prove Jesus rose from the dead to take away our sins. We just know He did because the Holy Spirit has worked faith in our hearts. It's the faith of the Old Testament heroes described in Hebrews 11. These great men of faith received special messages from God. They believed, and they did as God asked.

God sends us special messages too. He tells us about our Savior, Jesus, and how we can tell others about Him. He helps us follow Christ's command to make disciples of all nations (Matthew 28:19–20). God has given us great inventions like e-mail to make the job easier. Praise the Lord for His gift of Jesus! Praise the Lord for His gift of e-mail, another way to spread His Word!

_____Let's do: Write to a friend, using e-mail. Tell how Jesus died to take away your sins. You don't have e-mail? Share this news in person!

_____Let's pray: Thank You, Lord, for the faith the Holy Spirit has worked in each of us. Help us use the technology You have given us to spread the Good News. Amen.

G. F.

Get the Dust Off

Dust! Dust! Dust! Is there any chore worse than dusting? Every week you wipe all the furniture with a rag, then take the rag outside and shake out all the dust. And you know what? The dust comes right back in! So you have to do the job all over again the next week.

Have you ever watched the afternoon rays of the sun shining through a window? You can see the little particles of dust waiting to pounce on the tabletop you just polished. Every time you dust, more dust is waiting to take its place.

Dusting is a good thing to do during this season of Lent. It reminds us that sin, like dust, is everywhere. Our efforts to wipe away dust are never perfect. We always leave some specks behind, and in a matter of seconds more dust comes back. We can't wipe away sin either. No matter what we do, we're mired in more and more sin.

But God has given us the perfect cleaning method. Jesus suffered and died in our place. His blood washes away all our sins, every last one of them. And once they're gone, they stay gone—not just the sins we've committed, but also the sins we will commit. God has cleaned us through Jesus. In God's eyes we are spotless, now and forever!

────Let's do: Take turns volunteering to dust the furniture. When the rag wipes away the dust, thank Jesus for wiping away all your sins and the sins of every one in your family.

────Let's pray: Thank You, Jesus, for washing away our sins. Because You died and rose again, our sinful hearts are now clean. Amen.

G. F.

The Winning Team

Juli ran back to the bench. Her team had just finished warming up for their first game of the basketball tournament. "Those guys are giants!" Juli said to her teammates. "I bet they have to watch out for low-flying planes when they're close to the airport."

"That's okay," Juli's coach said. "We may not be tall, but we have other skills. Just relax and do what I tell you. We'll win the game."

Juli's team had a rough start, but soon they began to listen to the instructions their coach was giving. They found out they were much faster than the taller team. By using their speed and skill, the girls were soon outrunning and outscoring the taller, slower team. By the end of the game the taller girls were tired and out of breath, while Juli's team enjoyed the victory.

Read from God's Word

Then the eleven disciples went to Galilee, to the mountain where Jesus had told them to go. When they saw Him, they worshiped Him; but some doubted. Then Jesus came to them and said, "All authority in heaven and on earth has been given to Me. Therefore go and make disciples of all nations, baptizing them in the name of the Father and of the Son and of the Holy Spirit, and teaching them to obey everything I have commanded you. And surely I am with you always, to the very end of the age." Matthew 28:16–20

We also play on a team. And we have the greatest Coach of all. Jesus teaches us that we have sinned and need a Savior. He shows us God's plan for salvation, and how He completed the game plan, suffering a horrible death on the cross and rising victorious over the devil. Now we can rejoice because our team has won!

Our Coach tells us to spread the news of His victory all over the world. So we work as a team, sharing His message with all who will hear. And because of Jesus, our team continues to win!

———Let's talk: What are some skills Jesus gives us to spread His message?

———Let's pray: Thank You, Jesus, for being our Head Coach. Help us tell the Good News of Your great victory. Amen.

G. F.

No Hiding from God

Read from God's Word

For the word of God is living and active. Sharper than any double-edged sword, it penetrates even to dividing soul and spirit, joints and marrow; it judges the thoughts and attitudes of the heart. Nothing in all creation is hidden from God's sight. Everything is uncovered and laid bare before the eyes of Him to whom we must give account. Therefore, ... let us hold firmly to the faith we profess. ... Let us then approach the throne of grace with confidence, so that we may receive mercy and find grace to help us in our time of need. Hebrews 4:12–16 ✑

Lights, camera, action!" Letitia heard in the background Uh-oh! She wasn't going to get away with anything today. Her friend Angie had permission to bring the family's video camera to school.

Letitia's teacher started the day with devotions. "Nothing is hidden from God's sight," she said. Letitia knew that was true. *I'll be a wreck by the end of the day,* she thought. *God sees what Angie is recording on her video.*

It was easy to lie to Miss Smith, her teacher; easy to grab an extra cupcake at lunch. But sleeping would be tough.

Thankfully bedtime prayers helped. Dad read from chapter 4 of Hebrews. He read that Jesus, our High Priest, understands our weaknesses. *Did her dad know about her day?* she wondered. Then Dad read that Jesus knows our every fault. *Did her dad ever have days like hers?* Finally Dad said that Jesus isn't surprised by anything we do.

Letitia looked into her dad's eyes. Could she tell him about her day? It was only one cupcake. She didn't have the nerve tonight, but Letitia knew she could tell her heavenly Father. After all, He already knew everything about her and had already forgiven her through Jesus. She rested in God's mercy and forgiveness.

_____Let's talk: What kinds of things do you try to hide from one another? Think about the things you might not want to tell your parents, but you know you can tell your heavenly Father. How will your heavenly Father react to what you tell Him? How will your heavenly Father help you mend your ways?

_____Let's pray: Gracious High Priest, You know us so well. Not an inch of who we are is hidden from Your sight, yet You understand our weaknesses. Forgive us and strengthen us— today, tonight, and through each tomorrow. Amen.

G. R. W.

How to Get Really Clean

Read from God's Word

Surely I was sinful at birth, sinful from the time my mother conceived me. Surely You desire truth in the inner parts; You teach me wisdom in the inmost place. Cleanse me with hyssop, and I will be clean; wash me, and I will be whiter than snow. Let me hear joy and gladness; let the bones You have crushed rejoice. Hide Your face from my sins and blot out all my iniquity. Psalm 51:5–9

ara's finger trembled as it lay in her father's hand. "Ouch!" she cried. "Don't touch it there. That hurts!"

Dad gently probed around the black dot that marked the end of the splinter buried in Kara's skin. "I see it," Dad replied. "I think I can get it out pretty easily. You wait here."

Dad left the room and returned with a needle and a match. "What are you going to do with those?" asked Kara.

Dad carefully lit the match and held it under the needle until the tip turned black. "Now we're ready," he said.

"You made the needle dirty!" exclaimed Kara. "Don't stick me with that!"

Dad laughed. "I didn't make the needle dirty, Kara. I made it clean. The black covering on the point is carbon, just like ashes in the fireplace. It is what's left after the heat of the match kills the germs that were there. When I see the black coating, I know the needle is perfectly clean and safe to use."

Sin is like the germs on that needle. Sin causes pain, sadness, and even death. In Bible times, people rubbed ashes on themselves to serve as a reminder of their sins and to show God that they were sorry. Ashes also remind us of the way fire makes things clean. Just as the flame of the match killed the germs, Jesus' death took away the power of sin in our lives. He made us clean in God's eyes.

———Let's talk: Why did Kara's dad heat the needle with a match? When Jesus died on the cross, how did He do something like what Kara's dad did?

———Let's pray: Dear Jesus, thank You for cleaning our hearts from the power of sin by dying on the cross. Help us think about You often during this season of Lent and remember how much You love us. We love You too, Jesus. Amen.

C. S.

A Reason to Be Happy

Then Nehemiah the governor, Ezra the priest and scribe, and the Levites who were instructing the people said ... "This day is sacred to the LORD your God. Do not mourn or weep." For all the people had been weeping as they listened to the words of the Law. Nehemiah said, "Go and enjoy choice food and sweet drinks, and send some to those who have nothing prepared. This day is sacred to our LORD. Do not grieve, for the joy of the LORD is your strength." ... Then all the people went away to eat and drink, to send portions of food and to celebrate with great joy. ... Nehemiah 8:9–12

Willy was always the last one to be chosen for baseball. Once again he was stuck out in right field. No one ever hit the ball to right field. That's where they put guys like him. How he wished that today would be different. How he wished that today he would make the game-winning play.

Lost in his daydream, Willy looked up just in time to see the ball coming straight toward him. He closed his eyes, held up his glove, and prayed, "Please, God, let me catch it!"

The ball struck with a thud, right in the webbed pocket. Yes! No. Out it dropped like an egg falling to the sidewalk. And with it splattered Willy's hopes for glory.

Later, as Willy walked home, his stomach churned. Being a failure was hard to take.

Then he remembered something his Sunday school teacher, Mrs. Ross, had taught the class that week: "God tells us in His book, the Bible, that He loves us no matter what we do or who we are. He can make the bad and hurtful things in our lives work out for good. God sent His Son, Jesus, to give His life for us, taking away our sins and making us His children. We are very special because we belong to Him."

By this time, Willy was feeling better. His stomach didn't ache. His eyes didn't sting. Thinking about God and His love for him was like medicine for his hurt feelings.

_____Let's talk: What are you good at? What is hard for you to do? How does Jesus make it possible for you to be happy even when things go wrong?

_____Let's pray: Dear Jesus, thank You for cheering us up when we're feeling sad. Teach us what we need to know about You and Your love for us so we can deal with the disappointments and problems we face. We pray in Your powerful name. Amen.

C. S.

A Safe Place to Be

Mischief, the cat, was usually afraid of Jenna's dad. His size 13 shoes and deep voice kept the cat out of his way whenever possible.

One day, Mischief jumped up onto the table and landed in the middle of a stack of plates. The plates fell to the floor with a loud crash.

"You naughty cat!" Jenna yelled, looking at the broken pieces lying all around her. Mischief dashed off like a dart and leaped onto the lap of Jenna's dad, who was sitting in his favorite chair. Peering out from under his strong arm, Mischief knew she was safe—out of the reach of Jenna's anger.

Mischief's nature to be curious got her into trouble. We are born with the nature to do wrong. We call this sin. Sin causes us to get into trouble even when we don't intend to. We hurt people we don't want to hurt. We cause damage we can't fix. We make a mess of things in our own lives and in the lives of others.

When these things happen, we feel afraid. We want to run for help, just as Mischief did.

Some people are afraid of God because He is so strong and powerful. God wants us to know that His love is bigger than we could ever imagine. When we're in His strong arms, we are safe. Because Jesus died on the cross, God forgives us. We aren't in trouble with Him anymore. Aren't you glad that you're safe in His arms?

_____Let's talk: If you were a cat, you would purr as you lay securely in someone's lap. How can you show your Father that you're secure in His arms?

_____Let's pray: Dear God, thank You for loving us even when we do wrong. When we feel afraid, help us remember that You forgive us and protect us. We are safe in Your care. Amen.

C. S.

Read from God's Word

"My sheep listen to My voice; I know them, and they follow Me. I give them eternal life, and they shall never perish; no one can snatch them out of My hand. My Father, who has given them to Me, is greater than all; no one can snatch them out of My Father's hand. I and the Father are one." John 10:27–30

Best Friends

"I won't be your friend!" The words hurt. Rosa had been Maria's best friend since first grade.

Rosa was angry because Maria had gone to a movie with Beth. Maria's mom said, "You can all be friends together." But Maria knew that you could have only one best friend. Until yesterday that had been Rosa.

Why was Rosa so angry? Maria certainly wouldn't be jealous if Rosa and Beth had fun together. Or would she? Why did being friends have to be so complicated?

Jesus tells us in the Bible that He is our very best friend. His love for us does not change according to His mood or anything we do. He will never say the words to us that Rosa said to hurt Maria. Instead He promises, "I will never leave you nor forsake you."

Jealousy, hatred, selfishness, and pride are all sins. They keep us from being friends with God and make it hard for us to be friends with others. When Jesus died for us on the cross, He forgave all these sins. Now He lives in our hearts so we can also forgive and love one another.

When friends hurt your feelings, you probably feel like hurting them in return. Maria felt like calling Rosa names and never playing with her again. Then she remembered how God loved her and how He loved Rosa too. If God could be patient with her and keep on being her friend, then she could also forgive Rosa.

_____Let's talk: How is being friends with Jesus different from being friends with other people? Does Jesus' love ever change? Why not?

_____Let's pray: Dear Jesus, thank You for being our very best Friend and for giving us other friends with whom we can share Your love. Amen.

C. S.

Taking a Sock Walk

Read from God's Word

Finally brothers, whatever is true, whatever is noble, whatever is right, whatever is pure, whatever is lovely, whatever is admirable—if anything is excellent or praiseworthy—think about such things. Whatever you have learned or received or heard from me, or seen in me—put it into practice. And the God of peace will be with you. Philippians 4:8–9

Have you ever had things grow in your socks? Put a large pair of socks over your shoes and walk on the grass and on the sidewalk, through mud and even a water puddle. Then step in a tray filled with birdseed.

Take the socks off, place them in a plastic bag, set them in a sunny place, and wait. In a few days you will see things start to grow. Whatever you walked through will grow as the water and dirt nourish the seeds.

The Bible reminds us that what we see and experience makes a difference. The things we put into our minds grow there and are visible to everyone around us.

Jeremy thought it would be fun to watch an R-rated movie on the cable channel. His parents weren't home. It was easy. But that night he couldn't sleep. The things he had seen and the words he had heard troubled him.

Because Jesus died for us on the cross, He forgives us when we choose to do or say or think things that do not please Him. Jesus shows that He cares about what kind of people we are by sending us His Holy Spirit. As we read and study God's Word, His Spirit fills our minds with kind and loving thoughts. He helps us to see with our eyes the beauty He has placed in our world and to listen to joyful sounds that can be used to praise Him.

_____Let's talk: Can watching a movie or a television show be harmful? How? What kinds of experiences can help you fill your mind with the things mentioned in the Bible reading?

_____Let's pray: Dear Jesus, Your world is full of so many wonderful sights and sounds and ideas. Thank You. Please fill our minds and hearts with things that are good for us. Amen.

C. S.

Read from God's Word

How can a young man keep his way pure? By living according to Your Word. I seek You with all my heart; do not let me stray from Your commands. Psalm 119:9–11 ✍

The Yellow Lion

D on't step on the yellow lion!" Samantha warned her friend Toby. The "yellow lion" was really a dotted line marking the area where the school door swung when it opened and closed. Standing inside the "yellow lion" could be dangerous. The door often opened fast, and anyone in its path could be hit hard.

Toby jumped quickly out of the circle. "Thanks, Sam," he called. "I wasn't watching."

The school custodian painted that yellow line as a warning to keep children from being hurt. No one complained that they couldn't stand in that space. They were all glad that someone cared about them and wanted them to be safe.

God gives us warnings, too, about what is safe for us to do and not do. God's Laws tell us to honor His name, to worship Him, to obey our parents, and to be honest and helpful to others. God's rules are meant to be helpful to us, but we can never keep God's Laws perfectly. Only Jesus could do that. He died to take the punishment for the times we don't obey God.

We don't have to be afraid of God's Law. We can use it to help us in our lives, just the way God intended. He gives us these rules to keep us out of danger and to help us live in peace and happiness with others. The Holy Spirit helps us want to follow God's will and gives us the power to obey Him.

_____Let's talk: Can we obey all God's rules perfectly? Since Jesus died to forgive us when we disobey, why do we still keep trying to follow God's commandments?

_____Let's pray: Dear Father, thank You for loving us enough to give us rules by which to live. Thank You for forgiving us when we don't obey. Please give us the power to follow Your will. For Jesus' sake. Amen.

C. S.

The Cross that Wouldn't Move

The noisy backhoe stopped in its tracks. The construction workers scratched their heads, and the architect reached for her blueprints. Right there, where the wall of the new church building was supposed to go, stood an 18-foot-high cross embedded in a ton of concrete.

The cross had been donated to the congregation in memory of one of its first members. It was too big to move. It was too heavy to lift. And it had special meaning to the family who donated it—no one wanted to hurt their feelings by tearing it down. But the cross was right in the way!

The architect finally drew new plans so the wall of the building went around the cross. The building moved, but the cross stayed in place.

During this season of Lent, we remember another cross. Because Jesus died there to take away your sins, that cross is now part of our lives forever.

Read from God's Word

They brought Jesus to the place called Golgotha (which means The Place of the Skull). Then they offered Him wine mixed with myrrh, but He did not take it. And they crucified Him. ... With a loud cry, Jesus breathed His last. The curtain of the temple was torn in two from top to bottom. Mark 15:22–24, 37–39 ✑

When we are tempted to worry because we think we aren't good enough for God to love, Jesus' cross is there to remind us that He has forgiven all our sins. His love for us cannot be changed.

When we are frightened or sad or discouraged, Jesus' cross is there to remind us that He died and rose again and now lives in us. Any problems or troubles we face will have to go around Jesus and His cross. He will not move. We can depend on Him.

———Let's talk: What do you remember when you think of Jesus' cross? Is there anything that would cause God to stop loving and caring for you? Why not?

———Let's pray: Dear Jesus, thank You for dying on the cross to take away our sins and make us Yours forever. Please remind us of Your unchanging love when we feel worried or frightened. Help us show You our thanks in all that we do. Amen.

C. S.

What Makes You Afraid?

Some people are afraid of the dark. Others are afraid of loud noises or being in high places. Some people are afraid of being in a crowd or speaking in public. What makes *you* afraid?

Once a train was going along when a big storm came up. Most of the passengers were very afraid as they saw the lightning and heard the thunder. In one seat, however, was a little boy who seemed totally calm. One of the passengers asked, "Little boy, aren't you afraid to travel alone and in such a storm?"

The child answered, "No, I'm not afraid. My father is the conductor of this train!"

There are many "storms" in our lives. Some have to do with schoolwork and tests or with family worries. Some storms are the hurts we receive from others. Sometimes the storm of sickness or of losing someone we love comes upon us. Should we become worried when these storms surround us? Not if we know that the conductor of our life's train is our heavenly Father!

The storms of life may upset us, but that upset quickly goes away when we realize that all things are in God's hands. By faith in Jesus, who has saved us with His own life, we are children of God, members of His family.

How wonderful it is to know that even in the worst storms our heavenly Father is with us! We don't have to be afraid.

_____Let's talk: What are the storms in your life right now? How can you remain unafraid?

_____Let's pray: Heavenly Father, we thank You that we have become Your sons and daughters through Jesus, our Lord. Help us always remember that You are there in love whenever we need You. In Jesus' name. Amen.

P. T. M.

A Lesson from a Turtle

Read from God's Word

You see, at just the right time, when we were still powerless, Christ died for the ungodly. Very rarely will anyone die for a righteous man, though for a good man someone might possibly dare to die. But God demonstrates His own love for us in this: While we were still sinners, Christ died for us. Romans 5:6–8 ᴄ☙

Harry and his uncle found a turtle lying on a log. As Harry picked up the turtle, it pulled in its head and legs. He put the turtle down and picked up a stick to try to pry the creature open.

His uncle said, "No, that's not the way. You may kill it, but you won't get it open."

They took the turtle back home. Harry's uncle put a large bowl of water near the fireplace, placed a rock in the bowl, and set the turtle on the rock. Soon it pushed out its head and legs and began crawling around. After a while, the turtle became comfortable with Harry, its newfound friend.

Turtles are like that—and people too! We need to warm them up with kindness. But God did so much more to win us back! You and I were enemies of God, locked up in our shells of sin. God sent His Son, Jesus, to live and die for us. In the warmth of His great love, we could once more be open to God and His care for us.

Harry could have left the turtle on its own, but he didn't. God could have left us on our own, and in our sins we would surely have died. But St. Paul writes: "God demonstrates His own love for us in this: While we were still sinners, Christ died for us" (Romans 5:8).

_____Let's talk: Have you ever felt like a turtle, not wanting someone else to force you to do something? What won you over? How did God win us over? What does He still do today?

_____Let's pray: Heavenly Father, we were once tightly sealed in the shell of our sins. We thank You for the warmth of Your love in sending Jesus to be our Savior. Help us live in love toward You and others. In Your Son's name. Amen.

P. T. M.

Willing to Sacrifice

Read from God's Word

Everyone who loves has been born of God and knows God. Whoever does not love does not know God, because God is love. This is how God showed His love among us: He sent His one and only Son into the world that we might live through Him. This is love: not that we loved God, but that He loved us and sent His Son as an atoning sacrifice for our sins. Dear friends, since God so loved us, we also ought to love one another. No one has ever seen God; but if we love one another, God lives in us and His love is made complete in us. 1 John 4:7–12

The doctor looked at Dory lying in the hospital bed. She was very ill, and he knew that her only hope was to receive blood from someone whose blood matched closely.

Quickly the doctor found Dory's family and knelt beside a small boy. "Andy," he said, "your sister needs your kind of blood to make her well. Would you be willing to give your blood so she can live?"

"Sure, Doctor," he replied. After blood had been taken from Andy's small arm, he remained very quiet. Then he asked softly, "Doctor, when will I die?" Only then did the doctor realize that Andy had not only offered his blood to save his sister, he had been willing to offer his life.

Our Lord Jesus once said, "Greater love has no one than this, that he lay down his life for his friends" (John 15:13). Jesus knew the only way to pay the price for our sins was to suffer and die on the cross so we could all be brought back into a relationship of love with our heavenly Father.

Jesus did all this for His friends, and He tells us that we are His friends when we do what He commands. Jesus says, "This is My command: Love each other" (John 15:17).

It seems simple, doesn't it? But sometimes, as for little Andy, love means sacrifice. May we share the love of Jesus with others, no matter the cost.

_____Let's talk: Do you think it took a lot of courage for Andy to give blood so his sister could live? Where do we go to receive such courage?

_____Let's pray: Heavenly Father, help us be willing to sacrifice in love for others. In Jesus' name. Amen.

P. T. M.

God Doesn't Send Bills

Mom and Dad were sitting at the kitchen table, going over the family's bills. There were bills from the drugstore and the department store. There was a doctor's bill and a dentist's bill. Dad looked up and said, "Isn't it a good thing that God doesn't send bills?"

What if the Lord *did* decide to send a bill for this wonderful body? Think about what God has made:

The ears. A piano has 88 keys, but each of your ears has a keyboard with 1,500 finely tuned keys. The outside of your ear can catch up to 73,000 vibrations per second!

The eyes. They are microscopes and telescopes. They can gaze into the heavens and see a star millions of miles away, but they also can inspect very small insects.

The feet. Did you know that each foot contains 26 bones, and that the foot is put together with ligaments, tendons, muscles, and joints so that a 300-pound man can put all his weight on these tiny bones.

The heart. It's about the same size as your fist, but it pumps 4,320 times an hour. In a year that is nearly 38 million beats.

What if God were to send you a bill for the marvelous body He made for you? But God doesn't send us bills. He just loves us and takes care of us. When we think of this, we want to return His love and share it with others.

_____Let's talk: What are some other marvelous things that God gives you free of charge? What price could you put on a human life? on the life of the Son of God, Jesus, given for you?

_____Let's pray: Heavenly Father, Creator of all, we give You thanks for the wonderful bodies You have given us. Thanks especially for the gift of Your Son, who died to save us, both body and soul. In His name we pray. Amen.

P. T. M.

Read from God's Word

For You created my inmost being; You knit me together in my mother's womb. I praise You because I am fearfully and wonderfully made; Your works are wonderful. I know that full well. My frame was not hidden from You when I was made in the secret place. When I was woven together in the depths of the earth, Your eyes saw my unformed body. All the days ordained for me were written in Your book before one of them came to be. Psalm 139:13–16 ✍

april

Contributors for this month:

Mary Lou Krause

Jacqueline L. Loontjer

Phillip T. Miksad

Susan Waterman Voss

Christine S. Weerts

Soda-Pop Medicine

E very time eight-year-old Brandon tossed the plastic ring around a 2-liter bottle at the school fair he won a prize. He had three bottles of cola, but only one lemon-lime.

"Why did you get only one lemon-lime?" his friend asked.

"My brother likes lemon-lime, but I don't," said Brandon. "It has that nasty medicine in it."

"What medicine? Soda doesn't have medicine in it."

"Then why do they give it to you when you're sick?" Brandon asked.

Have you ever gotten your facts mixed up? April 1 is a day when we like to confuse people on purpose. We like to mix them up and then call out: "April fool!"

Having fun is one thing, but getting facts mixed up can sometimes cause problems. In today's Bible reading, even Jesus' disciples were confused. They saw someone who was blind and they thought his blindness was caused by sin. Jesus set them straight, and then He gave the blind man his sight.

Read from God's Word

As He went along, He saw a man blind from birth. His disciples asked Him, "Rabbi, who sinned, this man or his parents, that he was born blind?" "Neither this man nor his parents sinned," said Jesus, "but this happened so that the work of God might be displayed in his life. As long as it is day, we must do the work of Him who sent Me. Night is coming, when no one can work. While I am in the world, I am the light of the world." Having said this, He spit on the ground, made some mud with the saliva, and put in on the man's eyes. "Go," He told him, "wash in the Pool of Siloam" (this word means Sent). So the man went and washed, and came home seeing. John 9:1–7

Sometimes we might also get mixed up. We think we aren't "good enough" to go to heaven. But the Bible tells us that we are saved by grace through faith in Jesus Christ (Ephesians 2:8–9). Or maybe we think God won't forgive all our sins. But reading 1 John 1:9 helps us know that God forgives us for Jesus' sake.

We don't ever have to get our facts mixed up about Jesus, our Savior. He is our way to eternal life.

———Let's do: Check your salvation facts with John 3:16. How would you put this verse into your own words?

———Let's pray: Dear Jesus, keep Your truth ever living and active in us through Your Holy Spirit. Amen.

C. S. W.

Legend of the Dogwood

Read from God's Word

Then God said, "Let the land produce vegetation: seed-bearing plants and trees on the land that bear fruit with seed in it, according to their various kinds." And it was so. The land produced vegetation: plants bearing seed according to their kinds and trees bearing fruit with seed in it according to their kinds. And God saw that it was good. And there was evening, and there was morning—the third day. Genesis 1:11–13 ◁

In the South, dogwood trees blossom around Easter. The people who live there look for their snow-white blossoms to announce spring. Many churches use bouquets of dogwood branches instead of lilies to celebrate Easter.

The legend of the dogwood tree says that its blossoms tell the story of Jesus' crucifixion. The white outer leaves of the dogwood blossoms form a cross, with two long and two short petals. At the center of the outer edge of each petal is a "nail print" of brown rust stained with "blood." And in the center of the flower is a "crown of thorns." The white color reminds us of the righteousness of Christ.

Of course, legends are just stories. Trees can't really tell us about Jesus' passion and resurrection. But we can see God in nature as the almighty Creator. Martin Luther writes in his catechism that God has created everything in heaven and on earth, and He daily sustains it.

Many Christians like to look at the dogwood blossoms and "see" the story of the crucifixion of Christ. Each year, as they see their snow-white beauty blossom, they are reminded of the new life Jesus gives each of us through His painful death and victorious resurrection. How blessed we are to know that Jesus' victory over death brings new life—in all seasons and for all time.

_____Let's talk: Name other signs of new life around you. How do you see God's hand at work in His created world?

_____Let's pray: Precious Savior, through Your blood shed on the cross, we wear robes as white as snow, as white as dogwood blossoms. Thank You for our wonderful new life. Amen.

C. S. W.

Babylonian Junk Food

E von skipped lunch at school so he could spend money on snacks. He bought a soft drink, a chocolate cupcake, and potato chips. When he got home, Evon was still hungry. He went to the refrigerator and passed up fruit juice, milk, yogurt, and even grapes. He grabbed a piece of lemon pie.

By the time dinner was ready, Evon wasn't hungry. He felt too irritated to do all his math problems, and he finally fell asleep trying to write his English assignment.

Eating junk food can spoil our appetite for nutritious food and make us irritable. Though we feel full, we are not giving our body the vitamins and minerals it needs. So why do we eat such food? Because it tastes good!

This isn't a new problem. Even in 600 B.C., in the exotic and wealthy country of Babylonia, kings ate rich food and drank wine. When Daniel was taken captive with other Israelites, he said no to eating rich palace food. He asked to be given only vegetables and water. After 10 days they looked healthier and better nourished than those who ate rich food.

Read from God's Word

The king assigned them a daily amount of food and wine. ... But Daniel resolved not to defile himself with the royal food and wine, and he asked the chief official for permission not to defile himself this way. ... "Please test your servants for ten days: Give us nothing but vegetables to eat and water to drink. Then compare our appearance with that of the young men who eat the royal food, and treat your servants in accordance to what you see." ... At the end of the ten days they looked healthier and better nourished than any of the young men who ate the royal food. So the guard took away their choice food ... and gave them vegetables instead. Daniel 1:5–16 ✍

We don't have to follow strict food laws anymore, nor do we have to be vegetarians. But God does want us to take care of our bodies, and He provides healthful food for us to eat. We were bought with the price of Christ's own blood so we may honor God with our bodies.

———Let's talk: Keep a family food diary for a week. What did you eat? How did you feel? Plan nutritious snacks to have after school.

———Let's pray: Come, Lord Jesus, be our guest; and let Your bountiful and nutritious gifts to us be blessed. Amen.

C. S. W.

The Mirror Game

Read from God's Word

[Jesus said] "Now that I, your Lord and Teacher, have washed your feet, you also should wash one another's feet. I have set you an example that you should do as I have done for you. I tell you the truth, no servant is greater than his master, nor is a messenger greater than the one who sent him. Now that you know these things, you will be blessed if you do them." John 13:14–17

Have you ever played the mirror game? Here's how it works: Get a partner and stand facing each other. One is the mirror, and the other person looks into the mirror. The mirror must reflect everything that person does. You can act out fun things like combing your hair, jumping up and down, dancing, and exercising. After a few minutes, switch and let the other person be the mirror.

You may not realize it, but you probably have played another version of the mirror game. Here's how it works: If someone is nice to you, you are nice to him. If someone hits you, you want to hit her back. Stick out your tongue at someone, and he sticks out his tongue too! Too often, we simply reflect the bad things that others do.

Jesus wants us to play an entirely different mirror game. In today's story, Jesus surprised His disciples as He washed their feet. The roads were dusty and their feet certainly needed washing, but that was a servant's job—not a Savior's. As Jesus washed their feet, He said they were to wash one another's. This is the kind of mirror game Jesus wants us to play. Jesus is the mirror image we are to reflect. He even gave His life to save us.

Look at Jesus and see how He reflected God's love to everyone around Him. Then, with the Holy Spirit's power, play the mirror game with Jesus.

_____Let's talk: Can you think of anything you said, thought, or did today that reflected Christ? That reflected yourself? Read the whole story in John 13:3–17.

_____Let's pray: Guide our minds, our feet, and our hands today so we may reflect Your image, dear Jesus. Amen.

C. S. W.

Clunky Piano Neighbors

N ot another visit to Mrs. Milly's house!" Meagan whined. "I don't want to go. Her house is too hot, and her cat is mean. She always plays that clunky old piano and sings those boring hymns."

"But you promised to visit her for your school's neighbor-to-neighbor project," Meagan's mom reminded her.

"I'm sick of it! Can't I quit?"

"You made a commitment for six months."

"But, Mom, I have homework to do. We have a big spelling test tomorrow," Meagan said.

"We'll work on your spelling when you get home. Now, here's the juice, soup, and crackers we bought for her."

Meagan complained as she changed clothes. Mrs. Milly was nice, but Meagan had had a bad day. She was muttering "dumb old piano" as she grabbed the bag and walked to her neighbor's house.

Read from God's Word

Let no debt remain outstanding, except the continuing debt to love one another, for he who loves his fellowman has fulfilled the law. The commandments, "Do not commit adultery," "Do not murder," "Do not steal," "Do not covet," and whatever other commandment there may be, are summed up in this one rule: "Love your neighbor as yourself." Love does no harm to its neighbor. Therefore love is the fulfillment of the law. Romans 13:8–10 ☜

Mrs. Milly's eyes lit up when Meagan came, but she could tell Meagan was upset. "What's wrong?" Mrs. Milly asked kindly.

Meagan burst into tears as she told about her bad day. Mrs. Milly listened quietly and then went to the piano and began playing hymns. Meagan recognized "What a Friend We Have in Jesus." "Jesus really is our friend and Savior," Mrs. Milly commented. "He loves us all the time, even on bad days."

When Meagan got home, her mother asked how the visit went. "You know what?" Meagan said. "I think Mrs. Milly helped *me* today!"

_____Let's talk: Are you showing love to your neighbors? What more could you do for them?

_____Let's pray: Thank You, God, for our neighbors. Help us be good neighbors through the love of Your Son, Jesus Christ. Amen.

C. S. W.

Read from God's Word

I have fought the good fight. I have finished the race. I have kept the faith. Now there is in store for me the crown of righteousness, which the Lord, the righteous Judge, will award to me on that day—and not only to me, but also to all who have longed for His appearing.
2 Timothy 4:7–8

An Olympic Champion

Wilma was a sickly child from the time she was born. She caught every cold, and if someone got the flu, Wilma got pneumonia.

When she was four, Wilma had scarlet fever. Afterward, her left leg twisted inward. Doctors said she had polio and probably would never walk again. She couldn't play or go to school.

Her mother took her by bus for therapy to the closest hospital that accepted black patients, 50 miles away. Wilma got a metal leg brace to wear to school. Kids made fun of her. With hard work in therapy, Wilma walked into church without the brace for the first time when she was 10. Two years later, she got rid of the brace permanently.

From then on, Wilma didn't walk; she ran. In high school, she was a star basketball player. She became a track star in college. In 1960, Wilma was fast enough to win a spot on the U.S. Olympic team. It was hot and muggy in Rome that summer, but even spraining her ankle a few days before her first race didn't slow her down. Wilma knew how to overcome the odds.

Wilma won a gold medal and set a new world record. She repeated her victory and her world-record speed, winning a second gold. Wilma Rudolph became the first woman ever to win three gold medals in the summer Olympics. The girl who doctors said would never walk had become the fastest woman in the world.

_____Let's talk: What can we learn from the lives of people like Wilma Rudolph? What kind of race is St. Paul writing about? How do we win this race?

_____Let's pray: Dear Lord Jesus, You know trouble comes to all of us. Give us faith to keep running faithfully to the end, that we may receive the crown of life, which You won for us on the cross. Amen.

C. S. W.

Windy Reminders

Laronda was excited. It was her birthday. At school the class sang "Happy Birthday," and her teacher gave her a card. Her best friend gave her a necklace and a sucker. Laronda could hardly wait to get home and celebrate.

But when she got home, her mom had gone to work and there was no cake. Her sister Erika was fixing meat loaf, which Laronda didn't like one bit. Their family didn't have much, so birthdays were not big celebrations. Laronda had given up asking for a bicycle or even roller blades. But she had really wanted a piece of chocolate cake and some vanilla ice cream.

Laronda went outside, sat on the steps, and unwrapped her sucker. It was her favorite flavor—sour apple. The wind started to blow. As Laronda got up to go inside, she dropped her sucker in the dirt.

After her bath that night, she told Erika how unhappy she was. "Even God forgot me," she cried.

Read from God's Word

Praise the LORD, O my soul. O LORD my God, You are very great; You are clothed with splendor and majesty. He wraps Himself in light as with a garment; He stretches out the heavens like a tent and lays the beams of His upper chambers on their waters. He makes the clouds His chariot and rides on the wings of the wind. He makes winds His messengers, flames of fire His servants Psalm 104:1–4

Her sister said quietly, "Remember in Sunday school when Mrs. Holloway said God's always with us?"

Laronda sniffed. Suddenly she shouted, "The wind! I remember Mrs. Holloway told us that we can't see God, but He's still there. She said we can't see the air we breathe, but we know it's there. Sometimes we can feel it. She said the wind is a reminder that God gives us even the air we breathe. When the wind blew this afternoon, I guess God was blowing a 'happy birthday' wish my way!"

____Let's talk: How has God blown through your life today?

____Let's pray: Jesus, we know that even the wind obeys You. Help us remember You are always with us, on windy and calm days, on happy and sad days, on birthdays and every day. Amen.

C. S. W.

Who Are Your Heroes?

Read from God's Word

Then Jesus came to them and said, "All authority in heaven and on earth has been given to Me. Therefore go and make disciples of all nations, baptizing them in the name of the Father and of the Son and of the Holy Spirit, and teaching them to obey everything I have commanded you. And surely I am with you always, to the very end of the age." Matthew 28:18–20 ✍

"Dad, we have to write a paper about a hero in our family," Joel said. "No one in our family plays basketball or is rich and famous. I'm gonna flunk!"

"What about Aunt Elinor and Uncle Bill?" Dad asked.

"Hardly anyone knows them," Joel replied. "They spent most of their lives halfway around the world."

"Right. They were missionaries."

"How does that make them heroes?" Joel asked.

"Get out your Bible and look up Matthew 28:19. What does Jesus say we are supposed to do?"

"'Go and make disciples of all nations,'" Joel read. "Our Sunday school teacher calls that the Great Commission."

"Your aunt and uncle served God in Papua New Guinea as missionaries of the Gospel for 40 years," Dad said.

"Wow, I bet Uncle Bill baptized a lot of people in 40 years!"

"Yes, and he spread the Good News that Jesus died and rose to save all people. He translated the New Testament into the native language and started a seminary to train pastors. Aunt Elinor raised their seven children and worked with villagers."

"Dad, I think our family does have heroes," Joel said. "But now I've got another problem."

"What's that?" Dad asked.

"My teacher wants only one page, but I've got enough for a book!"

Note: This story is based on the work of Bill and Elinor Burce, who served on the mission field in Papua New Guinea from 1948 to 1988.

_____Let's talk: Who are some people our world would call heroes?
Are these the same kinds of heroes God recognizes?
Who are some heroes in your family?

_____Let's pray: Thank You, God, for heroes of the Great Commission. Bless their work for Jesus' sake. Amen.

C. S. W.

A Christian Easter Egg

Janice decided to plan an Easter-egg hunt for the neighborhood children, many of whom did not go to church. She got a silver coin, a rock, a purple ribbon, a cross, a nail, dice, a sponge, and a cinnamon stick and put them in a large plastic egg.

She asked her Sunday school friends to help. They made refreshments, brought more plastic eggs, and looked up the Bible passages. Each item in the egg would be used to tell the story of Jesus' death and resurrection: *Sponge (John 19:28–30); Spice (Mark 16:1); Empty egg (Mark 16:5–7); Cross (Mark 15:20–21); Rock (Luke 22:39–45); Purple ribbon (Mark 15:16–17); Dice (John 19:23–24); Coin (Matthew 26: 14–16); Nail (Mark 15:22–24).*

When the children arrived, Janice and her friends taught them songs and a Bible verse. Then they showed the egg. The kids were excited, thinking candy was inside. No, it was better than that, the Bible leaders said. It was the greatest gift of all.

As they pulled out each item, they read the Bible verses and described what had happened to Jesus. The children quietly listened. Some were sad to hear about the cruel things people did to Jesus.

The lesson ended with the Good News of Jesus' resurrection and His gift of salvation. The children learned to say, "He is risen indeed!" They hunted for empty plastic eggs, remembering the empty tomb. At the end of the party, each egg was filled with treats and small crosses to remind the children of Jesus' love.

_____Let's talk: How can you share the Good News this Easter?
How about when Easter is over?

_____Let's pray: Glory be to Jesus, Who in bitter pains
Poured for me the lifeblood, From His sacred veins.

C. S. W.

Read from God's Word

The women bowed down with their faces to the ground, but the men said to them, "Why do you look for the living among the dead? He is not here; He has risen! Remember what He told you, while He was still with you in Galilee: The Son of Man must be delivered into the hands of sinful men, be crucified and on the third day be raised again." Luke 24:5b–7

A Young Girl's Witness

So [Naaman] went down and dipped himself in the Jordan seven times, as the man of God had told him, and his flesh was restored and became clean like that of a young boy. Then Naaman and all his attendants went back to the man of God. He stood before him and said, "Now I know that there is no God in all the world except in Israel."
2 Kings 5:14–15

Imagine you live in Palestine. One day you're outside, maybe getting water from a well. Suddenly you hear thundering hoofbeats and shouts. Armed raiders from a nearby pagan country are invading your village. They grab you, stealing you from your family. You are made the slave of the military leader's wife.

What would you do? Would you witness to this military leader's family about the power of God? That's exactly what happened in today's Bible story. A young Israelite girl, who believed in God and the power He worked through the prophet Elisha, was captured by a raiding party from Aram (later known as Syria). She was forced to serve the wife of Naaman, the army commander.

When she saw that Naaman had leprosy, the girl told his wife about Elisha, God's prophet. Because of this one girl's witness, Naaman went to Elisha and was healed of his disease by God. Even better, Naaman learned of the true God and worshiped Him.

We don't know much about the young girl in the story. But we do know the most important thing about her: she had faith in God. Even in her trouble, she trusted in the Lord.

Today's story is a good reminder that even young people can witness to others about the power of God working in Jesus Christ, the Savior of the world. You can tell about the love of Jesus. You can say He died and rose for all.

_____Let's talk: Whom can you tell about Jesus? What can you say? Read the whole story of Naaman in 2 Kings 5:1–15.

_____Let's pray: Thank You, Lord, for this girl's witness, which speaks through the centuries. Help us see how You can use us to enlarge Your kingdom. In Jesus' name. Amen.

C. S. W.

Wishing Time Away

Taylor slammed the door. He threw his books on the table and went to the refrigerator to get some milk.

"Something wrong?" Mom asked.

"Yes! I'm so sick of school. I want summer to get here now. We have two whole months left. That's eight spelling tests, 40 math assignments, three social studies units . . ."

"I get the idea," said Mom. "I remember last August when you couldn't wait for school to start. You said summer was boring."

"Well . . . that was then."

"I used to feel a lot like you, Taylor. I'd wait and wait for something exciting to happen. But sometimes while I was waiting I missed out on other things because I wasn't looking for good things each day. God doesn't want us to wish time away. He wants us to enjoy all the things He gives us each day.

"The rest of the school year is also 40 noon recesses and an all-day field trip. You know what else?" Mom asked. "God gives us new surprises every day. He has great plans for you, Taylor."

We all have a great future because of our Savior. St. Peter assures us: "[God] has given us new birth into a living hope through the resurrection of Jesus Christ from the dead, and into an inheritance that can never perish, spoil or fade—kept in heaven for you" (1 Peter 1:3–4). Isn't that a wonderful promise to make all our days exciting?

_____Let's talk: What unexpected surprises has God given to you?
          Why is it important to enjoy each day God gives you?

_____Let's pray: Dear God, thank You for taking care of us each day. Help us look for and enjoy all the wonderful things You have planned for us. In Jesus' name. Amen.

S. W. V.

Read from God's Word

There is a time for everything, and a season for every activity under heaven. ... He has made everything beautiful in its time. He has also set eternity in the hearts of men; yet they cannot fathom what God has done from beginning to end. Ecclesiastes 3:1, 11

A Weird Collection

Read from God's Word

My dear children, I write this to you so that you will not sin. But if anybody does sin, we have one who speaks to the Father in our defense—Jesus Christ, the Righteous One. He is the atoning sacrifice for our sins, and not only for ours but also for the sins of the whole world. 1 John 2:1–2 ∽

Lots of people are collectors. There is one woman who collects cows. Not the milk-giving variety that say "Moo," but the smaller, nonliving kind. She has hundreds of cows in her home—big and small, stuffed, wooden, glass—every kind you could imagine. They are neatly displayed all through her house.

Many people have a collection. Do you? Maybe you collect toys or coins or stamps. Some people collect dolls, postcards, or baseball cards. Collections can be a lot of fun.

There's a story, though, of someone whose collection wasn't any fun at all. Sam collected grudges. Every time someone did something he didn't like, Sam became angry and formed a grudge. He never forgave anyone for anything. He just held the grudge inside himself. Every time he thought about it, he got angry all over again.

As Sam grew older he collected quite a lot of grudges. For days, months, and even years he remembered wrong things people did. Sometimes he was angry with people who didn't even know they had upset him. Sam's collection of grudges just made him angry, grouchy, and bitter all the time.

We can be grateful that God doesn't collect grudges. He washed our sins away through His Son's death and resurrection. Because Jesus completely removed all the wrongs we have done, God doesn't remember them anymore. He will never collect them. And that's fantastic!

_____Let's talk: Since God doesn't remember our sins, is it all right to keep on sinning? Why not? Since God forgives us, what can we do when others sin against us? Do you have any grudges to get rid of?

_____Let's pray: Thank You, Lord, for Your wonderful blessing of forgiveness. Help us forgive others as we have been forgiven. In the name of our Savior we ask this. Amen.

S. W. V.

Safe at Last

Tiger the kitten lay still, nestled against the warmth of the car's engine. He had been frightened by all the people who had come to visit. He didn't understand that no one would have hurt him.

When the car first drove up and stopped, Tiger had scurried under it. When the people walked away, he had climbed up inside to be safe and warm. No one would bother him here, he thought.

After a nap, Tiger decided to climb down to see if it was safe to come out. But the kitten was stuck. Tiger thought he had found warmth and safety beneath the hood of the car. Now he didn't feel nearly so safe.

Tiger started to cry. Loud and long meows were heard by the whole neighborhood. The owners of the car came to check out the problem. They found the extremely frightened kitten, very much in need of their help.

Read from God's Word

The salvation of the righteous comes from the LORD; He is their stronghold in time of trouble. The LORD helps them and delivers them; He delivers them from the wicked and saves them, because they take refuge in Him. Psalm 37:39–40 ✍

It took a long time to free Tiger, the rescuers had to work carefully. Parts of the car's engine were in the way, and the rescuers didn't want to hurt the kitten. Free at last, Tiger was given a bowl of milk. How wonderful to be safe again!

Today's reading says the Lord delivers us. He has delivered us from sin through Jesus. He delivers us from eternal death and promises us a forever place in heaven. There is nothing better than the safety of our Lord's love!

_____Let's talk: Have you ever tried to find safety and gotten yourself into a bigger problem? Who is our only source of safety? What did God do to rescue us from our sins? How does it feel to know that He is with you always?

_____Let's pray: Dear Lord Jesus, You not only keep us safe, but You saved us from all evil things as well. Thank You for loving us so very much. Amen.

S. W. V.

The Tunnel of Faith

Read from God's Word

The Lord had said to Abram, "... go to the land I will show you. I will make you into a great nation and I will bless you; I will make your name great. ... I will bless those who bless you, and whoever curses you I will curse; and all peoples on earth will be blessed through you." So Abram left, as the Lord had told him; and Lot went with him. Abram was seventy-five years old when he set out from Haran. He took his wife Sarai, his nephew Lot, all the possessions they had accumulated and the people they had acquired in Haran, and they set out for the land of Canaan, and they arrived there. Genesis 12:1–5

The underground tunnel was dark and damp. Sometimes water dripped from the ceiling and made puddles on the concrete floor. Small openings let in a little extra light and some fresh air. Some even said that bats lived in the tunnel.

Students at the college used the tunnel a lot because it connected two buildings. They appreciated having it there.

One day the electricity was cut off and the dimly lit tunnel suddenly became pitch-dark. Some of the students caught in the tunnel became frightened and had no idea how to get out.

But a blind girl was in the tunnel too. She was used to not being able to see, so it was easy for her to get out of the tunnel. She led the others to safety.

Abraham was led safely by God. He had faith to let God guide him even though he didn't know where God was taking him. The Lord led him from his former home to the beautiful land of Canaan.

We can have faith like that of Abraham. Even when we don't understand what is happening in our lives, we can trust God's love for us. He knows what is best, and He will guide us out of our dark "tunnels."

Romans 8:32 reminds us: "He who did not spare His own Son, but gave Him up for us all—how will He not also, along with Him, graciously give us all things?"

_____Let's talk: How do you know that you can rely on God to take care of you? How would you tell someone else what you believe about God's guidance in your life?

_____Let's pray: Dear God, we look to You for direction in our lives. Thank You for always watching over us and for leading us to safety. Bless us for Jesus' sake. Amen.

S. W. V.

Sowing and Reaping

Every year since Jacob could remember, he had helped plant the family's garden. This year his parents turned the job over to him.

Jacob went to the garden store and carefully chose the seeds he thought would be best. Dad had already tilled the ground to loosen the dirt. Jacob broke up the big clumps of soil and raked the ground smooth.

Jacob marked out both ends of each row. Then he carefully planted the seeds and smoothed the soil over each row.

Just then Karen, his little sister, came outside. "What will grow in the garden?" she asked.

"Carrots, corn, lettuce, green beans, and peas," Jacob replied.

"How do you know?" Karen asked.

"Because that's what I planted. The kinds of seeds you plant are the kinds of plants that grow."

Our Bible reading says that we will reap what we sow. But God wasn't talking about vegetables. He was talking about our actions. When we do harmful things, harmful things come back to us. When we, because of God's love in us, do kind and helpful things, kind and helpful things come back to us as blessings by the Lord.

God loved us so much that He sent Jesus to suffer and die for us. In thanks for that mercy, we do God pleasing works, and we reap what we sow.

_____Let's talk: How do you know that God loves you? What are some God-pleasing things you could do to show your love to others? Ask the Lord to help you do them.

_____Let's pray: Dear God, You love us so much. When we think about Your great love for us in Jesus, we want to show love for others. Help us think of new ways to share Your mercy every day. In our Savior's name we pray. Amen.

S. W. V.

Read from God's Word

Do not be deceived: God cannot be mocked. A man reaps what he sows. The one who sows to please his sinful nature, from that nature will reap destruction; the one who sows to please the Spirit, from the Spirit will reap eternal life. Let us not become weary in doing good, for at the proper time we will reap a harvest if we do not give up. Therefore, as we have opportunity, let us do good to all people, especially to those who belong to the family of believers. Galatians 6:7–10

Cheering or Jeering?

Read from God's Word

Jesus sent two disciples, saying to them, "Go to the village ahead of you, and at once you will find a donkey tied there, with her colt by her. Untie them and bring them to Me." ... The disciples ... brought the donkey and the colt, placed their cloaks on them, and Jesus sat on them. A very large crowd spread their cloaks on the road, while others cut branches from the trees and spread them on the road. The crowds ... shouted, "Hosanna to the Son of David!" "Blessed is He who comes in the name of the Lord!" "Hosanna in the highest!" Matthew 21:1–9

Some years ago, a runner named Rosie Ruiz finished first in the New York City Marathon. She came across the victory line in record time, and the crowds cheered as she was awarded many prizes.

Soon after, however, it was learned that Rosie had not run the whole race. She had taken the subway and other shortcuts to get to the finish line. She was disqualified and had to return the prizes and the title. All the cheers turned to jeers.

At the beginning of the week in which Jesus was to be crucified, He entered Jerusalem with great crowds of people cheering Him on. The spectators praised Him as the Messiah of God, who was to save His people Israel.

But in less than a week, the cheers turned to jeers. The echo of people singing His praises had barely faded when the cruel shouts of "Crucify Him!" began.

But Jesus had done no wrong.

Jesus' suffering and death on the cross took place so you and I and all others who believe in Christ might be saved for eternal life. The cheers for the triumphant but humble King had changed to jeers, but they would once again become triumphant cheers of "Hallelujah!" when He rose from the grave in Easter glory. And when that happened, there was no doubt who was the true victor over sin and death!

_____Let's talk: Can you remember any time when the wrong person was cheered as champion? In what way was Jesus' victory a victory for us as well?

_____Let's pray: Lord Jesus, always help us remember the great price You paid for our sinfulness. And then help us joyfully join in the cheers and alleluias of new life in You. We pray in Your name. Amen.

P. T. M.

Time-Out!

The whistle blew. The referee hollered, "Time-out, blue." The basketball game came to a standstill, and everyone got to rest. The teams could get drinks and the fans could relax for a while.

"It's recess time!" has been heard in schools all over the world. Students and teachers need some free time to release energy and frustration.

Jesus also grew weary at times and went off by Himself to rest. In Scripture we read that He left His disciples and the crowds and retreated to a quiet spot to rest. But He did more than rest—He prayed.

Jesus had been given the hardest job in history. He was to live a perfect life, and Satan was trying hard to ruin it. He was to die an innocent, painful death, loaded down with the sins of the whole world.

Jesus was a true man. That means He grew weary from doing His preaching and miracles. When people didn't listen to Him, He became sad. It would have been very easy, very human, to strike out in some way. But Jesus didn't because He asked the Father and the Spirit for help. And by His faithfulness to the tasks before Him, He won salvation for us.

Will going to the Lord for help work for us? Of course it will. Find a quiet spot. Relax, but don't forget to rest in the Lord. Pray. Read God's Word. Listen to what God is saying. It will be very refreshing.

_____Let's talk: For what do you sometimes need a time-out?

_____Let's pray: Dear Jesus, our Refuge, help us recognize weariness and stress. Lead us to restful things and places, especially closer to You. Only there can we truly receive the refreshment we need. In Your name. Amen.

J. L. L.

Read from God's Word

Immediately Jesus made the disciples get into the boat and go on ahead of Him to the other side, while He dismissed the crowd. After He had dismissed them, He went up on a mountainside by Himself to pray. When evening came, He was there alone. Matthew 14:22–23 ✍

Read from God's Word

For the LORD God is a sun and shield; the LORD bestows favor and honor; no good thing does He withhold from those whose walk is blameless. O LORD Almighty, blessed is the man who trusts in You. Psalm 84:11–12

We Need Sunshine

It had been raining or cloudy for 20 of the last 24 days. People were grouchy. Parents picked at their children, and children bickered among themselves.

"Ugh. There must be something to the 'amount of sunshine' theory," Jackie muttered to herself. This idea says that the amount of sunshine we get directly affects how we feel. The more sunshine, the happier people are. The more clouds and rain, the more "gloomy Guses" we find.

Our Christian lives are affected by the amount of *Son*-shine we see. When Christ, the Son of God, fills our life, we radiate a sunny faith. People see how much we love Jesus because we're loving to everybody around us.

On the other hand, if a storm suddenly hits in our life, what happens? Do we become a Moses and question God's actions? Do we act like Peter and try to hide our relationship to Jesus? Sadly, a lot of Christians do. They may even leave God's side forever.

Instead, let's take Job as our shining example. The Lord allowed Satan to destroy Job's prosperous life and health. But Job stayed strong in his faith, and God blessed him richly.

We may never have a lot of possessions or be wildly successful. That's not important. Staying close to God's Son is important. He lived, died, and rose again for us. So don't deprive yourself of the Son-light. Lay out your towel and soak up His rays.

_____Let's talk: How does sunshine make you feel? How much does it mean to you to have Son-shine in your life? Why do we need a lot of both kinds of warmth?

_____Let's pray: Dear Son of God and Sun of our life, shine into our hearts and souls. Keep us warm in Your love and forgiveness. Let this warmth radiate to others. In Your name, Lord. Amen.

J. L. L.

Is God in a Museum?

Museums are fascinating places. There are museums for art, science, and history. We can view displays of farming, mining, and industrial progress. There are even museums dedicated to toys and circuses!

A favorite kind of museum is a hands-on one. Most museums have their displays roped off or behind glass to keep the objects safe from harm. But to be able to touch, move, or experiment with things helps us learn so much more.

Have you put God into a museum? Do you think of Him as ancient history? Is He someone you visit on Christmas, Easter, and maybe Pentecost? Then do you put Him back behind glass until the next time you remember to visit Him?

It's true that God is the God of the world's past. After all, He created us all. (See Genesis 1 and 2.) But He is also the living God of today. He guides our everyday life and helps us grow. He knows how many hairs are on our heads. That makes Him a truly hands-on care provider.

Most important, He is the God of our future. He knows what we'll be and where we'll end up. Because of Jesus' death and resurrection, we are His. He shapes our lives while we work and play.

And where will you end up? Your future is heading right for heaven's door. After all, God made you; He saved you; and He lives in you.

_____Let's talk: What can help you remember that God is always with you? How can this knowledge help you in your daily decisions and struggles?

_____Let's pray: Living Lord, help us see Your presence and guidance in our lives. Make our life choices fit in with Your eternal plan for us. Live in us always. Amen.

J. L. L.

Read from God's Word

This is the account of the heavens and the earth when they were created. When the LORD God made the earth and the heavens—and no shrub of the field had yet appeared on the earth and no plant of the field had yet sprung up, for the LORD God had not sent rain on the earth and there was no man to work the ground, but streams came up from the earth and watered the whole surface of the ground—the LORD God formed the man from the dust of the ground and breathed into his nostrils the breath of life, and the man became a living being. Genesis 2:4–7

Track Events for Christians

Read from God's Word

Do you not know that in a race all the runners run, but only one gets the prize? Run in such a way as to get the prize. Everyone who competes in the games goes into strict training. They do it to get a crown that will not last; but we do it to get a crown that will last forever. 1 Corinthians 9:24–25 ✍

April 20th—the first track meet of the year. Everywhere you look students have numbers on their backs and school names on their fronts. They are stretching, jumping, sprinting, and practicing handoffs.

Suddenly a loudspeaker crackles to life. The person in charge shouts directions and announcements. The teams listen carefully for the places and times of their events. The speaker wishes them all a day of safe and fair competition.

In our Scripture reading, St. Paul compares our Christian lives to a race, a marathon with the heavenly prize as the goal. Along the way we come upon events that challenge us.

Our opponent has also been well trained. He's been putting up hurdles since the beginning in the Garden of Eden. Adam and Eve fell, as we all do. But we have a Coach to encourage us along the way.

There are times we find ourselves under heavy loads of sin or sorrow. We have learned how to throw the shot put of sin, but it's too heavy. A Substitute, the unbeatable Christ, steps forward and throws our sin away. In fact, He throws it so far that Satan has no chance to beat the record.

Finally, there are the relay events. We can't run the whole race alone. God has given us other team members for support—millions of other Christians, past and present. Someday we will hand off the baton to another generation of Christians. Then we'll sit on the eternal bleachers and cheer them on.

_____Let's talk: How does this devotion encourage you in your faith?

_____Let's pray: Heavenly Father, keep Your team running smoothly as we strain toward the finish line. Keep our eyes on the finish line. Forgive us when we stumble. In Jesus' name. Amen.

J. L. L.

The Hug of Hope

Read from God's Word

It was now about the sixth hour, and darkness came over the whole land until the ninth hour, for the sun stopped shining. And the curtain of the temple was torn in two. Jesus called out with a loud voice, "Father, into your hands I commit My spirit." When He had said this He breathed His last. The centurion, seeing what had happened, praised God and said, "Surely this was a righteous man." When all the people who had gathered to witness this sight saw what took place, they beat their breasts and went away. But all those who knew Him, including the women who had followed Him from Galilee, stood at a distance, watching these things. Luke 23:44–49 ✍

His eyes were closed, and his face winced with pain. He couldn't eat, and he couldn't even talk anymore. He lay very still in his hospital bed. Around this father were his children, taking turns at his side from morning through the dark, long night.

The children continued to hold his hand and pray. Down the hall, the nurses and caregivers heard them singing hymns. They sang simple words like "Jesus loves me, this I know" and comforting words like "Abide with me, fast falls the eventide. The darkness deepens; Lord, with me abide."

They spoke loving words to their father and cooled his head with a wet cloth. They didn't know how many of the words and songs he could hear, but his face lit up with a warm, bright smile when they reached down to hug him. He could feel the hug and the loving hands around him.

How Jesus longed for the heavenly Father's hug when He died on Good Friday! He knew He had to carry our burden of sin and He knew it separated Him from His Father. Yet He knew the loving, hugging arms of the Father were stretched out to receive Him as He cried, "Into Your hands I commit My spirit."

Jesus' victory over sin, death, and the devil means all our sins are forgiven. Because of Jesus, God's loving hands are ready to welcome us into His heavenly home.

_____Let's talk: Think of people you know who may be headed for death without knowing about the welcoming arms of Jesus. How could you tell them? What would you say? Why is it important to tell them?

_____Let's pray: Lord, thank You for faith in Jesus, which makes us certain that the moment we die the heavenly Father's loving hug will welcome us to heaven. Amen.

M. L. K.

Buried for Us

Read from God's Word

Or don't you know that all of us who were baptized into Christ Jesus were baptized into His death? We were therefore buried with Him through baptism into death in order that, just as Christ was raised from the dead through the glory of the Father, we too may live a new life. ... For we know that our old self was crucified with Him so that the body of sin might be done away with, that we should no longer be slaves to sin—because anyone who has died has been freed from sin. Now if we died with Christ, we believe that we will also live with Him. Romans 6:3–8 ✎

What's it like in a grave? Lazarus found out what it was like to be inside a grave and live to tell about it. It isn't a place where you want to go.

After He died on the cross, the body of Jesus rested in the grave—the same body that had carried away the sins of the world, the holy body that was whipped and hurt to pay our debt. Our lies, our angry words, our disobedience, and our selfish ways were piled onto our Savior. Jesus died and He was buried—for us.

The Bible tells us that we were *"buried with Him* through baptism into death" (Romans 6:4). Does that mean we were actually in the grave with Him? No, but let's try to explain it like this: Have you ever asked someone to stand in your place to pick up a ticket or to act as though they were you? Someone else is there in your place, but the ticket is still yours. The action is the same as if you yourself had done it. The action in our Baptism is the same as if we were experiencing burial with Christ. But He really did it all for us, in our place.

Jesus' work of suffering, dying, and rising has been done for our salvation. Our Baptism is a personal guarantee and reminder of God's power in our lives. With Jesus as our Savior, our life is a celebration of victory over the grave!

_____Let's talk: Why can you be sure that you will not be in the grave forever?

_____Let's pray: Lord, thank You for dying and being buried to pay the full debt of our sin. Help us be alive with Your power as we thank You with our life. Amen.

M. L. K.

From Sad to Glad!

A young missionary family served in a remote area of Europe. One day the mother and her children arrived home to find their house torn up. There were signs of struggle. They called out, but no one answered. The family knelt to pray, asking God to keep their dear father safe.

A few days later, shreds of the missionary's bloody shirt were found on a mountain path. After two weeks without any clues, the family made plans for a funeral service. The children cried as they remembered the hymns their dad loved to sing.

They were so sad they hardly noticed the opened door and the shabby, scarred person standing there. Could it be? Was it really? Yes! It was their father. In a second, their deepest sorrow turned into their greatest joy!

Something similar happened to Jesus' friends. As Jesus' body lay in the grave, it seemed all their hopes for heaven were gone. Mary was scared on Easter morning when she arrived to find the grave was empty. Then she heard His voice. JESUS IS ALIVE! She saw Him! He called her name. Bursting with joy, she ran to tell the others, "I've seen the Lord!"

This shout of celebration is the good news we need to hear when the devil tries to overwhelm us with sadness about our sins, fear of hell, or doubt about our faith. Rejoice! JESUS IS ALIVE! Hurry to tell others!

Read from God's Word

[Mary] saw two angels in white, seated where Jesus' body had been. ... They asked her, "Woman, why are you crying?" "They have taken my Lord away," she said. ... At this, she turned around and saw Jesus standing there, but ... thinking He was the gardener, she said, "Sir, if you have carried Him away, tell me where you have put Him, and I will get Him." Jesus said to her, "Mary." She ... cried out in Aramaic, "Rabboni!" (which means Teacher). ... Mary Magdalene went to the disciples with the news: "I have seen the Lord!" ... John 20:12–18

_____Let's talk: What are some things that make you sad? How does hearing about the risen Savior change those feelings? What could you say to someone who wants to know what Easter is all about?

_____Let's pray: Lord Jesus, help us hurry to tell others that You are the risen Savior, who gives us eternal life. Amen.

M. L. K.

Great News

A scraggly black cat jumped from behind the steps as the visitor team from the church approached the door. As the door opened, one of the visitors asked, "Would you mind . . . could we . . . talk to you about God?"

The young blond woman and the curly-haired man nodded. "I've been wanting to know more about God," Mindy said. "I went to church for a few years as a kid, but I blocked out everything I learned."

"Do you know that you'll go to heaven?" the visitor asked.

"Oh, yeah, because we try to be kind and generous to others. We've got jobs, and we try to pay our debts."

"Well, I have great news for you," said the visitor. "Heaven is a *free* gift! Romans 6:23 says, 'The gift of God is eternal life.' It can't be earned or deserved. In fact, all of us are sinners. The same verse says, 'The wages of sin is death.'"

The visitor continued, "But God had a wonderful plan. He sent His only Son, Jesus, to pay our debt of sin. He died on the cross and rose from the dead to prove His power over sin and death. By faith in Jesus we receive the gift of eternal life!"

Mindy replied, "I believe that Jesus can forgive me and take me to heaven." Tears of joy were rolling down her face. As the visitors left, Mindy and Jeff were making plans to go to church.

_____Let's do: Do you know people like Mindy and Jeff who need to hear that God's gift of eternal life is free through faith in Jesus? How might you share this wonderful Good News?

_____Let's pray: Lord, give us courage to share Your Word with others. Send Your Holy Spirit to give understanding and faith to those who listen. In Jesus' name. Amen.

M. L. K.

Easter Afterglow

Read from God's Word

John, To the seven churches in the province of Asia: Grace and peace to you from Him who is, and who was, and who is to come, and from the seven spirits before His throne, and from Jesus Christ, who is the faithful witness, the firstborn from the dead, and the ruler of the kings of the earth. To Him who loves us and has freed us from our sins by His blood, and has made us to be a kingdom and priests to serve His God and Father—to Him be glory and power for ever and ever! Amen. Revelation 1:4–6

Maybe you have a few minutes to make something special that will help you share your Easter joy. It might be fun to design a card or note telling about the meaning of Easter. Maybe you could decorate the card with a butterfly, a wonderful symbol of new life.

As you work to design your card, be sure to tell the following:

1. What Jesus did;

2. Why He did it;

3. Why it makes you happy.

Many people say Easter is the happiest time of the year. Do you agree? Frequently we forget to thank the Lord for His awesome victory. Instead we think about new clothes, Easter baskets and candy, and a big dinner. But Jesus died to forgive all our sins—even ungratefulness. He sends His Holy Spirit to help us rise each day to a new life that bears the fruits of faith aglow with Easter joy.

Look for ways to continue the victory celebration throughout this year. For starters, you can give your Easter card to someone who needs a lift.

_____Let's talk: What would you say to someone who asked, "Why is Easter the happiest day of the year?" What are some other things you could do to help people remember the joy of Easter?

_____Let's pray: Lord, forgive us for forgetting to thank You more for Your awesome victory over sin and death. Bless the words that we say when we share Your Easter gift with others. Amen.

M. L. K.

Bloom and Grow

Read from God's Word

We have not stopped praying for you and asking God to fill you with the knowledge of His will through all spiritual wisdom and understanding. And we pray this in order that you may live a life worthy of the Lord and may please Him in every way: bearing fruit in every good work, growing in the knowledge of God, being strengthened with all power according to His glorious might so that you may have great endurance and patience, and joyfully giving thanks to the Father. ... For He has rescued us from the dominion of darkness and brought us into the kingdom of the Son He loves, in whom we have redemption, the forgiveness of sins. Colossians 1:9–14 ✐

In some of the northern states, April is the time to plant sweet-pea seeds. The ground is still cool, and the seeds are small, round, and hard. They look quite different from the colorful blossoms pictured on the front of the seed package. It's quite a contrast.

What a far cry these dry, unattractive seeds are from the flowering plant in the picture! But you can be sure that the plants will grow and produce fragrant bouquets. After all, last year's batch ended up decorating the windowsill.

In some ways, that's how faith in the Lord Jesus grows. The kernel of faith was planted in your heart through the power of the Holy Spirit when you were baptized. As you learned more about God's love for you and God's will for your life, your faith grew. Now reading and hearing God's Word helps you understand God's plan of salvation and the gift of eternal life earned for us by Jesus.

With the Holy Spirit's blessing, the seed of faith is developing and growing stronger. Teachers, pastors, parents, and others explain God's Word to you. Your roots go deeper, and new spiritual growth takes place. You are strengthened to serve others with a fruit-bearing faith. Through the things you say and do to witness to your faith, others are attracted to God's love and want to know more about Him and His salvation.

Bloom and grow, young Christians!

_____Let's talk: How can you tell if your faith is growing? What are some ways that a "blooming faith hero" has influenced your life? How could you thank this person?

_____Let's pray: Heavenly Father, sometimes our faith seems to wilt. Forgive us, Lord, for not feeding it with more of Your Word. Send Your Holy Spirit to help our faith grow and bloom. Amen.

M. L. K.

Tech It Out!

When Jesus said that the message of salvation was to be carried "to the ends of the earth," sandals were in style and walking was the way to get from one place to another. Talking to someone face-to-face was the usual method of communication.

Today, messages and pictures bounce off satellites, and e-mail zips through cyberspace in a matter of seconds. With all this technology, it would seem that getting the Gospel message to the ends of the earth would be a snap. How can we use these modern devices to proclaim God's love in Jesus to all nations? Here are some ideas:

1. Does your family have a Web site? Many families are using their Web site to include a clear witness to their Christian faith. You could quote your favorite Bible verses and explain why they are meaningful to you.

2. If you have keypals or take part in approved chatrooms, you can talk about your faith. If you are writing or talking to someone who doesn't know about Jesus, explain that heaven is a free gift from God earned by our Savior when He suffered, died, and rose again to pay for our sins.

3. If you know missionaries, pastors, or teachers serving in a distant place, ask permission to send e-mail messages of encouragement. Many missionaries report being strengthened by knowing that other people care about them and pray for them.

4. Send prayer requests via e-mail to let others know of urgent needs or emergency situations.

_____Let's talk: What are some other ways that we can use our technology to get the Good News out to the world?

_____Let's pray: Lord, thank You for cyberage opportunities. Bless our efforts to use these gifts to Your glory. Amen.

M. L. K.

Read from God's Word

So when they met together, they asked Him, "Lord, are You at this time going to restore the kingdom to Israel?" He said to them, "It is not for you to know the times or dates the Father has set by His own authority. But you will receive power when the Holy Spirit comes on you, and you will be My witnesses in Jerusalem, and in all Judea and Samaria, and to the ends of the earth." Acts 1:6–8

The Worst Kind of Lost

Read from God's Word

*"In those days, at that time,"
declares the LORD, "the people of
Israel and the people of Judah
together will go in tears to seek
the LORD their God. They will
ask the way to Zion and turn
their faces toward it. They will
come and bind themselves to the
LORD in an everlasting covenant
that will not be forgotten."*
Jeremiah 50:4–7

A mom and her daughter were driving an unfamiliar road. They saw a road with a familiar-sounding name and thought they must be close to home, only to discover that they still had another 50 miles to go. For a few miles they were lost and didn't even know it.

Some people spend their lives lost and don't know it. They don't know they are headed for eternity without believing in Jesus Christ as their Savior. They are on the road leading to eternal punishment.

Some people may hear of the Bible, Jesus, or salvation, but they don't pay attention because they think there will always be time to get off the road to hell. Others see their friends headed that way and decide to follow along because they're having fun. Some people don't think there really is a hell.

We know from the story of the rich man and Lazarus that hell is a place of torment and fire. The road to eternity offers only two choices: heaven or hell. But God sent Jesus to put us on the path to heaven. Jesus said, "I am the Way" (John 14:6). He also said, "Follow Me" (Luke 5:27).

If you are not sure you're on the road to heaven, ask God to lead you there. Look in His Word for strength to go the right way. Jesus says, "My Father's will is that everyone who looks to the Son and believes in Him shall have eternal life, and I will raise him up at the last day" (John 6:40).

_____Let's talk: Why is it important to let people know about the road to heaven? Name three people you could tell about the way to heaven through Jesus.

_____Let's pray: Dear Jesus, it's so tempting to follow the wrong road. Keep us by Your side. Send Your Holy Spirit to strengthen us for the journey. Help us tell others that You are the only Way! Amen.

M. L. K.

When You Feel Forsaken

Read from God's Word

We do not want you to be uninformed, brothers, about the hardships we suffered.... We were under great pressure, far beyond our ability to endure, so that we despaired even of life. Indeed, in our hearts we felt the sentence of death. But this happened that we might not rely on ourselves but on God, who raises the dead. He has delivered us from such a deadly peril, and He will deliver us. On Him we have set our hope that He will continue to deliver us, as you help us by your prayers. Then many will give thanks on our behalf for the gracious favor granted us in answer to the prayers of many.
2 Corinthians 1:8–11 ✍

Jeremy wrote words of anger and despair in his journal. "How could he just walk out of my life? What did I do to deserve not having a dad? Doesn't he know that a dad is the most important thing a kid my age needs? I'd give anything to have my dad back."

When Jeremy's father left, it affected Jeremy's whole life. He dreamed of going to sports events with his dad. He longed to spend a quiet afternoon fishing. He hoped he could talk to his dad about the problems he faced as well as his hopes and dreams for the future. Nothing was the same now. Life was not fun, only sad.

The apostle Paul and his companions found themselves in a rough situation. They didn't think they could live through the pressures and the problems. But later Paul wrote, "This happened that we might not rely on ourselves but on God, who raises the dead" (2 Corinthians 1:9).

Life is full of changes and pressures. Some children are shuttled from one parent to another. Sometimes it seems like you will never get well from an illness or an injury. Or you may have a disability that you feel is more than you can bear. It's tempting to think that God has forsaken you.

When we feel forsaken, we can remember that God's love never stops. He solved our greatest need, the need for a Savior. He sent His only beloved Son to save us. Surely He can be trusted to help us with all our other needs.

_____Let's talk: Which verses from the Bible give you the most comfort when you're feeling sad? Share them with one another when you experience hard times.

_____Let's pray: Jesus, Savior, pilot me
Over life's tempestuous sea.

M. L. K.

The Story of People Pins

"Where did you get that pin?" asked the shopkeeper.

"Oh, that's a People Pin," the lady said. "Do you know the story of People Pins and House Pins?"

"No," the shopkeeper answered.

"No two pins are alike. They show different people or houses. Each one is handcrafted by an artist who once faced homelessness. After she was blessed with a home, she started making these pins as a way of helping other people. The money earned from the pins helps provide housing for the homeless in our community."

Together with others, we can make a difference for needy people in our communities. It's part of sharing the love that Jesus Christ showed to us.

A community effort to help those in need—that's what the early Christian church was all about. The Bible tells us that "much grace was upon them" (Acts 4:33). Christ's powerful resurrection was fresh in their minds. They knew they belonged to a mighty Savior and that they would never be let down by His love. They were amazed by God's love. Out of thanks they shared everything they had.

We are also standing in the light of Christ's powerful Easter resurrection. His love and His blessings are all around us. Much grace is upon us! How can we respond?

_____Let's talk: Why did the early Christians share everything they had? What are some things kids can do to help others in the community?

_____Let's pray: Heavenly Father, forgive us for closing our eyes to the needs of others. Thank You for giving Your Son so we can live in heaven's mansions. Fill us with Your love that we may share it with others. Amen.

M. L. K.

m a y

May Day

Read from God's Word

Remember this: whoever sows sparingly will also reap sparingly, and whoever sows generously will also reap generously. Each man should give what he has decided in his heart to give, not reluctantly or under compulsion, for God loves a cheerful giver. And God is able to make all grace abound to you, so that in all things at all times, having all that you need, you will abound in every good work. 2 Corinthians 9:6–8

Abby tiptoed to Mrs. Meyer's front door and gently laid a decorated basket on the mat. Inside the basket Abby and her mother had placed homemade cookies, a box of tea, and a bouquet of freshly picked daisies.

Abby rang the doorbell, scampered back down the steps, and hid behind a tree. She peeked out and watched Mrs. Meyer's delight when she spied the basket.

"May Day!" Mrs. Meyer exclaimed. "Today is the first of May. But who ...?" Then she heard a giggle from behind the tree and called out, "Abigail Johnson! I see you!"

Abby ran back up the steps. "How did you know it was me?"

"It was you I told about how we celebrated May Day when I was a girl," Mrs. Meyer laughed. "I didn't think anybody gave May baskets anymore."

"It was fun," answered Abby. "It's like backward trick or treat. Instead of going to neighbors to get something, you go to give them something."

"Giving makes people feel good," agreed Mrs. Meyer. "That reminds me of the way God gives to us."

"What do you mean?"

Mrs. Meyer continued, "Every day God gives us friends and neighbors, homes and families. Best of all, He gave us Jesus, our Savior, to forgive our sins and make us His children. Now come inside and share some of these cookies with me. I'd like to do some giving too. Happy May Day!"

_____Let's talk: What did Abby mean when she said May Day is like "backward trick or treat"? What gifts from God are your favorites? Think of some ways you could surprise your friends or family members with gifts this month.

_____Let's pray: Dear God, thank You for giving everything to us—especially for sending Jesus as our Savior. Please help us know the joy of giving to others, for Jesus' sake. Amen.

C. S.

Why Laughter Is Good

Read from God's Word

A cheerful heart is good medicine, but a crushed spirit dries up the bones. Proverbs 17:22

f April showers bring May flowers, what do May flowers bring? The answer: Pilgrims! It's an old joke. The Pilgrims came to America on the *Mayflower*—get it?

Laughter is a wonderful gift from God. The Bible reading says that laughter is like medicine for the soul. Laughter makes your heart beat in a healthy way and increases the circulation of your blood. It makes pain less intense and puts you in a good mood. Laughter has been called "internal jogging." That means it's good exercise for our hearts and minds.

What makes you laugh? A funny story? Good news? The antics of a puppy or kitten? The thrill of a roller coaster?

The Bible doesn't tell us what made Jesus laugh, but we know that He was a human being just as we are. He talked a lot about joy and the blessings that make people glad. Knowing that Jesus is our Savior and that He loves us even when we are saddened by sin makes us smile.

Some things, however, are not funny. Teasing others is harmful. Watching someone do wrong or get hurt is nothing to laugh about. Disturbing a class with actions or remarks is no joke. Instead of treating other people like that, think about ways God makes you happy. Think about ways you can make others happy too. Let the joy of God's love show in your face as you smile and laugh with your friends and family.

_____Let's talk: Why is making fun of others not funny? What do you think Jesus laughed about when He was your age? What could you say to make a sad person feel happy?

_____Let's pray: Dear Jesus, thank You for bringing joy to our lives. Please forgive us for the times we have used laughter in wrong ways. Help us spread Your joy to everyone we know. Amen.

C. S.

When I'm Afraid

Read from God's Word

When I am afraid, I will trust in You. In God, whose word I praise, in God I trust; I will not be afraid. What can mortal man do to me? Psalm 56:3–4 ✐

Calvin reached for the remote control. He hated watching the news on TV. Every story was about something bad. What if bad things happened to him?

Scary things do happen in our world. Ever since Adam and Eve disobeyed God, sin and the trouble it causes have been part of life. The devil wants us to be afraid and to worry about the evil he causes.

But you are a child of God. Your heavenly Father is in charge. He has the power to take care of His world and to take care of you. When Jesus died on the cross, He defeated the devil and proved that He is strong enough to win over every bad thing.

God promises that when bad things happen, He will turn them into good for those who love Him. Even if death would come, God has power to raise the dead and give us life.

Make a list of things that frighten you. Then draw a cross over the list as a reminder that because Jesus died to take away your sins, He will also take care of you in every other way.

King David was often in danger, but he knew that God was on his side. "When I am afraid," David prayed in Psalm 56, "I will trust in You [God]." Let that be your prayer at night when you cannot sleep or at school when you face a problem or at home when you watch TV. God is stronger than anything, and He lives to love and care for you. Ask Him to calm your fears and give you peace.

_____Let's talk: Tell about a time when you were frightened and God helped you. If a TV program or movie bothers you, what can you do to avoid becoming frightened?

_____Let's pray: Dear heavenly Father, thank You for protecting us. Send Your Holy Spirit into our hearts and give us peace. Just like David, when we are afraid, we will trust in You! Amen.

C. S.

Hiding Out

S punky was a scaredy-cat. She was afraid of dogs. She was afraid of loud noises. She was afraid of Dad's shoes. The day the workmen put a new roof on the house, Spunky was nowhere to be found. When nighttime came, Spunky didn't come when Katie called.

Katie was worried. That night, just as she was about to drift off to sleep, Katie heard a faint meow coming from right over her head. Spunky had crawled into the attic under the roof when the workers had the shingles off.

Dad opened the crawl hole and propped up a ladder so the cat could crawl down, but she was too afraid. Mom brought a piece of turkey to try to coax Spunky close enough to grab, but the cat ignored the bait. Finally Katie climbed up the ladder and crawled into the attic. She squeezed into the corner where Spunky was hiding, picked her up, and carried her back into the house.

Read from God's Word

Then Jesus told them this parable: "Suppose one of you has a hundred sheep and loses one of them. Does he not leave the ninety-nine in the open country and go after the lost sheep until he finds it? And when he finds it, he joyfully puts it on his shoulders and goes home. Then he calls his friends and neighbors together and says, 'Rejoice with me; I have found my lost sheep.' I tell you that in the same way there will be more rejoicing in heaven over one sinner who repents than over ninety-nine righteous persons who do not need to repent." Luke 15:3–7 ✐

Sometimes we too feel like hiding. When we do something wrong, we may be afraid to face our parents or teachers or even God.

But God doesn't let us stay in hiding. He comes after us. He finds us wherever we are and carries us back to His family. God forgives us and gives us courage for the future. He loves us, fears and all, and promises to take good care of us forever. Now, that's something to purr about!

_____Let's talk: Have you ever tried to hide from someone? Why? Who found you? How is the story about Spunky like the story of the caring shepherd that Jesus told?

_____Let's pray: Dear Jesus, thank You for finding us when we feel guilty and afraid. You are with us wherever we go. We know that we are safe because You are our Savior and friend. Amen.

C. S.

Read from God's Word

Therefore, I urge you, brothers, in view of God's mercy, to offer your bodies as living sacrifices, holy and pleasing to God—this is your spiritual act of worship. Do not conform any longer to the pattern of this world, but be transformed by the renewing of your mind. Then you will be able to test and approve what God's will is—His good, pleasing and perfect will. Romans 12:1-2 ✍

A Difficult Choice

Kim was excited when Pam asked her to go along to the mall. But as they passed the makeup display, Pam's hand swept a bottle of nail polish off the shelf and into Kim's pocket.

"Are you crazy?" Kim hissed. "You just shoplifted that nail polish. We've got to put it back."

"No way," replied Pam. "All the kids lift stuff from the stores. If you tell, you'll get in worse trouble. I'll say it was your idea. The polish is in your pocket."

Kim knew that the Seventh Commandment says, "You shall not steal." She knew it would be wrong to keep the polish. But how could she be strong enough to stand up to her friend and do what is right, although it might mean trouble for her?

When you became a child of God, the Holy Spirit gave you faith to trust in Jesus' forgiveness for all your sins. That same Holy Spirit came to live in your heart. He gives you the power to make good decisions and to do what pleases God. The more you read and study God's Word, the stronger your faith becomes and the more you want to do God's will.

When you see yourself trusting in God's promises and doing what is right, you know that the Holy Spirit is at work in your heart. With His strength, you will be able to stand firm when you're tempted to do wrong.

____Let's talk: What would you have done in Kim's situation? How can Christian friends help each other do things that please God?

____Let's pray: Heavenly Father, thank You for sending Jesus as our Savior and for sending the Holy Spirit to live in our hearts. Help us do what pleases You. Forgive us when we fail, and make our faith stronger. Help us honor You in all we do, for Jesus' sake. Amen.

C. S.

A Strong Grip

Three-year-old Juan begged and begged until his father bought him a bright red balloon. The balloon tugged on the end of the long white string and struggled toward the sky. It was a good thing that string was tied tightly.

But when Dad tried to fasten the other end of the string to Juan's wrist, the boy began to howl. "No!" he cried.

"You're not big enough to hold onto the balloon," his father explained. "You'll let go of the string, and the balloon will float away."

"No!" hollered Juan.

"Okay," said Dad. "But you'll be sorry."

Juan smiled and grasped the end of the string tightly in his chubby fist. But a few minutes later, his grip loosened. Slowly the balloon rose above his head and into the sky. Juan was left with an empty hand.

Sometimes we're like Juan. We think we're big and strong enough to hang onto God all by ourselves. We don't want to be tied to reading the Bible or going to church or praying. We just want to enjoy God's blessings and not be bothered by staying connected to Him. But when troubles or doubts come, we may find that our faith seems to be slipping away.

That's where the Holy Spirit comes in. We don't hold onto God; He holds onto us by His great power through His Word. We don't have to worry about losing God, because God will never let us go. We belong to Him now and forever.

Read from God's Word

[Jesus said] "My sheep listen to My voice; I know them, and they follow Me. I give them eternal life, and they shall never perish; no one can snatch them out of My hand. My father, who has given them to Me, is greater than all; no one can snatch them out of My Father's hand. I and the Father are one." John 10:27–30 ༄

———Let's talk: Why did Juan lose his balloon? How does God attach Himself to us? What does the Holy Spirit do for us?

———Let's pray: Dear Father, thank You for sending Your Spirit to connect us to You. We know that we could not believe in You by ourselves. Please help us remember that You will never let go of us. We are glad we belong to You! Amen.

C. S.

A Dangerous Secret

Alfredo had a dangerous secret. Deep in his pocket nestled a small silver pistol he had found in his father's dresser the night before. Alfredo could hardly wait to show it to his friends. "Awesome!" breathed Roger when he saw the weapon. "Let me hold it."

A small warning tugged at Alfredo's heart. Surely the gun must be safe, but he remembered all the warnings he had heard about playing with firearms. "I don't know," he hesitated.

"Come on," pleaded Roger. "I'll be careful."

Just then Wayne came up from behind. "What's that?" he asked. Alfredo jumped. He dropped the gun, and when it hit the pavement an explosion rang out. All three boys locked eyes in disbelief. The gun was loaded. They could have been killed.

A small crowd gathered, led by Mr. Stone, the principal. Alfredo knew he was in big trouble, but nothing could be any worse than the feeling he had in the pit of his stomach. Then he remembered some words from the Bible: "He will command His angels concerning you to guard you in all your ways."

God's angels were with Alfredo that morning. God protected him and his friends from the very real danger he had brought to school. He also knew that God would make him strong now to do the right thing.

_____Let's talk: Why did Alfredo take the gun to school? Why was that a bad idea? How did God protect Alfredo and his friends? What is the biggest trouble God protects us from because of Jesus?

_____Let's pray: Dear Jesus, thank You for protecting us from dangers of all kinds—especially for dying to save us from the power of sin. We know Your angels guard us every day. Help us make good decisions and do what is right. In Your name we pray. Amen.

C. S.

Overcoming Anger

Read from God's Word

"In your anger do not sin": Do not let the sun go down while you are still angry, and do not give the devil a foothold. He who has been stealing must steal no longer, but must work ... that he may have something to share with those in need. Do not let any unwholesome talk come out of your mouths, but only what is helpful for building others up. ... And do not grieve the Holy Spirit of God. ... Get rid of all bitterness, rage and anger, brawling and slander, along with every form of malice. Be kind and compassionate to one another, forgiving each other, just as in Christ God forgave you. Ephesians 4:26–32 ↩

Never let your mother brush your hair when she's upset with your dad. Those words of advice were offered by a child who found out the hard way just how painful anger can be. It's hard for an angry person to treat others gently.

What or who makes you angry? You may get upset when somebody cuts into line ahead of you or when you get teased. You may become angry when you aren't allowed to do something you want. What do you do then? Throw a tantrum? Start to hit or kick?

Anger hurts the person who is angry. It causes chemicals that make your heart work harder and raise your blood pressure. Anger can make you sick.

Counting to 10 or taking a walk may help control your anger, but those activities won't make it go away. Only God can help you overcome anger and replace it with feelings of peace, patience, and love.

The next time you feel angry, think about how God is patient with you even when you do something thoughtless or selfish. He never stops showing His love for you. All of God's anger was focused on Jesus when He died on the cross for us. Now we do not have to be angry with others.

God wants His children to live together in peace. This is especially important when you're brushing someone else's hair!

_____Let's talk: Think about the last time you were angry. How did you handle the situation? Why did Jesus have to die on the cross? Did He also die for the sins of those who anger you? Then how does He want you to treat them?

_____Let's pray: Dear Jesus, we know that our wrong behavior deserves Your anger. Thank You for loving us instead and forgiving our sins. Please take away all angry thoughts, words, and deeds, and help us treat others as You treat us. Amen.

C. S.

Finally, brothers, whatever is true, whatever is noble, whatever is right, whatever is pure, whatever is lovely, whatever is admirable—if anything is excellent or praiseworthy—think about such things. Whatever you have learned or received or heard from me, or seen in me—put it into practice. And the God of peace will be with you. Philippians 4:8–9

Living Inside Out

What color are flamingos? It all depends on what they eat. Flamingos that eat lots of deep pink shrimp become a deep pink color. The ones that eat more pale food remain white.

People are like flamingos. What is inside shows on the outside. A person who has a cheerful heart will wear a smile. A person who thinks about violence will probably look mean.

The Bible tells us to think about things that are pure, lovely, and right so we will act in pure, lovely, and right ways. When we focus on noble and positive things, our outlook will be positive too.

Jesus is at work in your heart and mind. He takes the impure thoughts and feelings that enter there and washes them in His blood so your heart and mind are clean in His eyes. The Holy Spirit works to keep you pure on the inside and makes you strong to do good on the outside.

Because God lives inside you, you can live for Him in all you think, say, and do. Be careful what you watch and think about. You are living inside out!

_____Let's talk: How can you decide if a movie or video game is good for you? How can you know what is in your heart? Think of several movies or books or games that would be healthy for you, as the Bible reading suggests.

_____Let's pray: Dear God, please make our hearts clean on the inside so we can live our lives for You. Take away our sins for Jesus' sake, and let everyone who sees us see You at work inside us. In Jesus' name we ask this. Amen.

C. S.

A Mother's Love

What do you call your mother? Do you call her "Mom" or "Mommy?" How about "Mama" or "Madre" or "Mum?"

Sean's mother died when he was just a baby. His dad is the person who hugs him and cares for him, drives him to school, helps him with his homework, and cooks healthful meals.

Moms and dads and grandmas and aunts and sometimes special friends are gifts from God to care for His children. As we celebrate Mother's Day, be sure to thank the person(s) God has given you.

God wants parents to love and care for their children the way He loves and cares for us. He loves us when we do good or bad, when we are clean or messy, when we are happy or sad. He teaches us how to live and protects us from harm. He provides us with many good things.

God wants children to love and honor their parents. Parents and children don't always do what God wants. Sin causes many problems in families everywhere. But God forgives our sins for Jesus' sake so we can forgive one another.

Sean gave his father a huge bear hug and made him a card that said, "Happy Parent's Day!" What do you suppose his father did with that card?

Read from God's Word

Children, obey your parents in the Lord, for this right. "Honor your father and mother"—which is the first commandment with a promise—"that it may go well with you and that you may enjoy long life on the earth." Ephesians 6:1–3

Let's talk: What do you think is the hardest part about being a parent? What do you think is the best part? Name some ways your family is like Jesus. How can you show your love for the people who care for you?

Let's pray: Dear God, thank You for giving us people to take care of us. We know that loving parents are a gift from You. Please forgive us when we don't do the things that make You happy. Help everyone in our family love and forgive one another. In Jesus' name. Amen.

C. S.

Read from God's Word

You are all sons of God through faith in Christ Jesus, for all of you who were baptized into Christ have clothed yourselves with Christ. There is neither Jew nor Greek, slave nor free, male nor female, for you are all one in Christ Jesus. If you belong to Christ, then you are Abraham's seed, and heirs according to the promise. Galatians 3:26–29 ✍

Oh, No! Not Her!

Bunny the cat was the ruler of the house—or so she thought. She let her family live there, but it was really her territory. The family belonged to her too, especially when she wanted some attention or a soft lap.

Then it happened! An intruder came into Bunny's territory. It was a small, wiggly bundle that made strange noises. The intruder was a baby girl named Madeline.

To make matters worse, everyone in the family wanted to hold Madeline, fuss over her, and play with her. Bunny was jealous and did everything she could to get their attention. She raced through the house, jumped on the furniture, or sat under the table and pouted. Each time Bunny looked at Madeline, you could almost hear Bunny thinking, *Oh, no! Not her!*

God doesn't want people to be jealous, but sometimes we may have to fight jealousy. It may seem that Mom or Dad is paying more attention to our brother or sister than to us. Maybe we're jealous of someone in school who always knows the right answers or someone who has lots of neat things we'd like to have.

We never, never need to feel jealous as far as God is concerned. He loves and cares for everyone the same. He watches over each of us and hears everyone's prayers. Christ died for the sins of *everyone*, and *everyone* who believes in Him will go to heaven when they die. God has no favorites, for He says, "You are all one in Christ Jesus" (Galatians 3:28). Isn't that wonderful?

———Let's do: On a sheet of paper, list some things that make you jealous. Then write Galatians 3:28 across the paper as a reminder that in God's sight everyone is equal.

———Let's pray: Jesus, help us fight jealousy. Thanks for loving each of us and for treating all of us fairly and equally. Amen.

J. A. D.

What a Friend!

Have you ever heard of Joseph Scriven? Probably not. But you may have heard something he wrote.

About 180 years ago Joseph was born in Ireland. He grew up there, went to school, graduated from college, and became engaged. But on the day before his wedding, Joseph's bride accidentally drowned.

Joseph was so terribly sad that he moved to Canada, where he taught school and tutored for a soldier's family. Joseph fell in love again and was about to be married. A short time before the wedding, the woman he loved became very ill and died. Joseph quit teaching and spent the rest of his life doing common, everyday work for elderly people.

You might think that Joseph became mad at God for all the bad things that had happened to him. But that wasn't how he felt. Joseph knew that no matter what happened, Jesus loved him. He knew that Jesus was his friend and was always ready to hear his prayers and help him. You see, Joseph Scriven wrote the hymn "What a Friend We Have in Jesus."

Jesus is our friend too—the very best friend we can ever have. Jesus hears us when we pray, watches over us, and takes care of us. Jesus loves us so much that He died for us. Because of His death and resurrection, our sins are forgiven and we can go to heaven when we die. What a marvelous friend!

Read from God's Word

[Jesus said] "My command is this: Love each other as I have loved you. Greater love has no one than this, that he lay down his life for his friends. You are My friends if you do what I command. I no longer call you servants, because a servant does not know his master's business. Instead, I have called you friends, for everything that I learned from My Father I have made known to you. You did not choose Me, but I chose you and appointed you to go and bear fruit—fruit that will last. Then the Father will give you whatever you ask in My name. This is My command: Love each other." John 15:12–15

_____Let's talk: What are some ways you can be a friend to someone
          who really needs a friend? How does it help to have
          Jesus as your "always friend?"

_____Let's pray: What a friend we have in Jesus,
          All our sins and griefs to bear!
          What a privilege to carry,
          Everything to God in prayer!

J. A. D.

Resurrected Bodies

Read from God's Word

But someone may ask, "How are the dead raised? With what kind of body will they come?" How foolish! What you sow does not come to life unless it dies. When you sow, you do not plant the body that will be, but just a seed. ... But God gives it a body as He has determined. ... Men have one kind of flesh, animals have another, birds another and fish another. There are also heavenly bodies and there are earthly bodies. ... So will it be with the resurrection of the dead. The body that is sown is perishable, it is raised imperishable; ... it is sown a natural body, it is raised a spiritual body. 1 Corinthians 15:35–44 🖎

Sara and Ben raced outside, eager to get started on their 4-H gardening project. Everything was ready for planting the seeds they had picked out.

"Row one will be carrots," declared Ben as he ripped open the top of the packet. A look of disappointment crossed Ben's face when he looked inside. "I think somebody made a big mistake. These seeds look like pepper! How can they grow into sweet, crunchy carrots?" he asked.

Sara was equally disappointed when she opened the packet of nasturtium seeds. "These look like dried-up peas!" she moaned.

When the kids complained to Mom, she reassured them. "The seeds *will* grow into carrots and nasturtiums. But they have to die before the new plants can come from them. You won't be disappointed."

One day some people asked St. Paul what their resurrected bodies would be like. Paul answered them by comparing a resurrected body to a seed dying and then growing into a plant. In 1 Corinthians 15:36–38, Paul explains, "What you sow does not come to life unless it dies. ... You do not plant the body that will be, but just a seed. ... God gives it a body as He has determined."

We will all die someday. But Jesus' death for our sins assures us that we will not stay dead. We will be raised and live with our Lord forever. That's a thousand times more wonderful than a dead-looking seed changing into a beautiful plant!

_____Let's do: Plant some seeds in your garden or a big container. As you watch them grow, they can remind you of the resurrected body you will have in heaven.

_____Let's pray: Thanks, Lord, for dying for our sins so we can have eternal life. Help us live in You, today and every day. Amen.

J. A. D.

Happy _____ Day

Read from God's Word

Imagine that kids from different countries were asked to fill in the blank above. Their answers might look something like this: Olga—*Mati's*; Gretchen—*Mutter's*; and Isamu—*Okasan's*. You would probably write *Mother's* or *Mom's* Day.

On the day mothers are honored, special things are done for them. That's great! Mom loves being fussed over. Flowers, cards, presents, or eating out are wonderful. They make Mom feel like "Queen for a Day."

Maybe *every* day should be Mom's day because she loves and cares for you 365 days of the year. Mom feels sad when you're sad, and she laughs with you when you're happy. At times Mom doesn't like some of the things you do, but she always loves you.

Of all the things Mom does for you, one stands out. Your mom tells you about Jesus. Like Timothy's mother, Eunice, she probably taught you

She took the boy ... to the house of the LORD at Shiloh. ... and she said to [Eli], ... "I prayed for this child, and the LORD has granted me what I asked of Him. So now I give him to the LORD. For his whole life he will be given over to the LORD." And he worshiped the LORD there. 1 Samuel 1:24–28

I have been reminded of your sincere faith, which first lived in your grandmother Lois and in your mother Eunice and, I am persuaded, now lives in you also. For this reason I remind you to fan into flame the gift of God. ... For God did not give us a spirit of timidity, but a spirit of power, of love and of self-discipline. 2 Timothy 1:5–7

Bible stories from the time you were little. Like Hannah, your mom often prays for you.

Mom wants you to know about Jesus' love and forgiveness. She wants you to be His child and follow Him, by the grace of God and the power of His Spirit. Mom wants you to live with Jesus forever. That's the most wonderful thing your mom can ever want for you!

_____Let's do: Make your mom a special tape recording or video. Get everyone in your family to record poems, funny stories, or music on a tape your mom can keep and enjoy all year.

_____Let's pray: Lord, thank You for Mom and for all the things she does for our family. We are especially thankful that she has told us about You and Your love. Amen.

J. A. D.

Fear Monsters

Read from God's Word

*An army with horses and chariots had surrounded the city. "Oh, my lord, what shall we do?" the servant asked. "Don't be afraid," the prophet answered. "Those who are with us are more than those who are with them." And Elisha prayed, "O LORD, open his eyes so he may see." Then the LORD opened the servant's eyes, and he looked and saw the hills full of horses and chariots of fire all around Elisha. As the enemy came down toward him, Elisha prayed to the LORD, "Strike these people with blindness." So He struck them with blindness, as Elisha had asked.
... 2 Kings 6:15–19*

About 2,000 kids from six countries were surveyed some years ago. They were asked to rate certain situations on a scale from 1 to 10, with 1 being the least fearful and 10 the scariest. The survey showed that, according to how children think, being afraid is normal. It doesn't mean we're bad; it means we need God's protection.

No matter what kind of fear monster attacks us, we can trust in God to protect us. Psalm 34:7 says, "The angel of the LORD encamps around those who fear Him, and He delivers them."

Jesus, our Savior, has delivered us from the worst dangers of all—sin, death, and hell. As children of God through Jesus' redemption, we can rely on our Father in heaven to watch over us. He will take care of us, just as He protected Elisha and his servant in today's Bible reading. Is there something that frightens you? Tell God about it and let Him take care of it!

_____Let's talk: Fight your fear monsters with God's Word. How do Psalm 34:17–19 and Psalm 23:4 assure us of God's protection?

_____Let's pray: God, sometimes we feel afraid. Help us trust You and know that You love us and will help us in every situation. Thanks for watching over us each and every day. In Jesus' name. Amen.

J. A. D.

Best Friends

Read from God's Word

The LORD said, "I have indeed seen the misery of My people in Egypt. I have heard them crying out because of their slave drivers, and I am concerned about their suffering. So I have come down to rescue them from the hand of the Egyptians and to bring them up out of that land into a good and spacious land, a land flowing with milk and honey. ... And now the cry of the Israelites has reached me, and I have seen the way the Egyptians are oppressing them. So now, go. I am sending you to Pharoah to bring My people the Israelites out of Egypt." Exodus 3:7–10 ✎

N ooo!" screeched Brandi at the top of her lungs. She covered her ears with her hands. "I don't want to hear it! Tell me it's not true! You're not moving!"

"It's true, and there's nothing I can do about it," replied April.

"But we're best friends! We ride the school bus together. We eat lunch together. You'll be going to a different school. How can you do this to me, April Forester?"

"Hey, don't blame me! It's not my fault. I feel bad about leaving you too."

During dinner that evening, Brandi's parents tried to comfort her. "You can write to each other. April can come and spend the weekend with us anytime," Dad told her.

Then her mother added, "There are other friends your age who live near us. When God shuts one door, he opens another."

"Does God really understand how I feel?" asked Brandi.

"Of course He does, Brandi. You remember the Bible reading we had today. It told us that God sees the misery of His people. When I feel bad, I remember the Bible verse from 1 Peter, 'Cast all your anxiety on Him because He cares for you' (1 Peter 5:7). Jesus cares about you so much that He was willing to die for you."

"Thanks, Mom. I guess I forgot who my best friend really is."

"Friends come and go, Brandi, but Jesus is with you always," Mom assured her.

_____Let's talk: Did you ever have a close friend who moved away? How did you feel? What does "Cast all your anxiety on Him" mean to you?

_____Let's pray: Dear Jesus, thank You for all the happy times we have in life. Thank You also for being there to help us during the difficult times. Amen.

E. R. S.

Read from God's Word

"Even now," declares the LORD, *"return to Me with all your heart, with fasting and weeping and mourning."* Rend *your heart and not your garments. Return to the* LORD *your God, for He is gracious and compassionate, slow to anger and abounding in love, and He relents from sending calamity. Who knows? He may turn and have pity and leave behind a blessing—grain offerings and drink offerings for the* LORD *your God. Joel 2:12–14*

Worst Enemies

Brandi's father was looking at his mail when he noticed a letter that belonged next door. "Brandi," he called, "will you please take this letter to Mrs. Clark? It came to our house by mistake."

"Okay, Dad," Brandi answered. She didn't like going to the Clarks because Lonnie Clark was the biggest tease in the fourth grade. At that very moment Lonnie was hiding between the two houses with a water balloon in his hand. He took careful aim. *Pow!* The balloon hit Brandi and she fell backward, hitting her head on the sidewalk.

Lonnie ran up to her and said, "Are you okay, Brandi? I'm sorry. I didn't mean to hurt you."

"Oh-h! My head! Here, take your stupid letter! I'm going home!" But Brandi felt so dizzy that Lonnie had to help her home. Lonnie told Brandi's father what had happened.

"It's all my fault, and I'm really sorry," he apologized.

Lonnie went home with a sick feeling in the pit of his stomach. This was one trick that wasn't funny.

"Stop tearing your clothes, Lonnie," said his brother, Lemay.

"What do you mean?" asked Lonnie. "I'm not tearing any clothes."

"Well, your glum face reminds me of Bible times, when people tore their clothes to show that they were sorry for their sins. God doesn't look at outward appearances but at the sinner's heart. He looks at us with love and always forgives us. So stop tearing your clothes!"

_____Let's talk: Where do we go to receive forgiveness? How did Jesus make our forgiveness possible?

_____Let's pray: Dear Jesus, sometimes we hurt people because we are selfish and think only of our own fun. Forgive us, and help us love others as You have loved us all. Amen.

E. R. S.

Moving Day

All too quickly, moving day arrived. The Foresters were packed and ready to leave. Brandi noticed that Lonnie was on his porch, watching everything. She was not going to let him see her cry.

Brandi hugged April. "Write to me every day," she urged.

"I promise, and you write to me too!"

"God be with you all," called Brandi's mother as the Sanchez family waved good-bye to their friends.

Just before April's car pulled away from the curb, she rolled down the window and yelled, "Stay away from Loony Lonnie!"

After April left, Brandi sat on the front steps, feeling very lonely. She noticed that Lonnie was still his porch. She hadn't talked to him since the day he threw the water balloon at her.

Maybe Mom's right, thought Brandi. *Maybe Lonnie just needs a friend.* Then she thought about these words in the Lord's Prayer: "Forgive us our trespasses as we forgive those who trespass against us."

Jesus forgives me every day. I ought to be able to forgive Lonnie, Brandi thought. "Hey, Lonnie, do you want to play Monopoly?" she called.

"I thought you were supposed to stay away from me. You heard what April said, didn't you?"

"Sure, I heard what she said. But she doesn't live here anymore. Come on over. I'll set up the game."

Read from God's Word

[Jesus said] "For your Father knows what you need before you ask Him. This then, is how you should pray: 'Our Father in heaven, hallowed be your name, your kingdom come, your will be done on earth as it is in heaven. Give us today our daily bread. Forgive us our debts, as we also have forgiven our debtors. And lead us not into temptation, but deliver us from the evil one.' For if you forgive men when they sin against you, your heavenly Father will also forgive you. But if you do not forgive men their sins, your Father will not forgive your sins." Matthew 6:6–15 ✑

_____Let's talk: How did Brandi show by her actions that she forgave Lonnie? How could you forgive someone who teases you?

_____Let's pray: Dear Jesus, thank You for forgiving all our sins. Empower us with Your Spirit to show kindness and forgiveness to others. Amen.

E. R. S.

The Heather Powell Story

Five days near death, Quincy teen recovers after being baptized during lengthy battle with meningitis. That was the news that was published in the Quincy, Illinois, *Herald-Whig* newspaper. The story told how Heather's sickness began with a stiff neck, headache, fever, and vomiting. She got worse. Soon she was fighting for her life.

Doctors told her parents that Heather had only a 1-in-10 chance of recovering. That's when her parents decided to have Heather baptized.

Heather lived across the street from Our Redeemer Church. When the people at church heard about her sickness, they began praying for her.

Mrs. Powell said that people in churches all over Quincy and throughout the United States prayed for her daughter. People as far away as Okinawa, Japan, also prayed.

The newspaper story went on to say, "Heather began to recover soon after her parents had her baptized."

We could easily change the title of this devotion to "The Holy Spirit Story." The Holy Spirit moved Heather's parents to have her baptized. And the Holy Spirit moved many people to pray for her. And God's Spirit healed Heather.

You too have the Holy Spirit at work in your life. This is something precious and to be desired. The Holy Spirit bears witness to Jesus, who spared us from God's anger and punishment. So reading the Bible and listening to God's Word whenever it is taught deserves our highest priority.

_____Let's talk: What are some times and places you can hear or read God's Word? How can you be a better listener?

_____Let's pray: Heavenly Father, thank You for bringing us to faith in Jesus Christ, our Savior. May Your Spirit be present in us as we reach out to others with Your love. Amen.

E. R. S.

The Ferris Wheel

Read from God's Word

By faith Abraham, when called to go to a place he would later receive as his inheritance, obeyed and went, even though he did not know where he was going. By faith he made his home in the Promised Land like a stranger in a foreign country; he lived in tents, as did Isaac and Jacob, who were heirs with him of the same promise. For he was looking forward to the city with foundations, whose architect and builder is God. Hebrews 11:8–10

A Ferris wheel has about 18 seats. Each seat can hold three people. That means today's Ferris wheels can hold as many as 54 people at one time.

The first Ferris wheel, invented by George Ferris in 1893, was enormous. There were 36 cars, and each car held 60 people. So George Ferris's machine could hold a total of 2,160 people at one time.

George Ferris invited his wife and a newspaper reporter to join him for the first ride. It was a windy day, but Ferris assured his wife and the reporter that his invention was safe. They believed him, and they willingly accompanied George on the first ride. The wheel turned perfectly, despite the wind, and the Ferris wheel was a success.

Faith means complete confidence or trust. By going on that ride, Mrs. Ferris and the reporter showed their faith in the inventor. They acted on their faith and did something that had never been done before.

In our Bible reading, we hear how Abraham believed God's promises and acted on his faith. He went on a long, difficult journey to a land that was strange and foreign to him.

We believe the promises of God, our Father. He promised that a Savior would come into the world to conquer sin, death, and the power of the devil. Through faith in this Savior, we have a promised home in heaven that will last forever. Let's follow Abraham's example and have faith!

_____Let's talk: What are some things you have done while acting on faith? What do you think is important for keeping your faith strong?

_____Let's pray: Lord, give us a strong faith so we can stand firm against the temptations that surround us. Give us a faith that will be a shining light leading others to You. In the Savior's name we pray. Amen.

E. R. S.

Then What?

Read from God's Word

Read from God's Word

And we know that in all things God works for the good of those who love Him, who have been called according to His purpose. For those God foreknew He also predestined to be conformed to the likeness of His Son, that He might be the firstborn among many brothers. And those He predestined, He also called; those He called, He also justified; those He justified, He also glorified. Romans 8:28–30

After the clay pot dried, Laura set it on a small table. As she went to get her paint set, she heard a crash. The small clay pot made for Grandma's birthday broke into pieces as it hit the floor.

Laura cried when her dad came home that night. "Daddy," she said, "you should have heard it! Crash, smash, boom!"

"Then what?" Dad asked. The cleanup. "Then what?" Tears. "Then what?" Dad asked again. Grief. "Then what?" Plans for clay pot number 2.

Have you ever played the "then what?" game? It can help when you don't know what to do next.

Laura's aunt was in a "then what?" situation, facing surgery. Her pastor said to her, "Lois, suppose everything goes well in surgery. Then what?"

Lois thought a bit and then replied, "I'd wake up in the recovery room and see my family again."

"Good," her pastor said. "But what if things don't go well in surgery? Then what?"

Lois was quiet. Then she tearfully answered, "I'd wake up in heaven and see my Savior. And I'd enjoy being in the Lord's presence forever." Lois trusted in Jesus' promise that "everyone who looks to the Son and believes in Him shall have eternal life" (John 6:40).

Now it's your turn. Play "then what?" with Romans 8:29–30 ("foreknew ... predestined ... called ... justified ... glorified").

_____Let's talk: According to Romans 8:28, what has God planned for your life? Can anything keep you from His purpose for you? Also see Romans 8:32, 38–39.

_____Let's pray: Dear Father, thank You for calling us to faith in Jesus Christ and for giving us the answer to what's next. Continue Your good work in us! Amen.

G. R. W.

"I'll Do It Later"

I think you need to clean your ears," Michael nagged at his sister. "Mom said to clean your room, not play video games."

"It doesn't have to be done now," Megan snapped back. "I'll do it later."

"It sounded like a *now* thing to me," Michael replied. "Mom said to have your room done when she got home."

Megan slammed the door and continued to play.

Does God care if children obey their parents? Sure He does. He even wrote a commandment about it. The Fourth Commandment talks about honoring parents.

Jesus honored and obeyed His earthly parents as He was growing up. His whole life and death showed obedience to His heavenly Father. He did everything for us to make us at peace with God.

God gives us parents or other people to care for us because of His love for us. Our caregivers are God's hands on earth. They serve God by caring for the children He has entrusted to them. Children serve God by obeying those placed over them.

Megan did eventually stop playing video games and clean her room. That was good, but her obedience was grudging and delayed. We honor God best when we obey willingly and quickly.

Read from God's Word

Finally, be strong in the Lord, and in His mighty power. Put on the full armor of God so that you can take your stand against the devil's schemes. For our struggle is not against flesh and blood, but against the rulers, against the authorities, against the powers of this dark world and against the spiritual forces of evil in the heavenly realms. Therefore put on the full armor of God, so that when the day of evil comes, you may be able to stand your ground, and after you have done everything, to stand. Ephesians 6:10–13

_____Let's talk: When is it the hardest to obey those in charge of you? What can you do to receive help and strength?

_____Let's pray: Thank You, dear Lord, for those who care *about* us and care *for* us. Thank You for being our loving Father in heaven. Help us to obey quickly and eagerly. Amen.

V. S.

Excuses, Excuses

Read from God's Word

Jesus replied: "A certain man was preparing a great banquet and invited many guests. ... But they all alike began to make excuses. The first said, 'I have just bought a field, and I must go and see it. Please excuse me.' Another said, 'I have just bought five yoke of oxen, and I'm on my way to try them out. Please excuse me.' Still another said, 'I just got married, so I can't come.' ... Then the owner of the house became angry and ordered his servant, 'Go out quickly into the streets and alleys ... and bring in the poor, the crippled, the blind and the lame ... not one of those men who were invited will get a taste of my banquet.'" Luke 14:16–24 ✎

Okay, class, it's time to turn in the social studies projects you've been working on for the last three weeks," Mr. Shepard announced.

"Mr. Shepard?" Jamie raised her hand meekly. "I don't have mine. It was all done, but my sister got sick last night and threw up all over it."

"I see," Mr. Shepard replied.

"I have a problem with mine too," Anthony chimed in. "I forgot to put my rabbit in his cage last night. This corner here is all he didn't chew up."

"Anybody else?" Mr. Shepard asked.

"I think my grandma might have put mine in her suitcase before she went back home," said Anita.

"My mom vacuumed mine up," said Felix. "We have a big vacuum."

"Are those reasons or excuses?" asked Mr. Shepard. "Reasons explain what really happened," he explained. "Excuses cover up what was never done."

God listens to lots of excuses. For instance—"I didn't invite my neighbor to church because he wasn't home Saturday afternoon when I called." "I can read my Bible anytime. This show is only on today." "It's okay if I forgot to pray for Roy. He has a lot of friends who probably prayed for him."

It's a good thing God isn't an excuse-giver. He could have thought of all kinds of excuses not to send His Son to earth to die for us, but He didn't hold back. Why not? Because He loves us!

_____Let's talk: What excuses do you like to use? Do you give those excuses to God?

_____Let's pray: Heavenly Father, thank You for loving us so much that You sent Jesus, not excuses. Help us serve You willingly—without excuses. Amen.

V. S.

Friends Again

arcie and Jacob were classmates. Each tried to outdo the other, and sometimes they got carried away. One day Marcie saw a chance to get the upper hand. Jacob had messed up big-time, and Marcie let him know it.

"Jacob," she exclaimed, "you're a terrible excuse for a human being! Even God doesn't love you!"

As she turned to flee, Marcie ran right into her pastor, who was walking through the hallway of their Christian school. "Pastor," she said. "How are you?"

"Marcie," he replied, "how could you do that? I heard what you said." Her red cheeks signaled her embarrassment, but her "I'm sorry" signaled that she had received a gift—God's gift of repentance.

Pastor said, "Marcie, you're forgiven for Jesus' sake. You know what to do next?"

Marcie didn't want to hear it. She'd "get to" apologize to Jacob, promising never to speak that way again. "I can't," Marcie confessed.

Read from God's Word

You, therefore, have no excuse, you who pass judgment on someone else, for at whatever point you judge the other, you are condemning yourself, because you who pass judgment do the same things. Now we know that God's judgment against those who do such things is based on truth. So when you, a mere man, pass judgment on them and yet do the same things, do you think you will escape God's judgment? Or do you show contempt for the riches of His kindness, tolerance and patience, not realizing that God's kindness leads you toward repentance? Romans 2:1–4 ✍

"You can," Pastor said, "because the Lord will strengthen you. Pray for that before you go."

Marcie's words to Jacob came slowly: "I'm sor...ry...for...what I...said."

Jacob thought for a moment and then answered, "I forgive you because I've been forgiven by Christ." His quick smile sealed the moment. The rivals were now friends.

_____Let's talk: Who have you wronged lately with your words or actions? How can God's power change things around? Who needs your forgiveness today?

_____Let's pray: Gracious Father, we know how much You have forgiven us through Your Son, Jesus Christ. Help us forgive others for Jesus' sake. Amen.

G.R.W.

Jesus Listens

"Jake," Amanda called. "You forgot to put my bike away after you used it. I'm going baby-sitting now. Please put the bike away before it rains. Jake! "

"Huh? Oh, sure," Jake called back, never taking his eyes off the TV.

"Jake, I have to run to the store. Will you get the towels off the clothesline before it rains?" Dad asked as he headed for the door. "Jake!"

"Oh, no problem, Dad," Jake mumbled.

"Jake, I can't get the dog's chain undone, and it's starting to rain. Will you help me so he doesn't get wet?" Kevin asked.

"I'll be right there," Jake promised.

An hour later Jake came down the stairs to find an unhappy family. Dad was holding a basket of wet towels, Kevin was drying a wet dog, and Amanda was just glaring at him.

"You weren't listening, were you, Jake?" Dad commented.

Jesus always listened to others. He also responded in love. When a father was worried about his sick daughter, Jesus listened and healed the girl. When a woman was sorry for something she had done, Jesus listened and forgave her. Jesus still listens. He listens every time we speak to Him, and He responds. He loves us so dearly that He gave up His life to save ours. He will never let us down.

_____Let's talk: What are some things that distract you from listening? Why is it important to listen well?

_____Let's pray: Thank You, Jesus, that You're a good listener—that You hear us and always answer. Help us listen to You too and follow Your will for us. Amen.

V. S.

Roy G. Biv

Have you ever heard of Roy G. Biv? He's very well known. He's been around since the time of Noah. But who is he?

Roy G. Biv isn't actually a person. The letters in his name are the first letters of the colors of the rainbow in the order they appear in the sky. Roy G. Biv is a little trick that can help us remember the colors: Red, Orange, Yellow, Green, Blue, Indigo, and Violet.

Do you have trouble remembering things? Maybe it's hard for you to remember what time you were supposed to be home for dinner. When was the last time you brought your gym clothes home to be washed? Where did you leave your pet hamster? Maybe you could use a trick to help you remember.

God put a rainbow in the sky as a reminder of His promise. He will never again destroy the earth with a flood. God doesn't need the rainbow. He never forgets His promises. He put His bow in the sky for those of us who may be forgetful.

The Bible is filled with promises God made to His people—promises of hope and blessings; promises of love and forgiveness; promises of salvation through His Son, Jesus. He has kept every one of them.

It's okay if you forget things sometimes. But God doesn't and He never will!

Read from God's Word

And God said, "This is the sign of the covenant I am making between Me and you and every living creature with you, a covenant for all generations to come: I have set My rainbow in the clouds, and it will be the sign of the covenant between Me and the earth. Whenever I bring clouds over the earth and the rainbow appears in the clouds, I will remember My covenant between Me and you and all living creatures of every kind. Never again will the waters become a flood to destroy all life." Genesis 9:12–15 ✍

_____Let's talk: What's the hardest thing for you to remember? What's the hardest thing for you to forget?

_____Let's pray: Dear God, thank You for reminding us each day, in so many ways, how much You love us. Help us never forget this. Amen.

V. S.

Never Alone

Read from God's Word

God is our refuge and strength, an ever-present help in trouble. Therefore we will not fear, though the earth give way and the mountains fall into the sea, though its waters roar and foam and the mountains quake with their surging. There is a river whose streams make glad the city of God, the holy place where the Most High dwells. God is within her, she will not fall; God will help her at break of day. ... The LORD Almighty is with us; the God of Jacob is our fortress. Psalm 46:1–7 ᔕ

Lindsay sat on the couch, her knees drawn up close. She had never realized how really dark it could get. A loud thunderclap made her jump.

"Better check the baby," Lindsay said to herself as she cautiously got up and made her way down the hallway. "It figures that the first time I baby-sit, a storm would knock out the power."

Lindsay sat down again after looking in on the sleeping baby. There was nothing she could do but sit there in the dark. She felt very much alone and frightened.

Lindsay closed her eyes and tried to think of something—anything—that would make her feel better. A Bible verse she had learned in Sunday school came to mind: "God is our refuge and strength, an ever-present help in trouble."

"Ever-present," Lindsay said out loud. "That means God is here now. I'm not alone." She could feel herself start to relax.

"God is my refuge," she continued. "A refuge is a place of safety." The cold, dark room didn't feel much like a place of safety. But knowing God was there made things a lot better.

Troubles come in many forms and situations. Some are harder to handle than others. God is dependable. He is ever-present. He may not make the trouble go away, but He will strengthen your heart and see you through it. He is a never-failing refuge.

_____Let's talk: What troubles or fears are on your mind? Have you entrusted them to God? How can He help?

_____Let's pray: Heavenly Father, thank You for always being with us, especially in times of troubles and problems. Thank You for always caring. In the name of Jesus, our Savior. Amen.

V. S.

Swaying Towers

T ired of doing the same old thing? Ready for something new and exciting? In towns and villages throughout Europe, a favorite pastime is building towers—human towers. The object is to see how high a tower can be built with people. Some towers can be more than 20 stories high!

How is this done? Several hundred people press together as tightly as they can. This forms the base. Then the next group climbs on top of them, stepping on heads, arms, shoulders, or whatever they can get a foot on. They put their arms on each other's shoulders and brace themselves for the next story to climb on top of them.

Group after group scampers up the human tower until someone's foot slips or someone's arm gets tired. Then the tower sways and falls. The problem is that there is no steady base on which to build. It is natural for people to shift their positions, to sway. In this case, a simple shift can cause disaster.

Read from God's Word

So then, just as you received Christ Jesus as Lord, continue to live in Him, rooted and built up in Him, strengthened in the faith as you were taught, and over-flowing with thankfulness. Colossians 2:6–7

Ever feel like a swaying tower in your faith? You may hear things from friends, music, or TV that may cause you to shift or sway in your faith. St. Paul reminds us in Colossians to live in Christ, rooted firmly in Him; built up in Him; strengthened in the faith that He is our Savior.

With Christ as our foundation there is no swaying, no shifting. Nothing can knock us down. Jesus lives to help us in every need and to quiet our fears.

_____Let's talk: What are some things you have heard that go against what you believe? How do you know they are wrong?

_____Let's pray: Dear Jesus, thank You for daily strength to face whatever may come. Give us a faith that doesn't shake or sway. Amen.

V. S.

Anything's Possible–Almost

For it is by grace you have been saved, through faith—and this is not from yourselves, it is the gift of God—not by works, so that no one can boast. Ephesians 2:8–9 ✐

Have you read the story about a train that had a big hill to climb? He was such a small train, and the hill looked much too high. He should have given up, but that little train believed he could do it. He tried as hard as he could, and he made it up that hill.

Do you ever feel like that train? There's something you have to do, and you decide it's impossible before you even try. Maybe you're standing behind a small lawn mower, looking at what appears to be a huge field of tall grass. Maybe you've been asked to sing a solo in the school musical, and you're sure there are tons of people in the audience. Perhaps it's your turn to bat. Your team is counting on you for a hit that will win the game, but you haven't hit the ball yet this year.

None of these things is impossible. They may be hard, but with the right attitude and your best effort, you can do *anything!* Well, actually, you can't do *everything.*

The Bible says you can't get to heaven by yourself, no matter how hard you try. You can't earn salvation by doing good things. You can't buy it or make a deal with God for it.

There's only one way to heaven—by faith in Christ Jesus as your Savior. It's a free gift from God. We can't brag about being saved. Jesus died on the cross so we could be in heaven with Him someday. With Him, heaven is not just possible, it's for certain!

_____Let's talk: Is it true or false that we have to do something special to earn God's favor? What do you think?

_____Let's pray: Dear God, how can we ever thank You for the wonderful gift You have given us in faith? Help us to always rely on Your love without question. Amen.

V. S.

I Was Soooo Embarrassed!

Today is the day you have to give your speech in front of the whole class. You're a little—make that *very*—nervous. As you begin to read your speech, you lose your place and say "uh" a lot. Then you drop your papers on the floor and have to pick them up. Your teacher is not smiling.

When you finally finish, you slip away to the restroom to have a minute alone. You look in the mirror to see that you didn't wash the milk mustache off your face after breakfast; toothpaste is dribbled down the front of your shirt; and your hair has a mind of its own. Embarrassed?

What are some things that don't embarrass you? Did you think of cool friends, nice clothes, the Word of God? Yes, I said the Word of God.

My dad is a pastor. As a kid I was afraid to bring friends home. I never knew what my dad might say. He might totally embarrass me by telling my friends, "Jesus loves you." But not one of my friends ever made fun of things my dad said.

Do you have a hard time talking to your friends about Jesus? It isn't always easy. God's Word, however, contains power. It gives us power to love, power to forgive, and power to tell others. We want them to know that Jesus makes us holy in God's sight and gives us a life that never ends. That's the best news of all!

Read from God's Word

I am not ashamed of the gospel, because it is the power of God for the salvation of everyone who believes: first for the Jew, then for the Gentile. For in the gospel a righteousness from God is revealed, a righteousness that is by faith from first to last, just as it is written: "The righteous will live by faith." Romans 1:16–17

———Let's talk: Which of your friends would you like to talk to about Jesus but are afraid to? Have you tried asking the Holy Spirit for help?

———Let's pray: Dear Jesus, we know we do a lot of things that would embarrass You. Thank You for not being ashamed of us. Help us never be embarrassed to talk about You. Amen.

V. S.

Read from God's Word

Therefore, since we have been justified through faith, we have peace with God through our Lord Jesus Christ, through whom we have gained access by faith into this grace in which we now stand. And we rejoice in the hope of the glory of God. Not only so, but we also rejoice in our sufferings, because we know that suffering produces perseverance; perseverance, character; and character, hope. And hope does not disappoint us, because God has poured out His love into our hearts by the Holy Spirit, whom He has given us. Romans 5:1–5 ✑

A Beautiful Paradise

"Are we really going in there?" Jess asked. A foggy mist hung over the portion of the island they were about to explore. "It may not look inviting from here," her dad said. "But if you stay with us, you're in for something special."

With that the family began their hike. At times the trail was difficult. Large branches often blocked the path, and rocks seemed to come up out of nowhere.

"Dad!" cried Jess as she tripped over an exposed tree root. "I scraped my leg."

"You'll be fine," Dad assured her as he checked her leg. "You just have to keep going. It will be worth it."

Other mishaps occurred along the way. Jared missed a rock while crossing a stream and got soaked. Jennifer walked through a spiderweb and screamed.

"It will be worth it," Dad kept saying. "Just keep going."

After a while, the family looked up to see tall mountains of hard volcanic rock. Beautiful flowers and ferns grew on and around them. A sparkling waterfall cascaded from the top of one peak. They just stood there and took in the wonder of it all. "Will heaven be this beautiful?" Jess asked.

Dad smiled. "I don't know exactly what heaven will be like. I do know that the trail leading to it is sometimes rough. Sometimes we may want to turn around or quit. But Jesus leads us onward. He paved the way for us with His sacrifice on the cross. And He sends His Holy Spirit to strengthen us along the way so we never give up. And I know the trip will be worth it!"

_____Let's talk: What do you find the hardest about following Jesus? How can you have joy when things seem bad?

_____Let's pray: Dear Jesus, thank You for sending Your Spirit to help us find joy when the day seems all bad. Amen.

V. S.

june

Sticking Together

Read from God's Word

Love is patient, love is kind. It does not envy, it does not boast, it is not proud. It is not rude, it is not self-seeking, it is not easily angered, it keeps no record of wrongs. Love does not delight in evil but rejoices with the truth. It always protects, always trusts, always hopes, always perseveres.
1 Corinthians 13:4–7 ✍

Rachel was angry at herself, her parents, and her puppy. Rachel's mom opened the screen door and said, "Honey, there's no reason to cry. The incident is over."

Rachel whined, "But, Mom, Dad is mad at me. I'm mad at the puppy and myself. Do we even love each other anymore?"

Hugging her daughter, Mom asked, "Rachel, what is love?"

The 10-year-old responded, "I'm not sure. I suppose it means to feel good about someone."

"Do you feel good about your puppy?"

Rachel answered, "Not right now. What a mess he made on the carpet! Dad was yelling at both of us. He made me clean everything up. Gross!"

Ruth smiled. "But you still love your puppy, don't you? And I know Dad loves you. Love is more than a feeling. It's a pledge to stick together."

"Stick together? Even when we're angry?" Rachel paused, then asked, "Mom, does God gets angry?"

"Yes, God gets angry at sin, " her mom explained, "But on Calvary God gave Jesus the anger we deserve. Our disobedience still angers God, but He forgives us each day."

Rachel said, "I guess love is like Krazy Glue—sticking together even when we don't always feel good about one another."

Ruth nodded. "Love is cleaning the mess on the carpet even though it was gross. By the way, I see a puppy outside needing love."

"Not anymore," said Rachel as she headed out the door.

_____Let's talk: Suppose a friend asks, "How can you be my friend and still be mad at me?" What would you say?

_____Let's pray: Father, through the cross of Your Son, You have restored us to Yourself. Let our love for You and for others be like Krazy Glue, never coming undone. In Jesus' name. Amen.

M. P.

Cut Again

Anthony threw his baseball glove to the ground. "Cut again?" his cousin David asked. "Yeah," Anthony replied, "just like last year. How about you?"

David sighed, "I didn't make it either. Too small to play in Little League."

Anthony looked oddly at David. "You act like you're happy to be cut from the team."

David responded, "I'm not happy. But I tried the best I could. It's not the end of the world."

Later, Anthony complained to his father, "I felt bad today when I was cut from the team. My Sunday school teacher told us that God wants us to have joy. I don't feel very joyful."

Anthony's dad picked up a baseball bat. "When Jesus was a boy, he probably played games with His friends. Do you suppose He won all the time?"

Read from God's Word

[Jesus said.] "Now is your time of grief, but I will see you again and you will rejoice, and no one will take away your joy. In that day you will no longer ask me anything. I tell you the truth. My Father will give you whatever you ask in My name. Until now you have not asked for anything in My name. Ask and you will receive, and your joy will be complete." John 16:22–24 ༺

Anthony hesitated and then answered, "Probably not."

Dad continued, "Jesus knew disappointment. Perhaps as a boy playing games in Nazareth. Certainly as our Savior on the cross."

"Well, He died. That *really* wasn't a very joyful thing," Anthony said.

His father explained, "His death was painful and humiliating. But from that terrible event came something of great joy for us. Jesus gives us forgiveness and life. God doesn't promise we won't experience disappointment. But He does promise to love us and to help us deal with disappointment."

_____Let's talk: When have you been disappointed? Why does God allow disappointment to come into our lives?

_____Let's pray: Holy Spirit, lead us to the cross, where we see the suffering and death of our Savior. Lead us to the cross, where in joy we see our sins forgiven. In Jesus' name. Amen.

M. P.

Read from God's Word

Find rest, O my soul, in God alone; my hope comes from Him. He alone is my rock and my salvation; He is my fortress, I will not be shaken. My salvation and my honor depend on God; He is my mighty rock, my refuge. Trust in Him at all times, O people; pour out your hearts to Him. For God is our refuge. Psalm 62:5–8

What Is Faith?

"Grandma, what is faith?" questioned Emily. "Honey, I'm not sure what you mean," answered Grandma Genny.

Emily explained, "We have a tough game next week with the Tigers. My softball coach told us to have faith. But Pastor talks about having faith in Jesus. Is faith in Jesus like playing ball?"

Grandma Genny sat next to Emily. "When your coach told you to have faith, he meant that you were to be confident—to play the best you can."

Emily replied, "So when we have faith in Jesus, we have confidence?"

Grandma responded, "Yes, but in a special way. Faith is a gift God gives to us. It is trust. We trust Jesus to forgive us, to answer our prayers, to help us. We know He will because His Word tells us so. Faith is a confidence that points to Jesus, not to ourselves."

Emily added, "So, softball faith is that we have confidence to play the best we can. Faith in Jesus is confidence that we know He will keep His promises, like forgiving us and giving us eternal life."

Grandma agreed. "Yes. But keep in mind that we can have confidence in ourselves and still fail. Your softball team might lose to the Tigers next week. But confidence in Jesus for forgiveness and eternal life will never fail because Jesus' love for us never fails. We can be sure of that."

_____Let's talk: Does confidence in Jesus mean that things will always go right? Give a reason for your answer.

_____Let's pray: Jesus, You are our confidence. Help us trust in You for all things and forever. Amen.

M. P.

A Matter of Courtesy

Jacob and Ann arrived at the class-room door at the exact same time. Jacob held the door open for the new girl in the class. As he followed the girl into the classroom, Jacob heard the other boys jeer: "Jacob, will you hold the door open for us?"

The Bible encourages us to let our gentleness be evident to all. However, gentleness is often seen as weakness. Jacob was mocked by his friends for being gentle to the new girl in class. But gentleness is not weakness. It is putting courtesy into action.

Do you suppose Jesus would have held the door open for Ann? Jesus wasn't weak or timid. He was firm, yet gentle. St. John tells us about a woman who was brought to Jesus and accused of many sins. First, Jesus tried to reach the hearts of the leaders who brought the woman to Him. They needed to see their own sin and their need for forgiveness.

Read from God's Word

The teachers of the law and the Pharisees brought in a woman caught in adultery. They made her stand before the group and said to Jesus, "Teacher, this woman was caught in the act of adultery. In the Law Moses commanded us to stone such women. Now what do you say?" .... [Jesus] said to them, "If any one of you is without sin, let him be the first to throw a stone at her." ... At this, those who heard began to go away one at a time. ... Jesus straightened up and asked her, "Woman, where are they? Has no one condemned you? ... Then neither do I condemn you. ... Go now and leave your life of sin." John 8:3–11 ✍

Second, Jesus didn't excuse the woman's behavior. He told her to leave her life of sin. But Jesus also demonstrated gentleness. He forgave the woman's sins. And He longed to reach out to the leaders with His love. This same Jesus, so gentle, willingly went to the cross to die so He might bring to us forgiveness and eternal life.

Jacob heard the laughter of his friends, but he didn't care. He knew that opening the door for Ann was the courteous thing to do.

_____Let's talk: If Jesus had opened the door for Ann, would the guys have jeered? Would you? Why or why not?

_____Let's pray: Lord Jesus, we know the kind thing to do is to be courteous. Forgive us when we sneer or laugh at the courtesy of others. In Your name. Amen.

M. P.

Jerry's Big Struggle

Read from God's Word

Do you not know? Have you not heard? The LORD is the everlasting God, the Creator of the ends of the earth. He will not grow tired or weary, and His understanding no one can fathom. He gives strength to the weary and increases the power of the weak. Even youths grow tired and weary, and young men stumble and fall; but those who hope in the LORD will renew their strength. They will soar on wings like eagles; they will run and not grow weary, they will walk and not be faint. Isaiah 40:28–31

Jerry, help me get up!" Jerry's mom cried. The 10-year-old reached down to help his mother. She had fallen over the coffee table while reaching for the remote.

Jerry hesitated at first; it was happening all over again. Mom was drinking again. Jerry thought about how hard it was to listen to Mom's weeping and the grumbling. He thought, *I wish Mom wouldn't drink so much. Why can't I have just one night of peace?*

Have you ever put together a difficult puzzle? Sometimes it can be a struggle. But when the puzzle is finally together, you have a sense of satisfaction, a sense of wholeness. Peace is a wholeness, like having every piece of a puzzle put together.

The Bible tells us we will have frustrations and struggles. Jerry knows! He struggles every day with his problems. And every day he pleads to God for help: *"Please, just one night of peace."*

God has not abandoned Jerry. Although Jerry is not aware of it now, God is using the problems he faces to help him grow stronger in his trust and relationship with God. God gives a special kind of peace through Jesus' death on the cross. Because of Jesus, Jerry is whole in God's sight. The things that matter most, like love and forgiveness, fit together just right. And God is helping Jerry learn to cope with a world that is filled with problems.

God loves us also. He gives us wholeness through the cross of Jesus. He gives us strength. He gives us peace.

_____Let's talk: If you were Jerry, where would you go for help? Talk as a family about what Jerry could do. Where does God fit in Jerry's situation? Where does God fit into your family?

_____Let's pray: Dear Father, help us keep our eyes on You as You put the pieces of our lives together. Help us grow and mature in You. In Jesus' name. Amen.

M. P.

Put on the Brakes!

Read from God's Word

But the fruit of the Spirit is love, joy, peace, patience, kindness, goodness, faithfulness, gentleness and self-control. Against such things there is no law. Those who belong to Christ Jesus have crucified the sinful nature with its passions and desires. Since we live by the Spirit, let us keep in step with the Spirit. Let us not become conceited, provoking and envying each other. Galatians 5:22-26 ✍

Have you ever been offered something that you knew wasn't good for you? Maybe someone has said to you, "I have some cigarettes. Want to try one?"

Saying no to drugs, alcohol, and cigarettes is the best way to deal with temptation. Saying no may take a lot of *self-control*, one of the fruit that the Holy Spirit produces in us. To be in control means knowing the difference between right and wrong; it means knowing when to stop or not to start at all.

Daniel, an Old Testament prophet, could have enjoyed rich food from King Nebuchadnezzar's table. But Daniel knew the king's delicacies were not only unhealthful but were also forbidden by God.

Around 600 B.C., Judah had been defeated by the Babylonians and taken into captivity. King Nebuchadnezzar was able to recognize the talent and intelligence of some of the Judean captives. The king ordered that these men be trained in the language and literature of the Babylonian Empire so they could serve in the king's court.

Daniel was privileged as one to be trained. Yet with such an honor, Daniel remembered the right and wrong of God's Word. He put on the brakes rather than eat unclean foods.

Daniel knew God's promises of a Savior who would come to forgive sins and give new life. Jesus was that Savior. He died for us and rose from the grave to assure our victory over Satan and sin. This Savior empowered Daniel to be in control. Our Savior empowers us to be in control also.

_____Let's talk: We know that when it comes to drugs and alcohol, we need to put on the brakes. When are other times the brakes need to be put on?

_____Let's pray: Father, teach me to know the difference between right and wrong. Forgive me when I fail to do Your will. Help me be like Daniel. In Jesus' name. Amen.

M. P.

Read from God's Word

In the same way, count your-selves dead to sin but alive to God in Christ Jesus. Therefore do not let sin reign in your mortal body so that you obey its evil desires. Do not offer the parts of your body to sin, as instruments of wickedness, but rather offer yourselves to God, as those who have been brought from death to life; and offer the parts of your body to Him as instruments of righteousness. For sin shall not be your master, because you are not under law, but under grace. Romans 6:11–14 ✍

Letting It Go

E mma tossed the soiled book on the table. "Dad, did you see what Andy did to my math book?" she asked. Her brother Andy had spilled soda on it. Emma clenched her jaw and said, "My math teacher will be mad at me. I'll get Andy for this."

Dad raised his eyebrows. "But, Emma, I thought you accepted Andy's apology. Don't you think this ought to be over now?"

Emma turned her head. "I know. But I'm still angry."

Dad motioned for Emma to sit down. "Remember last week when you lied about your homework?" Emma nodded as her father brought over some milk and cookies. "You were punished. But I also forgave you. Since then I've never brought it up again. When we accept the apology of some-one, we also need to let it go. Isn't that what God does with us?"

Emma picked up a cookie. "I guess so. But I'm not sure what you mean."

Her dad answered, "We live in God's grace. That means God loves us no matter what. Even when we break His Law, He still loves us. When He forgives us, He lets go of the things we have done wrong. He doesn't bring them back to haunt us."

Now Emma understood. "I should forgive Andy as Jesus has forgiven me." She picked up another cookie and headed outside. "I bet Andy would like a cookie too."

_____Let's talk: Is it easy or hard to forgive someone and really "let it go?" How can you learn to practice "letting it go?"

_____Let's pray: Dear Holy Spirit, lead us to the cross of Jesus for for-giveness. Then help us forgive others who hurt us. In Jesus' name. Amen.

M. P.

A Unique Defense

In the shallow water of the tropical seas lives the porcupine fish. Growing to a length of 24–35 inches, it gobbles up mussels and other shellfish. Its teeth are extra strong to tackle a diet of hard-shelled fish. You might think this fish also uses its teeth for protection. But instead it uses its prickly spines for self-defense.

When the fish is not in danger, its spines lie flat against its body. As soon as an enemy comes near, it swallows water. In just a few seconds, the fish fills out like a balloon. Its prickles become spikes and the enemy retreats. When the danger has passed, the fish returns to its normal size.

We can be threatened by our enemy, the devil. Satan tempts us and plots against us. And sometimes we give in. How can we defend ourselves against him?

The porcupine fish can handle its enemies on its own. But we can't tackle Satan by ourselves. God gives us protection in our struggle. He presents us with truth and righteousness, faith and salvation. God also gives us His Holy Spirit. Through the Word of God, He defends us against the devil's schemes. With God's armor we can stand on our ground of faith.

God gives the porcupine fish a unique defense mechanism. However, the armor He gives us is even more exceptional. And we don't have to swallow water and blow up like a balloon!

Read from God's Word

Finally, be strong in the Lord and in His mighty power. Put on the full armor of God so that you can take your stand against the devil's schemes. For our struggle is not against flesh and blood, but against the rulers, against the authorities, against the powers of this dark world and against the spiritual forces of evil in the heavenly realms. Therefore put on the full armor of God, so that when the day of evil comes, you may be able to stand your ground, and after you have done everything, to stand. Ephesians 6:10–13

_____Let's talk: Talk about times when Satan has tempted you. Plan how you can use God's armor when Satan returns.

_____Let's pray: Dear God, be with us in our struggles with sin and the devil. Remind us that You have given us full armor to wear. We ask this in Jesus' name. Amen.

J. D.

You Can't Hide

Read from God's Word

Then the man and his wife heard ... the LORD God as He was walking in the garden ... and they hid from the LORD God. ... But the LORD God called to the man, "Where are you?" He answered, "I heard You in the garden, and I was afraid because I was naked; so I hid." And [God] said, "Who told you that you were naked? Have you eaten from the tree that I commanded you not to eat from?" The man said, "The woman ... gave me some fruit from the tree, and I ate it." Then the LORD God said to the woman, "What is it you have done?" The woman said, "The serpent deceived me, and I ate." Genesis 3:8–13

It was time to redecorate the bathroom. Excitedly, Julie tore off the wallpaper—Uh-oh! Under the wallpaper was a multitude of holes. The walls were bumpy and uneven. Painting over the mess wouldn't hide the flaws. She knew she had a big job ahead of her, but she couldn't turn back.

We are like those bathroom walls, covered with flaws we can't hide. We don't want God to know that we're jealous of our best friend or that we say unkind things about some of the kids at school. Trying to hide our sins doesn't work. God can see them perfectly.

Today's Bible story about Adam and Eve shows this to be true. At first, their life in the Garden of Eden was flawless. God had created a perfect world for them to live in. Then Satan tempted Adam and Eve. They rebelled against God and tried to hide from Him. He sent them from the garden, but He never stopped loving them. He promised them a Savior who would rescue them.

Jesus came as God promised. He died on the cross for all our sins, even those we try to hide. Because we have His gift of forgiveness, we confess our sins and turn from them.

Julie didn't give up on the bathroom. She filled the holes and sanded down the bumps. Then she applied a fresh coat of paint. Praise God that He never gives up on us. The salvation won by Jesus has covered us with a new coat of righteousness. We are a brand new creation in Him.

_____Let's talk: What sins have you tried to hide from God? Why are you thankful for God's forgiveness?

_____Let's pray: Lord, forgive us for the times we've tried to cover up our sin. We are thankful for your unending mercy. In Jesus' name we pray. Amen.

J. D.

Honoring the Lord

Read the following sentences:
1. My grandma bakes cookies with sugar, *flower*, and butter.
2. My sister is afraid to fly in a *plain*.
3. Dad *one* his ballgame!
4. Ryan ate *for* more pancakes.
5. I like to have fun in the *son*.

Did you notice anything odd? These sentences sound right, but each contains a word that is spelled incorrectly. Words that sound alike but are spelled differently and have different meanings are called "homophones." Can you substitute the correct words in the five sentences?

Sometimes our actions are like homophones. Perhaps we say or do certain things to fit in with the right group. Some of the things we do may sound good at the time, but they don't fit who we are as Christians. They don't fit our Christian identity. We think we're having a good time, but are the things we do or say honoring the Lord? In times like these, we deceive ourselves, others, and God, too.

There is someone whose actions are always right and good. Jesus never deceives and He doesn't change. As the Bible reading states, "Jesus Christ is the same yesterday and today and forever." Jesus promises to love us always, even when we make the wrong choices and give into the world's temptations. He cared enough for us to die on the cross for our sins. His promise of forgiveness will always be there.

Jesus lives in us by faith. And He will help us honor Him in the way we live.

_____Let's do: Write other sentences with homophones. Challenge one another to find the incorrect words. Be alert for times that your actions don't fit your Christian life.

_____Let's pray: Lord Jesus, thank You for living in us. Help us live in a way that reflects Your love for us. Amen.

J. D.

Read from God's Word

So we say with confidence, "The Lord is my helper; I will not be afraid. What can man do to me?" Remember your leaders, who spoke the word of God to you. Consider the outcome of their way of life and imitate their faith. Jesus Christ is the same yesterday and today and forever. Hebrews 13:6–8

Read from God's Word

So then, just as you received Christ Jesus as Lord, continue to live in Him, rooted and built up in Him, strengthened in the faith as you were taught, and overflowing with thankfulness.
Colossians 2:6–7

Hold Your Horses

Two-year-old Maggie wiggled in her high chair, watching her mother prepare super. Playing with the toys on the tray in front of her did not interest her. Maggie wanted her mom's undivided attention.

"Mommy, Mommy," Maggie yelled. Maggie's mother heard her daughter's cry, but she needed to have a meal on the table soon. Maggie tried again—"Mommy, Mommy."

Overwhelmed, her mother replied, "Just hold your horses, Maggie!"

Maggie immediately became quiet. She sat oddly still in the high chair. Tears welled in her eyes as she blurted out, "But I don't have any horses!"

How many times have we told God to "hold His horses?" We get so busy in our day-to-day lives. Our conversations with God begin to dwindle. Sadly, we lose touch with Him.

God wants to be the number one priority in our lives. By our own strength, we cannot give Him our full attention. But He makes us *His* top priority. He sent His Son to die on the cross for our sins—including the sin of putting other things before Him.

Mom's instructions to "hold your horses" confused Maggie. God's Word for us in today's Bible reading is clear. Paul writes in verse 6, "Just as you received Christ Jesus as Lord, continue to live in Him." Take a moment each day to thank Jesus for His presence in your life.

_____Let's talk: What do you spend a lot of time doing? What can you put "on hold" in order to give God more attention?

_____Let's pray: Dear God, help us make time for you in our daily lives. Thank You for being patient with us. In Jesus' name. Amen.

J. D.

A New Home

Julio, Michele, and Anna were staying with Grandma. Mom and Dad were in another state, looking for a new home. "Grandma, do you think I'll have a place to roller blade when we move?" asked Julio.

"I hope I have some shelves to keep my books on," said Michele.

Anna said, "I want shelves too. I need a place for my stuffed animals."

Grandma shook her head. "Your parents haven't found the right place yet. What else do you think is important for your new home?"

There were a lot of answers—a big lawn, a place to keep their dog, other children to play with, room for their toys and bikes. When the children stopped for breath, Grandma said, "I think you're not telling me the most important thing."

The children guessed—a dishwasher, a bedroom for each child, a swimming pool?

"No," said their grandmother. "Don't you think the most important thing is that you'll be with your mom and dad?"

"Yes," they all agreed. "But it would be nice to have some of those other things too."

Sometimes we like to think about what heaven will be like. It's hard to imagine a place that's perfect. But we do know that Jesus will be there and that we will be with Him forever. He died and rose again so there could be a place in heaven prepared just for us. He will be there with us and we will praise Him all the time!

_____Let's talk: What do you think heaven will be like? What are some things the Bible tells us will *not* be in heaven?

_____Let's pray: Dear Jesus, thank You for dying so we can go to heaven. Thank You for going ahead of us to get a place ready for us. Thank You also for the homes we have here on earth. Amen.

E. P. L.

Wait Patiently

"It's time for lunch. Everyone line up at the door," said Mrs. Morales. Pete snatched his lunch bag and raced to be first in line. Most of the other children in the room did the same thing. There was a lot of pushing as each one tried to get first place.

Mrs. Morales had a way of taking care of "line rage." When all the children were in line, she had them face the end of the line. Then she had the last person lead them out of the room.

Most people don't like to wait. We don't like to stand in checkout lines or ticket lines. Sometimes we even wish people would move faster up the church aisle as they leave at the end of the service.

In Psalm 40, King David tells us how he handled frustration: "I waited patiently for the LORD; He turned to me and heard my cry." What happened then? David says that God "put a new song in my mouth, a hymn of praise to our God."

What can we do when we get impatient? We can try to look at some of the people around us and imagine how they feel. Then we can remember that God loves them too and that Jesus died for every person in the world.

The next time you are waiting, take some time to think about all the good things God has given you. Then say a silent "Thank You, God" prayer. Your wait may not get any shorter, but it won't seem as long.

_____Let's talk: Do you think time doesn't go by fast enough before a holiday or your birthday? Do you often say, "Are we there yet?" when you're riding in a car? What are some things you can do while you're waiting?

_____Let's pray: Dear Lord Jesus, we know that sometimes it's good for us to wait. Give us patience and a grateful heart. Amen.

E. P. L.

His Eyes Are on Us

"Joshua, come and keep an eye on your little sister," said Joshua's mother. "I have to go next door and call the telephone company. Our phone isn't working."

Joshua was playing with his toy trucks in his bedroom. He didn't mind leaving them to go downstairs. He was proud that his mother thought he was old enough to take care of Jeni for a little while. Joshua was nine, and Jeni was two.

Jeni was playing with her wooden blocks, so Joshua sat down to play with her. In a few minutes Jeni started to throw the blocks at Joshua.

Joshua said, "Let's put the blocks away and find your ball." He put away most of the blocks himself, and then they played with the ball.

When Joshua rolled the ball to Jeni, she picked it up and started to put it in her mouth. "No, Jeni," said Joshua. "That's dirty. Don't try to eat it." So she threw it to him. Then she got up and tried to open the door to go outside.

Joshua found her teddy bear and a storybook. He said, "Come and sit with me, Jeni. I'll read you a story."

Joshua did a good job of keeping an eye on his sister. Psalm 33:18 states, "The eyes of the LORD are on the righteous and His ears are attentive to their cry." This verse reassures us that God is watching over us and that He listens to our prayers. He loves us more than we can ever imagine. He loves us so much that He sent His Son to be a sacrifice for us. He will never take his eyes off of us and He will never let us go!

_____Let's talk: What did Mother mean when she asked him to "keep an eye on" Jeni? Why does God keep His eyes on us?

_____Let's pray: Dear Jesus, thank You for keeping Your eyes on us. Thank You for showing Your love for us by dying on the cross for our sins. Thank You for keeping us safe. Help us show Your love to the people around us. Amen.

E. P. L.

Read from God's Word

I lift up my eyes to You, to You whose throne is in heaven. As the eyes of slaves look to the hand of their master, as the eyes of a maid look to the hand of her mistress, so our eyes look to the LORD our God, till He shows us His mercy. Psalm 123:1–2 ∽

Where Should I Look?

A long time ago, boys and girls did not have television or video games. But they still had fun. They played many kinds of games.

One of the games kids loved to play was called "Hide the Thimble." Have you ever seen a thimble? It's a small, silver cap to wear on your finger when you sew. It isn't very big. The rules of the game were that the thimble had to be placed in plain sight in the room in which the children were playing. It couldn't really be hidden.

Because a thimble is small, the children had to look carefully to find it. Sometimes, when they had looked for a while and didn't see it, the leader would begin to look right at it. The others would look in the same direction and would soon find the thimble.

The Bible says we need to look at God. How do you know when you're looking at God?

Think about this. When you see an ice-cream cone, you think how good it would taste. When you see a swimming pool on a hot day, you think how good the water would feel. Well, we can tell our eyes are on Jesus when we think of how He died for our sins and when we thank Him for hearing our prayers. Every time we think of Jesus, our eyes are on Him.

How can other people know when we're looking at Jesus? They can tell by the things we do. If we're doing things that show the love of Jesus, others will know we must be looking at Him.

_____Let's talk: What kinds of things do we do that tell we are look-ing at Jesus? What things do we look at that make us forget to look at Jesus?

_____Let's pray: Dear Father in heaven, send Your Holy Spirit so we can keep our eyes on Jesus. Help us show You to oth-ers by reflecting Your love. Amen.

E. P. L.

Gifts from *A* to *Z*

Read from God's Word

Give thanks to the LORD, call on His name; make known among the nations what He has done. Sing to Him, sing praise to Him; tell of all His wonderful acts. Glory in His holy name; let the hearts of those who seek the LORD rejoice. Look to the LORD and His strength; seek His face always. Psalm 105:1–4

ere comes Grandma," shouted Max as he raced from the window to open the front door. "Happy birthday, Max," said Grandma. She gave Max a hug and handed him a box wrapped in birthday paper. "Here's something I made just for a boy who's 10 years old today," she said.

Max hurried to unwrap the box. His eyes opened wide when he saw that it was filled with chocolate-chip cookies. They were his favorite.

"Wow! Thank you," said Max. Then he gave Grandma a big hug. "May I take some of these to vacation Bible school to share with my class tomorrow? Then I can tell them about my grandma, the baker."

Jesus sends us His gifts every day. A fun thing to do is to go through the alphabet and list one gift for each letter. Your list could start with Apples, Brother, Church, Dogs, Easter, Flowers …

We can't give Jesus a hug when we thank Him for His gifts, but we can give our brother a hug. And we can remember to say thank You to Jesus in our prayers. He is our Savior and He gave us the gift of eternal life. By the way, did you put Jesus for *J* or Savior for *S?* If you didn't, you can add them now.

Max wanted to share his cookies so he could tell his friends about Grandma. We can share the gifts that God gives us with our friends. Then we can tell them about Jesus, who is the best gift of all. All we have, from *A* to *Z*, comes from Him.

_____Let's talk: What gifts on your list could you share with someone else? With whom could you share them?

_____Let's pray: Heavenly Father, thank You for sending Jesus to take our sins away. Thank You for all the gifts You give. Help us realize that everything we have comes from You. Amen.

E. P. L.

Never Out-of-Date

Read from God's Word

*Your word, O LORD, is eternal;
it stands firm in the heavens.
Your faithfulness continues
through all generations; You
established the earth, and it
endures. Your laws endure to this
day, for all things serve You.
Psalm 119:89–91* ✍

Matthew had to write a report for summer school. He was going to write about the flags of African countries. He already had a map in school to show the countries of Africa. Now he planned to use the computer in the library to get more information.

But Matthew couldn't go to the library because his family was visiting Grandma this weekend. Matthew's mom said, "Grandma has encyclopedias. You can get information from them."

Grandma's book showed an American flag with only 48 stars. There were flags from many other countries. Matthew saw that some of them were not on his map. And there were some countries on his map for which he could find no flags.

Matthew was disappointed. "This book doesn't show what's right. This is all old stuff. I think books aren't very good. Everything changes, but books just stay the same. Grandma, maybe you should throw all these books away."

Grandma looked at the book Matthew had opened. "Yes," she agreed, "that book has many things in it that aren't true anymore. But there is one book on my shelf that will always be true. It tells us about Someone who loves us and died to save us. Aren't you glad that Jesus is never out-of-date?"

_____Let's talk: What book was Grandma talking about? Why doesn't the Bible ever become "old stuff?" What is the main purpose of the Bible? (See John 20:31.)

_____Let's pray: Heavenly Father, thank You for giving us the Bible. Thank You for sending us the Holy Spirit so we can know Jesus and believe in Him, our one and only Savior. Amen.

E. P. L.

Heaven Is My Home

Tomo, Kirshna, Jasmyne, and Fumi all have something that unites them. Each was born in a different country. Tomo is a citizen of Japan. Kirshna is a citizen of India. Jasmyne is a citizen of France, and Fumi is a citizen of Nigeria. But each one is also an American citizen. These four children have dual citizenship. That means they are citizens of two countries.

Their parents are professors at a university. They all live in America during the school year, but they go to their home country during the summer. They use legal papers and passports to travel safely from country to country.

Did you know that we also have dual citizenship? It's true. God tells us we were once lost and wandering in sin. We had no place to go. But God rescued us. He made us His children through Baptism. Now we are also citizens of heaven. What an honor!

Read from God's Word

Consequently, you are no longer foreigners and aliens, but fellow citizens with God's people and members of God's household, built on the foundation of the apostles and prophets, with Christ Jesus Himself as the chief cornerstone. In Him the whole building is joined together and rises to become a holy temple in the Lord. And in Him you too are being built together to become a dwelling in which God lives by His Spirit. Ephesians 2:19–22 ❧

Our God loves us so much that He has provided a special place in heaven for us. We didn't do anything to deserve this honor. It's a gift. We don't even need any "legal papers and passports." All we need is faith in Jesus, God's Son who died in our place on the cross. Now we can enter heaven and say, "I'm home. My Father is expecting me."

Let's talk: Do you have any friends or relatives who are already living in heaven? Why are you certain they are in heaven?

Let's pray: Dear Father, thank You for rescuing us from sin. We look forward to coming home to heaven to be with You. Help us live as Your children while we are still here on this earth. In Jesus' name. Amen.

M. S.

Read from God's Word

Because those who are led by the Spirit of God are sons of God. For you did not receive a spirit that makes you a slave again to fear, but you received the Spirit of sonship. And by Him we cry, "Abba, Father." The Spirit Himself testifies with our spirit that we are God's children. Now if we are children, then we are heirs—heirs of God and co-heirs with Christ, if indeed we share in His sufferings in order that we may also share in His glory. Romans 8:14–17 ✑

A Real Dad

The little boy stood looking out the window, watching the rain. Excitedly he said, "Look, Daddy made it rain!"

His mom gently told him that only God can make it rain. The little boy thought about that and then declared, "Daddy helped God make it rain."

Dads are very special people. A dad is someone who fixes broken toys. He uses his paycheck to buy things the family needs. He wears old shoes so his children can have music lessons.

A dad plans surprises for his children. A dad will correct his children when they are wrong. He says he's sorry when he makes a mistake. A dad will teach his children the value of money but not that money is to be valued.

A dad will eat the food his children have prepared. He will let his children see him cry when he is sad. He will gently tease his children and make them laugh.

A dad will often tell his family how much he loves them. He will go with his family to church and Sunday school. He will introduce his children to God because he knows Him personally.

We can thank God for our dads. Even better, we can thank *God* for being our Father. In Romans 8:15, we call Him *Abba,* which means "Daddy."

God has made you His child. He knows you by name. He even knows how many hairs you have on your head. And He has given you an eternal inheritance. You are His, now and forever.

_____Let's talk: How does it feel to know that you can call your heavenly Father *Abba?* What would you like to tell Him?

_____Let's pray: Dear Father in heaven, thank You for making each one of us Your own special child. Comfort us when we're sad. Correct us when we're wrong. Teach us Your ways. And love us always. For Jesus' sake we ask it. Amen.

M. S.

The Prize

Jennifer and Shannon's favorite summer sport was sailing. It was summer and they couldn't wait to enter the regatta. They loved the special race where sailors use every possible skill to win the prize.

Jennifer and Shannon studied all the parts of the boat until they knew the stem from the bow, the jib from the jibe, and the sheets from the mast. Then they spent long hours perfecting their skills. It wasn't long before they could sail for hours without mishap. The work was hard, but they kept thinking of the prize they might win.

Jennifer and Shannon worked long hours to study and practice so they might win the prize. The good news is that, as Christians, we don't have to do anything to earn the prize that is ours already. God *gives us* the crown of righteousness that Jesus earned for us by His perfect life and His agonizing suffering and death.

Read from God's Word

For I am already being poured out like a drink offering, and the time has come for my departure. I have fought the good fight, I have finished the race, I have kept the faith. Now there is in store for me the crown of righteousness, which the Lord, the righteous Judge, will award to me on that day—and not only to me, but also to all who have longed for His appearing. 2 Timothy 4:6–8

The apostle Paul was near the end of his life when he wrote the words included in today's Bible reading. He called life a race. He knew that he would soon receive the crown of righteousness that Christ would award to him. He wrote these words to encourage us and other Christians to stay strong in the faith so we might all receive the prize Christ has earned for us. What better prize is there?

_____Let's talk: What race are we running? What is the prize? Can we do anything to earn this prize? How do we receive the prize?

_____Let's pray: Dear Father, thank You for the gift of Jesus and eternal life. Help us as we run the race of life. Keep us strong in our faith every day. In the name of Jesus, our Prize. Amen.

M. S.

Read from God's Word

But when the time had fully come, God sent His Son, born of a woman, born under law, to redeem those under law, that we might receive the full rights of sons. Because you are sons, God sent the Spirit of His Son into our hearts, the Spirit who calls out "Abba, Father." Galatians 4:4–5 ✍

It's Time!

The telephone rang. Would this be the call they had been waiting for? The rest of the Schmidt family watched as Mrs. Schmidt answered. They could hear her excited voice. Everyone laughed as they watched her jump up and down, saying, "Yes! Of course we'll be there. What time? Yes! Yes!"

By this time the whole family had gathered around her, waiting for the good news. She hung up the phone and squealed, "It's time!"

For a long time Mr. and Mrs. Schmidt had wanted a baby. They made plans to adopt a baby from Korea. Finally the time had come. They were to meet their new baby boy at the airport the next day. They were excited beyond words.

God's people waited a long time for the promised Savior. Finally the time had come. At Bethlehem, at the cross, and at the empty grave, Jesus carried out His Father's plan to save the world.

Jesus' great love for us reaches through time and into eternity. He has promised to come again. Perhaps today, tomorrow, or very soon, *we* will be jumping up and down, squealing, "It's time! Jesus has come for us, just like He said."

———Let's talk: How does it feel to wait for something exciting to happen? Name some ways you could share the great news that Jesus is coming again. Would you change anything in your life if you knew He was coming tomorrow? What would it be?

———Let's pray: Dear Jesus, thank You for Your love and forgiveness. Help us tell others of Your great love. We can't wait to join You in heaven when it's just the right time. Amen.

M. S.

Let's Keep Him!

The Schmidts were at the airport three hours early, waiting for their new baby to arrive from Korea. The three children were looking out the huge airport window, watching planes. The time seemed to pass so slowly!

Rachel asked, "Mom, what if we don't like this baby? Can we send him back?"

"No," her mother answered softly. "We'll love him and keep him, just like we love and keep all of you."

Suddenly the door opened and there stood Miss Fuller, holding a baby boy. She handed the baby to Mrs. Schmidt. The whole family gathered around and touched his tiny hands and feet. Everyone was very quiet until Rachel said, "Let's keep him, Mom!"

Have you ever wondered if anyone loves you enough to keep you? Have you ever done anything you believed was so bad you thought even God couldn't love you anymore? Always remember, God loves you no matter what you do. He forgives all your sins, daily and richly. He will never leave you. He will always keep you.

How can you know this for sure? Look at the Bible reading again. God promises, "I have loved you with an everlasting love; I have drawn you with loving kindness."

The proof of our Father's eternal love is Jesus. In His hands and side are the marks that convince us. He was wounded for us and He bought us back from our sinful ways. And He will never let us go.

Read from God's Word

"At that time," declares the LORD, "I will be the God of all the clans of Israel, and they will be My people." This is what the LORD says: "The people who survive the sword will find favor in the desert; I will come to give rest to Israel." The LORD appeared to us in the past, saying: "I have loved you with an everlasting love; I have drawn you with loving kindness." Jeremiah 31:1–3 ✍

_____Let's talk: Why might we sometimes think that God can't really love us? How does God show you that, despite such fears, nothing can ever separate you from Him?

_____Let's pray: Dear Father, we are so glad You will always love us. Thank You for keeping us as Your very own children, just as You promised. Amen.

M. S.

Adopted

Read from God's Word

But you are a chosen people, a royal priesthood, a holy nation, a people belonging to God, that you may declare the praises of Him who called you out of darkness into His wonderful light. Once you were not a people, but now you are the people of God; once you had not received mercy, but now you have received mercy.
1 Peter 2:9–10

Several months after the Schmidts brought their little boy home from the airport, they took him to the courthouse. A judge would make the adoption legal. The baby's Korean name was Wook Hun Cho. The family decided to name him Andrew Jonathan Cho Schmidt.

Once Andrew had no one to love him and care for him. Now he belongs to a family. Andrew is adopted. He is loved and cared for.

Do you know that you are adopted? God chose to make you part of His family when you were baptized. You too were given a new name: Christian. Now you can call God, the Creator of the universe, your Father. He calls you His child.

The Bible tells us: "God sent His Son ... to redeem those under law, that we might receive the full rights of sons" (Galatians 4:4–5). And St. Peter assures us in today's reading: "Once you were not a people, but now you are the people of God."

Remember, you always have a heavenly Father who loves you and cares for you. He chose you to be His very own. Being adopted is terrific!

─── Let's talk: What are some advantages of being adopted? Why is it good to be an adopted child of God?

─── Let's pray: Dear Father, thank You for adopting each one of us in Baptism. Remind us often that You love us and care about us, even when we do wrong things. We know You forgive us because of Jesus. Amen.

M. S.

Summer Vacation

Some people like Christmas vacation. Some people like spring vacation. But most kids like summer vacation the best.

No school! No hassles! Staying up late at night. Sleeping late in the morning.

Summer is a time to relax—no homework or tests. Summer is a time to try new activities. For some, summer is a time to do nothing but enjoy God's creation, and that's okay. (Of course, there may be a few chores to do at home, but that's okay too.)

Did you know Jesus took vacations? While on earth, He made sick people well. He spoke to thousands of people about God the Father. He taught His helpers. He worked hard! After each big event, He went off by Himself to pray, to relax, and to be refreshed.

Jesus also enjoyed hiking and sailing and eating dinner with His friends. Because He was born as a human, He understands our needs. He invites us to come to Him, not just for physical rest, but especially for rest for our souls. Because of His sacrifice on Calvary, we are forgiven! He grants us forgiveness and rest.

And one day all who believe will have a permanent vacation—eternal life in heaven. What a wonderful God!

Read from God's Word

After the people saw the miraculous sign that Jesus did, they began to say, "Surely this is the Prophet who is to come into the world." Jesus, knowing that they intended to come and make Him king by force, withdrew again to a mountain by Himself. John 6:14–15

_____Let's talk: Make a list of your favorite summer vacation activities. Did you remember to add taking time each day to enjoy creation and to thank God for summer vacation?

_____Let's pray: Dear Lord, thank You for understanding our needs. Thank You for forgiving us through Your suffering, dying, and rising again. And thank You for summer vacation. Amen.

M. S.

Old Faithful

Read from God's Word

O my Strength, I watch for You; You, O God, are my fortress, my loving God. God will go before me and will let me gloat over those who slander me. But do not kill them, O LORD our shield, or my people will forget. In Your might make them wander about, and bring them down. Psalm 59:9–11 ⌒

Aurora's family had saved money for two years. They wanted to take a special family vacation. They were headed to Yellowstone National Park.

Many winter evenings were spent planning for the trip. The family looked at book after book. Aurora decided that she especially wanted to see Old Faithful. That's the name given to a geyser in Yellowstone Park. It "blows" steam from the ground every 65 minutes—every day, year in and year out, without fail.

God is faithful too—every day, year in and year out, without fail.

But God is even better than Old Faithful. After all, the geyser has gotten smaller over the years, but God's promises have never changed. He has promised to love us. And He always will! He has promised to forgive us because of His Son, Jesus. And He always will!

And He promises to love us with a faithful love—today, tomorrow, and forever!

_____Let's talk: How can you respond to God's faithfulness? Do you know of anything in nature, besides Old Faithful, that reminds you of God?

Look around you. Make a list of what you see. Next to your list write how each item reminds you of God.

_____Let's pray: Faithful God, remind us daily that You love us and forgive us. Help us remember that we can trust You always. In Jesus' name we pray. Amen.

M. S.

A-a-a-a-a-h!

All young Sammy could utter was "hot" as he collapsed on the living-room chair. Sammy lives on a mountaintop in Tennessee. The high humidity combined with the high temperature had made him breathless. Climbing the steep driveway with his basset, Sheba, had taken a lot of effort.

Suddenly, Sammy said, "A-a-a-a-a-h!" His father had turned up the air conditioner. He also handed Sammy a pcool glass of lemonade with lots of ice.

There are times when we may feel as if we're going to collapse with worry, envy, fear, jealousy, or possibly persecution. Life can get pretty hard and can wear us out. Perhaps we even feel too tired to pray.

That's when the Holy Spirit reminds us of God's refreshing grace. That's His job. He has promised to renew us and restore us to the joy of His salvation.

Through Jesus, our Savior, we receive forgiveness and healing. He "redeems [our] life from the pit and crowns [us] with love and compassion." Like Sammy with his ice-cold lemonade and air conditioning, we feel great again. A-a-a-a-a-h!

Read from God's Word

Praise the LORD, O my soul; all my inmost being, praise His holy name. Praise the LORD, O my soul, and forget not all His benefits—who forgives all your sins and heals all your diseases, who redeems your life from the pit and crowns you with love and compassion, who satisfies your desires with good things so that your youth is renewed like the eagle's. Psalm 103:1–5

———Let's talk: When you feel spiritually tired, what can you do? What can help you remember God's refreshing love? How does going to church and Sunday school help you?

On an extremely hot day, sit in a cool place, drink a cool lemonade, and thank God for His mercy.

———Let's pray: Dear Holy Spirit, thank You for reminding me that Jesus loves me. Amen.

M. S.

Read from God's Word

Dear children, do not let anyone lead you astray. He who does what is right is righteous, just as He is righteous. He who does what is sinful is of the devil, because the devil has been sinning from the beginning. The reason the Son of God appeared was to destroy the devil's work. 1 John 3:7–8 ✐

Abracadabra

Manny swooped his sparkling wand in front of his sister Rita. "And now for my last trick," he said. "I'll drop this penny into this box, add dragon dust, and—abracadabra—the penny will multiply!"

Manny held the box to show her it was empty, then he dropped the penny. He sprinkled some "dragon dust" over it and put on the lid. Rita watched every move.

"I'll shake the box to spread the dust," Manny said. Then he lifted the cover, and Rita's eyes widened. Instead of one penny, she saw many.

"How did you do that?" she asked.

"That's a magician's secret," answered Manny.

Our Lord Jesus changed many things. He turned water into wine. He changed a few loaves of bread and some fish into enough food for more than 5,000 people. He made blind eyes to see and deaf ears to hear. Those works were miracles. Miracles are true changes because of God's power. Magic pretends to be true by using tricks.

Manny pretended to change one penny into many by using dragon dust. But the truth is, the dragon dust was only baking soda, and the box had a false lid where the other pennies were hidden. They fell to the bottom when Manny shook the box.

The devil tries to trick us into sin. But Jesus conquered the devil and sin—and that was not a trick! It was the greatest miracle of all. There are no secrets with God. He wants everyone to know about eternal life through His Son, Jesus Christ.

———Let's talk: What are some of the devil's tricks? How does God help us watch out for the devil and his evil ways?

———Let's pray: Dear Lord Jesus, we believe Your miracles. We believe You love us and want us to be saved. Keep us safe from the devil's tricks. Amen.

R. H. S.

Renee's Baseball Prayer

Renee's family had tickets for tomorrow's baseball game. Renee's brother Monty had quizzed her every night about player names and facts. But tonight Monty was sick.

"Mom, will Monty be able to go to the game tomorrow?" asked Renee.

"It doesn't look good," her mom said. "He didn't eat his supper, but we'll see how he feels in the morning."

Renee's voice quivered. "I hope he can go," she said. "Monty loves baseball more than I do."

Her mom gave her a hug and sent her off to bed. Renee tucked her glove under her pillow, took her Bible, and crawled into bed. She hugged her Bible close as tears streamed down her cheeks.

"Dear Jesus," Renee prayed, "You know Monty and I fight sometimes. But You know I love him. Please, if it be Your will, make him better so he can go to the game tomorrow."

The next morning sizzling sounds called Rita downstairs. She clapped her hands when she saw Monty devouring a tower of pancakes. "You're going to the game!" Renee shouted. Monty smiled.

Sickness came into the world when Adam and Eve sinned. But God our Father loves us and wants us to be healthy. He showed how much He loves us when He sent Jesus to die on the cross for us. He heals our bodies and, most important, He heals our sick souls. And God hears our prayers. He even hears prayers about baseball games.

_____Let's talk: Who needs your prayer for healing today? Why is no prayer too small to take to the Lord?

_____Let's pray: Heavenly Father, heal all of our loved ones when they are sick or hurt. Let us rest in Your forgiving arms when we are sick with sin. In Jesus' name. Amen.

R. H. S.

The Hayloft Episode

Tammy was helping her dad bale hay. "Wait in the hayloft while I bring in the next load," her dad said. "But stay away from that corner," he added. "I have to repair those rotting boards."

As she waited, Tammy heard a faint meow coming from the corner with the rotting boards. *Dad will understand if I go there to rescue that kitten,* she thought. She tiptoed toward the meow. The boards creaked and groaned. Her foot crashed through a floorboard. She pulled herself up and decided to wait for Dad.

Tammy waved and shouted at him when he returned. He laid a long piece of lumber over the hole and she walked on it like a balance beam. Tammy fell into her dad's open arms.

"I'm sorry, Dad," Tammy said. She felt his strong arms draw her closer. "I know you told me to stay away from that corner," she said, "but there's a kitten over there."

"I'm upset that you disobeyed me, Tammy. But I think your scare was a big enough punishment. And I don't think you have to worry about the kitten," her dad said as he pointed to the mother cat carrying the kitten away by the scruff of its neck.

We often disobey our heavenly Father. We fall into the devil's trap. But God gave us His Son, Jesus Christ, to rescue us from our sins. Jesus laid down His life for us so we can run to the Father and fall into His loving arms.

The Lord is "rich in mercy," the Bible tells us (Ephesians 2:4). Isn't that great?

_____Let's talk: Who gives you warnings? Why? Why does our heavenly Father warn us to stay away from sin? Why is Jesus the only one who can save us from our sins?

_____Let's pray: Dear Savior, keep us from anything that would hurt us or take us away from You. Thank You for laying down Your life for us. Amen.

R. H. S.

The Enemy Camp

Read from God's Word

You prepare a table before me in the presence of my enemies. You anoint my head with oil; my cup overflows. Surely goodness and love will follow me all the days of my life, and I will dwell in the house of the LORD forever. Psalm 23:5–6 ✑

Jerry and Stan sat on the camp's dock and skimmed stones across the lake's blue-green waters. "Tonight I'm rowing over to Thunderbird Lodge," Stan said as he pointed across the lake.

"But that's the enemy camp," Jerry said.

"Nobody talks to us here," Stan said. "Everybody knows each other from last year."

Jerry scratched his head and said, "The counselor warned us to stay away from the troublemakers at Thunderbird."

"I'll take my chances," said Stan. "You can come with me if you've got the guts."

At midnight they slipped out of their cabin. They stopped in their tracks at the sight of a patrol car's headlights. A ranger got out of the car and walked toward them.

"You'd better get back to your cabin before I report you," the ranger said.

The next morning the dining hall buzzed like a roomful of mosquitoes. Campers from Thunderbird Lodge had been caught spray painting the camp's entrance gate.

Sometimes we join the enemy camp when we feel rejected. We want to belong, so we unite with a group even though it's a bad one. Jesus knew what it felt like to be rejected. His friends left Him. His own Father let Him die on the cross so we might live forever in heaven. Jesus understands us. Go to Him and talk things over the next time you're tempted to run to an enemy camp.

_____Let's talk: How do you know if you're in an enemy camp? Why does Jesus want us to camp with Him?

_____Let's pray: Lord Jesus, comfort us when others reject us. Help us always turn to You, and give us Your Holy Spirit that we may stay close to You. In Your name. Amen.

R. H. S.

july

Contributors for this month:

Carol Brannan

Carol Delph

Phil Lang

Gloria Lessmann

Doris Schuchard

Beverly J. Soyk

Janet M. Wagner

Faith Overcomes Fear

Read from God's Word

Who shall separate us from the love of Christ? Shall trouble or hardship or persecution or famine or nakedness or danger or sword? ... For I am convinced that neither death nor life, neither angels nor demons, neither the present nor the future, nor any powers, neither height nor depth, nor anything else in all creation, will be able to separate us from the love of God that is in Christ Jesus our Lord. Romans 8:35–39 ⌒

Faith was in tears. She had just finished the 25-meter race in the butterfly and had clocked her slowest time ever. She looked up to see her father standing with open arms and a smile on his face.

"Faith, you did great!" he said. "Your form was excellent, and you didn't give up. I'm proud of you."

"Oh, Daddy, I don't know what happened. I saw all those people and got scared."

Later, Faith's dad showed her the Bible story of King Joash.

"When I read this story, Faith, I think about what it was like for seven-year-old Joash as he was crowned king before all those people. God did not leave him without help. It says, 'Joash did what was right in the eyes of the Lord' (2 Kings 12:2).

"I know you were scared seeing all those people today. Your coach has worked with you and taught you well. When you're ready to compete again, follow her instruction and do your best."

Like Faith, we all have times when we're scared and unsure of ourselves. Today's Bible reading tells of the great love our heavenly Father has for each of us. He loves us more than any coach ever could. He gave His own Son to die for us. His Word guides and directs us. He is *for* us, and nothing can separate us from the great love that is ours through Christ Jesus our Lord.

_____Let's talk: Spend some time reading the story of Joash in 2 Kings 11 and 12. Talk about how it feels to do something when others are watching. How can we turn to God for help?

_____Let's pray: Heavenly Father, thank You for Your love, which has no end. Thank You for Your free gift of forgiveness and salvation. Be with us as we struggle to do our best. Thank You for Your promise that we are more than conquerors through Him who loves us. Amen.

B. J. S.

Read from God's Word

The LORD is compassionate and gracious, slow to anger, abounding in love. He will not always accuse, nor will He harbor His anger forever; He does not treat us as our sins deserve or repay us according to our iniquities. For as high as the heavens are above the earth, so great is His love for those who fear Him; as far as the east is from the west, so far has He removed our transgressions from us. Psalm 103:8–12

Where Did It Go?

Karly sat at the computer, engrossed in her typing. She loved writing poetry, and in the summer months she had more time to journal her thoughts. Outside, the clouds gathered. Before long, rain splattered on the window beside her. Just as Karly's mom came into the room to tell her to shut down the computer, lightning flashed and thunder cracked. The power flickered and then went out.

"Oh, no!" Karly cried. "I hadn't saved that last page, and now it'll be gone."

"Don't worry, honey," her mom said. "Sometimes we can pull things back up. We'll wait until the storm passes and then try." But after everything had calmed down and the computer was working again, the poetry page was not to be found.

Our sins are like that missing page. When we confess our sins, God is faithful and just, and He promises to forgive us. As quickly as the page was deleted and gone, our sins are canceled and wiped away. They are not out there somewhere, waiting to be pulled back up for all the world to see.

God has promised that "as far as the east is from the west, so far has He removed our transgressions from us." In Jesus, our Savior, His forgiveness is complete.

———Let's talk: How far is the east from the west? How far has God removed our sins from us?

———Let's pray: "Have mercy on me, O God, according to Your unfailing love; according to Your great compassion blot out my transgressions. Wash away all my iniquity and cleanse me from my sin" (Psalm 51:1–2). In Your Son's name we pray. Amen.

B. J. S.

It Isn't Fair

Paul and Mark's dad stood at the door, ready to enter. He paused and listened. "I told you to leave my stuff alone!" yelled Paul.

"You're supposed to share!" Mark yelled right back.

"I bought these baseball cards with my own money, and you better not touch them," shouted Paul as he hit Mark on the shoulder.

"Ouch!" yelled Mark. Then he punched Paul in the arm.

"All right, boys, that's enough," said Dad as he entered their room. "What's going on here?"

Dad listened patiently and sorted out the facts. Then he sat each of them down for a talk.

Our heavenly Father is much like Paul and Mark's dad. Sometimes we feel unfairly treated. A sister or brother uses things without asking. "Everyone else" gets to do something except us.

Today's reading says that God

Read from God's Word

Be patient, then, brothers, until the Lord's coming. See how the farmer waits for the land to yield its valuable crop and how patient he is for the autumn and spring rains. You too, be patient and stand firm, because the Lord's coming is near. Don't grumble against each other, brothers, or you will be judged. The Judge is standing at the door! Brothers, as an example of patience in the face of suffering, take the prophets who spoke in the name of the Lord. As you know, we consider blessed those who have persevered. You have heard of Job's perseverance and have seen what the Lord finally brought about. The Lord is full of compassion and mercy. James 5:7–11

stands at the door, ready to judge. He knows our thoughts and feelings. He can help us through times when life just doesn't seem fair. God knows all about unfairness, for He gave His one and only Son to die for us, although Jesus had done no wrong. So great is God's love for us that He sent His Son to the cross to pay the price for us. Because of Christ's death and resurrection, we have a glorious future in heaven. Yes, the Judge is standing at the door, but He is full of love and mercy.

_____Let's talk: How have you handled times when you felt unfairly treated? How does it help realizing that God knows all about how you feel?

_____Let's pray: Lord God, we praise You for Your love and mercy. Thank You for giving Your Son so we may be saved. Be with us in the days ahead, and give us Your patience and understanding toward others. In Jesus' name. Amen.

B. J. S.

Freedom in Christ

Read from God's Word

It is for freedom that Christ has set us free. Stand firm, then, and do not let yourselves be burdened again by a yoke of slavery. ... You, my brothers, were called to be free. But do not use your freedom to indulge the sinful nature; rather, serve one another in love. The entire law is summed up in a single command: "Love your neighbor as yourself."
Galatians 5:1, 13–14 ✏

In the United States, July 4 marks a special occasion. It's the day on which America declared independence from England. The vote took place on July 2, 1776, but on July 4 the Declaration of Independence was actually signed.

Riders on horseback carried copies of the Declaration to the colonies. It took as long as two months until all the colonies had received the news. So that first Independence Day was celebrated on many different dates.

While it didn't end the war at once, the Declaration gave the colonists the courage needed to continue. Eventually it helped put an end to the American War for Independence. With that independence came freedom, a blessing that Americans still enjoy today.

No matter what country you live in, there is a freedom that everyone can have. It is much more important than the freedom from being ruled by another country. It's freedom from being ruled by sin. This freedom was bought and paid for with Jesus' precious blood.

All of us have been enslaved by sin, but Jesus set us free from the burden of slavery. Now we are free to love the One who died and rose for us. We are free to share His message with all those we meet. We are free to serve Jesus in joy until He takes us home. Celebrate this precious freedom, which is yours every day!

_____Let's talk: What does freedom mean to you? What does it mean to be free in Christ?

_____Let's pray: Dear Jesus, thank You for paying the price to set us free. Thank You for loving us beyond all cost. Help us stand firm and not become burdened by slavery to sin. In Your name we pray. Amen.

B. J. S.

Our Power Source

Read from God's Word

"Remain in me, and I will remain in you. No branch can bear fruit by itself; it must remain in the vine. Neither can you bear fruit unless you remain in Me. I am the vine; you are the branches. If a man remains in me and I in him, he will bear much fruit; apart from me you can do nothing." John 15:4–5

Screams and laughter filled the backyard as Dan and his friends squirted one another with water bottles. When his bottle was empty, Dan decided he needed bigger ammunition. Turning on the water hose, he sprayed the other boys. The cooling water was a relief from the heat of the day, and soon there was a battle to see who could control the hose.

Suddenly, the water supply was gone. All that remained was a dripping hose. Turning around, Dan discovered his sister standing by the faucet with a big grin on her face. The water source had been shut off.

Our lives can be like that hose. Jesus is our power source, and His Spirit is like water that flows through us and blesses others.

In today's reading Jesus teaches about how important it is to remain in Him. On our own we cannot produce the fruit of faith. But Jesus is the Vine and we are the branches. With Him—the Vine—as our power source, we will flourish and blossom and bear much fruit. Jesus bought our salvation with His love. And His love in us will produce much fruit. Our Savior gives us the strength to remain in Him, and He promises that He will always remain in us.

———Let's talk: When was the last time you enjoyed a water fight? How can the cooling water remind us of our ultimate "power source" and the blessings that Jesus gives us?

———Let's pray: Dear Jesus, thank You for loving us so much that You died so we might be saved. Thank You for Your promise to remain our Vine. Help us always to remain in you. Continue to fill us with Your Spirit so we may produce good fruit, which comes only from You. Amen.

B. J. S.

Read from God's Word

Now to Him who is able to do immeasurably more than all we ask or imagine, according to His power that is at work within us, to Him be glory in the church and in Christ Jesus throughout all generations, for ever and ever! Amen. Ephesians 3:20–21 ✍

Bursting with Thanks!

"Oh, Daddy, look at this beautiful, shiny pink purse! May I have it, please?" asked Rebecca. "I promise I'll pay you back when we get home."

Looking into Rebecca's pleading eyes, her dad just grinned. He said, "When I saw that purse, I just knew you'd love it. I will buy it for you, and you don't even have to repay me."

Rebecca hugged the purse close as they walked out of the store. Looking up into her dad's face, she exclaimed over and over again, "Oh, thank you, Daddy; thank you, thank you, thank you!"

Our heavenly Father has given us a far greater gift than Rebecca received from her father. Even if we tried really hard, we could never pay or do enough to earn salvation. But that's the beauty of God's grace. We don't have to do anything to earn salvation. Out of love, God has given the gift of eternal life to us through His Son, Jesus. In love and gratefulness, our hearts overflow with thanksgiving.

Every day God's goodness to us is overwhelming. He continually showers us with blessings far beyond what we could ever ask or imagine. Like Rebecca, we say, "Oh, thank You, Father; thank You, thank You, thank You!"

_____Let's talk: What is the best material gift you have ever received? How did you thank the giver? Will that gift last forever? Why are the gifts from God our best gifts of all?

_____Let's pray: O King of heaven, we praise You for gifting us with life everlasting. We thank You for all the blessings that You so freely give to us each day. May we always remember You as the Giver of all, and may all glory to You be given. Amen.

B. J. S.

Hidden on the Inside

Jalysa and Kirsten were excited! This was the first year the pear tree in their backyard was producing fruit. They had just brought in the perfect pear to show their mom. Mom promised she would slice it for lunch.

An hour later, as their mom called for the girls to wash up, Jalysa came running to see if the pear was ready to eat. To her surprise, something was wrong with their perfect pear. Little brown specks appeared on one side of the pear. As Jalysa watched, the specks seemed to get bigger.

"What's happening, Mom?" she asked.

Taking a knife, her mom sliced into the pear. Inside was a tiny worm working its way out. Carefully, her mother cut away all the bad spots and washed the rest of the pear.

"That's just like us and our sins—God cuts them all away and makes us clean again!" said Jalysa with a smile.

Read from God's Word

Search me, O God, and know my heart; test me and know my anxious thoughts. See if there is any offensive way in me, and lead me in the way everlasting. Psalm 139:23–24 ✐

In the Bible reading, David asks God to search him and know his heart. Only God can look on the inside. He sees our sins and by His word of forgiveness cleanses us from the inside out. He has given us our Savior and He continues to lead us in the way of everlasting life.

_____Let's talk: Are there times when you are smiling on the outside but thinking not-so-good thoughts on the inside? What do you think it means that God searches us from the inside? How might God's searching help us realize we have sinned and ask for forgiveness?

_____Let's pray: "Create in me a pure heart, O God, and renew a steadfast spirit within me. Do not cast me from Your presence or take Your Holy Spirit from me. Restore to me the joy of Your salvation and grant me a willing spirit, to sustain me" (Psalm 51:10–12). In Jesus' name we pray. Amen.

B. J. S.

Sharing a Song

The campfire crackled as a new log was thrown on top. Hannah sat by the fire, roasting some marshmallows. She listened as her grandfather called for everyone to gather around and sing some songs. One by one, everyone found a spot and sat down. Soon their music filled the air.

Matthew 26 tells of another time there was singing. Jesus had just shared the Last Supper with His disciples. But the special time they shared didn't end with the meal. They sang a hymn before they went out to the Mount of Olives.

How precious that hymn singing must have been as Jesus led His disciples in song! Jesus knew that in just a few short hours, He would be condemned to die so He could save all people. Yet He spent time in song with His disciples, praising God and giving thanks.

God's Word speaks to us, too, through the songs we sing. "What a Friend We Have in Jesus" comforts us when we're worried or feeling alone. In "Jesus, Savior, Pilot Me" we ask for guidance and acknowledge that all direction comes from Him. "The Lord's My Shepherd, I'll Not Want" helps us remember that Jesus is our Good Shepherd who is leading us to our eternal home.

When we sing these hymns and songs, God touches our hearts through the words that connect us to His Word. The comfort and joy He sends to us through song helps us face our struggles and celebrate our joys.

_____Let's do: What are some of the favorite hymns or songs your family enjoys? Choose one or two to sing together now.

_____Let's pray: Praise God, from whom all blessings flow;
Praise Him, all creatures here below;
Praise Him above, O heavenly host;
Praise Father, Son, and Holy Ghost.

B. J. S.

Which Hand?

Tim's dad stood with hands behind his back as he said, "Okay, Tim, you've worked hard, and I've got a treat for you. You can choose between two things. One I'll show you; the other I won't."

Slowly Tim's dad pulled his hand around for Tim to see. In it was a model of the racecar Tim's favorite driver liked to drive.

"Now you get to choose if you want the racecar or whatever is in my other hand," Tim's dad said.

Smiling, Tim replied, "I choose your other hand. I know you've always got something better for me than what I can see." As Tim's dad opened his other hand, two tickets fell out. They were tickets to a race so Tim could actually see his driver in action!

Sometimes our days are filled with troubles. And sometimes our days are so great that we can't imagine anything better. No matter what our day has been like, God promises us something even better. Our life here on earth will one day end. But our life with Jesus is eternal because He made us His own by shedding His blood for us.

We can't see Jesus' gift of eternal life right now, but it's a promise we can count on. Through the Holy Spirit, we trust that what we *can't* see is even better than what we *can* see. We know that what is waiting for us is the best gift Jesus has planned.

Read from God's Word

Therefore we do not lose heart. Though outwardly we are wasting away, yet inwardly we are being renewed day by day. For our light and momentary troubles are achieving for us an eternal glory that far outweighs them all. So we fix our eyes not on what is seen, but on what is unseen. For what is seen is temporary, but what is unseen is eternal.
2 Corinthians 4:16–18

———Let's talk: Think of someone you could surprise with a special treat. Do what Tim's dad did but keep it simple, and then share with that person the hope you have in Christ.

———Let's pray: Heavenly Father, thank You for the gift of eternal life. Grant that we may always remember this gift. Help us share with others the hope that is in us. In Jesus' name we pray. Amen.

B. J. S.

The Confidence Builder

Read from God's Word

[Jesus] said to Simon, "Put out into deep water, and let down the nets for a catch." Simon answered, "Master, we've worked hard all night and haven't caught anything. But because You say so, I will let down the nets." When they had done so, they caught such a large number of fish that their nets began to break. ... When Simon Peter saw this, he fell at Jesus' knees and said, "Go away from me, Lord; I am a sinful man!" For he and all his companions were astonished at the catch of fish. ... Then Jesus said to Simon, "Don't be afraid; from now on you will catch men." So they pulled their boats up on shore, left everything and followed Him. Luke 5:4–11 ⮎

M om," said eight-year-old Jake, "Dan and I are leaving now. Bye!"

"Hope you catch a lot," replied Mom.

"I do too," smiled Jake.

Jake was going fishing for the first time. He and his big brother were going to the best bass-fishing place: Joe's Lake.

After a long, hot day, Jake and Dan returned home. They were tired and happy. "I'm a fisherman," Jake said. "Actually, I'm a fisherman with a sore wrist. I caught 30 fish!"

"That's great!" Mom said. "How many did you catch, Dan?"

"I didn't put a pole in the lake," Dan replied. "I was too busy baiting the hooks and taking fish off Jake's line. I've never seen so many hungry fish. Fishing at Joe's Lake is a real confidence-builder!"

Just as Joe's Lake is full of hungry fish, the world is full of hungry people. They lack the Good News of God's love for them. They bite at anything to satisfy their hungry souls. They need to be filled with God's love. They need a Savior.

God sent His Son to die for the sins of the world. He wants all people to be saved. In our Bible reading we hear how the fishermen Peter, James, and John left everything for the best job ever: following Jesus. The Holy Spirit helps us to follow Jesus too. He gives us courage to share God's love with others. He tells us not to be afraid. He is always with us.

———Let's talk: Do you know someone who is hungry for God's love? Pray for the Holy Spirit to prepare their hearts and to give you the courage to witness to them.

———Let's pray: Dear God, help us follow Jesus this day. Help us tell others about Him. In His name we pray. Amen.

C. D.

E.R., O.R., D.R., R.R.

D o you know the meaning of the initials E.R. and O.R.? E.R. stands for Emergency Room. The initials O.R. mean Operating Room. Both are places in the hospital where people receive help after they get hurt. No one wants to get hurt and go to those rooms!

Does being a Christian guarantee a life free from getting hurt? Our Bible verses tell of the painful trials we suffer as Christians. We live in a sinful world and experience its pain each day. We ourselves are not free from sin, "for all have sinned and fall short of the glory of God" (Romans 3:23).

But God has several "hospital rooms" we can visit for healing. In the Examination Room, we see our sins. Without help, we face a scary future. We face eternal separation from God because of our sins.

But Jesus Christ, our Great Physician takes us from the Examination Room to the Delivery Room. He died on the cross and rose from the grave to deliver us from all our sins. Through Baptism we are reborn and named as God's children.

Jesus moves us to the Recovery Room. In this room, the forgiveness won by His precious blood heals us, restores us, and transfuses us with God's love.

Filled with God's love and strength, we are ready to face the world. With the Spirit's gentle aid, we can refer others who are hurting to our Great Physician.

_____Let's talk: How has believing in Jesus brought you into the "Living Room"? the "Waiting Room"? our "Heavenly Room"?

_____Let's pray: Thank You, Jesus, for healing us from sin. Help us serve You and others. We ask this in Your name. Amen.

C. D.

Read from God's Word

Dear friends, do not be surprised at the painful trial you are suffering, as though something strange were happening to you. But rejoice that you participate in the sufferings of Christ, so that you may be overjoyed when His glory is revealed. If you are insulted because of the name of Christ, you are blessed, for the Spirit of glory and of God rests on you. If you suffer, it should not be as a murderer or thief or any other kind of criminal, or even as a meddler. However, if you suffer as a Christian, do not be ashamed, but praise God that you bear that name. 1 Peter 4:12–16

Facing a Bear

Read from God's Word

I lift up my eyes to the hills—where does my help come from? My help comes from the LORD, the Maker of heaven and earth. He will not let your foot slip—He who watches over you will not slumber; indeed, He who watches over Israel will neither slumber nor sleep. The LORD watches over you—the LORD is your shade at your right hand; the sun will not harm you by day, nor the moon by night. The LORD will keep you from all harm—He will watch over your life; the LORD will watch over your coming and going both now and forevermore. Psalm 121 ✍

It's fun to go camping. Sleeping on the hard ground isn't as comfortable as sleeping at home. But it's a wonderful treat to roast marshmallows over a flickering fire, to hike through the woods, to view spectacular scenery, and most of all to spend time with your family.

One night Dad and Phil walked from their campground to an outdoor theater to watch a nature movie. Halfway through the movie Phil decided he wanted to go back to the tent. He was smart enough to take the flashlight and remember the trail they had come on.

However, he came to a stream that had to be crossed using a narrow bridge. As he started to cross the bridge, he looked up. There, standing nine-feet tall, was a great big black bear that was growling and looking very hungry.

Phil quickly turned around and went back to his dad. He waited and walked home safely, holding his father's hand!

This reminds us of the heavenly Father. Whenever we face a "big bear" of a problem or temptation, we need to realize that we can't handle it on our own. Instead we can return to our heavenly Father who gladly promises to hold our hand and lead us home safely.

May we always turn to our heavenly Father for help and comfort. May we also share with our friends the news of His love and protection. The Lord will keep us from all evil because we belong to Him through the rescuing work of Jesus, our Savior.

_____Let's talk: What's the worst danger you've ever faced? How did God keep evil from happening to you?

_____Let's pray: Dear Lord, thank You that we don't need to face the "big bears" of sin alone. We believe that You've defeated sin and that You're always watching over us. Amen.

P. L.

The Assembly Line

Read from God's Word

What, after all, is Apollos? And what is Paul? Only servants, through whom you came to believe—as the Lord has assigned to each his task. I planted the seed, Apollos watered it, but God made it grow. So neither he who plants nor he who waters is anything, but only God, who makes things grow. The man who plants and the man who waters have one purpose, and each will be rewarded according to his own labor. For we are God's fellow workers; you are God's field, God's building. 1 Corinthians 3:5–9 〰

Ryan's grandma works in a spice factory. One day a week the company runs an assembly line to package the products. One worker lines up the bottles; another fills them with fragrant spices. The next worker caps them; the following person seals them. Ryan's grandma is the last worker on the line. She puts the bottles into boxes for shipping. Through the work of many, the finished product is sent all over the world.

Being a Christian can be compared to working on an assembly line. For instance, our Bible reading explains that Paul planted the seed of God's message and Apollos watered it, but God made it grow.

At times, fear causes us to run away from our work. We lose the opportunity to share God's love. At other times, we may try to witness, but we stumble on the words. And sometimes we think we've done the work so well that we take pride in it. We fail to give God the credit.

Christ paid for our mistakes, failures, and prideful attitudes by His death on Calvary's cross. God forgives us and transforms our bungled job in ways that give Him glory.

The Holy Spirit unites us with fellow workers for the common purpose of spreading His words of love. He strengthens and prepares us for each day's work. He equips us with the patience to finish our tasks. And although we are God's workers, He completes the task. To Him be the glory!

_____Let's do: Pray for the people whom God places on your mind and in your life today.

_____Let's pray: Lord, help us enjoy each task You give us. May Your Word be spread to places all over the world. In Jesus' name. Amen.

C. D.

Read from God's Word

Then Jesus declared, "I am the Bread of Life. He who comes to Me will never go hungry, and he who believes in Me will never be thirsty. ... All that the Father gives Me will come to Me, and whoever comes to Me I will never drive away. For I have come down from heaven not to do My will but to do the will of Him who sent Me. And this is the will of Him who sent Me, that I shall ... raise them up at the last day. For My Father's will is that everyone who looks to the Son and believes in Him shall have eternal life."
John 6:35, 37–40

Mmm, Mmm, Good!

On warm days like today it's fun to reach into the freezer for a chocolate cornucopia or maybe an orange Epsicle.

The story says that it was a hot summer day at the 1904 World's Fair in St. Louis. A vendor ran out of dishes for his ice cream. Nearby was a man selling zalabia, a thin Persian waffle. He quickly rolled a waffle into a cone (or cornucopia) shape and scooped ice cream on top. It was an instant success!

In 1905 11-year-old Frank Epperson mixed soda water powder and water to make a favorite drink. He left his stirring stick in it and put the mixture outside on a cold night. The next morning he had a stick of frozen soda water. When Frank grew up, he began a business of selling seven flavors of Epsicles. Later the name was changed to Popsicle, a treat still enjoyed today.

Do you have the urge to head for the kitchen yet? There is another place to satisfy your hunger. Jesus said that whoever believes in Him will not be hungry or thirsty (John 6:35). Studying God's Word, hearing His Gospel of forgiveness, believing in Him, and receiving His love will refresh us. If we eat this "food," we won't be hungry for the sinful things in the world.

Are you hungry or thirsty? Go to Jesus, the Savior who takes away the sins of the world. His love will satisfy you completely.

_____Let's talk: Having devotion time with Jesus is one way we eat spiritual food. By what other ways can we fill up on heavenly food?

_____Let's pray: Dear Jesus, speak Your Gospel to us, that we may hunger only for You. Help us share Your Word with others who are spiritually hungry and thirsty too. Amen.

D. S.

Wired Shut

Can you talk without moving your jaw? Try it. Hold your bottom teeth tightly against your upper teeth. Now open your lips and try talking to someone near you.

How did it go? It can be done. The more you practice, the easier it is for people to understand you.

Some people have the chance to practice this kind of talking after breaking their jaw. The doctor wires the jaws together for at least six weeks so they can heal properly.

Talking isn't the only challenge. How do you think they eat their meals? They don't! They *drink* their meals. Everything has to be blended into a liquid and slurped through a straw. But with patience and perseverance they don't give up on talking or eating!

Life is full of challenges. Ever since Adam and Eve disobeyed God, we have been challenged by Satan, by sin. We are tempted to give up. We ask Jesus, God's Son and our Savior, the one who overcame all the devil's challenges, to help us.

Through His forgiveness and the power of the Gospel, Jesus helps us tell people about His love even when our mouths are wired shut. He shows us how to feed on His Word even when the doctor has confined us to a hospital. Jesus helps us share His love with our friends. He helps us overcome our challenges.

Read from God's Word

Now the serpent ... said to the woman, "Did God really say, 'You must not eat from any tree in the garden'?" The woman said to the serpent, "... God did say, 'You must not eat fruit from the tree that is in the middle of the garden, and you must not touch it, or you will die.'" "You will not surely die," the serpent said to the woman. "For God knows that when you eat of it ... you will be like God, knowing good and evil." ... the woman ... took some and ate it. She also gave some to her husband. ... Then the eyes of both of them were opened, and they realized they were naked. Genesis 3:1–7 ✐

———Let's talk: What challenges do you face in your life? Have you asked Jesus to help you with them?

———Let's pray: Dear Jesus, You know the problems and challenges we face. Thank You for overcoming sin, death, and the devil. Help us overcome our challenges by Your forgiveness. In Your name, Lord. Amen.

P. L.

Heat Relief

Read from God's Word

Jonah went out and sat down at a place east of the city. There he made himself a shelter, sat in its shade and waited to see what would happen to the city. Then the LORD God provided a vine and made it grow up over Jonah to give shade for his head to ease his discomfort, and Jonah was very happy about the vine. Jonah 4:5–6 ○

About now you may be experiencing some of the hottest days of summer. A tall glass of lemonade, extra sunblock, or feet propped up in front of a fan might bring relief as you wait for that first snowflake to fly.

How about using a parasol? Parasols were what people called umbrellas many years ago. The first umbrellas were invented more than 3,000 years ago in the Near East. They were used to keep the sun, not the rain, off their owners. Today umbrellas are used to protect people from both sun and rain.

One time God protected His prophet Jonah from the heat. Jonah had told people in the city of Nineveh to turn away from their sins and back to God or they would be destroyed in 40 days. As Jonah sat outside the city in the scorching sun, waiting to see what would happen, he became hotter and hotter. God saw how uncomfortable Jonah was and made a plant grow to give him shade. How glad Jonah must have felt to be in the cool shade!

In Psalm 121:5–6 God says He is our shade so "the sun will not harm you by day, nor the moon by night." God not only protects you from the sun's heat, but He also protects you from the evils that happen during the day and night. When Jesus died, He defeated the Evil One forever. Whenever evil does its worst, you can take refuge in Jesus. Through Him you now have the victory too!

_____Let's talk: Can you remember a time when God kept something from hurting you at night or during the day? How does it feel to know you always have God's shade over you? Read about Jonah's ministry in Nineveh in Jonah 3 and 4.

_____Let's pray: Dear Lord, thank You for being our "umbrella" to protect us from evil. It's good to know that whether we are awake or asleep, You are always there, watching over us. Amen.

D. S.

Wait for the Lord

"Are we there yet?" asked Jessie. "Is dinner ready yet?" drooled Drew.

"Why is this line for the roller coaster so long?" whined Winnie.

"When will it be my turn?" asked Omar.

Do we have to wait? For most of us, waiting is no fun. It feels like a waste of time.

Phil had to lay in a hospital bed for two and a half weeks. He was ready to go home. Then the doctor said, "Wait." *What?* Wait some more? Wait two more weeks? But he'd already waited long enough!

Little did he know the spiritual and educational experience God had in store for him during those extra weeks. God used the waiting time to show Phil His miracle of healing for the spirit and the body.

The next time you have to wait, try this: Instead of getting upset, say a prayer to Jesus. Thank Him that He waited until just the right time to come into our messed-up world of sin to be perfect for us. Thank Jesus for dying for your sins and disobedience. Thank Jesus for waiting for us with a heavenly home. Ask Jesus to help you show and tell His love to those around you.

Waiting time can be a good time to lean on God's grace. You may not even get your prayer finished before the waiting time is up.

_____Let's talk: Why is waiting sometimes good for us? How can waiting for God to act be a great blessing?

_____Let's pray: Dear Jesus, help us use our waiting time in prayer. Amen.

P. L.

Read from God's Word

I am still confident of this: I will see the goodness of the LORD in the land of the living. Wait for the LORD; be strong and take heart and wait for the LORD. Psalm 27:13–14

How We're Like Popcorn

Read from God's Word

But thanks be to God, who always leads us in triumphal procession in Christ and through us spreads everywhere the fragrance of the knowledge of Him. For we are to God the aroma of Christ among those who are being saved and those who are perishing. To the one we are the smell of death; to the other, the fragrance of life. And who is equal to such a task? 2 Corinthians 2:14–16

Imagine you are at the movie theater. You are standing next to the concession stand. You hear familiar poppity-pop-pop sounds above the crowd. Now, close your eyes and imagine what you smell. Hot, buttered popcorn!

There's no mistaking the smell of popcorn. Even if the theater workers tried to contain the aroma of popcorn (and they would never do that), they couldn't. The smell of popcorn spreads even into the movie auditorium, and it's irresistible. If you're like most other people, it makes you want to have some popcorn too.

Today's Bible reading calls the message of the Gospel "the fragrance of the knowledge of [Christ]" and it calls us "the aroma of Christ."

Just as the aroma of popcorn fills the theater, so are we to fill our surroundings with the knowledge of Jesus. Our words and actions are to be unmistakably Christlike. The love of Christ can't be contained or hidden. It spreads through us to the people who are around us each day. And that Christlike love, demonstrated by us, becomes so irresistible that others want it too.

But we don't always act Christlike. Our sinful words and actions sometimes take over. But read verse 14 again: "God … always leads us in triumphal procession." Jesus has forgiven our sins; He died and rose again to cover them. He will always be with us, leading us to be the "aroma" of His mercy in the world. That's how His love spreads!

_____Let's talk: Each time you smell fresh popcorn, remember who you are—the aroma of Christ—and share that thought with those around you.

_____Let's pray: Dear God, forgive us when the aroma of Christ from us to others is not as sweet as it could be. Lead us to be Your desired fragrance in the world. Amen.

G. L.

Down but Not Out

Read from God's Word

But we have this treasure in jars of clay to show that this all-surpassing power is from God and not from us. We are hard pressed on every side, but not crushed; perplexed, but not in despair; persecuted, but not abandoned; struck down, but not destroyed. We always carry around in our body the death of Jesus, so that the life of Jesus may also be revealed in our body. 2 Corinthians 4:7–10 ⌇

Jesse threw the first punch—a strong left jab to the face. Pete followed, landing a straight hit to the nose. Then Korrine stepped up and sent a barrage of swats right on target. The children's giggles and hoots got louder and louder as they slugged, hit, and punched away. But no matter how hard they hit, the threesome couldn't knock down the bop bag—that inflatable, four-foot-tall plastic clown with the weighted base.

Perhaps you have a bop bag. Because the bag is weighted at the base, it may weave, wobble, and bend to the floor when it is punched. But it will not topple over completely and stay down.

Christians have a lot in common with those bop bags. We, too, are sometimes punched—afflicted, perplexed, and struck down—but not completely destroyed. Our affliction could be a painful disease or sickness. We might be perplexed (confused) by tough choices when friends pressure us to do something we know is wrong. We may be struck down by arguing in our family or the death of someone we love. But no matter what, we are never destroyed completely!

That's because Jesus' death and resurrection is our solid base. Jesus Christ always brings us back up, just like a bop bag. We know that regardless of what comes our way in this life, we are God's forgiven children. We will someday live in heaven with Him because Jesus died and rose for each of us to take away pain, sorrow, and sin forever.

_____Let's talk: Read Romans 8:37. Make a list of times when you feel picked on, confused, sad, or disappointed. Read your list together and, after each one, repeat Romans 8:37.

_____Let's pray: Dear Jesus, thank You for winning eternal life for us. Pick us up when we are beaten down. Remind us always that we are winners in You. Amen.

G. L.

Christian Tag

Read from God's Word

*So when they met together,
they asked Him, "Lord, are You
at this time going to restore the
kingdom to Israel?" He said to
them: "It is not for you to know
the times or dates the Father has
set by His own authority. But you
will receive power when the Holy
Spirit comes on you; and you will
be My witnesses in Jerusalem,
and in all Judea and Samaria,
and to the ends of the earth."
Acts 1:6–8* ✎

"Tag—you're it!" How many times
do you suppose you've played that
familiar game? The rules of the game
are so simple anyone can play. Once
you're "it," you have a job to do—to go
and touch someone else so that person
can be "it."

Acts 1:8 is God's way of saying to
us, "Tag—you're it!" God has "caught"
us to be His children by sending His Son
to die for our sins and rise again so we
might have eternal life. He has touched
us with the Holy Spirit in our Baptism.

Now we're "it"—His witnesses. We
have a job to do—to catch others for
Christ, to touch them with His love,
and to tell them Jesus died to win their
salvation too. Whoever we are, whatever our age or abilities, we're "it."
Anyone can play!

Think about what happens when
the person who is "it" quits. The game
ends. As Christians, we don't want the
"tagging" to stop. We've been caught
by God's grace and we want to touch others with Jesus, even to the ends of
the earth.

That's quite a job, to catch all people to the ends of the earth. But
we're not alone. We have the help of other believers to catch people for
Christ. Most important, we always have Jesus on our side. So even when
we're tired of running, He'll be with us to keep us going.

_____Let's talk: Make a point of "catching someone" this week. Invite a
friend or relative to join you for Sunday school, church
services, or vacation Bible school. Share with a fellow
believer how you felt about "touching someone."

_____Let's pray: Dear God, thank You for touching us with Your love.
Give us the courage and strength to share Your love
as witnesses for You. Amen.

G. L.

Afraid of the Future?

Emily's dad was in the hospital. Emily was in high school, so she understood about heart attacks. Each day she became more frightened, since the news was never really good. Her mom, teachers, and other adults hugged her and said everything would be okay. But Emily was terrified. She loved her dad and the way life was, and she was afraid of all the ways everything could quickly change.

The younger children in the family needed Emily's care and reassurance. Emily would say, "Dad will be better soon, and everything will be fine." But even listening to her own voice didn't help her feel any better. What she needed was comfort and security because everything around her felt uncomfortable and insecure.

Sitting alone in her room, Emily began paging through her Bible. Quite accidentally she read, "'For I know the plans I have for you,' declares the LORD, 'plans to prosper you and not to harm you, plans to give you hope and a future'" (Jeremiah 29:11). God told Emily in the words of that verse that she could rely on Him to help her through this frightening time. She knew He would never leave her or her dad, and she could depend on His promise of a hopeful future.

In time, Emily's dad did recover. The experience changed the family and changed Emily. Her confidence in God had grown. She was sure He was with her and would always help her.

Read from God's Word

This is what the LORD says: "When seventy years are completed for Babylon, I will come to you and fulfill My gracious promise to bring you back to this place. For I know the plans I have for you," declares the LORD, "plans to prosper you and not to harm you, plans to give you hope and a future. Then you will call upon Me and come and pray to Me, and I will listen to you. You will seek Me and find Me when you seek Me with all your heart." Jeremiah 29:10–13 ✍

_____Let's talk: When was a time in your life that you had a fear of the future? What did you do about it? Could this verse have helped you then or could it help you in the future?

_____Let's pray: Thank You, Lord, for reassuring us that You have a plan for us and that we can trust You in all things. Amen.

C. B.

Read from God's Word

"Do not let your hearts be troubled. Trust in God; trust also in Me. In My Father's house are many rooms; if it were not so, I would have told you. I am going there to prepare a place for you. And if I go and prepare a place for you, I will come back and take you to be with me that you also may be where I am." John 14:1–3 ◌

A Place in Heaven

Ben was only four years old when Mrs. Hemp, the grandmother of his friend Davey, died. As was the custom in their town, all the friends and relatives gathered at the funeral home to comfort Mrs. Hemp's children and grandchildren.

Mrs. DeLeon, Davey's mom, was very sad to have lost her mother and was crying. Ben sat by his own mom on a chair and watched all the people coming and going. Finally, during a quiet moment, he said in a louder than necessary voice, "Why did she have to die?"

Several people heard him, including Davey's mom. Most of the people tried to ignore the question, but Mrs. DeLeon turned toward Ben. Everyone wondered what she would say. She walked over to where he was sitting, knelt down, and said, "She had to die to go to heaven to be with Jesus."

Ben said, "Oh." It was all the reason he needed. He knew about Jesus and about heaven.

It was all the reason Mrs. DeLeon needed too. She had been confident in her mother's faith in Jesus as Savior. When Mrs. DeLeon was a little girl, she had learned Bible stories about Jesus being born and dying for all of us. Her mom had taught her that we can be sure of going to heaven when we die because our sins are forgiven. She remembered hearing that Jesus even prepared a place for us. It was a wonderful comfort for Mrs. DeLeon to relive those moments.

_____Let's talk: Have you told the people you love that you know you're going to heaven? Which people in your life would like to hear such news?

_____Let's pray: Dear Jesus, thank You for living and dying for us. Thank You for going to prepare a place for us to be with You in heaven. Amen.

C. B.

Fitting In

Mike and Brian had moved a lot. Now they were faced with yet another new school. This was the fifth time they had started at a new school.

Mike didn't like leaving friends behind and facing the difficulty of making new friends. Much to Mike's surprise, this school was different. The kids in his sixth-grade class were friendly to him. They even invited him to join their soccer team. He met a girl named Cori and they became friends right away. She was kind and gentle and cared about Mike's stories. She listened to him and helped him understand how things were done at this school.

Other people also were kind. One parent drove Mike and Brian to and from school when transportation was a problem. Brian's teacher was humorous and helped him enjoy school. One day Brian's baseball coach invited him to supper before practice. Brian had a great time and became good friends with the coach's kids.

After some time Mike said to his mom, "It finally feels like we're part of a community. People here care about us and include us. We can depend on them."

Mike had always depended on God for strength. He knew God had put these people in his life at just this time to give him and his brother a safe feeling. That night he thanked God for always being with him and for sending Jesus to provide eternal safety.

> **Read from God's Word**
>
> "Do not let this Book of the Law depart from your mouth; meditate on it day and night, so that you may be careful to do everything written in it. Then you will be prosperous and successful. Have I not commanded you? Be strong and courageous. Do not be terrified; do not be discouraged, for the LORD your God will be with you wherever you go."
> Joshua 1:8–9

_____Let's talk: Are there any new kids in your neighborhood? There may be some new students in your class in the fall. What could you do to make them feel welcome and safe?

_____Let's pray: Dear Jesus, thank You for the special people who care for us. Help us share kindness with those we meet, for Your sake. Amen.

C. B.

Read from God's Word

Be joyful always; pray continually; give thanks in all circumstances, for this is God's will for you in Christ Jesus. ... May God himself, the God of peace, sanctify you through and through. May your whole spirit, soul and body be kept blameless at the coming of our Lord Jesus Christ. The One who calls you is faithful and He will do it. 1 Thessalonians 5:16–18, 23–24

Pray Continually

Laura was surprised when she was chosen to read a Bible verse at the prayer service her class was presenting. Laura was quiet and a little shy. She got good grades, but didn't like to raise her hand and volunteer. Her friends were happy for her, but she was nervous.

At the service, the school band played beautifully. The pastor said a few words. Five other students read very long Bible selections during the service. Laura was to be last. When it was her turn, she cautiously approached the microphone, waited for the choir to finish their song, and said, "Pray continually."

Some of her friends were worried that Laura's shyness had made her stop too soon and not finish her verse. So right after the service they looked up the Bible verse. Much to their surprise and delight, 1 Thessalonians 5:17 read, "Pray continually." Such a short verse was a perfect way to close the service of prayer.

Mrs. Anderson, their teacher, noticed the commotion. She brought the class together, and they all read verses 16–18: "Be joyful always; pray continually; give thanks in all circumstances, for this is God's will for you in Christ Jesus."

We can always be joyful and thankful because God has given His Son as a Savior for us. With Jesus' love surrounding us in the words of the Gospel, we are joined to Him at all times.

_____Let's talk: At what times in your day could you speak to God and share your concerns? How does it help to know He is listening to you all the time?

_____Let's pray: Dear Jesus, remind us to talk to You often. Stay with us all day, and guide our thoughts and actions. Amen.

C. B.

A Matter of Conformity

I n Aaron's neighborhood there was a lot of pressure to conform. A group of kids hung around together and pretty much did the same things. Aaron wanted to be part of this group, and they willingly accepted him. They enjoyed being with one another and had a great time.

But once in awhile some of the guys made Aaron uncomfortable with their language. Aaron knew such words weren't acceptable in his house, but he told himself it wasn't a big deal. *Everybody does it,* he thought. Besides, the other kids would think he was weird if he said anything.

Aaron and his little sister, Anne, got along well. Anne was used to tagging along, teasing, and playing with Aaron even when his friends were at their house. During dinner one evening she used a word she had heard Aaron's friends use. Aaron was horrified.

Dad asked, "Anne, what does that mean?"

"I don't know," she replied.

Read from God's Word

Therefore, I urge you, brothers, in view of God's mercy, to offer your bodies as living sacrifices, holy and pleasing to God—this is your spiritual act of worship. Do not conform any longer to the pattern of this world, but be transformed by the renewing of your mind. Then you will be able to test and approve what God's will is—His good, pleasing and perfect will. Romans 12:1–2

Mom and Dad talked to her about being sure what she was saying. They also told her to come to them whenever she heard new words or had a question about them.

Aaron knew where Anne had picked up that word. It made him feel sick to know that it was his fault. That night when he was talking to God, he asked for forgiveness and for help to make the right decisions with his friends. He fell asleep peacefully, knowing that his prayer would be answered.

———Let's talk: Are you ever faced with a hard decision about the friends you have? How can you avoid conforming to their behavior?

———Let's pray: Dear Jesus, be in our lives every day. Help us conform to Your will and not the will of the world. Thank You for earning forgiveness for each of us on the cross. Amen.

C. B.

Staying on Track

ncle Bob loves model trains. In his basement he has a large model railroad with tracks going over bridges, through tunnels, and around mountains. The tracks also crisscross each other.

Bob uses a control panel to direct where each train will go. He also can throw a switch so trains will change tracks. As he turned on one train at a time, the children watched it move around the table. When he finished, they asked, "Why don't you run all your trains at the same time?"

"Oh," said Uncle Bob, "I can't keep track of where two trains are going. I can't switch tracks in time to keep them from crashing or derailing."

When they looked at the control panel again, the children could see how it would be hard to remember which button to push and to do it quickly. Uncle Bob was in control, but they weren't sure they wanted to be passengers on his train.

Do you ever think about who is in control of you? Our loving Father in heaven has given us parents to care for us and He knows everything that happens in our lives.

What a blessing to know that our Father in heaven is in control! Nothing is too hard or complicated for Him. Even when sin and the devil try to derail us, the Lord keeps us on track through the forgiveness won for us by Jesus, our Savior.

_____Let's talk: Have you ever "crashed" or "derailed" because you ignored your parents? How can you stay on the right track?

_____Let's pray: Dear Jesus, take control of our lives and help us stay on the right track. Amen.

J. M. W.

The Algae Cover-Up

Uncle Bob's saltwater aquarium is pretty large. It takes up about one-fourth of a wall in his basement. He chose salt water instead of fresh water because the fish that live in salt water are more brightly colored: vivid blues, yellows, oranges, purples, and greens.

A few weeks ago the children noticed that they could hardly see the fish through the glass because of the algae growing on it. They asked, "How do you get rid of that algae?"

Uncle Bob told them he uses a plastic card to scrape the glass and remove the algae. They came back one day to discover that Uncle Bob had cleaned the glass. Now they could see all those brightly colored fish.

Our lives are a lot like that aquarium—overgrown with algae. This makes it difficult to see the beauty inside. The algae that covers us is sin—things like breaking promises, forgetting to do chores, calling others names, telling lies, cheating at games, or excluding a friend from play.

Every day the algae of sin grows. We must turn to Jesus, our Savior, to be cleansed. No matter how hard we try to stay clean we know that sin will always be there, but that our heavenly Father will continue to forgive us.

How wonderful for us that our heavenly Father welcomes us as did the father in today's Bible reading—with loving, open arms, always ready to forgive us.

Read from God's Word

"He said, '... I am starving to death! I will set out and go back to my father and say to him: Father, I have sinned against heaven and against you. I am no longer worthy to be called your son; make me like one of your hired men.' ... But while he was still a long way off, his father saw him and was filled with compassion for him; he ran to his son, threw his arms around him and kissed him. ... The father said to his servants, '... Let's have a feast and celebrate. For this son of mine was dead and is alive again; he was lost and is found.' So they began to celebrate." Luke 15:17–24

_____Let's talk: What things happen in your life that need forgiving? How did Jesus cleanse you from sin?

_____Let's pray: Dear Lord Jesus, wash away our sins. Help us be more loving and kind. Amen.

J. M. W.

Who Will Rescue Me?

"Mom!" shouted Aaron. "Make Brad stop hitting me!"

Mom entered the bedroom just as Brad pulled a model airplane away from Aaron and punched him on the arm. "What's going on?" Mom wanted to know.

Brad was so angry he was shaking. "Every day Aaron takes my models off the shelf and plays with them."

"Brad," Mom said, "Aaron's too little to understand how important these are to you. You need to control your temper."

"I know," Brad responded. "I seem to be losing my temper a lot lately. Yesterday I got mad at Jon because he missed a fly ball. We could have won the game if he had caught it. I felt awful for making such a scene."

"Brad, Paul says in the Bible that he had the same kind of problem. He wanted to do good things. But even though he tried hard, he did evil things. He called himself a 'wretched man.' *Wretched* means miserable and unhappy."

"That's how I feel, Mom. What can I do?"

"Paul said that only God could rescue him," Mom said. "Paul knew he needed to ask for Jesus' forgiveness and guidance and to trust that Jesus would help him. We can talk to Jesus in prayer. He forgives us too and helps us do better."

"Thanks, Mom," Brad replied.

_____Let's talk: Are there times when you intend to do good things but end up hurting someone? What could you say to Jesus when that happens?

_____Let's pray: Dear Jesus, we can't do anything good by ourselves. Guard us and guide us this day, and forgive whatever we do wrong. Amen.

J. M. W.

I Follow Christ

ebbie, will you read my paper?" asked Nathan. "Tell me if I spelled all the words correctly."

"Sure," said Debbie. "What are you writing about?"

"Mr. Ellert, my Sunday school teacher, is helping our class make a book that tells about our faith. He's going to put it in our church library."

"Oh, I see," Debbie said. "This looks pretty good. Oh, oh—you didn't spell *Christian* correctly. You wrote 'C-h-r-i-s-t-a-i-n.' You did fine spelling the first part: 'C-h-r-i-s-t.' Did Mr. Ellert tell you how to remember to spell *Christian?* The letter after Christ is *i.* Just remember that you are a follower of Christ. Then you can say, '*I follows Christ.*' The rest is easy! Try it."

Nathan thought about it. "That *is* easier," he said. "Wait till I tell the other kids. You know, Debbie, I thought the disciples were called Christians before Jesus died on the cross. I was surprised to learn that that happened later on. I wonder how the believers felt when others called them Christians?"

"Nathan, do you know when you were first called a Christian? It was when you were baptized. Jesus made you His own and gave you His name. That was a special day for you. "Now you can say, *I follows Christ.*"

_____Let's talk: How do you feel about being called a Christian? What does it mean to you?

_____Let's pray: Dear Jesus, thank You for giving each of us Your name at our Baptism. Help us follow You every day. Amen.

J. M. W.

Read from God's Word

Now those who had been scattered by the persecution in connection with Stephen traveled as far as Phoenicia, Cyprus and Antioch. ... The Lord's hand was with them, and a great number of people believed and turned to the Lord. ... When [Barnabas] arrived and saw the evidence of the grace of God, he was glad and encouraged them all to remain true to the Lord with all their hearts. ... A great number of people were brought to the Lord. ... For a whole year Barnabas and Saul ... taught great numbers of people. The disciples were called Christians first at Antioch. Acts 11:19–26

Someone Special

One February afternoon Mrs. Grant left school early because she didn't feel well. The next morning the students saw a substitute teacher when they arrived. On the chalkboard was a note: "Dear class, Chad arrived just before midnight. He has lots of dark hair and is a very special baby." Amy could hardly wait to tell her mother.

The next day the principal explained that Mrs. Grant's baby had Down syndrome. Chad would look different from other children. He would have a larger forehead and slanting eyes. He would learn things very slowly. The students were worried and upset. How could this happen?

When Amy came home, she went right to her room, laid on her bed, and cried. When her mother came in, Amy explained what the principal had told the class. "Oh, Mom, poor Mrs. Grant. She must feel awful that Chad is different. Did God make a mistake?"

Mother wiped Amy's tears and gave her a hug. "Amy, do you remember what the Bible says about God's creation—'God saw all that He had made, and it was very good.' You know that God makes all kinds of people, and not one of them is a mistake. The mistake is with us—how we treat people who are different. Children who have Down syndrome are very loving and happy. That's a very special thing. Chad is special! He too is loved and redeemed by Jesus."

———Let's talk: Do you know children who are "different" or "special"? How can you show God's love to them?

———Let's pray: Dear Lord, help us show Your love to all Your creation, but especially to Your special children. In Jesus' name we ask this. Amen.

J. M. W.

Lost and Found

This was David's first time to baby-sit Mark, his six-year-old brother. Mom gave some final instructions: "Be sure that Mark goes to bed by 8:30. You can read his new book—*The Lost Sheep*—to him."

Mark seemed very interested in the story. He asked, "Why didn't the little sheep stay with his mother?"

David scratched his head. "I guess the little sheep wasn't paying attention to where his mother was. He just wandered off. Remember when Mom took you to Target and asked you to hold onto the shopping cart while she chose a birthday card? You saw your friend Mike and went over to talk to him. Then you walked away with Mike and his dad."

"Oh, yes," remembered Mark. "Mom was really worried when she couldn't find me. She looked all over. Then she asked a man to call me on the loudspeaker. Mike's dad took me to find Mom. I knew I was in trouble!"

"Was Mom mad at you?" asked David.

"Well, yes-s-s, but she was really glad to see me too."

David added, "Jesus said that people are like sheep. They wander off and get into trouble or into dangerous situations. Jesus finds them and forgives them. He is happy when all His people are with Him."

"Just like Mom was glad to find me?" Mark wondered.

"Exactly. Jesus wants you with Him always."

_____Let's talk: Can you remember a time when you were lost? What did you do? Have you ever been lost from Jesus?

_____Let's pray: Thank You, Jesus, for loving us. Keep us close to You always. Amen.

J. M. W.

Read from God's Word

Jesus told them this parable: "Suppose one of you has a hundred sheep and loses one of them. Does he not leave the ninety-nine in the open country and go after the lost sheep until he finds it? And when he finds it, he joyfully puts it on his shoulders and goes home. Then he calls his friends and neighbors together and says, 'Rejoice with me; I have found my lost sheep.' I tell you that in the same way there will be more rejoicing in heaven over one sinner who repents than over ninety-nine righteous persons who do not need to repent." Luke 15:3

august

Contributors for this month:

Lisa Ellwein

Lisa A. Hahn

Jacqueline L. Loontjer

Nathan Monke

Eleanor Schlegl

Roger Sonnenberg

Our Ladder to the Sky

The sky is falling! The sky is falling!" Chicken Little is a silly story, but some people even today believe some very unusual things.

For example, a tribe in Africa believes that long ago the sky was close to the earth. It was so close, in fact, that people could reach up and touch it. They began to take little pieces out of the sky. They became greedy and took bigger and bigger chunks. This made their god angry, so he pulled the sky higher out of their reach.

A missionary came to Africa and heard this story. He told the people, "God is not angry anymore, and He brought the sky back down to you! The cross of Jesus is your ladder to the sky."

The missionary didn't mean that the people would be able to climb the ladder and touch the sky. He meant that Jesus brought God's love from heaven to us. That missionary followed St. Paul's example. Paul talked about something the people of Athens would understand—the statue marked "to an unknown god." Then he told the people about the one true God, who made the world and everything in it.

The missionary to Africa started with something familiar to the people, the sky. Then he taught them the truth about God's love for them. This is also a good way for us to do missionary work. Start with what a friend understands then lead him or her toward Jesus, the Savior.

Read from God's Word

[Paul] said: "... I see that in every way you are very religious. For as I walked around and looked carefully at your objects of worship, I even found an altar with this inscription: TO AN UNKNOWN GOD. Now what you worship as something unknown I am going to proclaim to you. ... [God] made every nation of men, that they should inhabit the whole earth. ... God did this so that man would seek Him and perhaps reach out for Him and find Him, though He is not far from each one of us. 'For in Him we live and move and have our being.' As some of your own poets have said, 'We are His offspring.'" Acts 17:22–28 ✍

_____Let's talk: Look up *atmosphere* in an encyclopedia. How many blessings of God that come from the sky can you think of?

_____Let's pray: Thank You, Jesus, for being our ladder to heaven. Empower us with Your Spirit so we might follow Paul's example and share Your love with others. Amen.

E. S.

Read from God's Word

O LORD. You have searched me and You know me. You know when I sit and when I rise; You perceive my thoughts from afar. You discern my going out and my lying down; You are familiar with all my ways. Before a word is on my tongue You know it completely. O LORD. ... For You created my inmost being; You knit me together in my mother's womb. I praise You because I am fearfully and wonderfully made; Your works are wonderful. I know that full well. Psalm 139:1–4, 13–14

My Favorite Adult

Who is a favorite adult in your life besides your parent(s)? It's probably someone who takes a very special interest in you. Maybe it's a teacher, pastor, family friend, or neighbor. Maybe it's your Godparent at Baptism. Maybe it's a special uncle who took you on your first roller coaster ride. Maybe it's a special aunt who helped you learn to write your name. Whoever it is, it is someone you will remember and cherish for the rest of your life.

There is a very special Someone who takes the greatest interest of all in each one of us. It's God, our heavenly Father. Psalm 139:13 tells us that God knew us before we were born. It says, "For You created my inmost being; You knit me together in my mother's womb."

God calls us by name and knows everything about us. This is not meant to scare us but to be a great comfort for us. God knows and cares about the time you fell off your bike and got hurt. He knows when your stomach aches. He knows and cares when someone is mean to you.

God loves us so much that He planned a way for us to be with Him in heaven forever. He sent His Son, Jesus, as a Savior—for each and every one of us!

_____Let's talk: God knew you and loved you before the creation of the world. Why is this a wonderful thing to remember?

_____Let's pray: Heavenly Father, thank You for caring for us and sending Jesus as our Savior from sin. Surround our loved ones with Your divine protection. Amen.

E. S.

God's Work of Art

Read from God's Word

Love never fails. But where there are prophecies, they will cease; where there are tongues, they will be stilled; where there is knowledge, it will pass away. For we know in part and we prophesy in part, but when perfection comes, the imperfect disappears. ... Now we see but a poor reflection as in a mirror; then we shall see face to face. Now I know in part; then I shall know fully, even as I am fully known. And now these three remain: faith, hope and love. But the greatest of these is love. 1 Corinthians 13:8–13 ᕙᕗ

H urry up, Jamien. You'll be late for your ball game!" "Get a move on, Rico. We want to leave by eight o'clock!" "Hurry, hurry!" Do these words sound familiar?

Way back in the year 1508, Michelangelo, a famous artist, was painting the ceiling of the Sistine Chapel in Rome. For four and a half years he painted while lying on his back. He'd reach up, using one hand and then the other. When people came into the Sistine Chapel and looked up, they saw boards and scaffolding. They could see only snatches of the great art being created above them. *Will he ever get done?* they wondered.

Then, in 1512, Michelangelo finally completed his work. The people looked up and marveled at the magnificent painting on the ceiling. It was worth the wait.

God's work of art is already complete. He looks down on us from heaven and sees the whole picture. His Son, Jesus, came to live a perfect life on earth. Jesus died on the cross for the sins of the world and rose in glorious victory. His work is done.

Here on earth we are like the people looking up and seeing only part of the picture. St. Paul tells us, "Now we see but a poor reflection as in a mirror; then we shall see face to face." Someday our view will be different. We will see God's complete and perfect work in heaven. "Now I know in part; then I shall know fully, even as I am fully known."

_____Let's talk: What were some things people waited for in Bible times? How was their waiting rewarded? How does God give us what we wait for?

_____Let's pray: Jesus, help us live our lives for You on earth and remember our promised life with You in heaven. Amen.

E. S.

Blue Belle

Read from God's Word

"Are not two sparrows sold for a penny? Yet not one of them will fall to the ground apart from the will of your Father. And even the very hairs of your head are all numbered. So don't be afraid; you are worth more than many sparrows." Matthew 10:29–31 ✍

All weekend Allison prayed and prayed that her missing parakeet would come home. Blue Belle had never been out of the house before. *How will he feed himself?* Allison wondered. There were so many things that could happen to a tame parakeet in the wild. Allison prayed that if he didn't come back to her, he would at least find a nice home.

Between Friday and Sunday, Blue Belle somehow flew 10 miles to a farm outside the city. He landed on the shoulder of Maria, a farmer's wife. He stayed on her shoulder and went right inside the farmhouse with her. Maria liked Blue Belle and gave him some cereal and water. The next day she called the radio station to ask if anyone had lost a parakeet.

Allison's neighbor was listening to the radio. She knew all about the missing bird and phoned to tell Allison that Blue Belle was safe. That day Allison and her mother drove to the farm to get Blue Belle. Allison believed that God had kept the little bird safe. She knew her prayers had been answered. She shared her story with others.

Since God cares so much about a small, helpless bird, just think how much more He cares about you! God rescued Blue Belle from living in the wild, and He rescued you from sin and the power of the devil. He cares so much about you that He sent His own Son, Jesus, to save you.

_____Let's talk: How does God protect you and your family every day? How can you thank Him?

_____Let's pray: Lord, thank You for saving us from sin and the power of the devil. Lead us to put all our trust in You. Amen.

E. S.

Clothes for Jesus

D ozens of cute, little dresses were on hangers in the hallway of the church. "Who is going to wear those dresses?" Bethany asked.

"They're going to be shipped to Papua New Guinea," her mother answered.

"You mean little New Guinea girls are going to be wearing them?"

"That's right," Mother replied. "And we're sending shirts and shorts for the boys."

Bethany went home and looked for Papua New Guinea on her globe. She found it just north of Australia. Two months later her church received a letter from a missionary in that country. He sounded excited that two boxes of dresses had arrived safely. But he was very sorry to say that the box with shirts and shorts was missing.

Bethany and her mother prayed that the missing box would somehow reach the children. It took three more

"Then the King will say to those on his right, 'Come, you who are blessed by My Father; take your inheritance, the kingdom prepared for you since the creation of the world. For I was hungry and you gave Me something to eat, I was thirsty and you gave Me something to drink, I was a stranger and you invited Me in, I needed clothes and you clothed Me, I was sick and you looked after Me, I was in prison and you came to visit Me. ... I tell you the truth, whatever you did for one of the least of these brothers of Mine, you did for Me.'" Matthew 25:34–40 ✍

months before they learned that their prayers were answered. News came that the last box had finally arrived at the mission station. When the missionary gave the clothes to the children, he told them that Christian friends in the United States had sent the dresses, shirts, and shorts for them.

It wasn't until Bethany saw pictures of the children wearing those clothes that she understood what had really happened. In Matthew 25:40 Jesus tells us, "Whatever you did for one of the least of these brothers of Mine, you did for Me." Making those clothes for the children of Papua New Guinea was like making them for Jesus.

_____Let's talk: What are some ways your church spreads the hope of Jesus to others through mission projects?

_____Let's pray: Dear Jesus, You are the Savior of the world. Help us share Your Gospel message with all nations. Amen.

E. S.

Read from God's Word

Endure hardship as discipline; God is treating you as sons. For what son is not disciplined by his father? If you are not disciplined (and everyone undergoes discipline), then you are illegitimate children and not true sons. Moreover, we have all had human fathers who disciplined us and we respected them for it. How much more should we submit to the Father of our spirits and live! Our fathers disciplined us for a little while as they thought best; but God disciplines us for our good, that we may share in His holiness. No discipline seems pleasant at the time, but painful. Later on, however, it produces a harvest of righteousness and peace for those who have been trained by it. Hebrews 12:7–11

Well Seasoned

Little Sarah stood on a chair in the kitchen and watched her mother make chili. Sarah saw the beans in the pot, the beef in the skillet, and the chopped onions on the counter. She also noticed small bottles of oregano, bay leaves, and chili powder. "Why did you put so little of that stuff in?" Sarah asked.

"Because if I put in too much, the chili will be ruined," her mom replied. "If I put in too little, the chili will be tasteless. Here, take a sniff."

Sarah pulled her nose back from the bottles. "Pretty strong, huh?" said Mom. Sarah nodded.

Perhaps you've tasted some food that had too many seasonings. Maybe you know a friend whose parents criticize or punish too harshly. Maybe your bike gets broken or stolen, or perhaps your best friend turns away from you. At times it seems like things just go against you. Maybe you even feel that sometimes God isn't treating you fairly.

Our God is always faithful to His Word. He promises to correct us without destroying us. In doing so He uses just the right seasoning in just the right amounts in our life.

The Bible assures us: "The Lord disciplines those He loves" (Hebrews 12:6). Our Father brought us to Himself through the death and resurrection of His Son, Jesus. Our Father continues to show us His love as He leads us through trials and setbacks to our home above.

_____Let's talk: Have you ever felt that God gave you too much to bear? How does today's Bible reading bring out God's wonderful plan for you?

_____Let's pray: Dear Lord, deal with us according to Your will. Correct us when we need correction, but help us always to remember that You treat us as Your dear children. We ask this in our Savior's name. Amen.

N. M.

Flying Blind

Read from God's Word

But now, this is what the LORD says—He who created you, O Jacob, He who formed you, O Israel: "Fear not, for I have redeemed you; I have summoned you by name; you are Mine. When you pass through the waters, I will be with you; and when you pass through the rivers, they will not sweep over you. When you walk through the fire, you will not be burned; the flames will not set you ablaze. For I am the LORD, your God. Isaiah 43:1–3a*

Marty Santos was flying alone at night in his airplane. Suddenly there was a severe thunderstorm. Marty couldn't see outside and he became confused and frightened. He took a few deep breaths and asked God to help him.

Then Marty radioed the control tower and told the commander that he was flying blind. Neal, who was commanding the tower, could see Marty's plane on his radar screen. "Just follow my orders, and I'll bring you down safely," he assured the frightened pilot. Neal kept speaking to Marty in a calm, easy voice, telling him exactly what to do. Marty put complete trust in Neal and followed all his orders. The plane landed right on target.

In our lives we sometimes feel like we are flying blind. We don't know what is ahead of us in our future. We can't see God's plan for us. When we feel like this, God's Word guides and comforts us. God tells us in Isaiah 43:2, "When you pass through the waters, I will be with you; and when you pass through the rivers, they will not sweep over you."

We can put our complete trust in our supreme Commander. God has kept every promise He ever made to us, especially the promise to rescue us from the dangers of sin and eternal death. Although we can't see Him, our Lord is always with us. We know this by faith, and we trust in His promises.

_____Let's talk: Suppose you are traveling in a car, train, or plane. What would you say to God if you were facing great danger?

_____Let's pray: Lord, You are indeed the Holy One of Israel, our Savior. Thank You for Your promise to be with us always. Amen.

E. S.

Read from God's Word

Jesus ... said to them, "Are you asking one another what I meant when I said, 'In a little while you will see Me no more, and then after a little while you will see Me'? I tell you the truth, you will weep and mourn while the world rejoices. You will grieve, but your grief will turn to joy. A woman giving birth to a child has pain because her time has come; but when her baby is born she forgets the anguish because of her joy that a child is born into the world. So with you: Now is your time of grief, but I will see you again and you will rejoice, and no one will take away your joy. John 16:19–22

From Sorrow to Joy

Franklin sat on the edge of his bed with a deep frown on his face. One foot was bare and the other had a sock pulled on halfway. His mother came into his room and said, "Franklin, you have to leave in half an hour. I know you're still sad, but it will pass."

Franklin was sad because his dad had backed the car over his bicycle in the driveway. Franklin's bicycle had been very special to him. It was painted blue and gold, and it really shined in the sun.

Franklin's friends had all admired the bike. Even some adults had complimented him on it. But now it was ruined. This morning Franklin felt that he would never get over his loss. His sorrow would last forever. He didn't want to go to school or even eat breakfast.

Jesus knew that we would be filled with sorrow at many different times and over many things. Soon after our Savior ascended into heaven, He sent the Holy Spirit to comfort us in our sorrows and to encourage us onward. He said, "You will grieve, but your grief will turn to joy" (John 16:20).

Jesus knew what it felt like to be sad. He bore the weight of the world's sins in Gethsemane and on the cross. But in doing so, He removed the biggest cause for worry, grief, and sadness from our lives—that is, the threat of being lost from God forever. Now we have real joy and hope. Jesus has won eternal salvation for us!

_____Let's talk: What kinds of things make you feel sad or fill you with sorrow? Where can you go for help when you need to talk to someone? Has God answered a prayer you prayed when you felt sad?

_____Let's pray: Dear Jesus, help us look to You in times of sorrow. Help us remember Your promise of love and support. We trust that in You we will find the joy that lasts. Amen.

N. M.

Kristi's Experiment

Kristi had two hamsters, Goldie and Hambone. She kept them in separate cages, but she treated them exactly the same way. She gave them exactly the same amount of food and water. She cleaned their cages on the same day and spent the same amount of time talking to each one. There was only one thing that was different— Goldie had an exercise wheel in his cage and Hambone did not.

How can a young man keep his way pure? By living according to Your word. I seek you with all my heart; do not let me stray from Your commands. I have hidden Your word in my heart that I might not sin against You. Praise be to You, O LORD; teach me Your decrees. With my lips I recount all the laws that come from Your mouth. I rejoice in following Your statutes as one rejoices in great riches. I meditate on Your precepts and consider your ways. I delight in Your decrees; I will not neglect Your word. Psalm 119:9–16

Kristi watched the two hamsters for six weeks and made notes. From the beginning of the experiment, she noticed that Goldie was more active during the day. He moved his shavings around and piled them up in one corner. Every time Kristi looked at Goldie's cage, the shavings had been moved.

Hambone slept most of the time. His shavings were spread out on the bottom of the cage, and they stayed that way. He moved around only a little. Kristi's experiment showed that exercise is important.

Christians also need exercise. We need exercise for our souls. The Holy Spirit works though God's Word and the Sacraments to keep us in faith. If we neglect these, our faith will not grow strong and healthy. That's why it is important to read our Bibles daily and listen to God's Word in church and Sunday school.

May God give us faith like that of Peter when he said to Jesus, "You have the words of eternal life. We believe and know that You are the Holy One of God" (John 6:68–69).

_____Let's talk: How do you exercise your body? How do you exercise your soul?

_____Let's pray: Lord Jesus, we can never thank You enough for coming into this world to rescue us from sin, death, and the power of the devil. Help us by Your Spirit to grow in Your Word and in loving You. Amen.

E. S.

Dirty Feet

Read from God's Word

[Jesus] poured water into a basin and began to wash His disciples' feet. ... He came to Simon Peter, who said to Him, "Lord, are You going to wash my feet?" Jesus replied, ... "Unless I wash you, you have no part with Me." ... "Do you understand what I have done for you?" He asked them. "You call Me 'Teacher' and 'Lord,' and rightly so, for that is what I am. Now that I, your Lord and Teacher, have washed your feet, you also should wash one another's feet. I have set you an example that you should do as I have done for you." John 13:5–9, 12–15 ⮐

During the summer we often wear sandals. By nighttime our feet are dirty from being outside in the hot, dusty air.

In Bible times, people wore sandals all year long. They lived in a hot, dry climate and walked on dirt roads. It was the custom in those days to wash your feet before entering a house. People kept large containers of water by their doors for this purpose.

It was the servant's job to wash the feet of visitors. It would certainly be amazing if a teacher washed the feet of his students. But that's exactly what Jesus did when He washed the feet of His disciples. No wonder Peter tried to stop Jesus.

Jesus teaches us that serving others is an honorable task. Whenever we feel proud and snobbish, we ought to stop for a minute to think about Jesus, the Mighty God and Prince of Peace who washed His disciples' feet.

With this simple act, Jesus taught His disciples two lessons. He taught them to serve others. He also showed them that He was going to wash their sins away.

Our Bible reading reminds us that Jesus washes us and makes us clean. He took the role of a servant for us when He humbled Himself and died on Calvary's cross. With grateful hearts, Jesus helps us follow His example and serve one another in love.

_____Let's talk: What are some ways we can show our thanks to Jesus? What are some ways we can be a servant to others?

_____Let's pray: Lord and Teacher, thank You for washing away our sins. Thank You for the example You have given us in Your Word. Help us by Your Spirit to live in humble service to others. Amen.

E. S.

Faith Is Free

D o these things: Clap your hands. Cross your legs. Shut your eyes. Say, "Good morning." If you were able to do these things, it was because of the way God made you. God gives you control of certain muscles like those in your arms and your mouth.

Now, try to make your heart stop beating. Can you do it? Of course not. Your heart doesn't beat because you tell it to—it works on its own! God has made your body so your heart's muscles are involuntary. That means you can do nothing to make those muscles move. Only God has control over your heart beat.

Paul's letter to the Romans says it is in your heart that you believe in Jesus as your Savior. It says your mouth can tell about your faith, but it's in your heart that God helps you believe in Him.

God alone did all the work of coming into your heart. Through His Word and through Baptism, He gave you the gift of faith and trust in Jesus, who was crucified to rescue you from eternal death.

Today, thank God that you didn't have to do anything to receive your faith in Jesus as your Savior. Pray that others will realize that faith is God's work, not theirs. Pray they will know that God works in our hearts and gives faith and eternal life for free.

Read from God's Word

That if you confess with Your mouth, "Jesus is Lord," and believe in your heart that God raised Him from the dead, you will be saved. For it is with your heart that you believe and are justified, and it is with your mouth that you confess and are saved. As the Scripture says, "Anyone who trusts in Him will never be put to shame." For there is no difference between Jew and Gentile—the same Lord is Lord of all and richly blesses all who call on Him, for, "Everyone who calls on the name of the Lord will be saved." Romans 10:9–13

_____Let's talk: Can you think of someone who doesn't know about God's free gift? Ask the Lord to help you tell them. When did God give you the gift of faith?

_____Let's pray: Thank You, God, that Your Word clearly tells us about Your wonderful love in Jesus. Give us words to clearly share this message with others. In Jesus' name. Amen.

L. A. H.

It's Good to Be Home

Read from God's Word

Join with others in following my example, brothers, and take note of those who live according to the pattern we gave you. For, as I have often told you before and now say again even with tears, many live as enemies of the cross of Christ. Their destiny is destruction, their god is their stomach, and their glory is in their shame. Their mind is on earthly things. But our citizenship is in heaven. And we eagerly await a Savior from there, the Lord Jesus Christ, who, by the power that enables Him to bring everything under His control, will transform our lowly bodies so that they will be like His glorious body. Philippians 3:17–21

"Home at last!" said Quentin. He plopped down on his bed and gazed around his room. He had had a great time with his family in Mexico, but some things had been difficult. He knew only a few Spanish words. He also had trouble paying for candy with *centavos* instead of pennies. He was glad to return to his old, familiar surroundings.

Have you ever felt like Quentin? No matter where you live, God has provided a place for you and your family to call home. If you've ever been away from home, you probably felt just like Quentin when you returned. It felt good to be home.

God has given you an earthly home. He's made a place where you and your family can enjoy life on earth. But did you know that the place you live right now isn't really your home? It's true that your room and all your things are there, but God's Word tells us that our real home is in heaven. We're only living on this earth until it's time to be with Him forever.

God prepared an eternal home for you before the world began, when He decided that His Son would give up His life to pay for all your sins. You can even look forward to the day you leave this earth. When you enter heaven and sit next to Jesus, you'll be able to exclaim, "It's good to be home!"

———Let's talk: Think about a time when you felt like you didn't fit in because you were a Christian. Now list three things you can look forward to in heaven.

———Let's pray: Father in heaven, please help us look forward to living with You forever in heaven. Thank You for forgiving us and for preparing our home with You. In Jesus' name. Amen.

L. A. H.

Forgive Completely

Read from God's Word

Therefore, as God's chosen people, holy and dearly loved, clothe yourselves with compassion, kindness, humility, gentleness and patience. Bear with each other and forgive whatever grievances you may have against one another. Forgive as the Lord forgave you. And over all these virtues put on love, which binds them all together in perfect unity. Colossians 3:12–14 ⌒

Marcell reached down to pick up his brother's rattle. He sighed as he put it into Michael's little hand. Michael smiled from his high chair. He played for a while. Then his rattle fell to the floor again. He began to cry and scream.

Marcell felt like he had handed back the rattle a hundred times. Sometimes it seemed like Michael was throwing it down on purpose, just to see what his big brother would do. Marcell was ready to give up and just let Michael cry.

Throughout the Bible there was something God's people kept dropping—their trust in Him. They would be happy and follow God for a while. Then they would just drop God out of their lives. This happened many times. Each time they turned away from Him, trouble came to them. They would cry out to God to save them. God would rescue them again and again.

We are blessed that God never gets tired of hearing our cries and never turns His back on us. Although we turn away from Him every day when we sin, He is always there to listen and forgive. He never gets tired of picking us up and setting us back on the right path. In turn, we can also forgive others. We do this because of Jesus, who took the punishment for our sins out of His great love for us. And He helps us to love and forgive others every day.

_____Let's talk: Are there times when is it hard for you to forgive? Practice saying some words to use the next time you need to forgive someone.

_____Let's pray: Lord Jesus, You forgave people who hurt You and even killed You. You forgive us every day. Please help us forgive in the way that You do. In Your name, Lord. Amen.

L. A. H.

Don't Be Fooled!

Read from God's Word

Finally, be strong in the Lord and in His mighty power. Put on the full armor of God so that you can take your stand against the devil's schemes. For our struggle is not against flesh and blood, but against the rulers, against the authorities, against the powers of this dark world and against the spiritual forces of evil in the heavenly realms. Therefore put on the full armor of God, so that when the day of evil comes, you may be able to stand your ground, and after you have done everything, to stand. Ephesians 6:10–13

One of Lisa's favorite things to do when traveling was to watch for special sights along the way. A huge church stood along one of the routes she and her family often took. It was made from smooth stones and had a very different design. It was lit up at night, making it even more impressive.

Lisa read the sign in front of the church. As she read it, her heart sank. For this incredible building was not a place for worshiping the one true God. It was a temple built for worshiping idols! She was sad that she would never be able to attend a service to see the inside.

There are things we come across each day that are like that beautiful temple. They look inviting from the outside but are not pleasing to God on the inside. Today's Bible reading reminds us how tricky Satan can be. He is very smooth and sly when it comes to deceiving us. He puts things in our paths such as gossiping, lying, and talking back to our parents. Satan makes such things look great on the outside. But that doesn't change how sinful they really are on the inside.

We can be thankful that God is always there to show us our sin, hear our confession, and forgive us. We're so dear to Him that He didn't spare His only Son but gave Him up to save us. Such great love moves us to resist temptation.

_____Let's talk: What are some evil things Satan tempts you to do? What can you do the next time he tries to trick you?

_____Let's pray: Dear God, thank You for parents and teachers who help us follow Your way. Teach us to watch out for Satan and to depend on Your guidance. In Jesus' name. Amen.

L. A. H.

Remember to Praise Him

When is your birthday? It probably didn't take you very long to answer that! Why do you suppose we remember birthdays? Maybe it's because birthdays are fun celebrations with a birthday cake, a favorite meal, gifts, or special guests.

In the Book of Psalms, God encourages us to remember His miracles of long ago and to consider His mighty deeds. God provides us with special places and times to worship Him and remember Him. Every Sunday we have an opportunity to go to church and do just that.

But sometimes we may not feel like going to church. Maybe we're too tired or have other things we'd like to do. If thoughts like these keep us away from church too many times, we could be tempted to drift away from fellowship with other Christians. We might even forget some of the things God has done for us, like His miracles or even His forgiveness. And we might even forget the joy of following Him.

We can be thankful that God doesn't ever forget about us. He is always loving us, caring for us, and giving us the great blessings Jesus won for us by His life, death, and resurrection. We can thank God for blessing us with a time to worship and remember His goodness and faithfulness. May we always remember to praise and thank Him.

Read from God's Word

I will remember the deeds of the LORD; yes, I will remember Your miracles of long ago. I will meditate on all Your works and consider all Your mighty deeds. Your ways, O God, are holy. What god is so great as our God? You are the God who performs miracles; You display Your power among the peoples. With Your mighty arm You redeemed Your people, the descendants of Jacob and Joseph. Psalm 77:11 15 ✐

_____Let's talk: What are some things that tempt you to dislike going to church? Talk about them as a family. What is your favorite part of church? Thank God for it.

_____Let's pray: Lord, we can think of so many things You do for us. Help us have a good attitude about going to church to praise You for them. May every breath and every beat of our hearts be dedicated to Your praise and glory. In Jesus' name. Amen.

L. A. H.

Read from God's Word

But you are a chosen people, a royal priesthood, a holy nation, a people belonging to God, that you may declare the praises of Him who called you out of darkness into His wonderful light. Once you were not a people, but now you are the people of God; once you had not received mercy, but now you have received mercy.
1 Peter 2:9–10

Chosen by God

It was the end of the first school day. Excitement filled the air—tonight was the back-to-school banquet. Mrs. Tran stood patiently in the front of the classroom. She was waiting to draw a name out of her blue basket. The chosen student would be the class representative at the principal's table at dinner that evening.

Mrs. Tran carefully unfolded the small square of paper she had chosen. The class was silent as she smiled and said, "Olivia Harris." Olivia's face beamed in surprise. As her friends congratulated her, she began to get excited about the special evening ahead.

Have you ever been chosen for something special at school? Maybe your parents choose you to do certain jobs at home. It's a good feeling to be chosen.

1 Peter 2:9 points out that as a Christian, you have been chosen by God. It says that you belong to Him. Wow! God loved you enough to plan that Jesus would die for you to give you a place in heaven. Besides that, He calls you royal and holy!

The Bible reading also tells about something you get to do because you are chosen and holy. It says you may declare God's praises. God loves to hear your praise in the way you think, talk, sing, and act as His child. Praising God in these ways is a great way to thank Him for calling you His own royal servant. Take time to enjoy your privilege today. Praise the Lord!

_____Let's talk: What are two ways you can praise the Lord? Do one of those things right now.

_____Let's pray: Lord God, it's so exciting that You have chosen us. Thank You for never changing Your mind about loving us. Help us praise You today for making us Your royal, holy children. In Jesus' name. Amen.

L. A. H.

Eyes upon Jesus

Once a young man saw a woman who was blind. She was walking downtown with her guide dog. He stood on the other side of the street, waiting to cross. He watched the woman and her dog as they walked down the busy sidewalk. Nothing special happened. *So what?* you ask. Why even mention such an unremarkable sight?

Actually, it was *very* remarkable. The fact that a dog can become the woman's eyes is cause for wonder. The blind woman would have a much harder time without her dog. She might cross the street in front of busy traffic or bump into a wall or another person. But with a Seeing Eye dog, she can safely cross streets and go wherever she wants.

Our God is very remarkable. In our blindness, we go our own way. Instead of obeying God, we turn against Him and against our neighbor. Through His Word, our Lord reminds us of Jesus and His death on the cross for our sins. By faith in God's Son, we become whole again.

Jesus healed a man who had been blind from birth by spitting in the dust and putting the mud on the man's eyes. We, too, are healed as we look to the Lord. He keeps us from stumbling in the darkness of our sinful ways. Praise God that He is leading us each and every day.

Read from God's Word

His disciples asked Him, "Rabbi, who sinned, this man or his parents, that he was born blind?" "Neither ..." said Jesus, "but this happened so that the work of God might be displayed in his life. As long as it is day, we must do the work of Him who sent Me. Night is coming, when no one can work. While I am in the world, I am the light of the world." Having said this, He spit on the ground, made some mud with the saliva, and put it on the man's eyes. "Go," He told him, "wash in the Pool of Siloam" (this word means Sent). So the man went and washed, and came home seeing. John 9:2–7 ✍

———Let's talk: A popular hymn tells us to fix our eyes upon Jesus. What happens to the things of this world when we look into our Savior's face? Why are His glory and grace better than anything on earth?

———Let's pray: Heavenly Father, give us eyes that see Your wonderful work in our daily lives. Help us focus on Jesus, who died and rose to save us from being lost in spiritual blindness. Amen.

N. M.

Keep On Climbing

Read from God's Word

"Blessed are those who are persecuted because of righteousness, for theirs is the kingdom of heaven. Blessed are you when people insult you, persecute you and falsely say all kinds of evil against you because of Me. Rejoice and be glad, because great is your reward in heaven, for in the same way they persecuted the prophets who were before you." Matthew 5:10–12 ✑

Bernie couldn't wait to see the waterfall. Someone had built stairs going up to the top of the cliff. It would be nice to stop and rest. It would be more comfortable to go back down and relax. But Bernie kept on climbing.

Soon his legs began to ache. His lungs felt tight. But the sound of the rushing water kept him climbing. He kept thinking about seeing the waterfall. When he finally reached the top, the view was incredible. The sun made the river sparkle and dance as it poured over rocks to the pool below. Bernie soon forgot about his long, hard climb.

Sometimes life can feel like a long, hard climb. We may have problems that don't seem to go away. We may try our very best at things and have them turn out all wrong. Maybe we even suffer at times because others know we are Christian.

Jesus knew what it was like to have a long, hard climb. He worked hard and was hated and rejected by many. Finally, He was killed. He did all this for us—so we would be eternally safe and happy.

Jesus knew these things were going to happen to Him. He knew He would suffer and He knew His followers would suffer too. So He gave us words of encouragement. He said we are blessed when we suffer for Him. He said that it means we are being powerful witnesses. He said to rejoice in this and to think about heaven. What a great idea!

_____Let's talk: What can you do to rejoice when it's hard for you to act as a Christian?

_____Let's pray: Lord God, we know that being a Christian isn't easy. Thank You for forgiving our sins. May the gift of Your forgiveness remind us to think about heaven when life on earth gets hard. In Jesus' name. Amen.

L. A. H.

Lighting the World

Thomas Edison perfected the light bulb. He was the first inventor to make electric lights available for homes and offices. Edison experimented with many materials for two years, trying to find the perfect filament. (The filament is the tiny wire in the bulb that lights up.) What finally worked was ordinary sewing thread. The first light bulb Edison used with the thread stayed lit for more than 24 hours. When the news got out, the rest of the world was astounded.

How much more astonished the world ought be with our God. He didn't need to experiment when He created light. He just said, "Let there be light." It happened instantly, and our world continues to depend on this natural light even more than on light bulbs.

You may have already learned in science class that nature would stop working if the sun stopped shining. Green plants would not be able to make food without sunlight. And if plants quit growing, animals and people wouldn't last long. We could live without Edison's light bulb but not without God's light.

There is another Light that is even more necessary. We were lost in the darkness of sin with no power to light our way out. God saw our need and sent the laser beam of His Son. Jesus cut through the darkness with His love and sacrifice. The darkness of Good Friday was replaced by the light of Easter Sunday. He is risen! His brilliance lights up each corner of our souls and drives out sin. We are forgiven—and filled with God's love.

_____Let's talk: What happens to plants without light? What happens to us without Jesus?

_____Let's pray: Dear Savior, take away the gloom of sin and fill us with Your radiance. Shine on us, Lord Jesus. Amen.

J. L. L.

Read from God's Word

And God said, "Let there be light," and there was light. God saw that the light was good, and He separated the light from the darkness. God called the light "day," and the darkness He called "night." And there was evening, and there was morning—the first day. Genesis 1:3–5

"Riding Shotgun"

Read from God's Word

"In my Father's house are many rooms. ... I am going there to prepare a place for you. And if I go and prepare a place for you, I will come back and take you to be with me that you also may be where I am. You know the way to the place where I am going." Thomas said to Him, "Lord, we don't know where You are going, so how can we know the way?" Jesus answered, "I am the Way and the Truth and the Life. No one comes to the Father except through Me. If you really knew Me, you would know My Father as well. From now on, you do know Him and have seen Him." John 14:2–6

When Jackie was growing up, one of her favorite things was "riding shotgun." This meant she got to sit in the front seat on road trips and read the maps. She became the second-most important person in the car. She had the honor of watching the highway signs and directing the driver. One challenge was keeping the driver on the right highway. The other was refolding the map.

The Bible is a much simpler road map to follow. It's all written there—the roads to heaven or hell. In His Word, God clearly shows the routes we can take. One road leads down the easy path. It's the road that looks wide and smooth, but it's really filled with potholes. These potholes, called sins, can lead to our eternal ruin.

Thank God that He also leads us to the exit from sin. Then He shows us the U-turn sign that brings us home to Him. This road may not be well paved or easy to follow, but God acts as our driver and steers us toward our final destination.

What is His map along the route? Jesus, His Son, is the Way to the Father. He is the *only* way to salvation, which He gained for us by His life, death, and resurrection. He knows about earthly temptations from first-hand experience. He will guide us through our own temptations and troubles. Through the death and resurrection of Jesus, all our sins are forgiven. As we keep our eyes on Him, we'll be going in the right direction.

_____Let's talk: What temptations are hard for you to avoid? How does Jesus help you in your daily struggles?

_____Let's pray: Lord Jesus, You are the Way, the Truth, and the Life. Lead us to know that Way, to keep that Truth, and to obtain that Life You won for us. Amen.

J. L. L.

Harvest Time

Read from God's Word

Jesus went though all the towns and villages, teaching in their synagogues, preaching the good news of the kingdom and healing every disease and sickness. When He saw the crowds, He had compassion on them, because they were harassed and helpless, like sheep without a shepherd. Then He said to His disciples, "The harvest is plentiful but the workers are few. Ask the Lord of the harvest, therefore, to send out workers into His harvest field." Matthew 9:35–38

When Jackie was 13, she stayed with her grandparents in Kansas. It was June, and that meant wheat harvest. When Granddad decided a wheat field was ripe, everyone got moving. Some drove combines and some drove grain trucks. Grandma, her aunts, and Jackie were the food detail. A big breakfast was on the table at 6 A.M. The men came home for a huge lunch at 12:00 sharp. And dinner was served after dark. The work was exhausting, but it was important. The money received from the harvest had to last a whole year.

In our Bible reading, Jesus called the crowds a harvest. He looked at them and saw how badly they needed a Savior. Then He told the disciples to pray for more harvest workers. Our world is crying out for the Good News of the Savior. More workers are needed to share the Gospel. God wants us to pray for that need and to consider being one of the workers.

Each of us works for Jesus when we show our Christian love. But He calls some of us to be specially trained for jobs in His kingdom. He calls pastors and missionaries to carry His message. He calls teachers and directors of Christian education to bring His love to the young. He uses Christian doctors and nurses to care for the ill.

Do you want to work in the communications field? Then you can help bring Jesus to people through TV, radio, or the Internet. Perhaps you will be a good writer, and He'll lead you to write Bible studies or Christian books. It will be hard work, but God will be using you to bring in His harvest.

———Let's talk: Have you considered a career in Christ's work? Talk to God and other Christians about the possibility.

———Let's pray: The harvest, Lord, is great. Send forth more workers into the world and help them speak Your Word, that people may be won for You. In Jesus' name. Amen.

J. L. L.

The Sand Dollar Legend

Read from God's Word

"For God so loved the world that He gave His one and only Son, that whoever believes in Him shall not perish but have eternal life. For God did not send His Son into the world to condemn the world, but to save the world through Him. Whoever believes in Him is not condemned, but whoever does not believe stands condemned already because he has not believed in the name of God's one and only Son. John 3:16–18 ✑

Taylor and Nicholas were enjoying their day at the beach, building sandcastles and playing in the waves. Later on, they decided to look for seashells. Soon Nicholas cried out, "Hey, look what I found! It's a sand dollar!"

Taylor ran to his side. "That's really cool. You know what? Once I heard my Sunday school teacher say that a sand dollar tells about the story of Jesus."

Taylor pointed to one side of the shell. "See, here's a picture of a Christmas poinsettia to remind us of Jesus' birth. Around the outside are five slits. Four represent the nail holes on Jesus' body from when He was crucified to save us from our sins. The fifth hole represents the mark on His body left by the Roman soldier's spear."

Taylor turned the sand dollar over. "On the back is a picture of an Easter lily to remind us of Christ's resurrection. In the center of the lily is the star that led the Wise Men to Jesus."

Taylor glanced at Nicholas. "You probably don't want to break the sand dollar open, do you?" Nicholas shook his head no. "Well, if you shake it, you can hear a rattling sound. Inside are five little pieces that symbolize doves waiting to spread the good news of Jesus' love!"

Nicholas looked at Taylor in amazement. "Who would have thought that a little sand dollar could be such a neat way to tell the story of Jesus?"

_____Let's talk: What other symbols can you think of that remind you of Jesus?

_____Let's pray: We praise You, O God, for Your beautiful creation. Thank You for the sand dollar and other reminders of Your love. Help us share Your message with others. Amen.

L. E.

Rescued from a Mess

When Mary was young, she lived on a farm in Montana. The family did not have indoor plumbing, so they had an outhouse behind their home. Mary also had a cat that she dearly loved. She and her cat were inseparable.

One day Mary's cat followed her into the outhouse and fell down one of the holes. Mary searched for her dad and told him what had happened. He said there was only one thing to do—they needed to rescue that cat!

Her dad followed Mary back to the outhouse, grabbed her by the ankles, and lowered her into the hole. She grabbed her cat, and he pulled them both back out to safety.

We are not perfect. Sometimes we get ourselves into some terrible messes. In fact, we may even consider the situation hopeless. When such times come, it's wise to remember a promise Jesus made to us: "Surely I am with you always, to the very end of the age" (Matthew 28:20). Jesus loves us and will never leave us. He rescued us from sin, death, and the power of the devil through His suffering on the cross. And He promises to help us get out of any messes we find ourselves in.

There is no sin too great for our Savior to forgive. There is no mess so big that He can't rescue us from it. He is all-loving, all-knowing, and all-powerful. He is better than Batman or Superman because He is real. Jesus is the best rescuer in the world!

Read from God's Word

I waited patiently for the LORD; He turned to me and heard my cry. He lifted me out of the slimy pit, ...He set my feet on a rock and gave me a firm place to stand. He put a new song in my mouth, a hymn of praise to our God. ...Do not withhold Your mercy from me, O LORD; may Your love and Your truth always protect me. For troubles without number surround me; my sins have overtaken me, and I cannot see. They are more than the hairs of my head, and my heart fails within me. Be pleased, O LORD, to save me; O LORD, come quickly to help me. Psalm 40:1–3, 11–13

_____Let's talk: What are some messes you have found yourself in? How has Jesus rescued you from them?

_____Let's pray: Jesus, forgive us when we don't follow You and we find ourselves in a bad situation. Help us remember the promise You made to be with us always and to rescue us. Thank You for Your great and powerful love. Amen.

L. E.

The Best "Package" of All

Read from God's Word

The city was laid out like a square, as long as it was wide. ... The wall was made of jasper, and the city of pure gold, as pure as glass. The foundations of the city walls were decorated with every kind of precious stone. The first foundation was jasper, the second sapphire, the third chalcedony, the fourth emerald, the fifth sardonyx, the sixth carnelian, the seventh chrysolite, the eighth beryl, the ninth topaz, the tenth chrysoprase, the eleventh jacinth, and the twelfth amethyst. The twelve gates were twelve pearls, each gate made of a single pearl. The great street of the city was of pure gold, like transparent glass. Revelation 21:16–21 ✎

ike was excited! He had been waiting for this package for three weeks. It all started when Mike bought a piece of bubble gum with an ad for army men on the wrapper. If he sent in 10 bubblegum wrappers and $5, a set of 50 plastic army men would be his. He saved his allowance and his wrappers, and then sent them in.

After ripping open the package, Mike was disappointed to see what was inside. There were 50 army men, just like the ad had promised. But they didn't look like the men in the picture. They were just 50 flat pieces of green plastic. "What a rip-off!" Mike said.

God makes many promises in the Bible. The best promise is that we will have eternal life with Him because of Jesus' death and resurrection. God tells us that heaven will have streets of pure gold. It's far better than Disneyland or any other place we have ever seen.

At times we may think this is just false advertising, like the ad for the army men. But we can believe God because He has a track record of keeping His promises. He promised to save Noah, and He did. He promised Abraham a son, and Abraham had a son. He promised to send a Messiah, and He sent Jesus. God does not falsely advertise. Everything He says in His Word is true. One day we will claim the best promise and package of all—heaven!

_____Let's talk: Have you ever been disappointed with something? What can you remember the next time you wonder about God's promises?

_____Let's pray: Heavenly Father, forgive us for the times we question and doubt You. Remind us of the promises You have faithfully kept. Help us look forward to our heavenly home with You. Amen.

L. E.

Can't Wait to Grow Up?

Clomp, clomp, thump, thump. Jason was stomping down the hallway in his father's large work shoes. Sandra, his big sister, came out of the kitchen to see Jason struggling forward, nearly walking right out of the shoes. Sandra burst into laughter and said, "You're not ready for those yet."

Jason looked hurt. He said, "Sure I am! I'm walking in them just like Dad does."

So often we can't get where we are going fast enough or get something soon enough. Everything around us teaches impatience. Gotta be it. Gotta have it—that new outfit, those expensive shoes, more video games, pierced-ears-and-noses-like-those-bigger-kids-have, NFL jackets, and on and on. We can't wait to grow up!

Jesus knew about patience and impatience. He was patient with His disciples as He taught them what they needed to understand for their Gospel ministry. He had to be patient in teaching them to be as trusting as little children.

Read from God's Word

To this you were called, because Christ suffered for you, leaving you an example, that you should follow in His steps. "He committed no sin, and no deceit was found in His mouth." When they hurled their insults at Him, He did not retaliate; when He suffered, He made no threats. Instead, He entrusted Himself to Him who judges justly. He Himself bore our sins in His body on the tree, so that we might die to sins and live for righteousness; by His wounds you have been healed. For you were like sheep going astray, but now you have returned to the Shepherd and Overseer of your souls. 1 Peter 2:21–25

With great patience, Jesus suffered insults and mockery from His enemies. He marched straight to His cross in order to suffer what we deserved because of our sins. By His wounds, says the Bible, we have been healed.

From Jesus Christ we learn to accept what comes our way in life with patience. He also helps us to be patient and helpful with others any way we can.

———Let's talk: What happens when you become too impatient for something? Why is patience so hard to learn? How can your faith in the Lord help you practice patience?

———Let's pray: Dear Lord, thank You for submitting to Your Father's will in Gethsemane and for patiently suffering for us on the cross. Where would we be without You? Amen.

N. M.

An Act of Kindness

Read from God's Word

Therefore, as God's chosen people, holy and dearly loved, clothe yourselves with compassion, kindness, humility, gentleness and patience. Bear with each other and forgive whatever grievances you may have against one another. Forgive as the Lord forgave you. And over all these virtues put on love, which binds them all together in perfect unity.
Colossians 3:12–14 ✎

A terrific thing happened at our school the end of last year. Students had received their school yearbooks and were eagerly passing them among their friends to be signed. But one student passed around an old notebook to be signed instead of a yearbook. His mom had said his family could not afford to buy a yearbook.

When the rest of the class heard this story, they pooled their money and bought a yearbook for their friend. They all signed it and presented it to him. He was astonished at the gift from his classmates. It was as if they had given him $1,000!

These students were wonderful witnesses of Jesus' love. When Jesus was here on earth, He performed many miracles and acts of kindness. He showed mercy to everyone—rich and poor, young and old, male and female. He even gave His life to save the whole world.

As God's children, we can show kindness and compassion to all people. We do this not to earn God's love, but as a thank-You to God for the love He has shown to us.

Sometimes we forget to be kind. It can be much easier to call people names or ignore them entirely. It's especially hard to be nice to someone who is mean to us. When this happens, God promises to help us do the right thing. Do you know someone who would benefit from your act of kindness?

_____Let's talk: What are some kind things people have done for you? What nice things could you do for others?

_____Let's pray: Thank You, Lord, for Your kindness to us. Help us be kind to all people. In Your precious name we pray. Amen.

L. E.

Make Lemonade!

[M]any, many years ago there lived a man who wrote some of the most famous music the world has ever known. Yet his life was filled with tragedy. His parents had died by the time he was 10 years old. His older brother raised him, but he wasn't very happy doing so.

His first wife died after 13 years of marriage. He had 20 children altogether, but 11 died. The man was paralyzed from a stroke and eventually went blind.

Who was this man who persevered through many difficult times and wrote some of the most wonderful music in praise to God? He was Johann Sebastian Bach, one of the world's greatest composers.

Life can be very painful at times because of sin. God didn't promise us a smooth flight, but He did promise us a safe landing. And He promises to be with us the whole way. He is there for us even in the worst of times. And He has a crown of eternal life ready for those who believe in Jesus as the Savior from sin.

Perseverance is a wonderful trait. Don't give up when things get tough. Remember that God is with you and ask Him to help you make the best of the blessings you've been given. After all, if Bach had been a quitter at any time along the way, the world would be missing some very beautiful music!

_____Let's talk: What are some gifts you have been given? How can you use them to God's glory?

_____Let's pray: O God, forgive us when we are overwhelmed with disappointments and feel like quitting. Thank You for always being with us. Help us to persevere and to use the blessings You have given us to Your honor and glory. Amen.

L. E.

Read from God's Word

Blessed is the man who perseveres under trial, because when he has stood the test, he will receive the crown of life that God has promised to those who love Him. James 1:12

Change Happens

The alarm clock buzzed. Emily pulled the sheet over her head. "Time to get up!" her mom called. "You don't want to be late for your first day at your new school."

Emily peeked her head out. "What if nobody likes me and the work is too hard? Why did we have to move? I loved my old school and all my friends."

Emily's mom sat on the edge of her bed. "Life is full of changes, Emily," she said. "Think about the seasons. My favorite part of fall is watching the leaves turn from green to red, gold, and orange. What's your favorite part about winter?"

Emily immediately replied, "Snow skiing and sledding!"

"What do you like about spring?" her mom continued.

"I love the pretty flowers and the warmer days," said Emily.

"And summer?"

"That's an easy one—no school and lots of free time," Emily grinned.

"Well," her mom said, "if there were no changes in the world, you wouldn't be able to enjoy the different parts of each season. There will most likely be many things about your new school that you will enjoy too. But you won't know what they are if you're not willing to try the place out. If you're still a little frightened, remember that Jesus and His love for you never change. He will be with you today and every day at your new school. And you won't know if you like it unless you try it!"

_____Let's talk: What are some changes you didn't like? What can you rely on the next time you face a change that makes you feel afraid?

_____Let's pray: Dear Jesus, please help us not to be afraid when we face changes in life. Remind us that You are with us every day. Thank You for Your unchanging love. Amen.

L. E.

Tough Questions

Read from God's Word

There are different kinds of gifts, but the same Spirit. ... Now to each one the manifestation of the Spirit is given for the common good. To one there is given through the Spirit the message of wisdom, to another the message of knowledge by means of the same Spirit, to another faith by the same Spirit, to another gifts of healing by that one Spirit, to another miraculous powers, to another prophecy, to another distinguishing between spirits, to another speaking in different kinds of tongues, and to still another the interpretation of tongues. All these are the work of ... the same Spirit, and He gives them to each one, just as He determines.
1 Corinthians 12:4–11

Experts tell us that 7 out of every 10 people like chocolate. Why do they like the taste of chocolate? What makes it taste good? Why do some people like raspberries more than strawberries? Why does ice cream taste better than alfalfa hay? Why does a hot dog taste better than sand on the beach?

Silly questions? Maybe. But they make us realize that not everyone is the same. People don't all like the same things. If each person were exactly like the next person, what a dull world this would be!

God made people different; He also gives each one different gifts or abilities. Some have the ability to make great speeches. Some can sing. Others can organize things.

If everyone could sing beautifully, who would be left to enjoy their singing? What would happen if everyone were good at making long speeches and wanted everyone else to listen?

Although people are different and have different gifts, God loves them all. He proved that by giving His Son to die for all people. Through the death and resurrection of Jesus, we are rescued from eternal damnation. Because we believe in Jesus as our Savior, we will someday live with Him in His home.

In the meantime, let's use our gifts to help and encourage one another. Wouldn't it be wonderful if as many people as possible came to Jesus and grew in faith in His love all their lives?

_____Let's talk: Do you think that in heaven some people will still like chocolate more than vanilla? Will we even need to eat in heaven? What will our main activity be?

_____Let's pray: Thank You, God, for making us all different and for loving us so much! Thank You for the gift of Your Son, our Savior. Amen.

R. S.

XOXOXO

Read from God's Word

And you also were included in Christ when you heard the word of truth, the gospel of your salvation. Having believed, you were marked in Him with a seal, the promised Holy Spirit, who is a deposit guaranteeing our inheritance until the redemption of those who are God's possession— to the praise of His glory. Ephesians 1:13–14 ✍

Do you ever write XOXOXO at the bottom of a letter or e-mail to represent kisses and hugs? The O symbolizes a hug because it looks like someone's encircling arms. But why does the X represent a kiss?

Actually, the practice of writing XOXOXO has been around for hundreds of years. It began way back in medieval times. In those days, saints were represented by different signs. St. Andrew's sign was the letter X.

In order to show that they were trustworthy, people would place the sign of St. Andrew after their signature on important papers. Then the signer would kiss the document to guarantee his good faith. The contract was not considered legal unless the signer included St. Andrew's X after his name. Through the centuries, this custom faded out, but people still associated the letter X with a kiss. It's still used that way today.

God has placed His seal or sign on you. At your Baptism, He filled you with His Holy Spirit. You are owned and protected by Him. Even when you sin and disobey God, that seal is there, a reminder of His forgiveness. It tells you over and over of His love for you. It reminds you of the promise of eternal life with Him in heaven.

God is trustworthy and of good faith. He keeps His promises. When you see something that reminds you of Baptism, remember that God has His seal on you.

_____Let's talk: How could you celebrate your Baptism day? How can you thank God for His seal of love and forgiveness?

_____Let's pray: Dear Savior, thank You for the gift of Your Holy Spirit. Thank You for our Baptism and for placing Your seal on us. Forgive us when we stray. We praise You for being trustworthy and always keeping Your promises. Amen.

L. E.

Very Special People

Tessa's creative writing assignment was going to be fun! She was supposed to write about her grandparents and what makes them special to her. Tessa was able to think of examples right away.

Grandma K. always had her favorite cookies in the cookie jar. Grandpa K. once drove her all over town in search of a certain type of paper doll. Although Grandma R. had died, Tessa will always remember how she taught her to cross-stitch and embroider. And Grandpa R. used to take her out for ice-cream cones.

As Tessa thought about her grandparents, she realized they all had something important in common. She remembered that Jesus was at the center of their lives. Before each meal they remembered to thank God for His many blessings. They had a cross and a picture of Jesus on their walls to help them remember His sacrifice to save them. They even took her along to church and Sunday school when she visited. Tessa decided to write how her grandparents had given her many examples of how to live her life for Jesus.

God has placed many special people in our lives that are living witnesses for Christ. They may be our relatives, neighbors, teachers, or best friends. We can give thanks to God for them. When life seems to get us down, we can turn to them for counsel and comfort. They are there to remind us of God's care and forgiveness. He put them in our lives for a reason!

_____Let's talk: What people are living examples of faith to you? How can you be an example of faith to others?

_____Let's pray: Thank You, Jesus, for the special people You have placed in our lives. Help us show our appreciation to them. Thank You for loving us every day. Amen.

L. E.

Read from God's Word

To Timothy, my dear son: Grace, mercy and peace from God the Father and Christ Jesus our Lord. ... I constantly remember you in my prayers. ... I have been reminded of your sincere faith, which first lived in your grandmother Lois and in your mother Eunice and, I am persuaded, now lives in you also. For this reason I remind you to fan into flame the gift of God, which is in you through the laying on of my hands. For God did not give us a spirit of timidity, but a spirit of power, of love and of self-discipline. 2 Timothy 1:2–7 ✍

september

Better Than Imagination

The Sunday school lesson was about how God saved Daniel from the hungry lions. The teacher explained that God is always with us too—just as He was with Daniel. During snack time, she heard Lauren and Patrick talking about the story. Patrick asked, "Is God really with me all the time?"

"Oh, yes," said Lauren.

Then Patrick wanted to know, "How does He do that?"

Lauren thought for a bit and then replied, "Well, I think it's kind of like imagination. You know, like an imaginary friend who goes wherever you go."

The teacher decided it was time to join the discussion. She explained to Lauren and Patrick that although we can't see Him, God is very real.

"That's cool!" said Patrick. "Even better than imagination."

There is nothing imaginary about God. He made the whole world and everything in it, and He is still in control of the world. God is hundreds of times more powerful than anyone or anything else. God knows all about each of us and cares for us.

God's love for you is very real too. He loves you so much that He sent Jesus to die for your sins and the sins of all other people. Now God forgives you when you sin and turn to Him again. You are God's child, and someday you will live with Him in heaven. That will be more wonderful than anyone can imagine!

Read from God's Word

But the LORD is the true God; He is the living God, the eternal King. When He is angry, the earth trembles; the nations cannot endure His wrath. "Tell them this: These gods, who did not make the heavens and the earth, will perish from the earth and from under the heavens.'" But God made the earth by His power; He founded the world by His wisdom and stretched out the heavens by His understanding. When He thunders, the waters in the heavens roar; He makes clouds rise from the ends of the earth. He sends lightning with the rain and brings out the wind from His storehouses. Jeremiah 10:10–13 ✍

_____Let's talk: On a piece of paper write 10 things that only God can do. Was forgiving your sins one of the things listed? How can knowing about God and His love for you help you when you're worried?

_____Let's pray: Dear God, we are so happy that You are real. Thanks for loving us and caring how we feel. For taking all our sins away, we will praise and thank You every day. Amen.

J. A. D.

Nearer to God

In the early 1800s two sisters wrote many of the hymns sung in their home church in England. Sarah Adams wrote the words and her sister Eliza composed the music. One week their pastor was searching for a hymn to go with his sermon. Together the sisters produced "Nearer, My God, to Thee," which tells about Jacob's dream of a stairway to heaven.

Two stories show how this beautiful hymn of faith has been comforting people for more than 150 years. An assassin shot U.S. President McKinley in 1901. As he lay dying, his family heard him whisper, "Nearer, my God, to Thee, nearer to Thee." Congregations around the country sang the hymn at memorial services, remembering President McKinley.

The second story happened when the *Titanic* sank on April 14, 1912. There weren't enough lifeboats on the ship to save everyone. More than 1,500 passengers were left on the deck of the *Titanic* to face death. As the lifeboats pulled away, the ship's band played "Nearer, My God, to Thee." Hundreds of voices joined in singing the hymn as the roaring sea pounded the battered ship.

The words of this hymn are just as true today as when they were written. The only way you can be nearer to God and eternal life is through the cross of Jesus. His death for your sins makes it possible for you to face life and death without fear. You are God's child, loved and forgiven.

_____Let's talk: What is your favorite hymn? Why do you like it? What does the hymn tell you about God and what He does for you?

_____Let's pray: Nearer, my God, to Thee, Nearer to Thee! Even though it be a cross that raiseth me; Still all my song shall be: Nearer, my God, to Thee, Nearer, my God, to Thee, Nearer to Thee!

J. A. D.

Too Medium

Read from God's Word

The LORD said, "I have indeed seen the misery of My people in Egypt. I have heard them crying out because of their slave drivers. … So I have come down to rescue them from the hand of the Egyptians and to bring them up out of that land into a good and spacious land, a land flowing with milk and honey. … I am sending you to Pharaoh to bring My people the Israelites out of Egypt." But Moses said to God, "Who am I, that I should go to Pharaoh and bring the Israelites out of Egypt?" And God said, "I will be with you. … When you have brought the people out of Egypt, you will worship God on this mountain." Exodus 3:7–12 ✑

Madeline always wanted to be a "big girl." She got upset when anyone said she was too little. When she was four years old, Madeline tried and tried to tie her shoes, but her fingers just wouldn't cooperate. Finally, she said, "Grammy, will you tie these shoes? I'm just too medium to do it." Madeline wasn't about to admit she was too little. But she also knew she wasn't big enough. So she settled for somewhere in between and decided she was "too medium."

Moses was tending his flocks when God appeared to him in a burning bush. God had a job for Moses to do—He wanted him to lead the Israelites out of Egypt. Moses didn't want to think he was "too little" for the job, but he didn't quite feel he was "big enough" to do it. Moses was in sort of a medium mood when he asked God, "Who am I, that I should … bring the Israelites out of Egypt?" God told Moses that He would be with him and help him.

Sometimes you probably feel pretty medium too. You don't know if you can do what God wants you to do. But God knows that you are big enough to do whatever job He gives you. And God is always there to help you. There is nothing little or medium about God's love. His love is super big—so big that He sent Jesus to die for your sins. Because of Jesus, you can know that God is ready to forgive and ready to lead.

_____Let's talk: What jobs make you feel "too medium" and not quite ready to do them? What special thing do you think God might want you to do?

_____Let's pray: Thank You, God, for Your super-big love and forgiveness. Please help us do what You want us to do in the best way we can. In Jesus' name. Amen.

J. A. D.

Lights Out

Read from God's Word

When Jesus spoke again to the people, He said, "I am the Light of the world. Whoever follows me will never walk in darkness, but will have the light of life." John 8:12

It was the worst ice storm Susan had ever seen. The freezing rain fastened onto everything in its path. Tree branches touched the ground as the weight of the ice bent or broke them. No one traveled for fear of accidents. Everyone stayed inside and looked out at the glistening wetness beyond the windows.

The next day was sunny and the world was beautiful. Sunlight sparkled on the ice, making it almost too bright to see. There was no electricity for a while because miles of electrical lines had fallen. Early that evening the lights came back on. When Susan went to the window, she saw only her side of the street had electricity. Across the street the houses were still dark and cold.

Do you know of someone living in the darkness? People around us may have all the electric lights they need, but do they all have Christ's light? In today's Bible verse, Jesus calls His light "the light of life." If we did not have Christ's light, we might be able to muddle through our earthly life, but we would not have eternal life in heaven.

But by God's grace we do have Christ's light and the promise of happiness with Him forever. And we can share His light with those who do not have it. God can turn the darkness of their sin into the light of life. He offers salvation to everyone. He can work through us to give His light to people still in darkness.

_____Let's talk: How can we tell whether someone believes in Jesus? In what ways might God use us to help those who do not believe?

_____Let's pray: Dear Jesus, thank You for Your precious gift of salvation. Please use us to share Your light with people still living in darkness. Amen.

S. W. V.

A Fresh Start

Happy New Year! Don't worry; you didn't sleep through four months of your life—it's still September. But it is a new year in school.

The beginning of a new school year is exciting—new clothes, new pencils, and new books. It's a time for a fresh start, and each student hopes for a perfect year. But after a few weeks, things are a little less exciting and not so perfect. The new shoes are scuffed, the pencils are short stubs, and some of the books are boring. Sometimes we don't understand the lessons and worry about getting bad grades. We want others to like us, so we try to be like everybody else. Does some of this sound like your school experiences?

In some ways, everyday life is like the beginning of a school year. We get excited about doing something and want it to be perfect. Then we goof up and things don't turn out the way we had planned. We feel like we need to start over.

Read from God's Word

He will not always accuse, nor will He harbor His anger forever; He does not treat us as our sins deserve or repay us according to our iniquities. For as high as the heavens are above the earth, so great is His love for those who fear Him; as far as the east is from the west, so far has He removed our transgressions from us. Psalm 103:9–12 ✍

We Christians want to please God and obey Him. We might try hard to do what is right, but then we sin and things get messed up. Jesus died for you and me and everyone else. Because of Jesus, our sins are forgiven and God gives us a fresh start.

You may get only one fresh start for each school year. But God gives you many fresh starts each day. Now, that's really exciting!

_____Let's talk: What are some things at school that may tempt you to sin? How does knowing that God forgives all your sins make you feel? How can you serve and obey God in school?

_____Let's pray: Dear Jesus, You went to school when You were growing up too. Help us follow Your example and be a good student. Thank You for giving us a fresh start by forgiving our sins. Amen.

J. A. D.

Forgiven and Forgiving

Read from God's Word

Get rid of all bitterness, rage and anger, brawling and slander, along with every form of malice. Be kind and compassionate to one another, forgiving each other, just as in Christ God forgave you. Be imitators of God, therefore, as dearly loved children and live a life of love, just as Christ loved us and gave Himself up for us as a fragrant offering and sacrifice to God. Ephesians 4:31–5:2 ✍

The ten Boom family lived in Holland during World War II. They watched as Jewish people were sent to suffer in concentration camps. Although it was dangerous, the ten Booms decided to hide some of their Jewish friends in their home. But they were arrested. Mr. ten Boom died. Corrie and Betsie were sent to a prison camp where life was horrible. They comforted themselves with words from the Bible and prayed for God's help and protection. Betsie died, but Corrie survived and after many years was released.

After the war, Corrie talked to groups of people about being in a prison camp. She told how Jesus was with her in that horrible place. She also talked about God's forgiveness. One night at the end of her talk, Corrie was shaking hands with people. A former guard from the prison camp was standing in front of her. "I'm so happy to know Jesus forgives me," he said.

Corrie remembered the cruel things that had happened at the camp. At first she didn't want to shake his hand. She prayed that God would help her forgive him. Then Corrie remembered God's love and forgiveness for all people. Corrie shook hands with the man and forgave him.

Through Jesus' death for your sins, you are forgiven. That love and forgiveness of God gives you the power to forgive others.

_____Let's talk: Is there someone whom you find hard to forgive? How can remembering that God forgives all your sins help you forgive others?

_____Let's pray: Forgiving God, we know that we sin and need Your forgiveness. Thank You for sending Jesus to die for our sins and the sins of all people. Help us forgive others, just as You forgive us. In Jesus' name. Amen.

J. A. D.

Lick, Don't Chew!

What's your favorite kind of candy? Do you like sweet chocolate that melts in your mouth? Or do you prefer lemon drops that make your mouth pucker? Maybe you like nuts or coconut in your candy. A favorite candy is a lollipop that is hard on the outside and has a chewy chocolate center. Yummy!

The problem with eating that lollipop is the really chewy center. It takes a while to get there when you have to lick the hard part. It's easy to get impatient and use your teeth instead of your tongue. After a few crunches you might be rewarded with the chocolate, but then you have hard candy stuck in your teeth. And the lollipop is gone in a flash.

Sometimes prayer is like that lollipop. Think of God as being the center and patience as the hard candy covering. Christians pray for many things for themselves and for others. We would like God to answer our prayers right away. And we often become impatient when we have to wait.

Read from God's Word

Trust in the LORD and do good; dwell in the land and enjoy safe pasture. Delight yourself in the LORD and He will give you the desires of your heart. Commit your way to the LORD; trust in Him and He will do this: He will make your righteousness shine like the dawn, the justice of your cause like the noonday sun.
Psalm 37:3–6

God hears and answers every prayer we pray. But He doesn't always answer them in the way we expect or want. Sometimes He says "yes," sometimes "no," and sometimes "wait." God loves us and knows what's best for us, so His answer is always good. Through Jesus, our dear Savior, we can speak to our Father at any time.

———Let's talk: What have you prayed for recently? Has your prayer been answered? Was it answered in the way you expected? If it hasn't been answered yet, how do you feel about waiting?

———Let's pray: Dear Lord, thank You for always hearing our prayers. Help us to wait patiently for Your answer. Also help us trust You to know what is best for us. In Jesus' name. Amen.

J. A. D.

No Favorites

Read from God's Word

Then Peter began to speak: "I now realize how true it is that God does not show favoritism but accepts men from every nation who fear Him and do what is right. You know the message God sent to the people of Israel, telling the good news of peace through Jesus Christ, who is Lord of all. Acts 10:34–36

"Favorites" lists are quite popular. There are favorite books, movies, TV shows, vacation spots, and restaurants. Each of us could make our own lists of favorite foods, favorite clothes, and favorite activities.

Favorites are things we really like. We keep using or doing our favorite things over and over. Some favorites change as we grow up, such as favorite blankets, but many favorites stay the same.

You probably have favorite people in your life too. These are people whom you enjoy being with and doing things with. Having favorite people is fine as long as it doesn't involve leaving out others.

In Old Testament times, the Jewish people were God's chosen people. When Christ was born, God revealed Him as Savior of the whole world. God has no favorites. No one is better or worse than another. Jesus died for the sins of *all* people, so everyone is equally loved in God's sight. The entire world became His chosen people. Everyone who believes in Jesus as their Savior receives forgiveness and eternal life.

Paul says in Galatians 3:27–28, "All of you who were baptized into Christ have clothed yourselves with Christ. There is neither Jew nor Greek, slave nor free, male nor female, for you are all one in Christ Jesus." That's the greatest list of all!

_____Let's talk: Who are some of your favorite people? Why? How can you follow God's example in how you act toward others?

_____Let's pray: Dear God, we are happy that You do not have a list of favorite people. Thank You for sending Jesus as the Savior of all and for making us Your own. Please help us be kind and forgiving to others, treating them as You treat us. Help us not to ignore or look down on others. In Jesus' name. Amen.

J. A. D.

Praise Him! Praise Him!

Jeanette grew up on a farm that had lots of animals, woods, and fields. She loved being outside. Now she lives in a suburb of a large city, and her "farm" is her yard. Jeanette still likes being outdoors, working in the garden and flowerbeds. And she still likes animals. She especially enjoys watching the birds that visit the bird feeders in her yard. There are also a few bushy-tailed squirrels that play tag up and down the trees.

Jeanette has never seen or heard a crabby bird. Birds sing and chirp as they go about finding food. Even in the coldest weather, they sound cheerful as they gather around the feeders. Their twittering and singing makes her feel cheerful and happy.

Mr. Squirrel also chatters cheerfully as he digs up buried goodies. And the beautiful flowers seem to dance joyfully as they sway in the breezes. These things remind her of Psalm 96:1: "Sing to the LORD a new song; sing to the LORD, all the earth." In their own way, the birds, animals, and plants praise God.

Read from God's Word

Worship the LORD in the splendor of His holiness; tremble before Him, all the earth. Say among the nations, "The LORD reigns." The world is firmly established, it cannot be moved; He will judge the peoples with equity. Let the heavens rejoice, let the earth be glad; let the sea resound, and all that is in it; let the fields be jubilant, and everything in them. Then all the trees of the forest will sing for joy. Psalm 96:9–12 ✏

Think of the many blessings we can praise God for. He created us and cares for us. But most important, He loves us so much that He sent Jesus to be our Savior. Through Jesus' death and resurrection, our sins are forgiven and we will live in heaven with God forever. Praise Him, praise Him—now and forever!

Let's do: Write PRAISE down the side of a piece of paper, one letter per line. Then think of something to praise God for that starts with each letter. Say "Thank You" to God for each thing you wrote.

Let's pray: Praise God, from whom all blessings flow;
Praise Him, all creatures here below;
Praise Him above, O heavenly host;
Praise Father, Son, and Holy Ghost.

J. A. D.

The Three P's

Read from God's Word

Not only so, but we also rejoice in our sufferings, because we know that suffering produces perseverance; perseverance, character; and character, hope. And hope does not disappoint us, because God has poured out His love into our hearts by the Holy Spirit, whom He has given us. Romans 5:3–5 ⌐⌐

can't do it! I can't learn this piano piece!" Keesha Kelly wailed. Her fingers banged on the keyboard. Her mother smiled. "Take it easy, Keesha. You need to remember the three P's."

"Three P's? What are these three P's?" Keesha asked.

"Practice, patience, and perseverance," Mrs. Kelly explained.

Keesha knew all about practice, and she understood patience. But *perseverance* was a new word.

"Perseverance is what keeps you going when you feel like quitting," her mother said. "It's sticking with something no matter what. Remember how long it took your brother to learn to ride his bike?"

Keesha rolled her eyes and laughed. "I remember," she said. "He looked awful, with all his scrapes and bruises."

"But he didn't give up. He persevered," Mrs. Kelly pointed out. "Now look at him. He rides like a pro."

Keesha was beginning to understand this new idea. Her mother continued, "God is there to help us when we feel like giving up and quitting. He helps us persevere and keep on going."

God is a perfect model of perseverance; He never gives up on us. No matter how many times we sin, God forgives us. Jesus brought us God's persevering love and forgiveness by dying for our sins. Because of this, we will live with Jesus in heaven someday.

_____Let's talk: Is there something you have trouble sticking with, like breaking a bad habit or completing a task? How can you persevere?

_____Let's pray: Dear God, thank You for persevering and not giving up on us. Thanks for loving and forgiving us. Please be with us and help us to learn to persevere. In Jesus' name. Amen.

J. A. D.

What Death Is Like

Along time ago, baby-sitters were not very common. Most moms stayed home while dads went to work. And when people visited other people in the evening, they took their kids along.

But kids can stay awake only so long before getting tired. The hosts placed the guests' coats on their bed. This pile grew according to the number of guests. The bed supporting the coats also welcomed kids when they started to fall asleep.

Sometimes kids would fall asleep on the mountain of coats but wake up back in their own beds. One moment they were in one place, and the next they were home.

Think about all that went on while they were asleep. Their dad had to pull them out of the clothes nest, put their flopping arms through the sleeves of their own coats, carry them to the car, and carry them to bed.

Read from God's Word

Brothers, ... we believe that God will bring with Jesus those who have fallen asleep in Him. According to the Lord's own word, ... the Lord Himself will come down from heaven, with a loud command, with the voice of the archangel and with the trumpet call of God, and the dead in Christ will rise first. After that, we who are still alive and are left will be caught up together with them in the clouds to meet the Lord in the air. And so we will be with the Lord forever. Therefore encourage each other with these words. 1 Thessalonians 4:13–18 ✍

Maybe that's what death is like. One second you fall asleep here, and the next you're home. Our heavenly Father has arranged for us to be brought to heaven by His Son. Jesus does all the work. Jesus says in the Bible that He will personally come and take us to be with Him. He has already prepared a place for us by *His* death in our place. Jesus Himself will carry us home.

_____Let's talk: Whom do you want to see first when you get to your real home in heaven? Why is that your answer? What do you think we'll do in heaven?

_____Let's pray: Dear Jesus, help us live knowing that not only when we die but also all through our lives we are in Your loving arms. In Your name and in love for You we pray. Amen.

G. T. Z.

The Bonus Army

Read from God's Word

This is how God showed His love among us: He sent His one and only Son into the world that we might live through Him. This is love: not that we loved God, but that He loved us and sent His Son as an atoning sacrifice for our sins. 1 John 4:9–10

Charge!" In the early part of the 20th century, many soldiers who fought in World War I came to Washington to receive a bonus check for serving in the army. The government promised to pay them this money years later, but the soldiers needed the money at once to feed their families.

Thousands marched up and down Pennsylvania Avenue. Herbert Hoover, who was the president, said no to their request. The men and their families, now called the "Bonus Army," camped out on the lawns. President Hoover didn't like the way that looked, so he sent out the army to drive these people away.

When Franklin Roosevelt became president, the Bonus Army returned. President Roosevelt didn't know what to do, so he asked his wife. Eleanor said, "I'll invite them in for tea and listen to their concerns." From then on the Bonus Army said, "Hoover gave us the army; Roosevelt gave us his wife."

Satan gives us death, and God gives us His Son, Jesus. We look pretty ugly in our sins, but God's answer is to invite us into His heart forever by Jesus' death on the cross. God decided to send Jesus. The Savior gives us life—*eternal* life. That's the greatest bonus any of us will ever receive, and it's already ours!

———Let's talk: If you receive an allowance, what would you consider a nice bonus? What can you do to share Jesus this week and give someone the best bonus of all?

———Let's pray: Dear God, thank You for sending Jesus to invite us to the greatest tea party ever. We want to be where You are, in Your heavenly home. Amen.

G. T. Z.

The Way Out

George and his family were in their family car, following in a funeral procession. There were many cars, and theirs was the last one. While cars in a funeral procession can go through red lights, they have to stop for trains. A railroad gate lowered right in the middle of the long string of cars. The gate cut the procession in two. It was a long, long freight train.

After the train had passed, the gate went up. But the first part of the procession was already gone. No one could see them. The people in the first car didn't know how to get to the cemetery. That's when George's dad said, "I know how to get there. Follow me." His car moved to the front, and everyone followed. George felt so proud of his dad! He knew the way, and everyone else followed behind.

In 1964 George's father died and made another trip to the cemetery. His tombstone is in Montrose Cemetery in Chicago, but he isn't really there. Jesus makes it possible for us to rise from the grave on the Last Day. In other words, He overcame death so it cannot hold us.

We all have a heavenly Dad. He is called our heavenly Father. When we were cut off from Him in our sins, He sent Jesus to bring us back to Himself. He made the way for us so we can follow Him.

Read from God's Word

It is better, if it is God's will, to suffer for doing good than for doing evil. For Christ died for sins once for all, the righteous for the unrighteous, to bring you to God. He was put to death in the body but made alive by the Spirit. 1 Peter 3:17–18 ∽

_____Let's talk: What could your family put on the grave of a Christian relative to show that your relative is with God in heaven? What does Jesus' empty tomb mean for you?

_____Let's pray: Dear Jesus, help us live in the joy of knowing we will never be lost from You or be stuck with a one-way ticket to the cemetery. Thank You for not only showing the way but also for being the way to our heavenly Father. Amen.

G. T. Z.

Breakfast in Bed

When He had finished washing their feet, He ... returned to His place. "Do you understand what I have done for you?" He asked them. "You call Me 'Teacher' and 'Lord,' and rightly so, for that is what I am. Now that I, your Lord and Teacher, have washed your feet, you also should do as I have done for you. I have set you an example that you should do as I have done for you. I tell you the truth, no servant is greater than his master, nor is a messenger greater than the one who sent him. Now that you know these things, you will be blessed if you do them." John 13:12–17

George and his wife have a favorite tradition. They go off by themselves for a week at the beach. Every day George makes breakfast in bed for them. And each evening they go out to eat at a restaurant. His wife never lifts a finger to make a meal all week. George enjoys serving her because he loves her.

Serving Jesus by serving others is also a joy because we love Jesus. Jesus sets the example. He tells us that He did not come into this world to be served but to serve and to give His life for everyone.

As Christians, we have a calling to feed people with the greatest food of all, the Gospel of Jesus Christ. This truly is "service with a smile."

We never lifted a finger to help Jesus with our salvation. He totally served us and continues to serve us today. His gifts of love, forgiveness, joy, and peace are new each day. Knowing this gives us the power to serve and the dignity of being truly useful for the Lord.

_____Let's talk: What reaction would you get if you made breakfast in bed for your family? What else could you do to serve others with the love of Jesus?

_____Let's pray: Dear Jesus, thank You for first saving us at the cross and then serving us each day with Your perfect love. Make us Your dedicated, joyful servants in this world. Amen.

G. T. Z.

Why Does He Love Me?

Let's start with two questions—one easy, one hard. First, the easy one: "Why did Jesus die on the cross for you?" Answer: He loves you. Good! Now for question number 2, the hard one: "Why does He love you?"

Let's look at a young boy named Nathan. He wouldn't go to bed without taking his favorite toy with him, a fire truck. Nathan played in the yard with his toy truck. Dirt, faded paint, and broken wheels began to appear on that shiny red truck. His dad could have junked the truck and bought Nathan a new one. But he didn't do that. In truth, the dirty truck was worthless. However, because Nathan loved it, it became valuable. We might say that Nathan created the value in the truck.

We belong in the same category. God doesn't look for value in us before He loves us. He creates value in us by loving us first.

Read from God's Word

Dear friends, let us love one another, for love comes from God. Everyone who loves has been born of God and knows God. Whoever does not love does not know God, because God is love. This is how God showed His love among us: He sent His one and only Son into the world that we might live through Him. This is love: not that we loved God, but that He loved us and sent His Son as an atoning sacrifice for our sins. 1 John 4:7–10 ✍

So how do we answer that second question? Jesus does not love us because of our good behavior and He does not take away His love because of our bad behavior. Why does He love us so? "Just because I choose to," says Jesus. "I want you to be with Me always. The heavenly Father made you, and I died on the cross for you because I love you. You belong to Me forever."

_____Let's talk: Why do you think your parents love you even when you disobey them? How can you return love to them?

_____Let's pray: Thank You, Jesus, for loving us completely and giving us value and worth. Help us love others with Your special kind of love. Amen.

G. T. Z.

Read from God's Word

"Four things on earth are small, yet they are extremely wise: Ants are creatures of little strength, yet they store up their food in the summer." Proverbs 30:24–25 ✐

Winter Is Coming

You may know the story of the grasshopper and the ant. The grasshopper played all summer, while the ant worked hard to prepare for the coming winter. The grasshopper did not survive, but the ant lived off the food he had stored up for himself.

The Bible verses from Proverbs point out that ants are wise creatures. They are diligent workers, and they have a keen sense of what time it is. They prepare for what is coming.

The season of winter is coming. We could give the name "winter" to any time that might come for which we need to be prepared. "Winter" might come in many different ways. You might become ill or be injured in an accident. Or maybe you are concerned about things to come during school this year.

Jesus never promised to make our winter storms go away. But He did promise that He will go through them with us. He will *never* leave us, whether it's winter or any other season.

What we need for the winter ahead is a real Helper, a real Savior, the real Jesus. He takes away our sins and makes us whole again. The joy of all this is that we don't have to seek out Jesus; He comes to us. He knows, like the ant, that winter is coming. But in Him, it will also pass.

———Let's talk: Is there a "winter" in your future about which you are concerned? Make time to read the Bible each day to store up God's wisdom in your heart.

———Let's pray: Dear Jesus, give us wisdom and strength to depend on You in every hardship we face. Thanks for Your promise to be with us always. Amen.

G. T. Z.

No Free Lunch

(O)ne day George was on vacation. He was fishing from a pier at the Outer Banks of North Carolina. He saw others catching skates (like a bleached-out stingray) and throwing them back into the water. So when he caught a skate, he planned to set it free and release it back into the ocean.

George's attempts to remove the hook from the skate's mouth only brought the flick of its long stinger into his arm. Moments later his arm started to go numb. He returned to the beach house where he told his wife what happened. She opened the phone book and found "Dial-a-Nurse." His wife called the number.

When the nurse answered, she wanted a certain kind of information even before finding out about the medical problem. She said, "First things first. What is your credit card number?" The call was going to cost $50!

"No free lunch" is a phrase people use to indicate that everything has a price. Certainly our salvation had a price, the very high price of Jesus' life given on the cross. However, Jesus doesn't require us to pay before He gives assistance and healing. We don't have to pay with good behavior or good works. What does Jesus charge for the forgiveness of all our sins and life eternal in heaven? Nothing on our part; everything on His. He comes to us in His love and mercy. We are truly blessed!

Read from God's Word

You see, at just the right time, when we were still powerless, Christ died for the ungodly. Very rarely will anyone die for a righteous man, though for a good man someone might possibly dare to die. But God demonstrates His own love for us in this: While we were still sinners, Christ died for us. Romans 5:6–8 ✎

_____Let's talk: Have you ever expected something to be free and found out later that it wasn't? How did that make you feel? How can you be an instrument of Jesus' love to others this week?

_____Let's pray: Dear God, thank You for sending Jesus to save us from the sting of death and giving us life with You forever. In Jesus' name. Amen.

G. T. Z.

Read from God's Word

We know that we live in Him and He in us, because He has given us of His Spirit. And we have seen and testify that the Father has sent His Son to be the Savior of the world. If anyone acknowledges that Jesus is the Son of God, God lives in him and he in God. And so we know and rely on the love God has for us. ... We love because He first loved us. 1 John 4:13–16, 19 ✐

Page 1

On January 27, 1986, the *Chicago Sun-Times* headline read "Number 1—Bears Shuffle to Title." Pictured on the front page was Mike Ditka, football coach for the Chicago Bears. The Windy City had won its first Super Bowl!

Page 2 was given over to more about the Bears' victory. So were pages 3, 4, 5, 6, 7, 8, 9, 10, 11, and 12. But on page 13 was an article titled "Fireman Saves 2, Dies Trying to Save More." Lt. Edmund Coglianese, age 42, of Engine Company 98 had died of burns and smoke inhalation after going back into the burning Mark Twain Hotel to look for more occupants.

Which story would you have put on page 1? The fireman who died saving lives or the Super Bowl? Jesus died on the cross to save all of us, yet we often forget to make Him page 1 in our life. We sometimes push Him to page 13.

But Jesus never makes us page 13 in His life. He calls us His brothers and sisters. What's more, He forgives us, even when we put Him on page 13 of our life.

We are called as Jesus' disciples in the world to "seek and save the lost." The world needs to see Jesus Christ, our rescuer, on page 1 in all we do and say.

———Let's talk: Why do you think things like sports or sales at stores get more attention than people like Lt. Coglianese? How can you show others that Jesus is page 1 in your life?

———Let's pray: Dear Jesus, may Your forgiveness inspire us to make You page 1, 2, 3, and all the other pages of our lives. In Your name we pray. Amen.

G. T. Z.

Don't Let It Go

For 130 years, the majestic 198-foot-tall lighthouse at Cape Hatteras has towered over Hatteras Island, North Carolina. Over the years, erosion had caused the Atlantic Ocean to move within 50 yards of the lighthouse.

Some people wanted to save the lighthouse from falling into the ocean. But others did not—they didn't want to spend the time and money necessary to save the largest lighthouse in America. Those who wanted to save the lighthouse worked hard getting money from Congress. They hired a company to move the lighthouse so it would be a safe distance from the ocean. They didn't let it go.

Jonah wanted the people of Nineveh to be let go. He didn't want to help them by warning them of God's punishment for their sins. He knew that if they were told about their sins, they might repent, and then the loving God would not destroy them. The story of Jonah ends with God telling Jonah that *He,* not Jonah, has the right to show mercy and decide what happens to His people.

God won't let us go either. God sent Jesus to die for us and bring us back to Himself as His own dear children. The Hatteras lighthouse couldn't pick itself up and move. Nor can we do anything to save ourselves. Someone has to do it for us. That someone is Jesus, who will never let go of us in this life or in the life to come.

Read from God's Word

But the LORD said, "You have been concerned about this vine, though you did not tend it or make it grow. It sprang up overnight and died overnight. But Nineveh has more than a hundred and twenty thousand people who cannot tell their right hand from their left, and many cattle as well. Should I not be concerned about that great city?" Jonah 4:10–11 ✐

———Let's talk: Why do you think Jonah didn't think the people of Nineveh should be spared? Why did God want the people to turn back to Him? What does this say about how much God loves us?

———Let's pray: Dear Jesus, thank You for never letting go of us. We are glad we can count on You to keep us safe. In Jesus' name. Amen.

G. T. Z.

Of Mice and Centipedes

D avid burst into the classroom, books and papers flying, shoelaces trailing behind like tails on mice. He scooped his stuff from the floor and scurried to his desk.

"Good morning, David. Please tie your shoes," said his teacher.

David was organizing stuff in his desk. The teacher and class waited. And waited.

"David, please tie your shoes," the teacher said again. "I'm glad you're not a centipede!"

David's friend raised his hand. "What if David *were* a centipede?"

David's eyes grew wide. "We wouldn't have money to buy all those shoes!" he said, smiling. He bent over to tie his only pair of shoes.

David's family had been struggling. His dad had lost his job and his mom had been in the hospital. They had lots of bills to pay. But David and his family tried not to worry because they knew God would care for them.

The Bible reminds us that birds and flowers don't worry. We are worth more than they, so surely God will give us all we need.

The Bible also tells us that God wants us to know that treasures in heaven are more valuable than treasures on earth. Jesus bought those heavenly treasures for us by His cross and empty tomb. So even if it seems like we don't have many treasures here on earth, we're rich in the things that really count.

_____Let's talk: What else would David need if he were a centipede? Why are you worth more than animals, birds, or flowers? How does God take care of your needs?

_____Let's pray: Dear Father in heaven, we praise You for our heavenly treasures—faith, forgiveness, and an eternal future with You. Thanks for sending Jesus to make these blessings possible. In His name we pray. Amen.

A. S.

Always with Us

Eric stared out the window at the sunny blue sky, remembering all the fun times he'd had during the summer. Today would be a perfect day for baseball! And here he was sitting in school, half listening to his teacher talk about all the great subjects they'd be studying this year.

I'd rather be playing baseball, Eric thought. Schoolwork is too hard.

The teacher's voice interrupted his daydreaming. "Please, students, always remember to raise your hand when you want to answer a question." She wrote *always* on the board for emphasis.

Always—where else had Eric seen that word recently? A moment later he remembered. His Sunday school teacher had written their memory verse on the board last Sunday: "Surely I am with you always" (Matthew 28:20).

She had explained that Jesus has promised to be with us at all times as we follow His command to tell others of His love. He lived and died for all so we can live with Him always in heaven.

Eric's thoughts were racing: *Jesus is with me always! That means He was with me when I struck out in June and when I hit that home run in July. And He'll be with me now as I do my work. Maybe school will be okay this year after all.*

_____Let's talk: Name some times and places when you're especially happy that Jesus is with you. How does His being with you help you?

_____Let's pray: Dear Jesus, please help us keep our minds on our schoolwork. Keep us in Your loving care. Thank You for being with us always. Amen.

A. S.

Read from God's Word

Then the eleven disciples went to Galilee, to the mountain where Jesus had told them to go. When they saw him, they worshiped Him; but some doubted. Then Jesus came to them and said, "All authority in heaven and on earth has been given to me. Therefore go and make disciples of all nations, baptizing them in the name of the Father and of the Son and of the Holy Spirit, and teaching them to obey everything I have commanded you. And surely I am with you always, to the very end of the age." Matthew 28:16–20

We Love by Being Loved

Read from God's Word

We love because He first loved us. If anyone says, "I love God," yet hates his brother, he is a liar. For anyone who does not love his brother, whom he has seen, cannot love God, whom he has not seen. And he has given us this command: Whoever loves God must also love his brother. 1 John 4:19–21 ✍

Brian sat on the bench with his teacher at recess, watching the other kids play ball.

"Why don't you join them?" suggested Mrs. Mullins as she motioned to the game.

"Nah," answered Brian. "They don't want me to play with them. I've never learned to play ball. I wish I had a dad or a big brother to teach me."

"I really liked the report you wrote on dinosaurs, Brian. You write very well!"

"Thanks," he mumbled.

"After recess would you like to read your report to the class?"

"Sure." Brian smiled and nodded his head. *At least his teacher was okay*, he thought.

Sometimes God works through teachers to show us His love. Jesus knew what it felt like to be rejected. He had also been rejected, but He did not reject others in return. Instead Jesus showed His great love for them and for all of us.

Whatever our nationality, race, abilities, or background, we are precious in our Savior's sight. How do we know? "This is how we know what love is: Jesus Christ laid down His life for us" (1 John 3:16). What a great reason to be kind to everyone we know!

———Let's talk: Is everyone in your class at school included in activities? What can you do to make everyone feel a part of your group?

———Let's pray: Dear God, thank You for sending many helpers to show Your love for us. Help us to love all those around us. In our Savior's name we pray. Amen.

A. S.

The Quiet Ones

Read from God's Word

Your beauty should not come from outward adornment, such as braided hair and the wearing of gold jewelry and fine clothes. Instead, it should be that of your inner self, the unfading beauty of a gentle and quiet spirit, which is of great worth in God's sight. 1 Peter 3:3–4

Susan shyly approached her teacher's desk. She waited patiently while the other children in front of her blurted out their stories about the weekend to the teacher. When the bell rang, the other students filed to their seats, and Susan turned to follow them.

"Susan, did you have something to tell me too?" asked the teacher.

Susan's face lit up as she whispered in her teacher's ear, "I have a new baby brother!"

The next week Susan walked into the classroom with her mom and new brother. All the children crowded around to see him and count his tiny fingers and toes. Susan didn't have to say anything. She just grinned.

Sometimes we don't hear the quiet ones like Susan. But God always hears them, even when they're not talking. The Bible says that a gentle and quiet person is very precious in God's sight. He sent His Son, Jesus, to die on the cross for everyone—the loud ones and the quiet ones.

Jesus Himself was quiet as He gave His life for us. The Bible tells us He was the uncomplaining Lamb of God. He gave Himself up for us in a gentle, quiet manner.

Here on earth some of us sing loud praises to God, while others may sing soft praises. God hears us all, even as we sing our loud and quiet praises all the way to eternity!

_____Let's talk: Do you know someone who's quiet? How can quiet persons share God's love? Why is being a good listener important too?

_____Let's pray: Dear God, thank You for those who have a gentle and quiet spirit. Help us love them and learn from them. In Jesus' name we pray. Amen.

A. S.

Read from God's Word

Each one should use whatever gift he has received to serve others, faithfully administering God's grace in its various forms. If anyone speaks, he should do it as one speaking the very words of God. If anyone serves, he should do it with the strength God provides, so that in all things God may be praised through Jesus Christ. To Him be the glory and the power for ever and ever. Amen. 1 Peter 4:10–11 ✍

Purple People?

Paul and his mom had just driven into the school parking lot. Suddenly Paul exclaimed, "Mom, I left my reading assignment at home! Could we please go back for it?"

"Paul, you've been reading a book all the way to school—and you forgot your *reading* assignment?"

"But, Mom, that homework was too easy, and this book is about dinosaurs and archaeology!"

Paul is very bright. He usually finishes his work quickly and then reads a book. In fact, he almost always has a book with him wherever he goes.

God has blessed Paul with a sharp mind. All of us have been blessed by God in different ways. Some are good in sports. Some find it easy to know when others are feeling sad and what to say to make them glad.

Wouldn't life be boring if we were all the same? What if all flowers were yellow? What if all people were purple? Although God loves us all the same, He has made us different so we can serve Him in different ways. When we use our talents from God, we give glory to Him.

We want to glorify God because of what Jesus has made us. Through Christ's great victory on Calvary, He has made us God's own children. That's the greatest blessing of all.

_____Let's talk: Answer the "what if" questions in today's devotion. How are you different from your friends? How can you serve God in special ways with your gifts?

_____Let's pray: Dear God, thank You for giving us different talents. Help us use them to glorify You. In our Savior's name we pray. Amen.

A. S.

God Provides

"But, Mom, I gotta have white soccer spikes," Michael pleaded. "The other guys will laugh at me if I play in these crummy old sneakers."

His mother tried to reason with him. "Michael, I know it's important for you to have spikes like the other boys. But since your dad was laid off, we have less money to spend. We can't afford new spikes. This is something we can pray about. God will provide an answer."

Michael looked doubtful. "How is God gonna buy me new spikes—especially white ones?" he asked.

"Let's pray and wait for an answer."

So they sat down and thanked God for all He had given them. Then they asked for a solution to the problem.

The next week, Michael's Aunt Carol called. "Joshua has outgrown his soccer spikes," she began. "We wondered if you'd like to have them, Michael."

"Are they white?" asked Michael.

"No, but maybe you could give them a few coats of white shoe polish."

Michael didn't get exactly what he wanted, but he was thankful for the answer to his prayer. Our heavenly Father doesn't always give us everything we ask for, but He gives us everything we need. God's best gift was His Son, Jesus. He came to search us out and to save us from being lost. We can surely trust Him to supply all our needs.

_____Let's talk: Why did Michael worry about the soccer shoes? What did he and his mom do that led to a solution to his problem?

_____Let's pray: Heavenly Father, thank You for all You have given us. Help us to trust You and not to worry. We are so thankful that we have Jesus because we need His love more than anything else. Amen.

S. M.

Read from God's Word

And my God will meet all your needs according to His glorious riches in Christ Jesus. To our God and Father be glory for ever and ever. Amen. Philippians 4:19–20

A Tough Decision

Maria was usually cheerful and talkative, but she had been very quiet during dinner. Later, Maria was studying in her room when her mother peeked in.

"Hi, hon, what's goin' on?"

"Mom, have you ever cheated at anything?" Maria looked down at her math book.

Hesitating, Mrs. Vasquez said, "I remember once at the grocery, the cashier gave me too much change. I didn't tell him. I prayed about it. After I talked with God, I returned the money."

"Some kids asked me to cheat on the math test tomorrow," Maria explained. "I know it's wrong to cheat, but I want to ace that test. I'm not sure just a prayer will help me do what's right."

Maria had a tough decision to make. She wasn't sure she could get an A without cheating. She studied hard and prayed for God's strength and guidance. Together, she and her mother read Hebrews 2:18: "Because He Himself suffered when He was tempted, He is able to help those who are being tempted."

Imagine! Jesus, who is God, has gone through temptation too. He not only conquered temptation, He also suffered the terrible consequences that we deserve for every time we give in to sin. We will face temptation every day. But through the Holy Spirit, God gives us His power and strength to resist temptation and sin.

The next morning, Maria had made her choice.

_____Let's talk: What do you think Maria did? How can you find help when you're tempted to do what you know is wrong?

_____Let's pray: Lord Jesus, every day we face temptations. Give us Your own strength so we might overcome temptation. Thanks, Lord. Amen.

S. M.

Signs along Life's Way

Signs are everywhere. Punch a code into the computer and up pops a sign. Go for a drive and you see lots of signs. Look at the signs in the stores. Some tell you where to buy; some say what to buy. And then there's the sign that tells you how much you bought!

Jesus gave signs for His disciples. We call them miracles. With each miracle He performed, He wanted His disciples to see something special.

In the story told in today's reading, Jesus performed a miracle. He made wine out of water. He did this to help some friends at a wedding, but the sign He wanted His disciples to see was much greater. John writes that Jesus "revealed" (or showed) His glory through this miracle. He revealed that He was God, not just man. The miracles of Jesus showed God's glory by revealing His power. He revealed this same glory when He died and rose again to defeat sin.

Read from God's Word

A wedding took place at Cana in Galilee. ... Jesus' mother said to Him, "They have no more wine." ... Nearby stood six stone water jars. ... Jesus said to the servants, "Fill the jars with water"; so they filled them to the brim. ... The master of the banquet tasted the water that had been turned into wine ... and said, "Everyone brings out the choice wine first ... but you have saved the best till now." ... [Jesus] thus revealed His glory, and His disciples put their faith in Him. John 2:1–11 ❧

God still gives us signs to read. The best ones are in His Word. Others come through people whom God uses to show His love: Parents who care for us, teachers who give us extra help, friends who spend time with us—these are signs of God's love.

Think of your life as a road. Along the way are many signs. Keep on the lookout for those that are from God. They show His marvelous love for you.

_____Let's talk: Look up Matthew 5:16. What are some things you can ask God to help you do that can show His love to others?

_____Let's pray: Dear Jesus, thank You for the many signs of Your love. Thank You for revealing them to us in ways we can understand. In Your name we pray. Amen.

J. K.

Hidden Colors

How great is the love the Father has lavished on us, that we should be called children of God! And that is what we are! The reason the world does not know us is that it did not know Him. Dear friends, now we are children of God, and what we will be has not yet been made known. But we know that when He appears, we shall be like Him, for we shall see Him as He is. Everyone who has this hope in Him purifies himself, just as He is pure. 1 John 3:1–3

In some places many trees are beginning to show that fall has arrived. The greens of summer turn to the reds, yellows, and browns of autumn. Where do these colors come from?

Scientists tell us that these colors are always there in leaves. We just can't see them because the green colors are so strong. But when the air gets cooler, the trees stop making the green color in their leaves. The other colors start to show.

Perhaps we can compare the colors in leaves to the message of St. John in today's reading. John is talking about the day Jesus will return. While on earth, Jesus looked like other people. They saw only that He looked like a man. But after His death and resurrection, they saw something more. His disciples finally believed that He was the Lord. When Jesus returns for us on the Last Day, all people will finally see Him and say, "Jesus is Lord."

What a wonderful day that will be! We will see Jesus as He really is. And other people will finally see who we are. They will see that we are God's sons and daughters. The colors of heaven that have been hidden in us will burst forth. Then we will go to live with our Savior in the eternal spring of heaven.

_____Let's talk: Can you think of times when your true, faith-filled colors can be seen by others even now?

_____Let's pray: Dear Lord Jesus, thank You for making it possible for each of us to become like You. Make that wonderful day when everyone will see that we are Yours come soon. Amen.

J. K.

Impressing Others

D id you know that Santa Claus moved from the North Pole to Lapland? Eleanor Roosevelt, wife of the U.S. president, wanted to tour Finland. While she was there, she also wanted to see Lapland, but the officials thought there was nothing to see in Lapland. They decided to build a house in Lapland and call it the home of Santa Claus. Now Mrs. Roosevelt would have something to see. These officials wanted to impress Mrs. Roosevelt.

Do we sometimes try too hard to impress others? When that happens, we often try to make ourselves look better than we really are.

Today's Bible reading warns us against placing too much importance on ourselves. It says: "In humility consider others better than yourselves" (Philippians 2:3). If you put others in the place of importance, you will not be able to occupy that same place.

How can we put others in the place of importance? By remembering what Jesus did for us! "Your attitude should be the same as that of Christ Jesus" (verse 5). Jesus is God, yet "He humbled Himself and became obedient to death—even death on a cross!" (verse 8)

Our Savior made Himself lower than us so we could be lifted up and be called God's children. We have forgiveness, heaven, and God's love, so we don't *have* to act big. God *makes* us big in His own special way—He makes us His very own. Now we can follow the example of Jesus in putting others first.

_____Let's talk: What does it mean to place others first? What are some ways to do this?

_____Let's pray: Lord Jesus, forgive us for the times we think too highly of ourselves. Forgive us for the times we try to make ourselves look the most important. Thank You, Jesus, for serving us and for helping us to be a servant to others. Amen.

M. J. G.

Read from God's Word

Do nothing out of selfish ambition or vain conceit, but in humility consider others better than yourselves. Each of you should look not only to your own interests, but also to the interests of others. Your attitude should be the same as that of Christ Jesus: Who, being in very nature God, did not consider equality with God something to be grasped, but made Himself nothing, taking the very nature of a servant, being made in human likeness. And being found in appearance as a man, He humbled Himself and became obedient to death—even death on a cross! Philippians 2:3–8 ✑

Read from God's Word

Let us draw near to God with a sincere heart in full assurance of faith, having our hearts sprinkled to cleanse us from a guilty conscience and having our bodies washed with pure water. Let us hold unswervingly to the hope we profess, for He who promised is faithful. And let us consider how we may spur one another on toward love and good deeds. Let us not give up meeting together, as some are in the habit of doing, but let us encourage one another—and all the more as you see the Day approaching. Hebrews 10:22–25

Staying Afloat in Your Faith

Imagine that you are aboard a large ship. But you have not boarded the ship to cross the ocean. You have boarded it to worship God. Why did some Christians worship aboard ship? In the early 19th century, the Dutch government passed laws that gave the government more control of the church.

Many Christians felt that the true Gospel was not being preached in the churches. They tried to worship in homes, but the government made it illegal for more than 20 men, women, and children to gather in a home for worship. If they did, the pastor and other leaders were arrested.

One day someone realized that there were no laws forbidding worship on a ship. On Sunday mornings, rowboats carried people out to a ship. They worshiped there until the government passed another new law forbidding worship on a ship. After that, many Christians moved to America, where they could worship freely.

These Christians were determined to worship together. They wanted to be reminded of God's love, faithfulness, and forgiveness. Some people even today may think it is not important for them to attend worship. They may even think no one would miss them if they weren't there. That is not true.

Coming to worship with other Christians gives us the opportunity to encourage one another and to receive once again God's words of love and forgiveness. He comes to us in worship and strengthens us. Then we are ready to face whatever the world has to offer.

_____Let's talk: Why did Christians in the Netherlands worship aboard ship? Do you place the same importance on worship?

_____Let's pray: Holy Spirit, work in our hearts so we will want to worship You each day. Help us encourage family and friends to stay close to You. In the name of our Savior. Amen.

M. J. G.

october

Read from God's Word

Therefore, as God's chosen people, holy and dearly loved, clothe yourselves with compassion, kindness, humility, gentleness and patience. Bear with each other and forgive whatever grievances you may have against one another. Forgive as the Lord forgave you. And over all these virtues put on love, which binds them all together in perfect unity.
Colossians 3:12–14 ✐

Spilled Milk

As Marisa passed the potatoes, her elbow tipped over her glass. Milk ran across the table.

"There goes Messy Marisa again," teased her brother Jamal.

"That's enough, Jamal," said Dad, returning to the table with a dishcloth to help with the cleanup.

"But she's always spilling her milk," Jamal complained.

"I don't mean to," said Marisa. "It just happens."

"You need to learn a little patience, Jamal," said Mom. "And forgiveness."

"But how many times are you going to forgive her for that same mistake?" Jamal insisted.

"We're going to forgive her all the times she makes that same mistake," replied Dad.

We are all like Marisa. We make the same mistakes over and over. We don't always plan to sin, but sin happens. We ask God to forgive us, and He does. We try to do better, and maybe for a while we do. But sin always happens again and again. That's why God sent Jesus to die for the forgiveness of our sins. Like Marisa's loving father, our Father in heaven patiently forgives us time and again, never putting a limit on the number of times He will forgive.

As God's children, we follow His example. He helps us to be patient and to forgive one another over and over, just as God, for Christ's sake, has forgiven us.

_____Let's talk: Is there something that you continually do wrong although you try not to? How many times will God forgive you for that same mistake?

_____Let's pray: Dear God, thank You for loving us enough to forgive all of our sins, even the ones we repeat over and over. Help us to be patient and forgiving to others who sin against us. In Jesus' name we pray. Amen.

C. L.

Someone to Hold Me

Three-year-old Crystal walked into the department store between her mom and grandma. "Someone needs to hold me," begged Crystal as they began to look around.

"I'll hold you, Sweetie," offered Grandma, holding out both hands.

Crystal shook her head and pulled away. "No, Mommy do it," she said matter-of-factly.

Grandma chuckled. "She always does that," said Crystal's brother, Jimmy. "She says, 'Someone hold me,' and when anyone but Mom offers to, she gives that same answer, 'No, Mommy do it!'"

"I'm beginning to think my name is 'Someone,'" smiled Mom.

"Yes," Grandma said, "Crystal knows you are someone—someone special who loves her."

We all need someone in our life who is special to us. Someone we can go to when we need to talk about a problem or to share good news or just to hold us. We need someone who will always be there for us. That someone could be a parent, a friend, a pastor, or a teacher.

Read from God's Word

People were bringing little children to Jesus to have Him touch them, but the disciples rebuked them. When Jesus saw this, He was indignant. He said to them, "Let the little children come to me, and do not hinder them, for the kingdom of God belongs to such as these. I tell you the truth, anyone who will not receive the kingdom of God like a little child will never enter it." And He took the children in His arms, put His hands on them and blessed them. Mark 10:13–16 ༄

We all have someone else to whom we can go at any time and about any matter. That "Someone" is Jesus. Jesus is that special Someone who loves us so much that He died and rose again to take away our sin. He has promised to be with us at all times and in all places. Jesus is never too busy or too far away to listen to us. What a comfort to know that Jesus is with us in everything we do.

_____Let's talk: Is there someone who needs you to be a good friend? Does this someone know the love of Jesus?

_____Let's pray: Dear Jesus, You are our very special friend. Thank You for always being there to hear and answer our prayers. Help us to see those around who might need one of us to be their special friend. In Your name we pray. Amen.

C. L.

Read from God's Word

For God did not appoint us to suffer wrath but to receive salvation through our Lord Jesus Christ. He died for us so that, whether we are awake or asleep, we may live together with Him. Therefore encourage one another and build each other up, just as in fact you are doing. 1 Thessalonians 5:9–11 ∾

Encourage One Another

It was the first game of the basketball season. After only three minutes of play, the coach could see that something was wrong. She called a time-out.

"What's going on out there?" asked the coach as the girls gathered.

"It's the other team," said Jessica. "They're saying mean things to us and calling us names."

"Well, girls," said the coach, "you know what they're doing. They're trying to distract you so your minds are not on the game. Now what are we going to do to concentrate on what's important?"

"We'll try to ignore them," said Heidi, "and we can encourage each other in the plays."

"We can think really hard about our plays and concentrate on our shots," volunteered Cathy.

"That sounds good," agreed the coach. "Now let's ask God to help us and get back out there and play."

Christians are a lot like the players on this basketball team. But the victory is already ours. God has already won it for us through His Son, Jesus Christ. By dying on the cross and rising again, Jesus has defeated our opponents—sin, death, and the devil.

As Christians, things that would try to distract us and keep us from the victory constantly surround us. Like the players on this team, we can pray to God for help and encourage one another. He will help us stay focused so we can share Christ's victory for eternity.

_____Let's talk: What temptations try to distract you from focusing on God? How can you help others stay focused?

_____Let's pray: Dear Lord, thank You for winning the victory for us over sin, death, and the devil. Help us to ignore sin. May we always remember to encourage others to stay strong as the Holy Spirit gives us strength. In Your name we pray. Amen.

C. L.

When I Am Afraid

Read from God's Word

The LORD is my light and my salvation—whom shall I fear? The LORD is the stronghold of my life—of whom shall I be afraid? Psalm 27:1 ✒

Susie's mom had just tucked her under the blankets in Grandma's guest bedroom. Moments later they heard a scream.

"That scream can mean only one thing," said Dad. "Spider."

"Spider!" exclaimed Grandma. "How could Susie see a spider in the dark?"

"Fear can make you see lots of things," replied Dad as he left the room.

Mom and Dad went into the bedroom and found Susie sitting up, hugging her pillow.

"Spiders, Mom," Susie whispered hoarsely. "Spiders all over the wall."

The flower pattern on the wallpaper, which was so pretty in the light, did indeed look like spiders in the dark. Dad turned on the light, and Susie saw the spiders turn back into flowers.

"It looks like spiders in the dark, but it's only flowers," said Dad. "Do you see?"

"Yes," replied Susie, "but I'm still scared of spiders. Daddy, will you sit with me till I fall asleep?"

Fear is a natural human emotion. People are afraid of all kinds of things—spiders, big dogs, high places. Our heavenly Father knows our fears. He understands that there are times when we feel weak and insecure. At these times, God invites us to come to Him for safety and strength. God has the power to defend us from anything that could hurt us—even sin. He sent Jesus to be our Savior and promises to be with us always. When we are afraid, we can pray to Him, knowing He loves us and will take care of us.

_____Let's talk: What are some things people are afraid of? Does worrying about these fears help? What will help us overcome our fears?

_____Let's pray: Dear Father, You know everything about us. You know when we are afraid and need Your protection. Help us to trust in Your strength, confident that You love us, forgive us, and care for us. In Jesus' name. Amen.

C. L.

Courage to Try

Read from God's Word

"Be strong and courageous. Do not be afraid or terrified because of them, for the LORD your God goes with you; He will never leave you nor forsake you." Deuteronomy 31:6 ✍

Mrs. Rickman smiled at the look of concentration on Matthew's face as he sounded out words in the first-grade reader. He had come a long way since the first day of school when he walked into the classroom and announced, "I'm Matthew Williams, and you're not going to teach me how to read!"

Obviously someone had told Matthew a few things about first grade. He knew some things would be expected of him. One would be to learn to read. Matthew didn't think he would succeed and was afraid to try.

We have many challenges in life. People expect certain things of us. Teachers expect us to do well in school. Parents expect us to be well behaved. And then there are the things we expect of ourselves. Sometimes we know what is expected and want to succeed. But we don't think we can, so we're afraid to try.

God expects some things of us too. He has blessed each of us with talents and abilities. He wants us to use them in ways that glorify Him. God wants us to develop our talents, not hide them or be afraid to use them. He also wants us to remember His great love for us. He promises to be with us in everything we attempt in life and He wants us to trust in that promise. Our God, who was willing to send His Son to die in our place for our sins, is also with us when we take a math test or audition for a play. We can have courage and not be afraid to try. God is with us.

_____Let's talk: When have you been afraid to try something new? What talents do you think God has given you? How can you use them to glorify God?

_____Let's pray: Dear Jesus, there are so many expectations put on each of us. Sometimes we feel afraid that we won't succeed. Give us the courage to try, and help us to trust that You will be with us in our successes and our failures. In Your name we pray. Amen.

C. L.

Winds and Waves Obey Him

The weather warning interrupted the TV movie. Emergency sirens began blaring while the Cortez family walked down the stairs to the basement.

"I'm scared," said little Carlita as the family settled on the couch.

"Me too," admitted Rico. "Remember that book we just read about tornadoes? Terrible things can happen to people in bad storms."

"Yes," said Mr. Cortez as he checked the batteries in the flashlight. "Severe weather can certainly cause problems. But let's remember that there is Someone who is more powerful than the weather. That Someone is God. God is in control of the weather. He knows we need His protection right now, and we trust that He will provide that protection for us."

Like all things, weather is a blessing from God. We enjoy the warm, sunny days that allow us to play outside. Rain showers water our lawns and gardens. But no one appreciates when the rain turns into raging floodwaters or clouds turn into tornadoes. This powerful side of the weather scares us until we are reminded of what the disciples learned about God's power on a boat one stormy night: "Even the wind and the waves obey Him!" (Matthew 8:27).

Believing this, there is no need to fear the weather. The God who created us, redeemed us, and brought us to faith will also take care of us through life's storms.

Read from God's Word

I know that the LORD is great, that our Lord is greater than all gods. The LORD does whatever pleases Him, in the heavens and on the earth, in the seas and all their depths. He makes clouds rise from the ends of the earth; He sends lighting with the rain and brings out the wind from His storehouses. Psalm 135:5–7

_____Let's talk: Does your family have a plan to follow in weather emergencies? Does that plan include prayer?

_____Let's pray: Dear Father, sometimes we get frightened by the force of the weather. Heavy rain and strong winds make us realize how weak we are. Help us to trust in the power of Your love to give us protection. In Jesus' name we pray. Amen.

C. L.

Read from God's Word

Then Jesus declared, "I am the Bread of Life. He who comes to Me will never go hungry, and he who believes in Me will never be thirsty. ... All that the Father gives Me will come to Me, and whoever comes to Me I will never drive away. ... And this is the will of Him who sent Me, that I shall lose none of all that He has given Me, but raise them up at the last day. For My Father's will is that everyone who looks to the Son and believes in Him shall have eternal life, and I will raise him up at the last day." John 6:35–40

Bread of Life

One morning, Kelsey and Mrs. Lawton were filling the bird feeders. "Mom," said Kelsey, "the yard is always full of finches, blue jays, and robins. But why not hummingbirds?"

"Some birds are easier to attract than others," replied Mrs. Lawton. "All the birds that have found us know they can get well-fed here. The hummingbirds just haven't found us yet."

"But we give them fresh nectar every week," continued Kelsey. "Don't they know we're waiting for them so we can help take care of them?"

"No, they don't know that yet," said Mrs. Lawton. "But we will fill their feeder and keep watching. Maybe someday they will come."

In our Bible reading, Jesus calls Himself the Bread of Life. He tells us that people who hunger after God's love and forgiveness will be satisfied as they come to know and believe in Him. Like the robins and finches in Kelsey's backyard, which are attracted easily, many people are led by the Holy Spirit to fill themselves with spiritual food by studying God's Word.

But like the hummingbirds, some people are hard to attract. They don't know that God's spiritual food is offered also to them. But God continues to offer the Bread of Life and waits patiently for all to receive His love and forgiveness.

———Let's talk: How can you satisfy your spiritual hunger for the Bread of Life? Do you know someone who is still spiritually hungry?

———Let's pray: Dear Father, thank You for providing everything we need. Thank You for giving us Jesus, the Bread of Life. Help us to tell those who don't know Jesus about God's love for them. In Jesus' name. Amen.

C. L.

Tribulation or Talent

The fourth graders were winding up their discussion on disabilities. "Now," said the teacher, "we've seen that there are many kinds of disabilities. Not every person with a disability uses a wheelchair. Do you know anyone with a disability?"

The teacher glanced around the room for a raised hand as she handed out the crossword puzzle that reviewed the lesson. Her eyes rested on Lori, who had been born with her right hand and arm misshapen and smaller than her left. Yet everyone knew she was the best artist in class. The teacher's gaze passed over Mike, who had epilepsy. Sometimes his nighttime seizures left him too exhausted to come to school. But he worked hard and was the class math whiz. Then there was Mindy, who had cystic fibrosis. She often had difficulty breathing, yet she sang like an angel.

Some would say these children have disabilities, thought the teacher. *Yet no one in the class viewed them that way, not even the children themselves.* In fact, God had helped them take what could have been a real tribulation in their lives and develop a wonderful talent. Each of these children had a strong faith, which trusted God to do what was best for their lives. They had learned that they were specially created by God and had been given distinct talents they could use to His glory. What a wonderful way to thank God for His gifts of love and forgiveness.

Read from God's Word

"For I know the plans I have for you," declares the LORD, "plans to prosper you and not to harm you, plans to give you hope and a future. Then you will call upon Me and come and pray to Me, and I will listen to you. You will seek Me and find Me when you seek Me with all your heart." Jeremiah 29:11–13

_____Let's talk: Do you or someone you love have a disability? How has God helped you or that person develop a special talent?

_____Let's pray: Dear God, You have created us and given us both strengths and weaknesses. Help us to seek Your strength to turn our tribulations into talents. In Your name. Amen.

C. L.

We're on an Adventure

Read from God's Word

I lift up my eyes to the hills—where does my help come from? My help comes from the LORD, the Maker of heaven and earth. He will not let your foot slip—He who watches over you will not slumber; indeed, He who watches over Israel will neither slumber nor sleep. The LORD watches over you—the LORD is your shade at your right hand; the sun will not harm you by day, nor the moon by night. The LORD will keep you from all harm—He will watch over your life; the LORD will watch over your coming and going both now and forevermore. Psalm 121 ✍

"Dad, do you know where we are?" asked Steve.

"Sure, I do. We're on this gravel road," replied Dad. "More important, I know where we want to be. This road is going to take us there."

"Why don't we stick to the main road, Ted?" suggested Mom.

"Nah," said Dad, "we're on an adventure!"

"I don't like it when he says we're on an adventure," grumbled Rachel. "That always means we're taking the slowest, most difficult route."

"Cheer up!" smiled Dad. "Just sit back and trust dear, old Dad."

As Christians, we are on an adventure. It's called *life*. And we have a destination. It's called *heaven*. Between the time we are born and the time we go to heaven, God allows us to travel many roads. Some days will be filled with successes. The road will seem smooth and the route will seem short. Other days will have troubles and the route will seem rocky and long.

God, our dear Father, always knows exactly where we are on this journey. We may encounter people who need our help. We may veer from His path and have to retrace our steps and start again. But whether the road is rocky or smooth, God is with us, helping us to reach our final destination, which He has prepared for us.

_____Let's talk: In His life on this earth, Jesus traveled many rocky roads. What did He do when the path seemed too rough? How can we follow His example?

_____Let's pray: Dear Lord, we know that You have a place reserved for us in heaven. Keep our faith in You strong even when the road of life is rocky. Thank You for Your Son, Jesus, who traveled the road to the cross to take away our sins. In Your name we pray. Amen.

C. L.

Beautiful Feet

Read from God's Word

How, then, can they call on the One they have not believed in? And how can they believe in the One of whom they have not heard? And how can they hear without someone preaching to them? And how can they preach unless they are sent? As it is written, "How beautiful are the feet of those who bring good news!" Romans 10:14–15 ⮌

"Welcome, students," said Mrs. Stanton. "The residents of Winter Haven Nursing Home are looking forward to your singing. They are always eager to see your young faces, especially when the message you bring is the message of God's love. Please come this way."

The students followed Mrs. Stanton into the room set up for their choir concert. As they lined up, one elderly woman smiled at Elena and said, "Children, you have beautiful feet."

Elena smiled back at her and then looked down at her scuffed, worn-out shoes. *My shoes are a mess,* she thought. *I wonder what she's talking about.*

The students sang one song of praise after another. Their enthusiastic audience smiled and clapped. After the last song, Mrs. Stanton said, "This morning in our devotion, we read about the need to hear the Good News of God's love in Christ. Romans 10 tells us, 'How beautiful are the feet of those who bring good news!' Children, there is no better news than the message you have proclaimed today through your music. And we are very thankful that God has sent you here to share that message with us."

Elena smiled at the audience as she followed the line of students to the refreshments. *Yes,* she thought, *the message of Jesus' life, death, and resurrection is the best news in the world. And I'm glad that God used me today to help tell these people that wonderful message.*

_____Let's talk: Do *you* have beautiful feet? How has God used you to spread His Good News of salvation?

_____Let's pray: Dear Jesus, knowing about Your love, forgiveness, and the gift of eternal life is the most important news in the world. Thank You for revealing this news to us. Please provide us with opportunities to share this Good News with others. In Your name we pray. Amen.

C. L.

Thank You!

Read from God's Word

For it is by grace you have been saved, through faith—and this not from yourselves, it is the gift of God—not by works, so that no one can boast. For we are God's workmanship, created in Christ Jesus to do good works, which God prepared in advance for us to do. Ephesians 2:8–10 ✍

Michael, a brave firefighter, lay in a hospital bed. He had rescued a sleeping boy from his burning home and had been burned badly. He was in pain, but the boy was safe. He heard a soft knock on the door. "Come in," Michael called.

Jason, the boy he had rescued, walked into the room with his mom. "I just wanted to say thank you," Jason said. "If it weren't for you, I would be in the hospital or maybe even dead." Jason swallowed and tried to go on, but he couldn't speak.

His mom stepped forward. "I'm so grateful to you for saving my son. What can we do for you? Would you like some magazines? A newspaper? Ice cream or candy? I know hospital food isn't the greatest. Please don't hesitate to ask for anything."

Jason and his mom were so thankful for the gift of Jason's life that they were willing to do anything to show the firefighter their gratitude. Jesus Christ has rescued us. We were dead in our sins and lost with no hope of salvation. Then our Savior came. He died on the cross and rose again so our sins might be forgiven and death would have no power over us. Praise God for that! He has saved us from eternal death. Our hearts are filled with joy for what He's done. As Christians, we want to show our thankfulness. Let's pray that we are as eager to show our gratitude to our Savior as Jason and his mom were to Michael.

_____Let's talk: From what has Jesus saved us? How can we show our gratitude? Do something today to show your thankfulness.

_____Let's pray: Dear Savior, we are so thankful for Your death and resurrection, which means our sins are forgiven and we have the gift of eternal life. Please help us to show our thanks every day by the way we live. In Your name we pray. Amen.

L. S.

Is It Time Yet?

Read from God's Word

And we know that in all things God works for the good of those who love Him, who have been called according to His purpose. Romans 8:28 ✎

Sam walked into his mother's office. Lunch had been cleared away just 30 minutes ago, but she suspected he wanted something to eat. "Mom? Is it time for a snack yet?"

Mom smiled. "Honey, we just finished lunch a little while ago. It's not time yet. Go outside and ride your bike or play in the tree house."

"All right," Sam replied and left reluctantly. A half hour later, Sam came back again. "Is it time yet, Mom? I'm really hungry. I rode my bike like you wanted me to."

"It's still too soon, Sam. Please wait a little while longer."

Sam grumbled. "I can't wait until I'm big. Then I'll eat whatever I want when I want it."

Mom asked, "Would that be good for you, Sam? Although you don't like it, I'm doing what is best for you. You need to wait."

Often when we pray, we expect God to answer immediately. Like Sam, we want answers right away. God knows all that we need and wisely answers our prayers with "yes," "wait awhile," or "no." No matter how God answers our prayers, we can trust Him to do what is best. After all, He has done the best thing for us by sending Jesus into the world as our Savior from sin. And heaven will be worth waiting for!

———Let's talk: Think of a time when God answered a prayer with a yes. Think of a time when it seemed like God wasn't answering a prayer. Looking back, can you understand why He answered these prayers the way He did?

———Let's pray: Dear Lord, we do not see the big picture like You do. Forgive us when we grumble and think that You do not hear us. Please help us always to trust that You will do what is best for us. In Jesus' name. Amen.

L. S.

Watermelons and Trust

Bonnie calmly sat in the car eating a slice of watermelon. She had been swimming in the lake, but Dad called her out when the sky started getting dark. Picnickers hustled to gather things together. Bonnie grabbed a slice of watermelon and headed for the car.

As the family left the park, Bonnie rolled her window down to spit out the seeds. The sky grew darker. A few raindrops fell, and then a few more. The little girl quickly put up the window, but she continued to eat. The wind grew stronger and shook the car forcefully.

Barbie, Bonnie's older sister, asked, "Why are you eating watermelon at a time like this? Don't you know it's storming?"

Bonnie rode in the car, eating her watermelon, confident her father would get them home safely through the storm. Bonnie's trust in her father kept her calm. But Barbie focused on the storm and the potential danger to the family.

Storms of different kinds come into our lives—friends that hurt us, problems with teachers, even arguments with parents. Jesus asks us to trust Him, and He will see us through. He weathered the storm of sin for us; and with Christ at our side, we can weather any storm.

———Let's talk: What kind of storms are you facing right now? What does the Bible reading tell us about tough times?

———Let's pray: Dear Lord, Master of all things, when we fail to trust You to help us through our problems, forgive us. Remind us that You love us and will help us always. In Jesus' name. Amen.

L. S.

Come and Go

Read from God's Word

And be content with what you have, because God has said, "Never will I leave you; never will I forsake you." So we say with confidence, "The Lord is my helper; I will not be afraid. What can man do to me?" Remember your leaders, who spoke the word of God to you. Consider the outcome of their way of life and imitate their faith. Jesus Christ is the same yesterday and today and forever. Hebrews 13:5b–8 ⌇

Janet rummaged through a box in the closet. She and her mother were cleaning. "Hey, Mom, what's this?" she asked, pulling out a wall hanging made of heavy yarn and beads.

Mom laughed. "That? That's called *macramé*. It was a popular craft quite a few years ago. Everyone did macramé projects, and then they stopped. I liked it at the time. Now I wonder why. What else is in there?" she asked.

Janet dug deeper. "Oh, look. Here are Ray's Power Rangers! They aren't as popular as they used to be. I remember when Ray had a Power Ranger lunch box, backpack, pajamas, and everything else. I bet he doesn't even know these are in here."

"Probably not," said Mom. "I'm always amazed how quickly things come and go. One minute something is popular, and then people forget about it completely."

Clothing styles, toy fads, and other trends come and go. Their popularity often lasts for a short time and then it is gone. But our Lord and Savior is different. Verse 8 of the Bible reading says, "Jesus Christ is the same yesterday and today and forever." The Bible promises us that Jesus will never change. If we sin and do wrong, He still loves us. If we start to drift away from Him, He is still there. What a wonderful gift we have, knowing He remains the same no matter how we change or what we go through. His love and forgiveness remain constant.

_____Let's talk: What toys or activities are popular right now? How long do you think they will be popular? How do you feel knowing that Jesus never changes? What does that mean for you?

_____Let's pray: Dear Lord, we live in a world of constant change. We thank You for not changing and for loving us no matter what happens. In Jesus' name. Amen.

L. S.

Turned Around

"Brother Saul, the Lord—Jesus, who appeared to you on the road as you were coming here—has sent me so that you may see again and be filled with the Holy Spirit." Immediately, something like scales fell from Saul's eyes, and he could see again. He got up and was baptized, and after taking some food, he regained his strength.
Acts 9:17b–19 ✍

"Don't put those in the trash!" said Mrs. Brown. Her son was throwing away a bag of old Christmas cards. "What good are they?" asked Brian. "Christmas was so long ago!"

"I want to use them to make place mats for my preschoolers. We glue the cards onto construction paper and then laminate them," said Mrs. Brown.

"Oh, I never thought of that."

Mrs. Brown walked over to the trash with some scraps of construction paper. She saw Brian had also thrown away butter tubs. "Oh, Brian. These need to be recycled. The symbol on the bottom shows they can be turned into something useful."

Brian smiled, "Sorry, Mom. I didn't realize they were in that bag too."

When we recycle things, we make it possible to use them again in a new and different way. In the Bible reading, we see how God changed Saul and gave him a new opportunity to serve Him. Saul had been a persecutor of Christians. When God entered Saul's heart, he became Paul, a preacher and teacher for Christ. In the same way, God takes us sinners, showers us with His love and forgiveness, and turns us into new creatures. We belong to Him. Now that we are changed by His love, we can reach out to others.

———Let's talk: Think of something that seems useless or worthless. Can you think of another way to use it? How has God changed you to help others? You can read the whole story about Paul's conversion in Acts 9:1–19.

———Let's pray: Dear Lord, thank You for forgiving our sins, washing us clean, and turning us into useful people. Please help us find ways to help other people and show them Your love. In Jesus' name. Amen.

L. S.

What You Deserve

Read from God's Word

For the wages of sin is death, but the gift of God is eternal life in Christ Jesus our Lord. Romans 6:23 ✑

Pam looked over her shoulder. No one was around. She quietly opened the garage door and wheeled out her brother's bike. Her bike was old, but Mark's bike was brand new and so cool. *I'm almost safe*, she thought.

"Hi, Pam," called Mrs. Thornton. "How are you today?"

"Just fine," Pam answered with a nervous glance at the house. She hoped Dad hadn't heard their neighbor. Right then Dad walked around the corner of the garage.

He looked disappointed. "What are you doing?" he asked.

"I'm sorry, Dad," said Pam, looking guilty. "I wouldn't hurt Mark's bike, honest."

"That's not the point," said Dad. "You were told not to take Mark's bike again or what would happen?"

Pam hung her head. "You said I wouldn't be able to go anywhere for a week."

Today's Bible verse tells us that because we sin, we deserve to be punished. And the punishment for sin is eternal death. But the verse doesn't stop there. It goes on to give us hope. Although we do not deserve it, God gives us a gift. His gift to us is eternal life, not because of anything we have done but because of what His Son did on our behalf. Jesus lived a perfect life, died, and rose again for us! He loves us that much!

_____Let's talk: When have you done something wrong and gotten what you deserved? Can you think of a time when your parents did not punish you as you deserved?

_____Let's pray: Dear Savior, we thank You for Your great love and mercy toward us. We ask Your forgiveness for our sins and failures. Keep us strong in our faith. In Jesus' name. Amen.

L. S.

Read from God's Word

Like newborn babies, crave pure spiritual milk, so that by it you may grow up in your salvation, now that you have tasted that the Lord is good. 1 Peter 2:2–3 ✍

Got Milk?

Jacob opened the refrigerator door and grabbed the milk. He poured a big glass and drank it down. After he filled it up again, he put the jug back into the fridge.

Mom smiled, "I'm glad to see you drinking milk."

"You are? Why?" Jacob answered.

"I'm sure you've learned in school why milk is important," said Mom.

Jacob grinned. "Yeah, that's an easy one. The calcium in milk helps build strong bones and teeth."

"That's right." Mom continued, "Milk is important for people of all ages, but especially for you. You'll soon be going through a big growth spurt when you will need lots of calcium to help your bones grow."

Healthy babies want and need milk. If children or teens don't get milk, their bones will not grow properly. In the same way, as Christians we need God's Word. God wants us to spend time reading His Word and studying it. God's Word nourishes our faith and helps it grow. In His Word we discover God's promise to provide a Savior from sin. In His Word we discover how Jesus came to be that Savior. And in His Word we discover that all who believe in Jesus as Savior will live forever in heaven. How wonderful it is to learn more and more about God's love in His Word!

_____Let's talk: Why is milk important for babies? Why is God's Word important for people? How are you nourished by God's Word?

_____Let's pray: Dear Lord, we thank You for Your Holy Word, given to us in the Bible. We ask that You help us spend more time reading and studying the Word so we grow in faith. In Jesus' name. Amen.

L. S.

Lights Out

Read from God's Word

The LORD is my light and my salvation—whom shall I fear? The LORD is the stronghold of my life—of whom shall I be afraid? Psalm 27:1 ⊲

Each week Lisa and her family drove to a church that was not close to home. It was in the inner city. They helped tutor neighborhood children in math or reading. Lisa liked helping, but sometimes she felt nervous. She wasn't always certain she was safe in the unfamiliar neighborhood.

As usual, a lady named Florence waited for them at the door. "Come in, folks," she welcomed. "We're almost ready to start."

The family walked downstairs to the basement where children and other adults had gathered. They sat down. After the opening devotion and prayer, they separated into groups and started working.

Suddenly, the lights went out. The basement windows were covered, so the room was completely dark. Florence's voice rang out. "Stay calm, everyone. I'll go to the kitchen for candles. Form a circle and hold hands with the little ones." Lisa tried to stay calm. She wanted to be home—*now!* Carefully, she made her way to the circle and held hands with two small children. *They are probably more frightened than I am,* she thought.

It can be frightening to be in the dark. Other situations can be frightening, too, like when parents fight or a family has money problems. God promises to be with us no matter what. With Him on our side, we have nothing to fear. Jesus came to break through the darkness of sin. He gives us strength to carry on through any and every situation.

_____Let's talk: When have you been frightened by something? How did God help you through?

_____Let's pray: Dear God, there are times when we are afraid. Remind us that You are always with us. With You by our side, we have nothing to fear. In Jesus' name. Amen.

L. S.

Fire!

Read from God's Word

When we put bits into the mouths of horses to make them obey us, we can turn the whole animal. Or take ships as an example. Although they are so large and are driven by strong winds, they are steered by a very small rudder wherever the pilot wants to go. Likewise the tongue is a small part of the body, but it makes great boasts. Consider what a great forest is set on fire by a small spark. The tongue also is a fire, a world of evil among the parts of the body. It corrupts the whole person, sets the whole course of his life on fire, and is itself set on fire by hell. James 3:3–6 〜

"Only *you* can prevent forest fires," says Smokey the Bear, a character seen in books, commercials, and ads. He encourages people to be careful with fire when they are in the woods.

Fire is useful if it is handled properly. It gives warmth and cooks food. If it is not handled right, a small spark can start a big fire. A raging forest fire destroys many things. People and animals lose their homes, and sometimes their life. Valuable lumber is lost. God's creation is wounded.

Our tongues can be as dangerous as a spark that starts a fire. A friend or classmate says something that may or may not be true. Another person repeats it and adds a little more to the story. Before long, the original statement has been repeated and changed so many times that it is hard to recognize. By this time, a person's feelings may be hurt or reputation may be ruined.

The Bible encourages us to be careful with our tongue, which can get out of control quickly. It is important to keep a tight reign on what we say. The Bible also tells us our tongue can be used for good, like singing praises to God, encouraging family and friends, and telling others about Jesus, our Lord and Savior. With God's help we can control our tongue. He forgives us when we fail and reminds us that He is with us always, helping us to use our tongues to spread His love to others.

_____Let's talk: How recently have you repeated something about a friend or classmate? Did it need to be repeated? How can you avoid the temptation to gossip?

_____Let's pray: Dear Lord, we are sorry that our tongue sometimes gets away from us. Please forgive us. Help us not to repeat things that may hurt or damage others. In Jesus' name. Amen.

L. S.

Crosses in the Cloth

Read from God's Word

Day after day every priest stands and performs his religious duties; again and again he offers the same sacrifices, which can never take away sins. But when this Priest had offered for all time one sacrifice for sins, He sat down at the right hand of God. Since that time He waits for His enemies to be made His footstool, because by one sacrifice He has made perfect forever those who are being made holy. Hebrews 10:11–14 ↝

Alena watched as her mother changed the colored cloths on the altar. She noticed the crosses in all four corners. She held one end and Mom held the other as they carefully laid the long piece of linen across the altar. Then Alena checked the cross design in the center. Her mom noticed how she looked at the large metal cross on the wall behind the altar to check that they lined up exactly.

"Our pastor taught us all about the altar cloth in Bible class," said Mom. "He explained that the linen material helps us remember the cloth wrapped around Jesus' body for His burial. The crosses on one end represent the nail marks in His hands. The crosses on the other end would be the nail marks in His feet. The cross in the center is for the wound in Jesus' side."

"That's really something," said Alena. "It all has a special meaning!"

"There are deeper meanings too," Mom said. "In the Old Testament, altars were for sacrifices of animals. Remember when Abraham was almost ready to sacrifice his son, Isaac? God stopped him and provided a lamb instead. Well, Jesus is called the Lamb of God. He sacrificed Himself in our place, for our sins. The linen cloth on the altar reminds us of all that."

"Thanks for telling me, Mom. Coming along to help with the altar cloths was more interesting than I thought it would be." Alena smiled. "I'll be thinking about this tomorrow during church."

_____Let's do: Look up Mark 15:46, John 19:34–37, and John 20:24–28. How do these verses fit with the crosses on the altar cloth? Try looking for shapes like crosses in things you see every day.

_____Let's pray: O Christ, the Lamb of God, You sacrificed Yourself on account of our sins. May we always call You Savior. Amen.

M. K.

The Path of the Shrew

Read from God's Word

O LORD, You have searched me and You know me. Psalm 139:1 ✑

Joe likes animals. When he mows the yard, he watches for toads. He knows their special places and sometimes pets them. Joe likes to sit on the front step when he's done with his work. Rabbits crouch in the grass. After a while they get brave and move a little closer, but they are always on the lookout for danger.

A person can learn a lot by watching animals. But the Lord knows much more about each of us. In Psalm 139, we learn that the Lord watches our paths all the time. He knows what we think. He knows everything we say and do, even before we say or do it.

A small animal in the wild can be overcome by one of its natural enemies. We have natural enemies too. At times we follow the ways of the world around us. We give in to our sinful hearts and to the devil. We go off the paths God has laid out for us in His Word.

However, these enemies need not destroy us. God sent His Son to travel life's way perfectly for us. Jesus defeated the powers of evil when He died for us. He lives again to give us a new life with Him. He surrounds us with His love. The Holy Spirit helps us follow the right paths. He offers us forgiveness when we stray. How wonderful that the God who knows us completely is also our forgiving friend!

_____Let's talk: In what ways do we act like wild creatures? How does God "tame" us? What pathways does God see you following in your everyday life?

_____Let's pray: Lord, You know us better than we know ourselves. Thank You for loving us even though we are sinners. Please keep us on the path to our eternal home with You. Amen.

M. K.

A Tale of Two Peaches

Read from God's Word

All day long he craves for more, but the righteous give without sparing. Proverbs 21:26 ✍

Mr. Nelson had a peach tree. Sometimes on Saturdays, Mike went to see Mr. Nelson. They would walk all around his yard. They'd look to see how the peaches were doing and check out the corn, tomatoes, carrots, and onions in his garden. Mr. Nelson would fill a sack with fresh vegetables and ripe peaches for Mike to take home.

One spring only two peaches blossomed. "One for you and one for me," Mr. Nelson said with a smile. He invited Mike to choose which one would be his. In August, the peaches were ready. Mr. Nelson gave Mike the one he had chosen. It was large and juicy. And it was half of his crop.

Mr. Nelson enjoyed giving. When he had lots of peaches, he shared lots of them. When he had only two, he still shared. He knew that God is the most generous Giver of all. The peaches were some of God's gifts. Sharing the crop was one way for Mr. Nelson to show his thankfulness. That gave other people a special reason to thank God too.

All of us have received much from God. He has given us life with all its blessings. Out of love He sent His Son, Jesus, who gave His life to save us from our sin. The Holy Spirit gives us faith in Jesus. By faith we receive the precious gifts of forgiveness and eternal life. God also gives us thankful hearts to share His gifts with others.

——Let's talk: What makes it hard sometimes to share God's gifts? What makes it easy? What can you share with others? Think of someone who needs something you can give.

——Let's pray: We thank You, dear God, for the gift of salvation and for all Your other blessings. Please forgive us when we're selfish with Your gifts. Lead us to share joyfully with other people because You love us all. Amen.

M. K.

Making Music to the Lord

Read from God's Word

Sing joyfully to the LORD, you righteous; it is fitting for the upright to praise Him. Praise the LORD with the harp; make music to Him on the ten-stringed lyre. Sing to Him a new song; play skillfully, and shout for joy. For the word of the LORD is right and true; He is faithful in all He does. The LORD loves righteousness and justice; the earth is full of His unfailing love. Psalm 33:1–5 ✍

Trinh sat on the patio. When his sisters were done watching TV, he'd be able to practice his piano lesson. He hoped to play the organ someday, just like his teacher did at church.

Trinh thought he heard something. There it was again, this time louder. It was the call of the tree frogs, and the sound was coming from inside one of the hollow poles extending to the patio roof. Trinh examined the metal framework supporting the patio roof. There were lots of little resting places that were just right for tree frogs.

The next afternoon he told his music teacher about the frog's music. She smiled. "One of these days you can make music in a pipe too," she said. "An organ has many pipes—long wooden ones and tiny metal ones. With hands and feet and switches, an organist controls the air going to the pipes. You'll be able to make all kinds of sounds.

"Think of it this way," she continued. "Your little frog friend was making his kind of music last night. It's the song God put into him. God also put music into you. Through Jesus, He has saved you and given you a new kind of song. You can praise Him as your Savior forever. You can help other people praise Him too."

_____Let's talk: Why do we praise God? (Check verses 4 and 5 of
          Psalm 33.) How can you make music for the Lord?

_____Let's pray: All creatures that have breath and motion,
          That throng the earth, the sea, the sky,
          Come, share with me my heart's devotion,
          Help me to sing God's praises high.
          My utmost pow'rs can never quite
          Declare the wonders of His might.

                                                      M. K.

Better Than a Million Dollars

The church parking lot was full of cars. Everyone was working to get the church ready for a special service. Some pulled weeds, others washed windows. Many hands were helping.

Kelsey ran through the doorway. "Mom," she grinned, "I took the aluminum cans I've been collecting to the recycling center." She plunked some money on the counter. "Look— $2.14. I'm going to put it all in the offering tomorrow. I wish it were a million dollars."

Jesus cares about *you*—so much that He loved you to His death. And He cares about your love for Him. There are many ways to show your love in response to His. The adults were serving to make the church, God's house, a beautiful place. And Kelsey was happy to give Jesus every penny she had, just because she loved Him.

Giving back to Jesus is a wonderful way to say thank You for the gift of His love. It might be a dollar or a nickel or a penny. It might be a song or a prayer. He thinks your love is better than a million dollars!

Read from God's Word

As He looked up, Jesus saw the rich putting their gifts into the temple treasury. He also saw a poor widow put in two very small copper coins. "I tell you the truth," He said, "this poor widow has put in more than all the others. All these people gave their gifts out of their wealth; but she out of her poverty put in all she had to live on." Luke 21:1–4 ✑

———Let's talk: If you could give Jesus anything in the world, what would you give Him? What did Jesus do to show His love for you? What can you give to Him right now?

———Let's pray: Take my love; my Lord, I pour
At Your feet its treasure store;
Take my self, Lord, let me be
Yours alone eternally.

R. G.

It's Fun to Laugh

Read from God's Word

A cheerful heart is good medicine, but a crushed spirit dries up the bones. Proverbs 17:22

"Who can think of a word that begins with the letters *sn?*" Mrs. Courtney asked. Jon raised his hand. He was planning to say "snake," but instead he sneezed!

"Very good, Jon. 'Sneeze' starts with *sn,*" the teacher laughed. All the kids laughed, and Jon laughed too.

Jon had been laughing all day. It started when he accidentally poured orange juice on his cereal. "Uh-oh," his grandma laughed, "you're going to have a funny day."

At recess when Jon kicked the ball to Lien, his shoe came off and flew farther than the ball. Jon and Lien laughed until they fell to the ground. By the time Jon got home from school, he was laughing at words like *pepperoni pizza* that usually don't seem funny at all.

It feels great to laugh and be silly. Sometimes you might laugh all day like Jon. Sometimes you might be surprised by something funny when you aren't expecting it.

You have an even better reason to be happy and joyful. You have a God who loves you so much that He sent His Son to die on the cross for you. Because of Jesus, God forgives your sins and promises to take you to heaven. He will always take care of you and give you what you need. That Good News gives you an inner joy that will last forever.

_____Let's talk: What did you laugh at today? Why is it good to be able to laugh? Why is laughter one of God's blessings?

_____Let's pray: Lord, thank You for all the things that made us happy today. Fill our hearts with joy each day and help us be mindful of the blessings You surprise us with each day. In Your name we pray. Amen.

R. G.

I Could Eat a Whole Pizza!

Read from God's Word

Taste and see that the LORD is good; blessed is the man who takes refuge in Him. Fear the LORD, you His saints, for those who fear Him lack nothing. The lions may grow weak and hungry, but those who seek the LORD lack no good thing. Psalm 34:8–10

The campers started their hike down the mountain at 8:00 in the morning. By 10 o'clock no one was talking about squirrels or pinecones anymore.

"I could eat a mountain of chocolate ice cream," Matthew sighed.

"I'd like to drink a barrel of soda," Barb said.

"I'd like to jump into a barrel of soda," laughed Brandon.

At noon everyone yelled, "There's my favorite food!" when they saw hot dogs cooking on the fire by the lake. All the campers agreed—the hot dogs were the best thing they had ever tasted.

In the psalm for today, King David talked about God as if he were talking about food. He said, "Taste and see that the LORD is good!" That's a great thing to say about God, isn't it?

Think about the campers and how good the hot dogs tasted after being so very hungry. Now think about God and how empty you would feel without Him. Think about one thing God has done for you. Maybe it's how He sent His Son to die for you, or about the family He has given you, or about a time He helped you. Doesn't even one "taste" of God's love feel great?

Sometimes you might get so hungry that you wish you could eat a whole pizza or a whole carton of ice cream. With God's love you never have to stop with one little taste. His love and goodness will keep filling you up.

_____Let's talk: Plan a meal together. Include a favorite food of each person. After you eat, have a circle prayer and let each person thank God for His goodness.

_____Let's pray: Thanks, Lord, for pizza and hot dogs and ice cream, for hikes and campouts, for friends and family. Thank You most for Your love in Jesus, which truly satisfies us. Amen.

R. G.

Afraid of Falling Away?

Read from God's Word

"My sheep listen to My voice; I know them, and they follow Me. I give them eternal life, and they shall never perish; no one can snatch them out of My hand." John 10:27–28

Candice started to worry. She loved Jesus a lot. But what if something happened when she got older? What if she forgot about Jesus? What if she stopped believing in Him? Then she wouldn't be able to go to heaven.

The next Sunday Candice sat in church and noticed a picture of little lambs. She listened as the pastor read, "My sheep listen to My voice; I know them, and they follow Me. I give them eternal life, and they shall never perish; no one can snatch them out of My hand."

Candice remembered that she used to sing, "I am Jesus' Little Lamb." She liked to pretend Jesus was holding her in His arms. Suddenly Candice sat up straight. She realized what the words of Jesus meant. She really was Jesus' lamb, and He really was holding her. She didn't have to be afraid about forgetting Jesus. He would always hold her and never let her go.

Have you ever worried about falling away from the Savior? You don't need to worry. Jesus loves you so much that He gave His own life for you. He promises to take you to heaven. He's holding you right now, and He will never let you go. And no matter who tries to pull you away, He'll hold you close, for you are one of His lambs.

_____Let's talk: What do you think is the greatest danger to a Christian's faith today? How can you prepare to fight against this danger?

_____Let's pray: Thank You, Jesus, for promising to keep us close to You. Your love fills me with joy, knowing that You forgive me and have a place for me in heaven. Amen.

R. G.

A Story about Scars

Read from God's Word

A week later His disciples were in the house again, and Thomas was with them. Though the doors were locked, Jesus came and stood among them and said, "Peace be with you!" Then He said to Thomas, "Put your finger here; see my hands. Reach out your hand and put it into my side. Stop doubting and believe." Thomas said to Him, "My Lord and my God!" Then Jesus told him, "Because you have seen Me, you have believed; blessed are those who have not seen and yet have believed." John 20:26–29 ✍

One day Matthew decided to walk his large dog, Ozzie, down the road. He got a leash so Ozzie could not run away.

As they walked Matthew noticed that Ozzie was pulling the leash very hard. He wrapped the leash around his arm until it was tight. Suddenly a rabbit ran right in front of the dog. Ozzie pulled so hard that Matthew fell to his knees on the gravel road. He was hurt so badly that he tried to let go, but the leash was too tight around his arm. Finally Matthew was able to let go and Ozzie ran off into the woods. He cried because his dog was lost and his knees were bleeding.

After his knees had healed, Matthew thought about what had happened. He had a new dog, but he still missed Ozzie. And although his knees felt better, he still had scars on them.

Scars on our body usually have a story that explains how they got there. When Jesus was nailed to the cross for us, He, too, received scars from His wounds. And He has an explanation for us as to why He got those scars: *I love you.*

When He showed Thomas the nail marks in His hands and feet, Jesus encouraged His disciple: "Stop doubting and believe" (John 20:27). To us, too, the Savior says: "Believe that I received these scars for your sake. Trust Me for your salvation."

———Let's talk: Do you have a story about a time when your feelings were hurt or you got some scars? How did God help you recover from such injuries?

———Let's pray: Dear God, sometimes life isn't easy. But we know that You are always with us and that You send special people to love us. Thank You for the gift of Your grace and the loving help You give us each day. In Jesus' name. Amen.

D. P.

Read from God's Word

Do you not know? Have you not heard? The LORD is the everlasting God, the Creator of the ends of the earth. He will not grow tired or weary, and His understanding no one can fathom. He gives strength to the weary and increases the power of the weak. Even youths grow tired and weary, and young men stumble and fall; but those who hope in the LORD will renew their strength. They will soar on wings like eagles; they will run and not grow weary, they will walk and not be faint. Isaiah 40:28–31

Strength to Go On

Elizabeth was the star pitcher on her softball team. It was the championship game of the season and the game was close. Her team was winning 3 to 2 in the final inning. Elizabeth was pitching well, but she was tired.

After two outs, the other team got a hit. Then came another one. Elizabeth walked the next batter, and the bases were loaded. Her arm was tired, so the coach switched Elizabeth and the left fielder. The left fielder didn't pitch as well, but she was the only other player who could pitch. Elizabeth was now playing left field.

The new pitcher threw the ball five times, and the count ran to three balls and two strikes. The batter hit the next pitch hard to left field. Elizabeth ran as fast as she could and caught the ball. Her team won!

Many people at the game said it was the best catch they had ever seen. Elizabeth told them that sometimes Jesus gives her strength she doesn't even know she has. Someone asked her how she would have felt if she had missed the ball. She said that God would have given her the strength to accept that too.

Sometimes life can be tough. During the good and the bad times, we know Jesus is always with us. He loves us so much that He gave Himself—His very life—to rescue us from our sins and failures. Through trust in the Savior, we have the most important victory of all—heaven.

_____Let's talk: Can you name some times God was there when you really needed Him? How has He given you comfort during hard times?

_____Let's pray: Dear Lord, some days we feel tired and wonder how we can find strength. Give us Your love and power at all times—good and bad. In Jesus' name, help us to overcome and live victoriously. Amen.

D. P.

No More Punishment

Read from God's Word

Therefore, there is now no condemnation for those who are in Christ Jesus. Romans 8:1 ✐

Martin Luther's parents loved him very much, but they punished him harshly when he got out of line. He learned that if he did not do what was right, he would receive harsh punishment. When he grew up, he went to a place of prayer and meditation called a monastery to fulfill a promise he had made. He felt that God would punish him for his sins, and he was afraid of God.

Martin tried his best to be perfect, but he would find himself doing something sinful no matter how hard he worked. He even began to punish himself because he was so angry and sad that he couldn't be perfect.

Martin was thinking that God the Father in heaven would treat him the same way as his father on earth. He had been punished as a child for doing wrong, and now he thought that God would never forgive his sin. Then he read something wonderful in the Bible. He discovered that God had sent His own Son to be punished for our sins. God's own Son—God Himself—had suffered the punishment we should have had. Our debt has been paid, and God's grace and mercy are ours.

Although Martin Luther was sinful, he now knew that he was loved and forgiven by God. The Word of God teaches that our heavenly Father forgives us all our sins for Jesus' sake. Ask, and you will receive His forgiveness.

_____Let's talk: How do you think Martin Luther felt when he discovered how much God his Father loved him? How does God's love and forgiveness make you feel?

_____Let's pray: Our God, thank You for the message of grace You have sent to us through Your servant Martin Luther. We praise You for the Good News of forgiveness through the blood of Christ. In His name. Amen.

D. P.

No More Indulgences

Therefore, since we have been justified through faith, we have peace with God through our Lord Jesus Christ, through whom we have gained access by faith into this grace in which we now stand. And we rejoice in the hope of the glory of God. Romans 5:1–2

At the time of Martin Luther, the Christian church in Europe had something called "indulgences." These were pieces of paper people could buy to receive forgiveness. Or they might buy indulgences for loved ones who had died. Many people believed in a place called purgatory where they would go after they died to be purged, or cleansed. They thought if they gave money, their loved ones would get out of purgatory and go to heaven.

Martin Luther knew that we do not have to buy indulgences to be forgiven or to get into heaven. All we need do is to believe in Jesus as our Savior. So on October 31, 1517, he nailed a list of 95 statements to a church door in Wittenberg, Germany. He said that we are justified (or saved) by God's grace, through faith alone. People cannot buy or earn their way to heaven. Heaven is a gift from God through the death of Jesus Christ on the cross.

When Luther was asked to take all this back, he said: "Here I stand. I can do no other. God help me. Amen."

We can all remember this great Reformation theme from Romans 5:1: "Since we have been justified through faith, we have peace with God through our Lord Jesus Christ."

———Let's talk: What does the Reformation begun by Martin Luther mean in your life? Why do we still need the Bible truths that Luther taught?

———Let's pray: Lord God, we love You so much. We pray that You will reform us every day to be more like You. Make us strong in what we believe and comfort us with Your love. In Jesus' name. Amen.

D. P.

november

Read from God's Word

"He will wipe every tear from their eyes. There will be no more death or mourning or crying or pain, for the old order of things has passed away." Revelation 21:4 ✍

Who's a Saint?

Today is the church festival known as All Saints' Day. It is when we think of Christians who lived here on earth but now live with God in heaven. Maybe you have a grandparent, or another family member or friend, who is now a saint.

Today's Bible verse tells us that in heaven no one will be hungry or sad anymore. There will be no pain or tears. But the Bible doesn't tell us very much about what heaven is like.

TV shows, movies, books, or cartoons may give the impression that those who have died are all angels. They sit on clouds or fly around trying to help humans still on earth. But that is just someone's imagination.

Mostly we know that after they die on earth, whoever believes in Christ lives forever in the presence of God.

Does a person have to die to become a saint? No. You became one at Baptism when God named you as one of His children. We are sinners because of our sinful nature, but we are saints because Jesus died on the cross for the forgiveness of our sins. All who believe in Him will live as saints forever in heaven.

So on All Saints' Day we think of millions of saints who have already died in Christ. But we can also think of ourselves, the saints who will join them someday.

_____Let's talk: How might knowing that you are already a saint make a difference in the way you act?

_____Let's pray: Praise to You, God, for the faithful witness of all the saints who have ever lived. Keep us strong in our faith in Jesus so someday we too might be heavenly saints. Amen.

D. N.

Evergreen Christians

At this time of year, some people spend hours raking leaves. Green leaves turn lovely shades of red, yellow, or gold, and then fall to the ground. Walking in crisp, fallen leaves makes a nice crunching sound, and driving through the countryside when the colors change is a great way to see nature's beauty. When the weather turns cold, these trees lose their leaves and look lifeless.

Trees that lose their leaves are called *deciduous*, a word that comes from a Latin word that means "to fall." These trees must wait until spring before they once again show their glory. Yet, conifers, or "cone trees," stay green the year round—we call them *evergreens*. Conifers do not change color from season to season (except when they're decorated as Christmas trees, that is!). They seem to stay the same, year after year.

The difference between these two types of trees can remind us of how Christians are sometimes different. Some seem to have a splash of color! They attract attention as they proclaim their faith in Jesus Christ by what they say and do. But then temptations or discouragements come along, and they give up. As far as others can tell, their faith is gone.

Evergreen Christians witness to faith in the Savior, but they do it in a quiet, steady way. When they face troubles, they keep right on trusting in God's love and trying to do His will. Which tree do you wish to be?

_____Let's talk: Can you think of any Christians who seem to have lost their faith? How might you pray for them? What would you say?

_____Let's pray: Thank You, God, for the gift of Your Son, Jesus. Help us to be an evergreen Christian. Amen.

D. N.

Read from God's Word

"Do not be afraid of what you are about to suffer. I tell you, the devil will put some of you in prison to test you, and you will suffer persecution for ten days. Be faithful, even to the point of death, and I will give you the crown of life." Revelation 2:10 ❧

Read from God's Word

This is good, and pleases God our Savior, who wants all men to be saved and to come to a knowledge of the truth. For there is one God and one mediator between God and men, the man Christ Jesus, who gave Himself as a ransom for all men—the testimony given in its proper time.
1 Timothy 2:3–6

Being Different

Are you left-handed? Or do you know others who write or throw a ball with their left hand? Many famous people were left-handed. Julius Caesar, Queen Victoria, Napoleon, Henry Ford, and Joan of Arc are thought to be on the lefties honor roll. Three recent American presidents—Reagan, Bush, and Clinton—are all left-handed. And along with leaders, many athletes, artists, and other creative people use their left hand more than their right one.

The reason for left-handedness is a mystery of the human brain. Scientists are still trying to figure out why some brains work differently than others.

Being different isn't easy. Southpaws, as left-handed people are sometimes called, get teased a lot. In times past, many parents and teachers tried to force children to use their right hand. They thought it wasn't good to be different from the majority. Some people even wrongly thought that things on the left side were evil.

Now people realize that God has simply made each of us different. We aren't all the same color or the same height or the same in any other trait. But Christ died for every one of us, not just for the majority. God loves us all the same. So we also want to love those who are different from ourselves.

_____Let's talk: Are there some ways that you are different from the majority? Is that okay in God's eyes?

_____Let's pray: Forgive us, Lord, for the times we have looked down on people who are not the same as us. Help us remember that we are all Your children and that You love us equally. In Jesus' name. Amen.

D. N.

Visiting Granny Annie

Read from God's Word

"Honor your father and your mother, so that you may live long in the land the LORD your God is giving you." Exodus 20:12 ✍

H urry up, twins," Mom called up the stairs. "We don't want to keep Granny Annie waiting." Today was Granny Annie's 90th birthday. Kanesha and Kenny and Mom had planned a big celebration. Mom baked a cake and the twins helped decorate it with candy. They could hardly wait for a taste!

Granny Annie wasn't really their grandmother, but they loved her just the same. She had lived in a home for retired teachers for a long time. The twins' mother, who was also a teacher, started visiting Granny Annie even before Kanesha and Kenny were born, so they had known her their whole life.

Once they asked Mom why Granny Annie lived there. It was more like a dormitory or a hospital than a house. She moved there when she retired, Mom explained. She sometimes forgot to take her medicine, so she couldn't live alone. But she had no relatives, and she needed others to care for her.

Some elderly people in retirement and nursing homes are not as fortunate as Granny Annie. They don't have anyone who comes to visit them. Sometimes they feel alone and forgotten.

Jesus reminds us to honor our parents. That includes all older people, especially fellow Christians. The Good News about Jesus has been passed from one generation to the next. After all, if older folks had not been faithful to God, we might not know about Jesus.

_____Let's talk: Is there a home for older people in your area or neighborhood? Could your family make plans to visit? (Perhaps you could go Christmas caroling there.)

_____Let's pray: Thank You, dear Lord, for the faithfulness of earlier generations. Help us to find ways to honor them, for Jesus' sake. Amen.

D. N.

Read from God's Word

You, my brothers, were called to be free. But do not use your freedom to indulge the sinful nature; rather, serve one another in love. The entire law is summed up in a single command: "Love your neighbor as yourself." Galatians 5:13–14 ✍

A Man of Many Talents

Albert Schweitzer was born in France more than 125 years ago and lived to age 90. As a young man, Albert studied music, religion, and philosophy. By the time he was 30, Schweitzer was a pastor. He had written three books and become a professor. This talented man was known throughout the world as a wonderful organist and music scholar.

But Albert was troubled. He had learned that people in Africa were suffering. They had many diseases but no hospitals and only a few doctors. So the world-famous teacher and musician decided to become a doctor himself. After studying medicine, he and Mrs. Schweitzer went to Africa to build a hospital and care for people there.

Some people thought he was foolish. A man with so many talents, they said, should not hide away in a far-off land. But Albert continued writing books and took several trips abroad. He was awarded the Nobel Peace Prize. But he continued to work with people in Africa. He believed God wanted him to.

This is a prayer Dr. Schweitzer wrote: "Here, Lord, is my life. I place it on the altar today. Use it as You will."

God would also have us use our God-given abilities to serve others. This is one way in which we can glorify God and spread the Good News about Jesus and His love.

_____Let's talk: God gave all of us talents to use for Him. What are some of yours?

_____Let's pray: Thank You, heavenly Father, for the talents You have granted to each of us. Use our lives as You will, for Jesus' sake. Amen.

D. N.

High Flyers

Read from God's Word

Here is a trustworthy saying that deserves full acceptance: Christ Jesus came into the world to save sinners—of whom I am the worst. 1 Timothy 1:15

Wow, Dad," Janeen shouted, "Look at those birds! They look like they're aiming straight at us!" In July Janeen's family had moved to a small city from Chicago, where she had lived her entire life. Because of the tall apartment buildings in her neighborhood, Janeen had never noticed the wild geese flying south in the fall.

Now she watched the flight in amazement. "Do they always stay together in a *V* like that?"

Janeen's father explained that God had given the birds something called *instinct*. It makes them know when they should fly south to escape the cold winter. They also know they should follow their leader.

Janeen wanted to know if people have instincts too. "No," said her dad, "people never all act the same way unless we've been taught what to do. God gave us minds so we can think for ourselves, not just follow a human leader."

Of course that means we can make mistakes and get into trouble. Only people know the difference between right and wrong, so only people are sinners. That's why God let His Son, Jesus, come to earth and become human—so He could die for us.

If you have a pet, it might seem at times that it can think. Animals learn to react to situations, but they don't think the way humans do. Pets don't need a Savior. People do.

———Let's talk: What is the difference between using instinct and using your mind? Aren't you glad God gave you a mind?

———Let's pray: Thank You, Jesus, for being born as both God and man. Thank You for saving us from our sins. Amen.

D. N.

Popcorn People

Read from God's Word

"Do not judge, and you will not be judged. Do not condemn, and you will not be condemned. Forgive, and you will be forgiven." Luke 6:37

Popcorn—everybody seems to love it. The town of Valparaiso, Indiana, has a popcorn festival every fall. The floats in the parade use popcorn as decoration. Popcorn machines are found on nearly every downtown street corner. The newspaper prints popcorn recipes. And people enjoy an arts-and-crafts fair with popcorn as the theme.

The funny thing about popcorn is that it looks just like tiny cobs of regular sweet corn, although we can't eat it that way. Only when the hard, dry kernels are heated do they "explode" and become light, fluffy, and delicious. What a surprise it must have been the first time someone tried to cook popcorn. Imagine the look on everyone's face when it burst into those little, fluffy things!

Popcorn reminds us of the saying: "You can't judge a book by its cover." In other words, you can't tell what is inside a book just by looking at the outside. The saying is true for people too. You can't judge what a person is like by what shows on the outside. Someone from a different background might seem strange at first. Or a person who is shy might seem unfriendly. But maybe they are popcorn people, just waiting to get warmed up!

Jesus told us not to judge others but to love them as God loves us. Only God can know what's inside our heart and mind. And only God knows who believes in Jesus as Savior.

_____Let's talk: Do you know someone who needed to get warmed up before you became friends? Are you ever like popcorn, not showing what's inside of you?

_____Let's pray: Forgive us, dear Lord, when we judge others instead of looking at them as Your children. In Jesus' name. Amen.

D. N.

The Game of Life

Read from God's Word

If you, O LORD, kept a record of sins, O Lord, who could stand? But with You there is forgiveness; therefore You are feared. Psalm 130:3–4

In some sports, including football, hockey, and basketball, people wearing black-and-white striped shirts are right in the middle of the action. We call them referees, and they make sure everyone plays according to the rules.

When someone makes a mistake, the referees signal what the penalty will be. In football, for example, the ball may be moved to give the opposite team an advantage. Hockey players might get a penalty and have to leave the game for a while if they've done something wrong.

Some people think God is like a referee—always watching for what we do wrong so He can punish us or give us penalties. But that's not true at all.

Oh, yes, we have "rules" for the "game" of life. We know them as commandments. And God certainly wants us to obey those rules. But at the same time, He is a loving God. He knows that no matter how hard we try, we will fail. We will sin because we are sinful creatures.

That is why God sent His Son into this world. Jesus lived a perfect life, and although He was innocent, He died on the cross in our place. When we believe in Jesus as our Savior, God doesn't act like a referee. He gives us forgiveness instead of the punishment we deserve.

_____Let's talk: Why do games have referees? Would people follow the rules if there were no one present to make sure they did?

_____Let's pray: Thank You, Jesus, for living and dying for us. Be with us as we try to follow Your way. Amen.

D. N.

Read from God's Word

If you make the Most High your dwelling—even the LORD, who is my refuge—then no harm will befall you, no disaster will come near your tent. For He will command His angels concerning you to guard you in all your ways; they will lift you up in their hands, so that you will not strike your foot against a stone. Psalm 91:9–12 ✍

Meet Isaac

I wish you could meet Isaac. He is a "leader dog," trained to help and protect a disabled person. Maybe you've noticed Seeing Eye dogs with people who are vision impaired, helping them do things like crossing busy streets. Leader dogs are similar, but their humans can see—they just can't always manage by themselves.

Isaac is a large black dog that helps a woman in a scooter, which is a motorized wheelchair. He is with her everywhere she goes. When she goes to church, Isaac is there too. When they go to a party, Isaac gets dressed up. He is usually the center of attention.

When leader dogs are out in public, they are working. They should not be petted or distracted from the job of keeping guard. They know their duty is to protect and serve.

When we see dogs like Isaac on the job, we can be reminded of angels. We don't know a lot about angels, and we can't see them. But the Bible speaks of them as beings that watch over us. They are a symbol of God's constant care for us, His children. He loves us and wants what is best for us. He sent Jesus to be our Savior from sin because we could not save ourselves. And He sends angels to take care of us when we cannot take care of ourselves. Our God is a loving, caring God. He leads, guides, and directs us out of love for us.

_____Let's do: Make a list of the ways you think a leader dog can be of help. Thank God for creating dogs that can be trained to help people.

_____Let's pray: God, we know You always watch over us. Protect us in all our ways until we live with You in heaven. In the name of Jesus. Amen.

D. N.

"No School Today!"

An early winter storm knocked down power lines and disrupted traffic. Everyone listened to battery-operated radios, waiting for the anticipated announcement: "No school today!"

Pete and his neighborhood friends had a ball. They put on boots and dressed in their warmest jackets. They spent the day building a snow fort in Pete's backyard. When they finally felt chilly, Pete's mom called them in to sit by the fireplace and drink hot chocolate. Everyone agreed it was the perfect way to spend an unexpected day off.

We all enjoy getting out of our routine and having the time to do something different. That's one reason why holidays and vacations are so popular. Even when we love school and enjoy our work, we appreciate a change now and then.

But God never goes on vacation or takes a break. He is eternal, and there are no such things as hours and days and years in eternity. Our human minds can't figure out what that is like. But we do know that God's love for us is eternal—it will never end.

This means there is never a time when God doesn't care for us or hear our prayers. He is always there to forgive us when we sin. It is God's plan that we should live eternally with Him. As was promised, all who believe in Jesus will share a heavenly home forever. And we won't ever want to take a break from that!

Read from God's Word

And be content with what you have, because God has said, "Never will I leave you; never will I forsake you." Hebrews 13:5b

_____Let's talk: Is there anything in your life you don't ever want to take a break from? Does that give you any idea of what eternity might be like?

_____Let's pray: Dear heavenly Father, we can't really understand eternity. But we believe Your promise that all who die believing in Jesus will share it with You. Thanks for being such a great, loving God. Amen.

D. N.

The Right Trail

Have you ever stooped down to watch an ant trail? How do the ants know how to go in the right direction? Scientists tell us that it's because of a pheromone, a chemical the insects place as they walk along. It helps the ants following to know that they're on the right trail.

Suppose an ant could suddenly grow giant-size and look down at people. What would it see? You guessed it—confusion everywhere, people going in many different directions, and most of them not even sure of where they came from or where they're going. And we thought ants had it tough!

We Christians are to stand apart from this confusion. When others see us going to church, caring about strangers, sharing with neighbors, and working cheerfully, they see us following a trail. They might ask, "How do you know how to go in the right direction?"

We can come right out and tell people about our trail. We want them to know Jesus as the Savior of the world and the only way to eternal life. Jesus is our leader on the path of forgiveness, love, and service to others.

By studying Scripture and by living our faith, we follow God's way. As we walk His trail, St. Paul's words become our guideline: "Live a life of love, just as Christ loved us and gave Himself up for us" (Ephesians 5:2).

"Come along," we call to those we meet. "Join us! Follow the right trail, the Jesus trail."

———Let's talk: How do you make decisions about which trail to follow each day? Did you stay on the Jesus trail today? Did you invite someone else to join you?

———Let's pray: Dear Jesus, we thank You for Your guiding Word and Holy Spirit. We ask for strength and wisdom to follow Your way as You guide us through this week. In Your holy name. Amen.

K. M. M.

Give Me a Break!

Read from God's Word

Thus the heavens and the earth were completed in all their vast array. By the seventh day God had finished the work He had been doing: so on the seventh day He rested from all His work. And God blessed the seventh day and made it holy, because on it He rested from all the work of creating that He had done. Genesis 2:1–3

Winter time is wet and dreary in Juneau, Alaska. One winter, clouds parted to let the long-forgotten sun shine through. Everyone was excited. The governor declared a "sun holiday" so everyone could stop working and enjoy a welcome change of weather.

People often get tired of the same old things. Too much rain, too much sun, too many responsibilities, or too many problems can make a person feel like yelling, "Where will it all end? Give me a break!"

It isn't easy to live in our sinful world. We need to take time from our confusion, dreary days, or busy schedule to appreciate the good things around us that remind us of our loving heavenly Father. Psalm 84:11 promises, "The LORD God is a sun and shield; the LORD bestows favor and honor; no good thing does He withhold from those whose walk is blameless."

Sunday, or "Sun-day," is meant to give us a break from our routine. As we stop to remember good things on that day, we remember the best thing of all: God's Son, Jesus, died on the cross and rose again for us. Because of Jesus' sacrifice, we will someday have an eternal holiday with Him in heaven. Maybe then we will spell it "Son-day."

Whenever you hear the pastor say, "The LORD make His face shine on you," he is comparing Jesus to a bright light, like the shining sun. Then remember that Sunday is a good day to take a rest.

_____Let's talk: What has been keeping you busy this week? Why does God give us a day of rest? How will you praise God this Sunday?

_____Let's pray: Heavenly Father, we praise You for giving us weekly tasks. We also praise You for giving us a day apart from them. Refresh us and renew us, Lord, each "Sun-day." In Jesus' name. Amen.

K. M. M.

God's Own Sheep

For an hour Gretchen had been watching the meadow high up on a steep Alaskan mountain. Suddenly a wild ewe and lamb moved close to her hiding place.

Click! went Gretchen's camera. After all her waiting, Gretchen was rewarded with a good photograph. After many hikes and photos, she had learned to identify individual sheep. She knew that by counting the rings on their horns, she could figure out their age.

Imagine what it would be like if God had to sit quietly for an hour for us to come close enough to Him in order to find out about us. If He spent one hour per person, in one week He would learn a little about only 168 people. But the world population is over six billion, with people dying and babies being born every day. It would be impossible for God to find out about each of us.

The good news is that our heavenly Father already knows us because He made us. He doesn't have to wait for us to come close to Him. Jesus said, "The very hairs of your head are all numbered" (Luke 12:7).

God comes to us through Jesus. The Savior even laid down His life to make us God's own sheep. "I am the Good Shepherd," Christ said. "I know My sheep and My sheep know Me" (John 10:14).

Gretchen had to leave the wild sheep behind, but God is with us all the time. He made us, and we are His.

———Let's talk: Does God know how you feel today? Why does God stay with you all the time? Name some ways that you are reminded this week that God is with you.

———Let's pray: Heavenly Father, thank You for making us Yours and for being with us. As we graze and run through the meadows of our week, help us remember that You love us. In Jesus' name. Amen.

K. M. M.

Vital Signs

When animals hibernate for the winter, their vital signs, such as heartbeat, breathing, and normal body temperature, change. Normally, a woodchuck breathes 6,000 times per hour. But its breathing slows to only 10 times an hour during hibernation.

Your Christian faith also has vital signs that lead you to study God's Word and help you to share the Gospel with other people. The Holy Spirit makes you strong in Christ's love so you care about your friends and even your enemies.

A strong faith never hibernates. And it's a good thing that a strong faith does not depend on anything we can do. We say with the psalm writer, "Find rest, O my soul, in God alone; my hope comes from Him. He alone is my rock and my salvation. ... I will never be shaken" (Psalm 62:5–6).

We can be certain of God's help because Jesus lives and reigns eternal-ly. He won the victory over sin, death, and hell. And He gives complete victory to us who are joined to Him in Baptism. Now no evil can harm or destroy us.

When the woodchuck wakes up in spring, he'll feel revitalized. By God's Spirit and through His Word, we are renewed and revitalized all year long.

_____Let's talk: What might be some signs that a person's faith is going into hibernation? How does the Holy Spirit keep your faith alive today?

_____Let's pray: Dear Lord, thank You for giving us life, inside and out. Help our faith stay alive and strong all year long. We depend on You alone, O Lord. We put our hope in You. Amen.

K. M. M.

Read from God's Word

My soul finds rest in God alone; my salvation comes from Him. He alone is my rock and my salvation; He is my fortress, I will never be shaken. How long will you assault a man? Would all of you throw him down? ... They fully intend to topple him from his lofty place; they take delight in lies. With their mouths they bless, but in their hearts they curse. Find rest, O my soul, in God alone; my hope comes from Him. He alone is my rock and my salvation. ... He is my mighty rock, my refuge. Trust in Him at all times, O people; pour out your hearts to Him, for God is our refuge. Psalm 62:1–8

Read from God's Word

No, in all these things we are more than conquerors through Him who loved us. For I am convinced that neither death nor life, neither angels nor demons, neither the present nor the future, nor any powers, neither height nor depth, nor anything else in all creation, will be able to separate us from the love of God that is in Christ Jesus our Lord. Romans 8:37–39

Our Glorious Future

A scientist tried to get rid of colds and runny noses. He invented tissues made from a germ-killing substance. When used, the tissues would kill germs on a person's hands and face. Then sickness wouldn't spread to other people. Some people named this idea the "Killer Kleenex."

But the scientist soon realized that cold germs would spread in other ways. Even a "Killer Kleenex" couldn't solve the problem. It seems as if no world problems are ever solved simply or completely. No matter how we may try to make life easier, there is always sin. Because of sin in others and in ourselves, we live in a mixed-up world.

Accidents, death, war, and even natural disasters are part of sin in our surroundings. But our loving heavenly Father gives us a wonderful promise. He promises us an eternal home in heaven after this world passes away. There will be no death there, and our joy with God will last forever. This glorious future is ours because of Jesus, who destroyed the power of sin and gives us daily forgiveness.

Yet that's only part of God's promise. He also stays with us here and now. When bad things happen, God will give us strength to get through them. He will never leave us all alone. His love sustains us every moment.

There will be times when we might wish for easy solutions like a "Killer Kleenex." But having God forever is far better.

_____Let's talk: Why do bad things happen in the world? When was the last time you were sick and wanted to be well again? How does God keep us well in our hearts?

_____Let's pray: Heavenly Father, we thank You for Your love and care, especially during hard times. Please keep us safe in Your love, for Jesus' sake. Amen.

K. M. M.

The Line Is Open

Read from God's Word

Praise awaits You, O God, in Zion; to You our vows will be fulfilled. Psalm 65:1 ✍

Marcus impatiently dialed the telephone for the fifth time. He held his breath as he waited for the ring. The line was still busy. Angry and disappointed, Marcus hung up the phone. He really wanted to talk to his grandfather about the trouble he was having at school. Grandpa always had time to listen, but not now. Today his phone was busy.

Marcus paced around the living room, trying to think of someone he could talk to. His dad was on a business trip, his mom wouldn't be home until late, and his friends wouldn't be able to help him with this problem.

On his third circle around the living room, Marcus paused in front of a picture of Jesus. As he stood there, he could hear in his mind his grandfather saying, "Marcus, remember that you are never alone. You can always talk to Jesus. You can count on Him to hear your prayer."

Jesus always has a clear "telephone" line. He died to take away the barriers created by our sins. Now we have "toll-free" access to our Lord at all times.

Like Marcus, we can talk to our Savior when we're having trouble at school or at home. We can also praise Him when we're having good times. We can tell Him that we had fun playing and thank Him for giving us good friends. Whenever we need help and guidance, Jesus is there to assist us.

_____Let's do: Get a piece of paper and three markers of different colors. Make three columns and label them "Troubles," "Good Things," and "Help Needed." Then list something in each column that you can talk to Jesus about.

_____Let's pray: Dear Savior, help us remember that You can always be reached and that You're never too busy when we call to You. Amen.

D. L. B.

Read from God's Word

Now to each one the manifestation of the Spirit is given for the common good. To one there is given through the Spirit the message of wisdom, to another the message of knowledge by means of the same Spirit, to another faith by the same Spirit, to another gifts of healing by that one Spirit, to another miraculous powers, to another prophecy, to another distinguishing between spirits, to another speaking in different kinds of tongues, and to still another the interpretation of tongues. All these are the work of one and the same Spirit, and He gives them to each one, just as He determines. 1 Corinthians 12:7–11 ✐

Pretty Packages

"Happy birthday, Danielle; happy birthday to you." Danielle blew out the candles on her cake. She selected a brightly wrapped gift with a purple bow. She knew it was from Jan, her best friend. It would be something only she would know to give. Danielle carefully unwrapped the box and peeked inside. She looked up and gave Jan a big smile as she unfolded a purple shirt.

"Thank you, Jan," she said. "It's just what I wanted. Purple is my favorite color."

Did you know that God gives each Christian a particular gift or gifts so we can work together like a team? Our gifts don't come brightly packaged with purple bows on top. Some of us even have to search and look deep into ourselves for our special gifts.

You may have the gift of wisdom so you can see God's plan at work in your life and the lives of others. Through the gift of faith, you can help others know Jesus. You can tell them that He is the one way to God and that He saved us by giving His life for us. Are you able to make friends feel better about a bad grade or a lost dog by talking and praying with them?

There are many gifts God gives to us through the Holy Spirit. If you don't know what yours is, ask the Lord to help you discover it and use it for His glory and the good of others.

_____Let's talk: Read 1 Corinthians 12:7–11 one more time. How many spiritual gifts are listed in this passage? Can you close the Bible and name them all?

_____Let's pray: Holy Spirit, please help us find and use our gifts for the good of Your people. Thank You for making us part of Christ's body, eager to serve one another. Amen.

D. L. B.

The Right Equipment

Read from God's Word

But you, man of God, flee from all this, and pursue righteousness, godliness, faith, love, endurance and gentleness. Fight the good fight of the faith. Take hold of the eternal life to which you were called when you made your good confession in the presence of many witnesses.
1 Timothy 6:11–12

Charles and Peter love football. The brothers enjoy watching college and pro games on TV. Even more fun is playing football with their friends in the neighborhood. The large lot next to their house is perfect for games.

They are planning a big game on Saturday. The boys have been talking about it for days. Peter's team is ready to play Charles's team to see who will be champs. Before the game, the boys went to the garage to check their equipment.

Charles got out his baseball mitt and pounded it a few times to see if it was in good shape. He found the tennis racket and saw that no strings were broken. Peter found the perfect ball for their game—his red and blue soccer ball. And he thought the team would definitely need his baseball bat. Now they had their equipment ready for the big football game, right?

Wrong! What a funny football game they'd be playing with such equipment. And so it is with the Christian life. Jesus tells us we need the right equipment to be His disciples. By reading and studying the Bible, we grow in the love and grace of God. We receive the joy of forgiveness through Jesus Christ. We have the hope of heaven.

Our Lord is always **present** to help us in our daily struggles. It's a privilege to play on His team.

_____Let's talk: What's the best time for you to read your Bible? What does Bible study do for your faith? How does it help you live for Jesus?

_____Let's pray: Dear God, please help us win our battles against the devil and our sinful self. Give us Your Spirit, that we may grow closer to our Savior and walk in His ways. Amen.

L. A.

Read from God's Word

Above all, love each other deeply, because love covers over a multitude of sins. Offer hospitality to one another without grumbling. Each one should use whatever gift he has received to serve others, faithfully administering God's grace in its various forms. If anyone speaks, he should do it as one speaking the very words of God. If anyone serves, he should do it with the strength God provides, so that in all things God may be praised through Jesus Christ. To Him be the glory and the power for ever and ever. Amen. 1 Peter 4:8–11

Lisa's Gift

Marta woke up feeling sad. She didn't want to go to Sunday school at her new church. Marta knew what it would be like. Everyone would stare. No one would talk to her. Marta had to wear thick glasses because of eye problems. Some of the girls would probably giggle and point. The boys would probably tease her. When Marta heard her mother calling for breakfast, she tried to crawl under the covers and disappear.

Have you ever felt like Marta? Let's find out what happened to Marta at Sunday school that morning.

When she arrived, a helper took her to the third-grade room and introduced her. "Welcome to our Sunday school, Marta," said Mrs. Williams. "Who wants to be Marta's partner for today?" she asked the class.

Lisa stepped forward. "Come and sit with me, Marta," she said. She got her book. Marta began to relax.

Lisa whispered in her ear, "You're going to like Mrs. Williams. By the way, I like your glasses, Marta." The two girls smiled at each other. Lisa wore glasses too.

For Marta the difference between liking Sunday school and not liking it was a girl named Lisa. Lisa gave her the gift of love. God tells us to "love each other deeply" and to practice "hospitality." When Jesus lived on earth, He reached out to all kinds of people to make them feel loved. He gave Himself completely when He died on the cross for the sins of the world. Now He encourages us to share the gift of love, as Lisa did.

_____Let's talk: Think of someone at school or church who sits alone. What can you do to show the love of Jesus to this person? How can you make a difference in this person's life?

_____Let's pray: Dear Jesus, thank You for the people who show love to us. Help us reach out and share Your love with others. Amen.

L. A.

Solving a Mystery

Two police officers stopped a car for a traffic violation. They noticed a new TV in the back seat, so they asked about it. The driver said, "It's a surprise for my mother. My dad bought it at Famous-Barr (a department store) at 9:30 this morning."

The police officers immediately arrested the man. What was the clue that tipped them off?

"I used to work at Famous-Barr," said one of the officers. "It's not open at 9:30 in the morning. It opens at 10:00."

Have you ever heard the saying "life is a mystery?" Almost everyone wants to know what life is all about. But some people search in the wrong places. They turn to money or drugs to feel better about themselves. They look for answers in cults or false religions, but they find no clues to happiness.

Read from God's Word

This is love: not that we loved God, but that He loved us and sent His Son as an atoning sacrifice for our sins. Dear friends, since God so loved us, we also ought to love one another. No one has ever seen God; but if we love one another, God lives in us and His love is made complete in us. We know that we live in Him and He in us, because He has given us of His Spirit. And we have seen and testify that the Father has sent His Son to be the Savior of the world. 1 John 4:10–14 ✑

The Bible tells us to turn to God and His love. In Him the mystery is solved. All around us are clues of His care. He has given us so many blessings that if we tried to list them, we wouldn't have enough time.

God has given us Jesus to take care of our biggest problem—sin. Our Bible reading says Jesus is the payment for our sins. He took them on Himself because He loves us.

Jesus is the best clue to the meaning of life. We believe in Him because God sent the Holy Spirit to live in us and give us faith. Because of our Savior, it is no mystery that God loves us.

_____Let's talk: How have you told others about your faith? What else can you do to help them learn about the meaning of life?

_____Let's pray: We pray, Lord Jesus, that as You live in us, we will be witnesses of Your love to others. Thank You for all the clues of Your care that You have given us. Help us live for You every day. Amen.

L. A.

Read from God's Word

Search me, O God, and know my heart; test me and know my anxious thoughts. See if there is any offensive way in me, and lead me in the way everlasting. Psalm 139:23–24 ✍

Shine a Light on Your Heart

Did you know a flashlight can "x-ray" the bones in your hand? Hold the palm of your hand over a lighted flashlight. The light travels through the thin parts of your skin but is stopped by the thickness of your bones. They leave a shadow just like they do on x-ray film.

Wouldn't it be cool if we could shine a light into our heart? There are machines that show a doctor what the heart is doing, but there is no machine that can search the heart the Bible talks about. This heart is the center of our human spirit and is the place where we would see our thoughts, emotions, motivations, courage, and faith.

Just like a flashlight is a poor substitute for a real x-ray, we cannot search our own hearts completely. We know what we feel and think, but only God knows what is really there. We think we are being brave, but God knows the worries that lurk in the corner. We think we are doing something kind, but God knows the real motive for the deed. He sees the sins we don't even know we are planning.

God's light shines into every corner of our heart, but He does not shut off the light in disgust at what He finds there. God calms the fears, washes away the sin, and fills our heart with His love. The Holy Spirit's work in our heart leads us to salvation and makes us servants.

It can be scary to know that we cannot hide anything from God's searching flashlight. God's search is so thorough, but our salvation is complete.

_____Let's talk: What does God see when He shines His light on your heart?

_____Let's pray: Search our hearts, dear God, and lead us in the way of everlasting life. In Jesus' name. Amen.

K. D. M.

Faith Magnification

A simple index card can act as a microscope. Make a pinhole in the center of the card. Close one eye and look through the hole with your open eye. Examine something small like a pin or a toothpick. It will look larger than it really is. Because of the pinhole, not as much light gets through to your eye. The concentration of light makes the object appear larger.

When we face big problems in our life, like a test at school, a fight with a good friend, or perhaps a family problem such as illness or divorce, we can feel very small. We may feel we don't have enough of what it takes to tackle this big problem. We worry we are not smart enough, quick enough, kind enough, or wise enough to get through a tough time.

The truth is we aren't big enough to take on even little problems by ourselves. But with the gift of faith, we

Read from God's Word

He told them another parable: "The kingdom of heaven is like a mustard seed, which a man took and planted in his field. Though it is the smallest of all your seeds, yet when it grows, it is the largest of garden plants and becomes a tree. ..." He told them still another parable: "The kingdom of heaven is like yeast that a woman took and mixed ... all through the dough." Jesus spoke all these things to the crowd in parables; He did not say anything to them without using a parable. So was fulfilled what was spoken through the prophet: "I will open my mouth in parables, I will utter things hidden since the creation of the world." Matthew 13:31–35

have what it takes. Jesus compares our faith to a mustard seed. A mustard seed is so tiny it is barely big enough to be seen with our eyes. However, just as that tiny seed can grow into a plant that is 10 feet tall, God magnifies our faith and promises that nothing is impossible for us.

The next time you are faced with a problem that seems impossibly big, remember your faith is magnified with the power of God. Know that with Him you are strengthened to be able to do all things.

——Let's talk: Read Matthew 17:21 and Philippians 4:13. What do these verses tell you about faith in Jesus?

——Let's pray: Thank You, Lord, for Your strength, which magnifies our faith. Help us to live as Your dear children. In Jesus' name. Amen.

K. D. M.

A Thankful Heart Reflects

Read from God's Word

You will be made rich in every way so that you can be generous on every occasion, and through us your generosity will result in thanksgiving to God. This service that you perform is not only sup-plying the needs of God's people but is also overflowing in many expressions of thanks to God. ... Men will praise God for the obe-dience that accompanies your confession of the gospel of Christ, and for your generosity in shar-ing with them and with everyone else. And in their prayers for you their hearts will go out to you, because of the surpassing grace God has given you. Thanks be to God for His indescribable gift! 2 Corinthians 9:11–15 ∽

Take two paper cups. Leave one white and color the other cup with a black marker. Fill both cups with equal amounts of water (at the same temperature), and set them in the sun. After 30 minutes compare the temper-ature of the water in the cups.

The black cup absorbed heat, which raised the temperature of the water. The white reflected the heat and kept its contents cool. The color of the cup does not create the heat on its own. Heat must come from a different source—in this case, the sun. The color just determines where the heat will go.

Thanksgiving is a time when we are reminded to give thanks for our many blessings from God. But what is the source of our thankfulness? Just as the cups cannot create heat, we cannot create thankfulness in our heart. Thankfulness is a blessing from God. When thankfulness fills our heart, it becomes absorbed and remains for a long time. God reminds us of His love and care for us and turns our hearts to Him with love and gratitude.

But thankfulness is more than something to be absorbed. We can also reflect thankfulness. When God's love fills our hearts, we respond with gen-erosity toward others. He helps us supply the needs of His people through gifts, acts of kindness, and words of love. His Word assures that our reflec-tion of thankfulness will result in more thanksgiving to God.

———Let's talk: Make a list of how God has blessed you. How can you reflect thankfulness toward other people?

———Let's pray: Thank You for Your many blessings, Lord. Make our hearts ready to absorb Your thankfulness and reflect Your generosity. In Jesus' name. Amen.

K. D. M.

The Power of Words

Read from God's Word

But since we belong to the day, let us be self-controlled, putting on faith and love as a breast-plate, and the hope of salvation as a helmet. For God did not appoint us to suffer wrath but to receive salvation through our Lord Jesus Christ. He died for us so that, whether we are awake or asleep, we may live together with Him. Therefore encourage one another and build each other up, just as in fact you are doing.
1 Thessalonians 5:8–11*

ut a penny-sized hole in the middle of the lid of an oatmeal box. Put the lid back on the box and set it on its side about four inches away from a lit candle. (Any activity that involves an open flame should also involve an adult.) Tap the bottom of the oatmeal box like a drum. You will notice that the sound waves make the flame flicker. If you have the oatmeal box in just the right spot, the flame will go out.

It may be a surprise to see that sound has an effect on the flame of a candle. Sometimes it is also a surprise to see the effect our words have on other people. When we use words of hate, we tear people down. When we use words of love, we build people up. There are times in our lives when we are angry and need to talk. When we tell a friend that he has made us angry, our words should express our anger but should not insult him. We may need to make the flame flicker, but we should not blow it out.

With God's help and with God's Word we can encourage and build up our friends with our words. We can offer God's peace when a friend is sad or worried. We rejoice when a friend is excited. Our words have the power to hurt or to heal. God loves us when we are angry, and when we are happy. His love shows us how we can encourage and support one another with our words and actions. For God loves us in every situation, forgiving us through His Son, our Lord and Savior, Jesus Christ. It is His love that heals.

_____Let's talk: Think of three times in the Bible when Jesus' words had the power to heal. How have you been built up by the words of a friend this past week?

_____Let's pray: Dear Lord, may our words be from Your Word so they may be words of healing, not hurt. In Jesus' name. Amen.

K. D. M.

Read from God's Word

Then Peter, filled with the Holy Spirit, said to them: "... Know this, you and all the people of Israel: It is by the name of Jesus Christ of Nazareth, whom you crucified but whom God raised from the dead, that this man stands before you healed. ... Salvation is found in no one else, for there is no other name under heaven given to men by which we must be saved." ... Peter and John replied, "Judge for yourselves whether it is right in God's sight to obey you rather than God. For we cannot help speaking about what we have seen and heard." Acts 4:8–20 ↩

Just Can't Keep a Secret

Take an empty drinking glass and put the open end against a door. Put your ear against the bottom of the glass. Can you hear what is happening inside the room on the other side of the door? The glass against the door helps your ears catch the sound vibrations in the room on the other side. Could this trick help you to find out any secrets?

Secrets are hard to keep because they are so intriguing. We are curious about secrets and want to know about them. When news is very exciting, it is especially hard to keep the secret. Everyone knows not to tell a little sister or brother what Mom is getting from the family for her birthday. Otherwise, it won't stay a secret for long.

The news about God's love should be as hard to keep quiet as a really good secret. In the Bible reading, Peter and John told the judge they could not help speaking about what they had seen and heard. When we read the Bible, God shows us how much He loves us and what His Son, Jesus, has done for us. From the time of our Baptism, the Holy Spirit has filled our hearts and we cannot keep God's love a secret. The people we meet each day will not need a glass to hear the secret of the peace, joy, and love of God.

———Let's talk: Think of three ways God helps you tell others about Him.

———Let's pray: Lord, let the story of Your death and resurrection burst from our hearts in everything we do or say. Amen.

K. D. M.

Refuel Your Faith

Electric batteries are not the only things that make electricity. Straighten one end of a paper clip and insert it into a lemon. Take some copper wire without insulation and stick that into the lemon also. Touch your tongue to the exposed ends of both wires at the same time. Your tongue is like a switch that completes the electric circuit, and you feel the tingle of electricity. It works because you used two different metals and the lemon supplied a bit of citric acid.

We use electricity to fuel many different things in our world. If you have ever been in a big storm and had to live without electricity for a while, you know all too well how we depend on it for our everyday lives.

Our faith needs fuel too. During His temptation, Jesus told the devil that "man does not live on bread alone, but on every word that comes from the mouth of God" (Matthew 4:4). Our faith grows and is strengthened each time we hear, read, or sing the Word of God. His Word is the fuel that keeps our faith growing. Reading His Word each day will keep the tingle in our faith.

When batteries lose their power, we don't always notice it at first. When we are separated from God's Word, we may not notice it at first either. We can go a week or two and not feel a difference in our faith. But unlike a smoke alarm that chirps when the battery is running low, we do not have a heart that chirps when our faith needs fueling. We need to take every opportunity to feed our faith because it is saving faith in Jesus. God is always ready to feed us with His Word and Spirit.

_____Let's talk: Make a list of how many different ways you hear the Word of God. Make a plan to study God's Word as a family.

_____Let's pray: Dear Lord, we cannot live by bread alone. Bless us and help us grow with the power of Your Word. In Jesus' name. Amen.

K. D. M.

Read from God's Word

Jesus answered, "It is written: 'Man does not live on bread alone, but on every word that comes from the mouth of God.'" Matthew 4:4

Therefore, rid yourselves of all malice and all deceit, hypocrisy, envy, and slander of every kind. Like newborn babies, crave pure spiritual milk, so that by it you may grow up in your salvation, now that you have tasted that the Lord is good. 1 Peter 2:1–3

Read from God's Word

But as surely as God is faithful, our message to you is not "Yes" and "No." For the Son of God, Jesus Christ, who was preached among you by me and Silas and Timothy, was not "Yes" and "No," but in Him it has always been "Yes." For no matter how many promises God has made, they are "Yes" in Christ. And so through Him the "Amen" is spoken by us to the glory of God. Now it is God who makes both us and you stand firm in Christ. He anointed us, set His seal of ownership on us, and put His Spirit in our hearts as a deposit, guaranteeing what is to come. 2 Corinthians 1:18–22 ✍

Rainbows and Promises

H ere is an activity for early in the morning or late in the afternoon when the sun is close to the horizon. Drag out the water hose, and while standing with your back to the sun spray the water upward and toward something dark, like a car or van. Experiment with the angle of spray a bit until you make a rainbow. Rainbows remind us of God's promises.

Our promises are not always faithful. We make a promise to our parents or a friend and then either because we forget or because we can't keep it, the promise is often broken. The Spirit of God is working in our hearts to create faithfulness, but because we are sinful, we are not always faithful.

"Jesus Christ is the same yesterday and today and forever" (Hebrews 13:8). The promises found in the Bible are absolutely reliable. The rainbow was for Noah, and is for us, a reminder of God's love and faithfulness. His promises are always kept. Every promise—from God's first promise to send His Son until His final promise of eternal life—is true.

_____Let's talk: How does a rainbow remind you of God? Can you name a promise from God for each color of the rainbow?

_____Let's pray: Lord, You are the same yesterday and today and forever. Thank You for Your faithful promises. Amen.

K. D. M.

Everything I Need

Float a piece of notebook paper in a small bowl of water. Gently place a needle on the paper. Now carefully push the edges of the paper down into the water. The paper will sink as it gets wet, and the needle will be left floating on top of the water.

Normally, a needle will not float in water. In this case, the needle is supported by surface tension. The surface of the water has molecules that cling close enough together so they support the needle. Something as small as a drop of dish soap will break the tension and sink the needle.

God created us and knows our needs. He knows we need food, sleep, clothing, loving parents, and a way to learn about His world and His Word. Just like the surface tension supports the needle, God supports us with all that we need.

The world makes us tense about getting enough stuff. Advertisements try to make us think we need many things to be happy. Jesus tells us not to worry about our needs or wants. That kind of tension will not support us. God the Father knows us and loves us, and He will provide for us. With the power of the Holy Spirit, we are to set our eyes on His kingdom, and the rest will be provided. With our eyes set on God's kingdom, our needs are met in Him. That is a much stronger support than surface tension.

Read from God's Word

Then Jesus said to His disciples: "Therefore I tell you, do not worry about your life, what you will eat; or about your body, what you will wear. Life is more than food, and the body more than clothes. Consider the ravens: They do not sow or reap, they have no storeroom or barn; yet God feeds them. And how much more valuable you are than birds! ... Your Father knows that you need them. But seek His kingdom, and these things will be given to you as well. Luke 12:22–31 ✎

_____ Let's talk: What is the difference between things you need and things you want? Think of a time when God gave you something you didn't even know you needed.

_____ Let's pray: Thank You, Lord, for caring for our every need. Help us to share our blessings with others. Amen.

K. D. M.

Fellows Together in a Ship

Read from God's Word

Dear friend, you are faithful in what you are doing for the brothers, even though they are strangers to you. They have told the church about your love. You will do well to send them on their way in a manner worthy of God. It was for the sake of the Name that they went out, receiving no help from the pagans. We ought therefore to show hospitality to such men so that we may work together for the truth. 3 John 1:5–8 ✐

Making boats and experimenting with them can be a good way to learn about sinking and floating. Try using clay, paper, cardboard, or aluminum foil as material to make boats. Test the boats by loading them with pennies to see how much weight they can sustain.

There is a boat or a ship that is a part of our Christian life. That "ship" is the word *fellowship*. Fellowship may be easiest to remember by thinking of yourself as one of many fellows in the same ship. Having fellowship means you work, learn, and celebrate together because you have the same beliefs.

As Christians, we have the blessing of fellowship. We read the same Bible and worship at the same church with people who share the same faith in Jesus as Savior. We all feel the same way about our wonderful God. Fellowship means we help one another and work together to build God's kingdom. Fellowship is a way to feel the love of God through the words and actions of other people.

Fellowship is a gift from God. Our sins of selfishness and pride often get in the way of fellowship. Only God can work a spirit of unity in His church so all the fellows in a ship can work together for God's purposes.

_____Let's talk: How does God bless you with fellowship? What activities help people to fellowship?

_____Let's pray: We thank You, Lord, for our fellow Christians. Help us to be a blessing to one another. Amen.

K. D. M.

As the Pendulum Swings

Read from God's Word

Do not think of yourself more highly than you ought, but rather think of yourself with sober judgment, in accordance with the measure of faith God has given you. ... We have different gifts, according to the grace given us. If a man's gift is prophesying, let him use it in proportion to his faith. If it is serving, let him serve; if it is teaching, let him teach; if it is encouraging, let him encourage; if it is contributing to the needs of others, let him give generously; if it is leadership, let him govern diligently; if it is showing mercy, let him do it cheerfully. Romans 12:3–8 ✐

The swing on a playground is a pendulum, an object hung from a fixed point that can swing freely. Pick two people of different weights and have them take turns on a swing. Count the number of swings each completes in exactly one minute. If you are careful about how you count the swings, you should find the same number of swings for each swinger. Each swing takes the same amount of time for the same pendulum. The different weights do not change the work of the pendulum. This is why a pendulum keeps good time.

Our Bible reading shows us that God has blessed each of us with gifts to use in His kingdom. Sometimes those gifts do not seem to be given equally. Some kids seem to be good at everything, and there are days when you may wonder if you can do *anything* well. Maybe you think you can't help with God's work.

Each of us is blessed with different gifts, but it is good to know that no one gift is more important than another. God does not need us to make His work happen here on earth, but He gives us gifts and uses us to spread His Gospel. Your gift, whether it is encouraging, leading, giving, or being merciful, is a useful and important gift. He has a plan for you and is happy to use you for His purpose.

_____Let's talk: With what gifts has God blessed you? How might He ask you to serve Him with these gifts?

_____Let's pray: Lord, You have made us members of one body. Help us to serve You always with our gifts. Amen.

K. D. M.

december

Night Hike

Before departing on a forest hike, Cheryl and her friends decided to take flashlights. They didn't think they'd need them because it was mid-afternoon. However, for the sake of precaution, they decided to take the flashlights.

The path led the group along a gurgling mountain stream. They walked through thick forests and along rocky ledges. The trail led up and down many slopes. After walking for a couple of hours, the friends realized that they would not get back to their car before sunset. They turned around and headed back to the trailhead.

Cheryl and her friends walked a little faster and the forest around them began to fade into shadows. Soon they were unable to see the path clearly and had to turn on the flashlights. The flashlights guided them over fallen tree limbs and around holes. By their light, they avoided running into boulders or off the side of the ledge. And eventually, those flashlights guided the hikers back to the safety of their car.

God's Word is like that. His Word is a light to our path. When we struggle on our journey, Satan tries to trip us by putting temptations in our way. With God's Word guiding us, we can see clearly the tricks and temptations Satan hopes will make us fall. God's Word lights our path and helps us avoid falling. It will guide us to the safety of our final destination.

Read from God's Word

Your word is a lamp to my feet and a light for my path. Psalm 119:105 ✍

_____Let's talk: Have you ever been lost? How did it feel to find your way back to safety?

_____Let's pray: Dear Father, when Satan tries to trip us with his temptations, help us to follow the path lit for us by Your Word. Amen.

C. H.

Read from God's Word

Then they cried out to the LORD in their trouble, and He brought them out of their distress. He stilled the storm to a whisper; the waves of the sea were hushed. Psalm 107:28–29 ↩

Take Shelter

In Southern Louisiana, land and water mix together and become very marshy. These wetlands are full of tall cypress trees. Bright green water lilies blend with the many colorful wildflowers. Many tourists come to take boat rides so they can view the swamp's beauty up close.

While visiting the area, two friends took one of these tours. They were thrilled with the natural beauty surrounding them. On their way back to the dock, a storm hit.

They spotted a cabin on the shore and aimed their boat for it. The rain started. Lightning and the sound of thunder filled the air around them. The winds began to blow with fury. Unable to get into the cabin, they huddled together on the porch until the storm stopped.

One night the disciples of Jesus were in a similar situation. The wild storm around them threatened to sink their boat. The waves tossed them back and forth. But Jesus understood their fears. Psalm 107:28–29 says, "Then they cried out to the LORD in their trouble, and He brought them out of their distress. He stilled the storm to a whisper; the waves of the sea were hushed."

Jesus also understands our fears. During times of difficulty, we can call on Jesus. He will be with us through our troubles. He will still the storm and hush the waves.

_____Let's talk: How would you have felt if you had been on the boat with the disciples? How do you feel knowing Jesus understands our fears?

_____Let's pray: Dear Jesus, thank You for understanding when we are afraid. Thank You for helping us at those times. Amen.

C. H.

Hide-and-Seek

Have you ever played "Hide and Seek?" One person is "it." This person covers his or her eyes and counts while the rest of the players hide. Often the person who is "it" does not have to look very hard or very long because the other players break into giggles.

In our Bible reading for today, Jesus' disciples were hiding. But they were not playing a game. They had seen Jesus arrested, tried, and put to death. They were afraid they would be arrested too. So they hid.

Maybe you have felt the same way. Someone at school has been teasing you, so you "hide" by avoiding them. Or maybe you are afraid of a big test at school, so you "hide" by feeling sick that day. Or maybe you are afraid of thunderstorms, so you "hide" by closing all the curtains. There are many things that can make us fearful.

Read from God's Word

On the evening of that first day of the week, when the disciples were together, with the doors locked for fear of the Jews, Jesus came and stood among them and said, "Peace be with you!" After He said this, He showed them His hands and side. The disciples were overjoyed when they saw the Lord. John 20:19–20

The story of the hiding disciples did not stop with their fear. In the midst of the room, with all the doors and windows locked, Jesus came and stood among them. He said, "Peace be with you." With Jesus standing there, the disciples did not think their fears were quite so big anymore.

The next time you are afraid and the walls of fear are pushing in on you, remember that Jesus stands with you. And remember that He has said, "Peace be with you."

_____ Let's talk: When have you been afraid? How did Jesus help you to be at peace?

_____ Let's pray: Dear Jesus, thank You for being with us when we are afraid. Help us to remember that You always care for us. Amen.

C. H.

Read from God's Word

"And teaching them to obey everything I have commanded you. And surely I am with you always, to the very end of the age." Matthew 28:20 ✐

Advent Adventure

During Advent we think of Jesus' coming. This season reminds us that He has already come and that He will come again. When we think of His first coming, we think of Mary and Joseph, shepherds and Wise Men. Each was involved in the great ADVENT-ure of the coming of the Christ Child.

An adventure may mean taking a risk or being exposed to danger. Mary and Joseph risked ridicule because Mary was pregnant. The shepherds risked being considered foolish for listening to singing angels. The Wise Men risked their own deaths by disobeying Herod.

Now as we await the Second Coming of Christ, we are all involved in the ADVENT-ure. Each day we face risks because of our faith in Jesus. When we stand up to our classmates and tell them we will not make fun of someone, we are taking a risk. When we invite a friend to be our guest at Sunday school, we are taking a risk. When we help someone who is unable to help himself, we are taking a risk.

Always keep in mind that we have a Wonderful Counselor and a Mighty God. He promises in Matthew 28:20, "And surely I will be with you always, to the very end of the age." In other words, He will be with us until the end of this earthly ADVENT-ure.

_____Let's talk: List the letters in ADVENT. Try to write a promise from God that starts with each of the letters in ADVENT.

_____Let's pray: Heavenly Father, thank You for being with us as we face our earthly ADVENT-ure. Help us prepare for Your coming. In Jesus' name. Amen.

C. H.

Learning to Float

Ⓞn a recent white water rafting trip, the group was instructed about the importance of the equipment and the life jacket each would wear. They were told that if they fell into the water, they should lie back and let the life jacket do its job.

Their journey began. They guided the raft through many exciting rapids, paddling furiously as they went. Then they came to Dimple Rock. It was a dangerous spot. They discussed their strategy and guided their raft through the rapids. Suddenly the raft jerked, stopped, and spun around. They had become lodged on a rock and could no longer control the raft. The four friends were thrown out of the raft.

One tried to tread water and kick his feet. Another started to panic. Yet another was afraid that he might drown. Then they remembered what the instructor had said. Could it really be as easy as relaxing and letting the life jacket do its job? They relaxed and felt secure.

We often approach life's difficulties the same way. We try to struggle and kick our way out. We see the "rushing waters" around us. We get scared and start to panic. But the solution is quite simple. All we need to do is relax and lie back into the surrounding love of our heavenly Father. He will help us through our difficulties. He will lift us up.

_____Let's talk: How has trusting in God's love helped you?

_____Let's pray: Dear Father, when we try to solve our problems on our own, remind us that You solved the biggest problem of all when You sent Jesus to die for our sins. Amen.

C. H.

Read from God's Word

When you pass through the waters, I will be with you; and when you pass through the rivers, they will not sweep over you. When you walk through the fire, you will not be burned; the flames will not set you ablaze. Isaiah 43:2 ✑

What a View

Read from God's Word

Now faith is being sure of what we hope for and certain of what we do not see. Hebrews 11:1 ✐

The Great Smoky Mountains is a popular vacation spot. They were named for the blue "smoke" that hides the peaks each evening. During a trip, the family arrived late at night. It was very dark, but finally they found the cabin they had rented. They heard the gurgling of a nearby mountain stream, but everything else was hidden by darkness.

The next morning Mom woke up early. She wanted to see the mountains they weren't able to see the night before. But the whole area was covered in gray. The mountain stream was there, just a few feet away, but there was no view of the mountain peaks. She knew that the mountains had to be there, but she couldn't see them. Several hours later the fog lifted. And on the other side of the stream was a glorious mountain peak. Behind the first peak they could see many others rising high into the sky.

Sometimes we look for God's love in a similar way. We seek His love, but our own sins cloud our vision and we just can't see it. His love is there, but we seem to be looking through a haze. At these times it is important to remember Hebrews 11: "Faith is being sure of what we hope for and certain of what we do not see." Through faith, even when our vision is clouded by our own sinfulness, we can be certain that the love of God is always there for us.

———Let's talk: Make a family list of the many ways you can see God's love. Post it on the refrigerator where you can remember His love each time you see the list.

———Let's pray: Dear Jesus, thank You for always loving us, even when we cannot see it. Amen.

C. H.

Full Moon

Have you ever seen a full moon brighten a dark field or whiten a field of snow? Yet the full moon does not have an energy source of its own. There is nothing in or on the moon that helps it give off the bright glow. In its natural state, the moon is nothing more than a dull piece of gray rock.

The moon gets its light from the sun. When the sun is at the correct angle, the reflection can be seen here on earth as a full moon. When we look at the moon, we should really be giving credit to the sun, the true light source.

In Matthew 5, Jesus is preaching the Sermon on the Mount. He is teaching His disciples that it is important to let their lights shine. He tells them to let their good deeds show before others.

The disciples did not have their own energy source. And neither do we. Because of sin, we are like nothing more than dull pieces of gray rock. We have nothing of any worth to shine before others.

But Jesus never asks something of us without giving us the resources we need to accomplish it. He asks us to shine in the world, and then He gives us the light source with which to do it Himself. In John 8:12, Jesus says, "I am the light of the world." Because of what He did for us on the cross, all of His faithful believers have the ability to reflect His light.

Read from God's Word

"In the same way, let your light shine before men, that they may see your good deeds and praise your Father in heaven." Matthew 5:16 ✑

_____Let's talk: What do you think it means to let our light shine? Why do we call Jesus the Light of the world?

_____Let's pray: Dear Jesus, thank You for coming into this dark world to bring us Your heavenly light. Help us to reflect Your light to others. In Jesus' name. Amen.

C. H.

Read from God's Word

The LORD is my rock, my fortress and my deliverer; my God is my rock, in whom I take refuge. He is my shield and the horn of my salvation, my stronghold. Psalm 18:2 ✑

Rock Building

Eight hundred years ago, a group of American Indians called the Anasazi lived in the Southwest. They were an advanced culture. They developed new ways to farm. They built roads and learned to trade things with their neighbors.

Some of their most amazing achievements were the homes they built. In order to protect themselves from enemies, they built pueblos, or villages, high into the solid sandstone cliffs. These villages could be as long as 22 miles and contain as many as 200 rooms. One of these pueblos may have supported as many as 5,000 people.

In Psalm 18:2, David calls the Lord his Rock, his Fortress, and his Stronghold. David wrote this psalm after God had delivered him from his enemy Saul. David understood the power of God to protect His people. He knew God would shield him in times of difficulty.

Many things come into our lives and threaten us. Problems develop at school. Arguments happen between friends. We have troubles within our family. Loved ones get sick and even die. At these times we can remember, as David did, the stronghold we have in God. Just like the Anasazi, we are safe and secure in our fortress. But unlike the Anasazi pueblos, made of sandstone that will erode, we have a rock in God that will never erode.

_____Let's talk: What other hymns or Bible verses can you think of that use the symbol of a rock? To what do they compare the rock?

_____Let's pray: Dear Father, thank You for the strength You are for us. Help me always to trust in You. Amen.

C. H.

Soaring

Traveling through the beautiful mountains of West Virginia, a group of friends was treated to a wonderful yet rare sight. Soaring gracefully high above were several bald eagles. It was amazing to watch these birds gliding through the air.

With a huge wingspan of seven feet, the eagle has been a symbol of power and freedom for thousands of years. Eagles' wings, covered with strong, stiff feathers, are easily capable of carrying their heavy bodies. These long feathers create a unique airflow that enables the bird to glide long distances. The special wing design allows the air to flow smoothly over the wings.

In Isaiah 40:31, we read that "those who hope in the LORD ... will soar on wings like eagles." With our hope in the Lord Jesus Christ and the salvation He brings, we are able to soar. We will have the strong wings that will help us carry all our burdens.

Just as the eagle is a symbol of power and freedom, so it is that the Lord, based on what He has done for us, brings to us the power of the Holy Spirit and freedom for the forgiveness of sins, won for us by Christ Himself.

_____Let's talk: Who are the people in your life that help you soar? Say a prayer of thanks for them today.

_____Let's pray: Heavenly Father, thank You for the hope You have given us through Your Son, Jesus Christ. Amen.

C. H.

Read from God's Word

But those who hope in the LORD will renew their strength. They will soar on wings like eagles; they will run and not grow weary, they will walk and not be faint. Isaiah 40:31 ✍

Suddenly!

Suddenly a great company of the heavenly host appeared with the angel, praising God and saying, "Glory to God in the highest, and on earth peace to men on whom His favor rests." Luke 2:13–14 ✍

John swung the door open and walked into the quiet, dark house. He flicked the switch, to hear "Surprise!" Once his heart stopped racing, John looked around the room. All his friends were there, smiling brightly. There were streamers, balloons, and decorations. And on a table in the middle of the room was a huge cake.

Have you ever been surprised? The shepherds in Luke 2:8–14 certainly were. They were quietly watching their sheep on a dark evening. Suddenly an angel brought an unexpected surprise for these sleepy shepherds. Once their hearts stopped racing, they heard the angel's message, "Do not be afraid. I bring you good news."

This sudden celebration, however, was too big for one angel. This was the celebration of the birth of the promised Christ Child! The sky was suddenly filled with a multitude of angels. The night sky was filled with the celebration of the birth of a long-awaited Savior.

As you prepare your home for Christmas, ask God to help you prepare your heart as well for the celebration of pure joy that we receive in Jesus Christ. Just as the angels filled the night sky with the sound of song and praise, we also sing, "Glory to God in the highest, and on earth peace to men on whom His favor rests."

_____Let's talk: Tell about a sudden celebration you have experienced. How will you celebrate Christ's birth this year?

_____Let's pray: Dear Jesus, thank You for being our reason to celebrate during this season. Amen.

C. H.

The Scoffers

I saw what you picked up!" Jared was startled. He had picked up some litter while waiting for the school doors to open. Cleaning up seemed like a good thing to do.

"That's nasty! I bet it's crawling with ants," called a second voice.

"You must be the new janitor!" called a third voice, and the three boys burst out laughing.

Jared was new to this school. He didn't want to be known as the "janitor." He dropped the litter and slunk off to get over his embarrassment.

That afternoon Jared noticed someone picking up the piece of litter he had dropped. *It must be the real janitor*, he thought. But wait! It was Mrs. Feldman, the principal. That night, Jared shared the incident with his father.

"I'm glad your principal was not ashamed to pick up someone else's trash," Dad said thoughtfully. "Jesus said that the greatest among us would be those who serve. But there are always scoffers who try to discourage you from doing what is right."

Jared prayed that night for forgiveness for letting the scoffers get to him. He asked Jesus for courage not to be intimidated by the older boys. Jesus answered this prayer, and Jared made several good friends who admired his willingness to do what was right.

____Let's talk: Has anyone ever made fun of you for doing what was right?

_____Let's pray: O Lord, we know scoffers in our school or neighborhood. Change their hearts so they will do and say what is right, and until then, help us to not be afraid of them. Amen.

R. Z.

Read from God's Word

Blessed is the man who does not walk in the counsel of the wicked or stand in the way of sinners or sit in the seat of mockers. Psalm 1:1

Read from God's Word

Praise be to the God and Father of our Lord Jesus Christ, who has blessed us in the heavenly realms with every spiritual blessing in Christ. For He chose us in Him before the creation of the world to be holy and blameless in His sight. In love He predestined us to be adopted as His sons through Jesus Christ, in accordance with His pleasure and will—to the praise of His glorious grace, which He has freely given us in the One He loves. In Him we have redemption through His blood, the forgiveness of sins, in accordance with the riches of God's grace that He lavished on us with all wisdom and understanding. Ephesians 1:3–8

Guaranteed Offers

Have you ever ordered something from a catalog? It looks so easy. Find the picture, then call or mail in the form, wait a few days, and you have your package.

Have you ever sat down and paged through the Bible as though it were a catalog? Could you find anything in it you'd like to have? What's being offered in God's Word?

How about the forgiveness of sins in Psalm 130:8? You could sure use some of that, right? Romans 5:8 says we can get love. And John 14:2–3 shares the promise of a new home, guaranteed forever!

If you've ever enjoyed ordering from a catalog, think how much more wonderful it is to receive things from God's Word. It's all free, and we don't have to pick and choose. God gives all His gifts and promises to us. Jesus Christ has already paid the total price for salvation. He paid for it on the cross with His life.

To get all these wonderful promises, all you need is faith in Jesus as Savior. That too is a gift from the Holy Spirit, who works in our hearts. On top of all this, we can contact our Lord anytime, toll-free, 24 hours a day, seven days a week, as long as we live. What a bargain!

_____Let's talk: What are some promises offered for free in the Bible? How long will these promises last?

_____Let's pray: Lord, thank You for giving us eternal salvation with You in heaven. Keep us always in Your care, for Jesus' sake. Amen.

K. M. M.

Emmanuel—God with Us

Jonathan was the spelling champ. One day he asked, "Dad, why is that sometimes I see the word *Emmanuel* that starts with *E*, and sometimes I see the word *Immanuel* that starts with *I*. Are they the same?"

"Yes," Dad replied, "both mean 'God with us.'"

"Then why are they different?" persisted Jonathan.

"The Old Testament and the New Testament were originally written in different languages. Translators use different spellings for the same word. God gave the promise of *Immanuel* to King Ahaz of the house or family of David when Jerusalem was attacked by an enemy. The family of David would have *Immanuel*, 'God with us,' born to them. This promise was to remind Ahaz that he and his kingdom would survive the attack."

"In the New Testament, God kept this promise when Jesus was conceived and born to the Virgin Mary, of the house of David. Now, God is with us in Jesus Christ. When we are afraid or worried about the future, we can always remember that God kept His promise by sending *Emmanuel* to be our Savior from sin."

Read from God's Word

Again the LORD spoke to Ahaz, "Ask the LORD your God for a sign, whether in the deepest depths or in the highest heights." But Ahaz said, "I will not ask; I will not put the LORD to the test." Then Isaiah said, "Hear now, you house of David! Is it not enough to try the patience of men? Will you try the patience of my God also? Therefore the Lord Himself will give you a sign: The virgin will be with child and will give birth to a son, and will call Him Immanuel." Isaiah 7:10–14 ✍

_____Let's talk: Why is it good to know that God is with us? When do you think Jesus was with you today?

_____Let's pray: Thank You, Father in heaven, for keeping Your promise to send Jesus, our Emmanuel. Help us trust all Your promises. Amen.

R. Z.

Read from God's Word

For there is one God and one mediator between God and men, the man Christ Jesus, who gave Himself as a ransom for all men—the testimony given in its proper time. 1 Timothy 2:5–6

Ransom Captive Israel

Perry was in trouble! He had ignored two warnings from his teacher about his behavior in class, and now he had an in-school suspension. He could not go to his other classes and had to wait for his mom to meet with the principal.

He was missing music class, which was rehearsing for the Christmas program. He heard his classmates singing:

Oh, come, oh, come Emmanuel,
And ransom captive Israel,
That mourns in lonely exile here
Until the Son of God appear.
Rejoice! Rejoice!
Emmanuel shall come to you, O Israel!

Perry realized that he was in his own kind of "exile," sent out from his class. He realized how much he needed Emmanuel—Jesus—God with us. He needed Jesus to forgive him for the behavior that got him into trouble and to help him make better choices. But most of all, he knew he needed the love of Jesus, who had taken his sins to the cross. Now Christmas, the birth of Emmanuel, would mean so much more!

_____Let's talk: Have you ever been "exiled" for misbehavior? What does the Bible call our misbehavior? Who will save us from our misbehavior?

_____Let's pray: Lord Jesus, Emmanuel, save us from wrong choices that lead to misbehavior. Be with us and forgive us. Amen.

R. Z.

Wisdom from on High

Read from God's Word

"ook for the pattern!" Esperanza's teacher would say in math class. Esperanza had no idea what Miss Euclid meant until one day when she did a particular assignment. Esperanza had to write out all of the math facts she had been memorizing in order. 1 + 1 = 2; 1 + 2 = 3; and so on. She began to see the pattern, that 3 contained 1 and 2. That is if you took 2 from 3, you had to get 1. Now she realized that this was true for all the problems. Math started to make sense. Wow!

"For wisdom is more precious than rubies, and nothing you desire can compare with her. I, wisdom, dwell together with prudence; I possess knowledge and discretion. To fear the LORD is to hate evil; I hate pride and arrogance, evil behavior and perverse speech. Counsel and sound judgment are mine; I have understanding and power." Proverbs 8:11–14

Patterns like the one Esperanza discovered in her math facts exist throughout the world God made. The ability to recognize these patterns in God's world is what the Bible calls "wisdom." The world God made bears the marks of His wisdom as surely as your sandbox might show your footprint.

Our world often doesn't "make sense" because sin has messed things up. To make things right, God sent His Wisdom, His own Son, to be born as a man in Jesus Christ. Faith in Him sets us right with God and makes it possible for us to begin to understand the patterns in His world.

_____Let's pray: Oh, come, our Wisdom from on high,
Who ordered all things mightily;
To us the path of knowledge show,
And teach us in her ways to go.
Rejoice! Rejoice!
Emmanuel shall come to you, O Israel!

R. Z.

Lord Almighty

Sandy and Andy were visiting their grandparents in southern California. They were watching television with Grandpa when a TV character exclaimed, "Lord Almighty!" Sandy and Andy started to laugh when Grandpa turned off the TV. That got their attention.

"I wonder if you know what those words *Lord Almighty* really mean?" Grandpa asked. "The Lord appeared to Moses and all Israel. He gave them the Law, the Ten Commandments, on Mount Sinai, amid earthquakes and thundering. Calling on the Lord Almighty is no laughing matter."

Andy and Sandy became a little worried, thinking that they had laughed at God. Grandpa explained, "We live in a world that laughs at God, and sometimes we become guilty of it too. But the Lord Almighty, who gave the Law, also came to bring forgiveness. Each of us who has broken His Law, laughed at His name, or sinned in any other way can look to Jesus, the Son of God, who kept the Law in our place. Now we can call on the Lord Almighty in every need."

A few days later, a mild earthquake struck Southern California. Grandpa, who had experienced them before, knew their house was built for it. He only looked up in concern when a picture fell off the wall. But Andy and Sandy were frightened. They prayed, "Lord Almighty, save us!" Nobody laughed then.

———Let's pray: Oh, come, oh, come, our Lord of might,
Who to Your tribes on Sinai's height
In ancient times gave holy law,
In cloud and majesty and awe.
Rejoice! Rejoice!
Emmanuel shall come to you, O Israel!

R. Z.

Rod of Jesse

Read from God's Word

A shoot will come up from the stump of Jesse; from his roots a Branch will bear fruit. The Spirit of the LORD will rest on Him ... and He will delight in the fear of the LORD. He will not judge by what He sees with His eyes, or decide by what He hears with His ear; but with righteousness He will judge the needy, with justice He will give decisions for the poor of the earth. He will strike the earth with the rod of His mouth; with the breath of His lips He will slay the wicked. Righteousness will be His belt and faithfulness the sash around His waist. Isaiah 11:1–5 ᥱ᥎

Kris remembered that particular stump. Several years ago he had gone with his uncle to cut a tree for Christmas and had left that stump behind. Kris had thought the tree was dead, but now a new branch had sprouted from the old stump. If anything, it was taller than the original tree. Kris knew enough about plants to recognize that this new branch was giving life to the old stump.

Isaiah spoke of Jesus, the promised Savior, as a branch or rod of Jesse's stump. Jesse was the father of King David and was an ancestor of Jesus. In Isaiah's day, it looked like the family of David might be cut off. They were defeated by foreigners and made slaves for a time. But from this stump of a family, Jesus was born, in keeping with God's promise.

Like His ancestor King David, Jesus is a King who saves His people from their enemies. But while David fought against temporary enemies like neighboring kingdoms and tribes, Jesus fought single-handedly against sin, death, and the devil. By His cross He overcame them all. It seemed at the time that Jesus Himself was cut off when He died on the tree. But He came to life again and gives new life to His people, just as the branch Kris had seen gave life to the old stump.

_____Let's pray: Oh, come, O Rod of Jesse's stem,
From ev'ry foe deliver them
That trust Your mighty pow'r to save;
Bring them in vict'ry through the grave.
Rejoice! Rejoice!
Emmanuel shall come to you, O Israel!

R. Z.

Key of David–Paradise Opened

Read from God's Word

"To the angel of the church in Philadelphia write: These are the words of Him who is holy and true, who holds the key of David. What He opens no one can shut, and what He shuts no one can open." Revelation 3:7

Josey loved to play basketball. Her team had practiced for weeks and they were going to play their first game. But there was a problem.

School was closed for Christmas vacation. Her coach had no key and the custodian was not working. Parents and members of the visiting team suggested canceling the game and going home. Josey and her teammates had been looking forward to this game almost as much as they looked forward to Christmas. Tears of disappointment came to her eyes.

Then Mr. Clavis, the principal, came. It was his vacation too, but he came to school with the key to open the gym so the girls could play their game. He even stayed to cheer and seemed to enjoy the afternoon. Afterward, he locked up to make sure the gym would be secure over vacation.

Jesus is the Key of David. He opens heaven, or paradise, for those who wait for Him. He came at Christmas for those who waited for God's promises to be kept. He opened their understanding of God's plan. He is coming at the end of the world for His children who are waiting for paradise. He comes to be with His people when they hear His Word and pray. He makes heaven secure from evil-minded people and opens it to those who believe.

_____Let's pray: Oh, come, O Key of David, come,
And open wide our heav'nly home;
Make safe the way that leads on high,
And close the path to misery.
Rejoice! Rejoice!
Emmanuel shall come to you, O Israel!

R. Z.

Dayspring

Jillian's family had just lit their Advent wreath and had sung a stanza of "Oh, Come, Oh, Come, Emmanuel." Jillian asked, "What's a Dayspring?"

"It's a word poets sometimes use for the dawn, the rising of the sun," her mother replied.

"I don't understand why people are so excited about the dawn," said Jillian.

Her grandfather spoke up. "I used to work the midnight shift on the oil rig. I had to stay up all night and watch out for dangers in the dark. I was pretty happy to see the dawn because it meant I could soon go home."

Her brother John joined in. "I remember lying in bed once in the dark. I'd had a bad dream and was so afraid. Then the dawn came, and I could see that all was safe."

"And what about last Christmas morning?" asked Mother. "You weren't allowed to open any presents until daylight on Christmas Day. You were pretty happy to see the rising sun— you shouted it to your sister before you ran to see what was under the tree."

Jillian now understood that Jesus, our Dayspring, comes to satisfy our longing, chase away our fears, and give us joy.

_____Let's pray: Oh, come, our Dayspring from on high,
And cheer us by Your drawing nigh;
Disperse the gloomy clouds of night,
And death's dark shadows put to flight.
Rejoice! Rejoice!
Emmanuel shall come to you, O Israel!

R. Z.

Read from God's Word

"And you, my child, will be called a prophet of the Most High; for you will go on before the Lord to prepare the way for Him, to give His people the knowledge of salvation through the forgiveness of their sins, because of the tender mercy of our God, by which the rising sun will come to us from heaven to shine on those living in darkness and in the shadow of death, to guide our feet into the path of peace." Luke 1:76–79

Read from God's Word

"This is what the LORD Almighty says: 'In a little while I will once more shake the heavens and the earth, the sea and the dry land. I will shake all nations, and the desired of all nations will come, and I will fill this house with glory, says the LORD Almighty. 'The silver is mine and the gold is mine,' declares the LORD Almighty. 'The glory of this present house will be greater than the glory of the former house,' says the LORD Almighty. 'And in this place I will grant peace,' declares the LORD Almighty." Haggai 2:6–9 ◠

Desire of Nations

Now Mandy was glad that Mrs. Beatrice was her teacher! Mandy had wanted her all along, although she didn't know it.

Last year's teacher had seemed nice. She made promises of all the things they would do that year, but they actually did very few of those things. Some kids would misbehave and the whole class would lose out. She let kids talk or bother others, and didn't seem able to stop it. Finally, she seemed too busy dealing with fights and quarrels to help Mandy with her math.

But Mrs. Beatrice was different. At first the children were a little afraid of her because she meant what she said. Kids that bothered others weren't allowed to continue. She had time to help Mandy with math. After the class had learned to behave, Mrs. Beatrice took them to the science museum.

"I didn't know I wanted that kind of teacher," Mandy told her mother. "But we do things together now that we never could before."

"Yes, Mrs. Beatrice brought peace and unity to your class," replied her mother. "In one way or another all people long for peace and unity."

"Is that what we mean when we call Jesus the Prince of Peace?" asked Mandy.

"Yes. He is what all people and nations need and desire, whether they realize it or not," said her mother. "He came at the first Christmas to be the Savior, and people from all nations have been rejoicing in Him ever since."

———Let's pray: Oh, come, Desire of nations, bind
In one the hearts of all mankind;
Oh, bid our sad divisions cease,
And be Yourself our King of Peace.
Rejoice! Rejoice!
Emmanuel shall come to you, O Israel!

R. Z.

Pass It On!

Laura's heart thumped. She watched the relay runners move around the track. Soon they would hand the batons to the next set of runners. Laura took a deep breath and held out her hand. There was the baton. Laura took it and she was off. The other team dropped the baton during the handoff. By the time they picked it up, they were behind and never caught up. Laura's team won the race.

The most important moment in a relay race comes when the baton is handed from one runner to the next. If the handoff doesn't go smoothly, the race can be lost.

Christians are in a special kind of relay race. The baton we hand to others is the Good News that Jesus was born into the world and that He died to take away our sins. Parents hand off this Good News to their children. Teachers pass it on to their students. We all have friends and family who need to hear about Jesus.

Read from God's Word

Therefore, since we are surrounded by such a great cloud of witnesses, let us throw off everything that hinders and the sin that so easily entangles, and let us run with perseverance the race marked out for us. Let us fix our eyes on Jesus, the Author and Perfecter of our faith, who for the joy set before Him endured the cross, scorning its shame, and sat down at the right hand of the throne of God. Hebrews 12:1–2 ✐

Christmas can be a great time to hand off the Gospel, but we need to be careful. Runners in a race are careful to avoid distractions that might make them fumble the baton. Christmas has many distractions. Gifts, parties, stress, and busy times may make us look away from the important message. Keep your eyes on Jesus as you run through these last days before Christmas.

———Let's talk: Think of someone you know who needs to hear about Jesus. What are some ways you can use this Christmas season to hand off the Good News to them?

———Let's pray: Dear Father, keep our thoughts on Your Son this Christmas. Give us opportunities to share Him with others. Send Your Holy Spirit to prepare their hearts to hear. In Jesus' name. Amen.

D. N.

Read from God's Word

To this you were called, because Christ suffered for you, leaving you an example, that you should follow in His steps. "He committed no sin, and no deceit was found in His mouth." When they hurled their insults at Him, He did not retaliate; when He suffered, He made no threats. Instead, He entrusted Himself to Him who judges justly. He Himself bore our sins in His body on the tree, so that we might die to sins and live for righteousness; by His wounds you have been healed. For you were like sheep going astray, but now you have returned to the Shepherd and Overseer of your souls. 1 Peter 2:21–25 ✒

The Candy Cane

Did you know that candy canes were first made to tell people about Jesus? A candy maker carefully made the candy cane to remind his customers of Jesus' birth, life, and death.

He started with a stick of hard, white candy. The white stands for purity. Jesus was born without sin. All of us are sinful because sin came into the world through Adam and Eve. But Jesus was fully God as well as fully human and was without sin.

The hard texture of the candy cane reminds us that God's love and promises are firm. Already in the Garden of Eden, God promised to send a Savior to take away our sins.

The candy maker made the candy in the form of a *J* because the precious name of Jesus begins with a *J*. Jesus is the Savior God had promised to send.

The cane is also shaped like a shepherd's crook. The Bible calls Jesus the Good Shepherd. He cares for us, guides us, and protects us from evil, just as a shepherd cares for his sheep.

Finally, the red stripes symbolize Jesus' suffering and death. The small stripes stand for the stripes on His back where He was beaten. The large red stripe represents His blood, which was shed for us. When Jesus died on the cross, He earned forgiveness for the sins of the world. We now have the promise of eternal life.

What a sweet story of love there is in this sweet treat!

_____Let's talk: What are some things you can think about while you eat a candy cane? Give a friend a candy cane and share the story.

_____Let's pray: Thank You, Father, for sending Your dear Son to suffer and die for us. Help us to always remember Your great love. In Jesus' name. Amen.

D. N.

The Truth Test

"Today we're going to learn how our senses can trick us," Mr. Sanchez told the class. "Sometimes things aren't what they seem."

The teacher tied a blindfold on Joel. Then he peeled a red apple and handed Joel a slice. "Can you tell me what this is?"

Joel sampled it and said, "It's an apple."

Then Mr. Sanchez handed him a slice from a yellow apple. Joel guessed right again. Then Mr. Sanchez handed him a slice of a potato. He guessed apple again. Joel ate it. The class giggled. Mr. Sanchez explained, "The potato has the same texture as an apple. You assumed it was an apple. Your senses tricked you.

"It's just as easy for our spiritual senses to trick us," he continued. "There are many false teachers and lies about God. False teachers may even use Bible verses to lead you away from the truth. But Jesus said, 'I am the Way and the Truth and the Life.' He is the Son of God, who died for the sins of the whole world. The truth will always proclaim that Jesus is the Savior of the world. Anything that disagrees with that is false."

Mr. Sanchez asked one last question. "Now do you see why it's important to study God's Word and know what it says?" They all nodded.

Read from God's Word

Dear friends, do not believe every spirit, but test the spirits to see whether they are from God, because many false prophets have gone out into the world. This is how you can recognize the Spirit of God: Every spirit that acknowledges that Jesus Christ has come in the flesh is from God, but every spirit that does not acknowledge Jesus is not from God. This is the spirit of the antichrist, which you have heard is coming and even now is already in the world. 1 John 4:1–3 ✍

_____Let's talk: Some government workers learn to recognize counterfeit money by carefully studying real money. Knowing the real thing helps them pick out the fake. How can you recognize that something is a false teaching? What did Jesus mean by saying He is the truth?

_____Let's pray: Thank You for Your holy Word, Lord. Send Your Spirit to plant its truth in our hearts. Guard us from evil. In Your Son's name. Amen.

D. N.

The Wait Is Over

A week before Christmas, presents arrived from Richard's grandparents. Mom arranged them under the Christmas tree.

Finally Christmas Eve arrived. After Richard's family went to church and celebrated the birth of Jesus, they let the family open the gifts from Grandma and Grandpa. What fun to finally see what the gifts were! One package had a watch inside. He knew he would really enjoy wearing it.

Long ago God promised Adam and Eve that He would send a Savior to take away the sins of the world. They passed that promise on. For 4,000 years God's people remembered and waited. Over the years God repeated the promise. Each time it must have felt like looking at wrapped gifts. God's people wondered when the Savior would come.

"But when the time had fully come, God sent His Son, born of a woman, born under law, to redeem those under law, that we might receive the full rights of sons" (Galatians 4:4–5).

Jesus, God's Son, our Brother, was born at the perfect time in God's plan. The small group of people in the stable knew the waiting was over. They joyously spread the news.

That little baby grew up. He lived a perfect life of love. He died and rose to save all people. Joy to the world! The Lord is come!

_____Let's talk: Have you ever waited for something for a long time? Was it hard to be patient as time passed? Were you surprised at how things worked out?

_____Let's pray: Dear Lord, fill our hearts with joy at the news of Your birth. Help us to never forget why You came to be our Savior. Forgive our sins, we pray. Amen.

D. N.

Special Delivery

K ara's dad drove a delivery truck. He had to work on Christmas Day. Many packages still had to be delivered so people would get them on time.

Mr. Meyer spent the day driving from house to house. "Special delivery," he called as he knocked on each door. The people inside were always delighted to see him and receive their gifts. By late afternoon Mr. Meyer had finished the work. He went home to have Christmas dinner with his family.

Later Mr. Meyer read the Christmas story from the Bible. His children listened carefully to the story of Jesus' birth.

"I made many deliveries today," he told them as he closed the Bible. "But this story tells of the most important delivery. The most wonderful gift we have ever received is Jesus Christ, our Savior. God the Father sent His Son to earth special delivery. Jesus wasn't wrapped in pretty paper but in a blanket of love."

Kara smiled at her father.

Mr. Meyer continued. "Jesus made special deliveries too. He delivered healing to suffering people. He gave love and forgiveness to sinners. Then our Lord went to the cross and delivered the whole world from the curse of sin. What an amazing and wonderful gift!"

_____Let's talk: Did you receive any Christmas gifts by special delivery? In His great love, God special-delivers many blessings to us every day. What are some of these? You can read the whole story in Luke 2:1–20.

_____Let's pray: Heavenly Father, we praise You for delivering Your Son to be our Savior. Thank You for this awesome gift. And some day, special-deliver us to eternal life in heaven with You. For Jesus' sake. Amen.

D. N.

Read from God's Word

But the angel said to them, "Do not be afraid. I bring you good news of great joy that will be for all the people. Today in the town of David a Savior has been born to you; He is Christ the Lord. This will be a sign to you: You will find a baby wrapped in cloths and lying in a manger." Suddenly a great company of the heavenly host appeared with the angel, praising God and saying, "Glory to God in the highest, and on earth peace to men on whom His favor rests." Luke 2:10–14 ✑

God Does the Unexpected

Would you choose a big engine or a little one to pull a train up a mountain? Remember the story about a little engine that did the job? He believed he could do it.

Then there's the story of David and Goliath. No one except David believed he could really defeat the giant. Yet with God's help he did.

Jesus' birth in a lowly stable was a surprise to many. The long-awaited Son of God lying on dirty straw. His parents were poor, not rich or important. There were smelly animals nearby.

As an adult, Jesus didn't always do what others expected. He spent time with sinners and others who were not well liked. Important religious leaders opposed Him and He was chased out of town. Even His own disciples wondered when Jesus would set up a kingdom on earth.

Jesus' death accomplished the most unexpected thing of all. Our sins are forgiven. Our relationship with God is restored. We have been given eternal life. Who would ever have expected it to turn out that way?

The Bible is full of events where God does the unexpected. Often He chooses something weak and lowly to do great things. That way His great power and love are clear for all to see.

_____Let's do: Look up these verses and remember them to help you when you feel weak or small: Luke 1:37 and Philippians 4:13.

_____Let's pray: We praise You, Lord, for Your great power and Your wonderful way of working. Help us trust You when things seem impossible. In Jesus' name. Amen.

D. N.

Patient Simeon

Simeon was a man who had spent his life serving God. God promised Simeon that he would not die before seeing the Savior. God kept that promise as He keeps every promise.

When Jesus was only 40 days old, Joseph and Mary brought Him to the temple. When Simeon saw Jesus, he was filled with joy. He knew in his heart that this child was the Savior of the world. He took Jesus in his arms and thanked God for letting him see the One who would bring light to a world dark with sin.

Like Simeon, we can trust God to keep His promises. We are at peace with God because Jesus came into the world.

Also like Simeon, we may have to wait a long time to see how God will work something out. There are things about God that we can't understand. We may not have the answers to all our questions until we live with God in heaven.

Read from God's Word

Now there was a man in Jerusalem called Simeon, who was righteous and devout. He was waiting for the consolation of Israel, and the Holy Spirit was upon him. It had been revealed to him by the Holy Spirit that he would not die before he had seen the Lord's Christ. Moved by the Spirit, he went into the temple courts. When the parents brought in the child Jesus to do for Him what the custom of the Law required, Simeon took Him in his arms and praised God, saying: "Sovereign Lord, as You have promised, You now dismiss Your servant in peace. For my eyes have seen Your salvation which you have prepared in the sight of all people, a light for revelation to the Gentiles and for glory to Your people Israel." Luke 2:25–32 ✍

Simeon looked forward to the Savior's coming. We look forward to His Second Coming. This time Jesus will come not as a baby but as the glorious Son of God.

_____Let's talk: Why was Simeon happy to see Jesus? What makes you happiest about Jesus?

_____Let's pray: "Lord, as You have promised, You now dismiss Your servant in peace. For my eyes have seen Your salvation, which You have prepared in the sight of all people, a light for revelation to the Gentiles and for glory to Your people Israel" (Luke 2:29–32).

D. N.

Soldiers for Christ

Tyrone's older brother had joined the army. Next week he would take a bus to boot camp to begin his training to become a good soldier.

"Why do you have to go so far away?" asked Tyrone. "We won't even be able to see you."

"The training is very hard and important," his brother explained. "I can't be distracted by other things. For these weeks I must think only about what I'm learning. I want to become the very best soldier I can be."

At times Jesus went away by Himself. He wasn't training to become a soldier, but He was in a battle against sin. He needed time away to pray and prepare for what He had to do. The Bible says that Jesus came "to serve, and to give His life as a ransom for many" (Mark 10:45).

Christians find it helpful to get away sometimes. But you don't need to go very far away to tune out life's distractions. You can sit in a quiet room. Turn off the TV or radio. Pray, read the Bible, and think about what God's message means in your life. Ask the Holy Spirit to help you say no to sin. Praise God for His great love. Thank Him for Jesus, who has given us the victory.

_____Let's talk: Are you on Christmas or winter vacation this week? Think of the time you're away from your normal routine as a boot camp.

_____Let's pray: Father, help us to glorify You in all we do. Strengthen us by Your Word to know Your will. In Jesus' name. Amen.

D. N.

How God Says Yes

Read from God's Word

For the Son of God, Jesus Christ, who was preached among you by me and Silas and Timothy, was not "Yes" and "No," but in Him it has always been "Yes." For no matter how many promises God has made, they are "Yes" in Christ. And so through Him the "Amen" is spoken by us to the glory of God. 2 Corinthians 1:19–20

When Jenna learned to crawl, she got into everything. She especially loved electrical wires. She squeezed behind furniture and pulled at TV, VCR, or lamp cords.

One day when her mom found her with a cord, she very sternly said "no!"

Jenna's brother, John, was just four years old. He had never seen his mom warn Jenna before. He asked, "You still love our baby, right?"

"I sure do!" she answered. "I'm warning her *because* I love her. Electrical wires could shock or burn Jenna. Someday she will understand. For now it's my job to keep her safe."

"No" is a hard thing to take. It's even harder when we don't understand why. Disappointment may cause us to wonder if we are still loved.

Today's Bible reading assures us of a big yes! We are loved so much that God sent His Son to snatch us from eternal danger. God said yes when He created each of us. He said yes as He gave those who take care of us. He said yes when He sent His Son to suffer and die for us. He says yes when we ask for forgiveness. He says yes to many things big and small.

Adults may say no to us because they love us. We can also be sure God's decisions for us are never wrong. Remembering the yes of God's great love helps us deal with those times in life when we hear no.

_____Let's talk: When was a no answer especially hard for you to accept? How has this devotion helped you?

_____Let's pray: Loving God, help us accept Your will for us in all things, especially those things to which You say no. In Jesus' name. Amen.

D. N.

Read from God's Word

As for you, you were dead in your transgressions and sins, in which you used to live when you followed the ways of this world. ... All of us also lived among them at one time, gratifying the cravings of our sinful nature and following its desires and thoughts. ... But because of His great love for us, God, who is rich in mercy, made us alive with Christ even when we were dead in transgressions—it is by grace you have been saved. Ephesians 2:1–5 ✍

The Real World

"Shontay, didn't you hear me?"

Shontay jerked her head up from the mystery book she was reading. "Did you say something, Mom?" Shontay had been so busy living in her story's dream world that she had forgotten the real world!

This can happen to anyone. Sometimes it even seems to happen in church. People sing hymns, listen to the sermon, go to Sunday school, and read the Bible. Then they go home. They feel like getting back into the real world outside of church.

The funny thing is, that idea is backward. God's Word and worship are the "real world." After all, nothing in life has any meaning or true purpose apart from the Lord. To be alive in Christ is to know every minute that the Creator of the Universe is your own loving Lord. Being alive in Christ is knowing that daily forgiveness can be shared with those around you. It is knowing that Christ died for you, rose again, and walks with you each day.

Living with God at the center of your life and activities is the only real way to live, like coming back to reality after reading a book.

———Let's talk: How does it feel to be alive in Christ? How can you daily remind yourselves about your life in Christ?

———Let's pray: Dear Jesus, thank You for dying on the cross to give us life. By Your Spirit, help us live this life for You. Amen.

K. M. M.

The Salvation Parade

"Oh, boy, tomorrow we get to watch New Year's Day parades," said Julie. "They're the best parades of the whole year. I hope I'm in one someday."

Have you ever thought of the characters in the Bible as being in a parade? All the people and events of Scripture make a fascinating parade—showing God's love and mercy.

Imagine that at the head of the parade is Jesus! "He was with God in the beginning" (John 1:2). Right behind Him come Adam and Eve, carrying flowers and fruit from the Garden of Eden. And here comes Noah and his family. They're all leading animals.

From Adam to the apostles, thousands and thousands of Israelites and Gentiles from Scripture fill the parade, all of them believers in the Lord of creation, all of them sinners in need of salvation through Christ, just like you.

Look—there's a gap in the parade, a space right behind the apostle Paul. That space is reserved for you. When you follow Jesus, you don't just walk off the screen like people in parades on television do. Jesus leads you to everlasting life. Your heavenly Father gives you this prize with His grace.

So if you see any parades tomorrow, remember God's salvation parade. You may not see it on TV, but it remains the most spectacular one of all time. And you're in it!

Read from God's Word

Therefore, since we are surrounded by such a great cloud of witnesses, let us throw off everything that hinders and the sin that so easily entangles, and let us run with perseverance the race marked out for us. Let us fix our eyes on Jesus, the Author and Perfecter of our faith, who for the joy set before Him endured the cross, scorning its shame, and sat down at the right hand of the throne of God. Hebrews 12:1-2 ꙮ

———Let's talk: Name some other biblical characters who are in the salvation parade. Are you part of God's parade? Why are you glad to be in it?

———Let's pray: Heavenly Father, thank You for making me Your very own. Now I can be in the parade of all Christians who love and worship You. Help me hold onto You as I live by Your Word. In Jesus' name. Amen.

D. N.